The
Westminster Confession Of Faith
Study Book

The Westminster Confession Of Faith Study Book

A Study Guide for Churches

Joseph A. Pipa Jr.

CHRISTIAN FOCUS

Joseph A. Pipa Jr. is President and Professor of Historical and Systematic Theology at Greenville Presbyterian Theological Seminary, Greenville, South Carolina. He hold degrees from Belhaven College (B.A.), Reformed Theological Seminary (M. Div) and Westminster Theological Seminary (Ph. D) and has previously taught at Westminster Theological Seminary, Philadelphia and Westminster Theological Seminary in California. His previous books include '*The Lord's Day*' (ISBN 978-1-85792-201-1) and a Focus on the Bible commentary on *Galatians* (ISBN 978-1-84550-558-5).

ISBN 978-1-84550-030-6

10 9 8 7 6 5 4

Published in 2005,
Reprinted 2008, 2012 and 2017
by
Christian Focus Publications Ltd.,
Geanies House, Fearn, Tain,
Ross-shire, IV20 1TW, Great Britain.

www.christianfocus.com

Cover Design by Alister MacInnes

Printed by Bell & Bain, Glasgow

MIX
Paper from responsible sources
FSC® C007785

CONTENTS

TEACHER'S GUIDE

APPENDICES

INTRODUCTION

The work of discipleship is a lost art in many of our modern Churches. This work, however, is commended by scripture both in precept and by example. The Psalmist lays out the work of family and generational discipleship in Ps. 78:1-6 – a work commanded in the law, Deut. 6:7 and 11:19-21. Paul commends this work to Timothy in 2 Tim. 2:1, 2. The Bible is replete with examples: Moses and Joshua; Elijah and Elisha; the school of the prophets; Christ and the disciples (Mark tells us that He chose them in order that they might be with Him 3:14. In addition to qualifying them to bear witness, Jesus was training them.); and Paul with his band of traveling evangelists.

Unfortunately in our day the work of discipleship is not being practiced in many churches. Such neglect (clearly in violation of Scripture) will only result in the harm of God's people and to the detriment of God's church.

The content of discipleship is quite broad: the doctrines and practice of the Christian faith; pre-marital and marital counseling; preparation for child rearing; managing a household; preparation for the ministry, the eldership, and the deaconate. It includes the work of parents with children and older (spiritually) men and women with younger (spiritually) men and women (2 Tim. 2:1, 2; Titus 2:3-5). It is a work that may be done one on one; couple with couple; or one person with a group.

I have written this material to train Christians in the basic doctrines and practices of biblical Christianity. The study is a series of inductive Bible studies keyed to the Westminster

Standards. (I have added the Three Forms of Unity so people in churches holding to these standards may adapt the material.)

The material is suitable for a number of different applications. It is designed to be used in one on one or in couple on couple relationships. I chose the word relationship deliberately. The best discipleship takes place in a relationship. Normally the study should take place in a context of prayer and mutual accountability. In the Teacher's Guide I suggest methods of accountability. I suggest meeting twice a month for a least an hour per session.

We have used the material on a number of occasions as the formative Bible study for a group of people meeting to begin a Church. (I know of four congregations that began using this material.) The study enables everybody to understand and own the doctrines and practices; thus the group is on the same page. Meanwhile, through the discussion, a doctrinal and personal cohesiveness develops within the group, which is essential to their continuing together to form a congregation.

The material has been used effectively as part of the training of men to serve as elders or deacons. We have used it as well in Sunday school classes and in men's and women's Bible Study groups in order to train people in the congregation and to equip a larger number to use the material to disciple others.

It may be used a number of ways with young people. One man used it with his Senior High Youth Group. It could be used as part of a curriculum in Home Schooling or in Christian Schools. It is a good tool to use in Campus ministry.

The first part is the student book. The student will need to use a notebook to write his answers. We also provide a teacher's guide, which gives brief answers for each question and suggestions for accountability. In preparing the lesson the student should first read the assigned sections from the Westminster Standards or the Three Forms of Unity. The student then should do the topical Bible study. One can complete a lesson in one and a half to two hours. Memorization assignments enable the student to memorize some foundational passages of Scripture and a portion of the Shorter Catechism. (One could substitute appropriate questions and answers from the Heidelberg Catechism.)

The teacher or mentor then meets with student(s) or class and leads a discussion of the lesson. In discipleship relationships the people should pray together and the teacher/mentor will share how he or she has dealt with the various situations and practices discussed. The teacher/mentor holds the student accountable to complete the lesson and the memory work and helps the student work out plans to deal with the various applicatory elements of the material. In the situation where there is no teacher/mentor, a person may use both the student book and the teacher's guide to complete the material.

I recommend the Harmony of the Westminster Confession and Catechisms, compiled by Dr. Morton H. Smith and published by Southern Presbyterian Press (the publishing arm of Greenville Presbyterian Theological Seminary) or Reformed Confessions Harmonized, compiled by Joel Beeke and Sinclair Ferguson and published by Baker Books.

In the back of the book there is a teacher's guide, a Personal Information Sheet and a Bible and Sermon Record Keeper. There are also appendices with the full text of the Westminster Confession of Faith, the Larger Catechism, the Shorter Catechism, the Belgic Confession, the Heidelberg Catechism and the Canons of Dordt.

Abbreviations

Old Testament

Genesis	Gen.
Exodus	Exod.
Leviticus	Lev.
Numbers	Num.
Deuteronomy	Deut.
Joshua	Josh.
Judges	Judg.
Ruth	Ruth
1 Samuel	1 Sam.
2 Samuel	2 Sam.
1 Kings	1 Kings
2 Kings	2 Kings
1 Chronicles	1 Chron.
2 Chronicles	2 Chron.
Ezra	Ezra
Nehemiah	Neh.
Esther	Esther
Job	Job.
Psalms	Ps.
Proverbs	Prov.
Ecclesiastes	Eccles.
Song of Solomon	Song
Isaiah	Isa.
Jeremiah	Jer.
Lamentations	Lam.
Ezekiel	Ezek.
Daniel	Dan.
Hosea	Hosea
Joel	Joel
Amos	Amos
Obadiah	Obad.
Jonah	Jonah
Micah	Micah
Nahum	Nahum
Habakkuk	Hab.
Zephaniah	Zeph.
Haggai	Hag.
Zechariah	Zech.
Malachi	Mal.

New Testament

Matthew	Matt.
Mark	Mark
Luke	Luke
John	John
The Acts	Acts
Romans	Rom.
1 Corinthians	1 Cor.
2 Corinthians	2 Cor.
Galatians	Gal.
Ephesians	Eph.
Philippians	Phil.
Colossians	Col.
1 Thessalonians	1 Thess.
2 Thessalonians	2 Thess.
1 Timothy	1 Tim.
2 Timothy	2 Tim.
Titus	Titus
Philemon	Philem.
Hebrews	Heb.
James	James
1 Peter	1 Pet.
2 Peter	2 Pet.
1 John	1 John
2 John	2 John
3 John	3 John
Jude	Jude
Revelation	Rev.

Other

W.C.F.	Westminster Confession of Faith
L.C.	Larger Catechism
S.C.	Shorter Catechism
B.C.	Belgic Confession
H.C.	Heidelberg Catechism
C.D.	Canons of Dordt

LESSON 1:

GOD'S WORD OUR RULE

Assignment:

Read:

W.C.F. 1; L.C. 1-6; S.C. 1-3;
B.C. 2-7; H.C. 19;
C.D. ; I, article 3; II, article 5; III, IV,
articles 6, 7, 8, 17; V, article 14.
Complete this study

Memorize:

2 Tim. 3:16, 17
S.C. 1-3.

As you begin this study pray that the Holy Spirit will enable you to understand the Bible and its message.

General Revelation

1. Read Ps. 19:1-6. What physical activity is David describing in verses 1-6?
2. Who is speaking through these activities?
3. Compare Rom. 1:19-21 and 2:14, 15 with Ps. 19:1, 2.
   a. What can we learn from the creation? (Compare your answer with W.C.F. 1.1.)
   b. According to Rom. 2:14, 15, what do we know innately?
   c. This is called General or Natural Revelation.

4. According to Rom. 1:32; 2:1, 2, 14, 15, of what use is this revelation to man?

5. According to Rom. 10:13, 14; Acts 4:12, what does the creation not reveal to man?

Special Revelation

6. Go back to Ps. 19. According to verses 7-9 in what other way does God speak to men?

7. Read Num. 12:6-8.

   a. What are three ways prophets received God's message?

   b. According to Heb. 1:1, 2, what is the ultimate face to face (mouth to mouth) revelation?

8. If these revelations were to be preserved, what needed to be done? Look at Deut. 31:24; Jer. 36:1, 2; Luke 1:1-4.

9. Where do we find God's Word today?

10. Now read 2 Tim. 3:16, 17.

    a. According to verse 16, how was Scripture given?

    b. Look up "inspiration" in a dictionary. What are some possible meanings?

    c. What do you think "inspiration" means here?

    d. According to Rom. 1:2; 15:4; 1 Tim. 5:18; 2 Peter 3:15, 16, what books does the term "Scripture" include?

11. Writers of Scripture were under the direct influence of the Holy Spirit. Look at 2 Peter 1:20, 21. Write this verse in your own words. (Note: in this verse, the word interpretation means initiative).

12. Read 2 Sam. 23:1-3. When David wrote the Psalms, who spoke through him?

13. What claim does Paul make in Gal. 1:1, 11, and 12? Do you think Paul knew he was writing God's Word?

14. What term does Peter use to describe Paul's letters in 2 Peter 3:15, 16?

Authority of the Bible

15. Whose Word is the Bible?

16. From whom then does the Bible derive its authority? (Look at 1 Thess. 2:13; W.C.F. 1:4; L.C, 4.)

17. According to W.C.F. 1:5 and L.C. 4 what are some other evidences that the Bible is the Word of God?

18. According to John 16:13, 14; 1 John 2:20; and W.C.F. 1:5, what ultimately persuades men that the Bible is the Word of God?

19. Go back to 2 Tim. 3:16. What are the things for which the Bible is useful or profitable?

20. These things are summarized by W.C.F. 1:6; L.C. 3, 5; S.C. 2, 3. According to these references what does the Bible teach?

21. According to 2 Tim. 3:17 and Ps. 19:11-14, why should we study the Bible?

22. All Presbyterian and Reformed churches have a secondary authority based on the Scriptures. Presbyterian Churches have The Westminster Confession of Faith, The Larger and Shorter Catechisms. Churches from the Dutch and German tradition have the Three Forms of Unity: The Belgic Confession, The Heidelberg Catechism, and The Canons of Dordt. Presbyterian and Reformed Churches also have a book or manual of Church Order. The Confession and Catechism are the doctrinal standards of the church. The Book of Church Order gives procedures for the proper government, discipline, and worship of the Church. All officers must take an oath that they believe that the things taught in these documents are scriptural and that they believe them. Furthermore, the doctrines summarized in these documents are the standard for the preaching, teaching, and ordering of the church. In the Presbyterian Church, members do not have to hold to all the doctrines as they are set forth in these standards, but they may in no way work against

these truths and practices. In the Reformed Churches, officers and members must hold to the doctrines set forth in the standards.

Matthew Henry in volume V of his commentary wrote on the usefulness of Creeds: "Brief summaries of Christian doctrine are of great use to young beginners. The principles of the oracles of God brought into a little compass in creeds and catechisms have, like the beams of the sun contracted in a burning glass, conveyed divine light and heat with a wonderful power" (p. 1146).

LESSON 2:

THE STUDY OF GOD'S WORD

Assignment:

Read:

W.C.F. 1:7, 9; L.C. 156, 157, 160, 178-196;
S.C. 98-107; H.C. 118-129.
Complete this study.

Memorize:

the titles of the books of the Bible;
review S.C. 1-3 and begin to learn 4-6.

Background for Bible Study

1. Read Ps. 119:105, 130.

   a. What figure is used in these verses to describe the Bible?

   b. To what kind of person does the Bible give understanding?

   c. What does "simple" mean in Ps. 119:130?

   d. If the Bible is compared to light and if it gives understanding to the simple, do you think that a Christian ought to be able to understand the Bible for himself? (Compare your answer with W.C.F. 1: 7.)

2. According to Ps. 119:18 and Acts 17:11, 12, what two things are necessary to gain a correct understanding of God's Word?

3. How does one receive the enlightenment mentioned in Ps. 119:18?
   a. What should we do every time we begin to study the Bible or to listen to a sermon or Bible lesson?
   b. Did you do this as you began this study? If not, pause now and seek the illumination of the Holy Spirit.
4. What does it mean to examine the Scriptures? (Compare your answer with L.C. 157.)
5. For profitable Bible study, it is helpful to have a good Bible. Preferably the Bible should be a modern translation (This study uses the New American Standard Version. The New King James Version and the English Standard Version are also very useful.) It also should have a thorough cross-reference system and maps. An English language dictionary is needed as well. You need to know the meaning of all the words in a verse before you can expect to understand what the verse means. It is also helpful to make notes in a notebook or the Bible and Sermon Record Keeper.

   Some other useful reference tools are a concordance, a Bible Dictionary, commentaries and a Bible Atlas.

   One of the greatest difficulties in effective Bible Study is consistency. You will need to seek God's grace in order to be consistent, but there are some practical things that help. First, have a time planned in your daily schedule. (If you have not been regular, start about twenty minutes a day, ten for Bible study and ten for prayer). Second, set aside a regular place for daily study and prayer. Third, have a plan. Basically, there are four approaches to Bible Study: survey, in-depth book study, thematic study, or work through a commentary like Matthew Henry. We recommend that you use a Bible Reading Calendar and begin with the survey approach.

Principles for Bible Study

6. The goal is to be able to answer three questions about the verse or passage you read:

a. What is going on in this passage? This is observation. What kind of literature is it (prose, poetry, narrative, didactic, figurative, prophetic, etc.)? Does it contain promises or doctrines? Who is speaking? To whom is he speaking?

b. What does it mean? This is interpretation. What is God communicating in this passage? Be able to state the truth in your own words.

c. What does it mean to me? This is application. What lessons, promises, commandments, truths are here for me? This should include meditation. Meditation is explained in Ps. 143:5; to muse, to talk to oneself, to mull over something. Meditation is mulling over who God is, what He does, and what that means to us, Ps. 145:5.

7. There are four basic principles of interpretation to be used in accomplishing our goal:

a. The context – How does this verse or passage fit with what was written before and after it? What is there in the context that will help me to understand the passage I am studying?

b. Linguistic analysis – Identify the type of literature; know the meaning of the words and the basic sentence structure. (Is it a statement of fact, a command or a question? Are the verbs past, present or future?)

c. Cross references – Use the footnotes to look at parallel passages and other uses of words, phrases and concepts.

d. Analogy of faith, W.C.F. 1:9 – The Bible does not contradict itself. An individual passage must be interpreted in light of what the Bible teaches throughout. The Westminster Confession and Catechisms are very useful at this point.

Practice of Bible Study (an example)

8. Bible study on Matt. 6:9-15.

   a. Read verses 1-18 to get the context.

      (1) What is Jesus' purpose in verses 1-18?

      (2) What are the three elements of personal religion that He discusses?

      (3) In verses 5-8, what principles does He lay down concerning prayer?

      (4) What do you think was His purpose in giving the prayer we are studying in verses 9-13?

   b. Linguistic analysis.

      (1) What type of literature is this in verses 9-15?

      (2) Look up in a dictionary any words in verses 9-13 that you don't know.

   (3) List the main verbs. Beside each write if it is a statement, commandment, or a question.

   c. Cross References.

      (1) Look at the parallel passage in Luke 11:2-4.

         (a) Are there any major differences?

         (b) Is there anything in the Luke 11 passage that will help you better understand Matt. 6?

      (2) Some cross references for the word "kingdom" are Matt. 3:2; 4:17; John 3:5. How do these verses help you to define what Jesus means by "kingdom come?"

      (3) Look at Ps. 103:20.

         (a) How do angels perform God's will?

         (b) On the basis of this verse what does Jesus mean when He says "Your will be done on earth as it is in heaven"? (Compare your answer with S.C. 103.)

d. Analogy of faith.

   (1) Verses 14, 15 could be interpreted to mean that our salvation can be earned. In light of what the Bible says of salvation being of grace alone, can this be a proper interpretation (Eph. 2:8, 9)?

   (2) What do you think Jesus means here? (Compare Matt. 18:21-35 and S.C. 105.)

e. Answer the three questions.

   (1) What is going on?

      (a) Why does Jesus teach this prayer?

      (b) To whom does He teach the prayer?

   (2) What does it mean?

      (a) List the petitions that are found here?

      (b) What elements of prayer do thcy include? (Look at S.C. 98-107.)

   (3) What does it mean to me?

      (a) Do you have a regular time of prayer and Bible study each day? If not, take time now to schedule a time.

      (b) Do your prayers include the four elements taught by Christ (adoration, confession, thanksgiving and supplication)? Keep these four things in mind as you pray.

      (c) Note: It is very useful to use a prayer journal. Write down daily, weekly, and monthly prayer items. Keep a list of answered prayers.

How to Listen to a Sermon

9. Read L.C. 160.

   a. What is required of those that hear the Word preach?

b. How should you approach listening to a sermon (three things)? Define each thing.

c. How should you listen (two things)?

d. What four things should mark how you receive the Word preached?

e. What should be your response (four things)?

f. "Confer" means to talk about the sermon. How do you do this with your family? With others?

g. What are you to do with the content of the sermon during the following week?

10. Keep a record of both Sunday sermons. Include Scripture; main theme; the outline; a paragraph that tells about the passage or doctrine explained; and the lessons and applications you received through the sermons. You may use the "Bible and Sermon Record Keeper".

11. If you are the head of a household you also should be practicing regular family worship. Have a set time with your wife and children. (Mothers who are heads of family should do so as well.) Sing a Psalm or hymn, read and discuss a portion of Scripture, and pray.

LESSON 3:

THE NATURE OF GOD

Assignment:

Read:

the W.C.F. 2:1, 2; L.C. 6, 7; S.C. 4; B.C. article 1.
Complete this study.

Memorize:

Deut. 6:4; Exod. 34:6, 7; S.C. 4-6.

As you begin read Heb. 11:6. Ask God to bless you with knowledge of Himself as you seek to know Him through His Bible.

1. Read Deut. 6:4. What three things does this verse tell us about God? (You may check your answer in the following questions.)
   a.

   b.

   c.

2. The first thing we learn about God is that He is "our God." What does this phrase teach us about God?
   a. Since God is personal, we must be able to know Him. If you are to know someone personally what are some things that you need to know about Him.
   b. Are we able to know these things about God?

3. Because God is a spirit we do not know what He looks like, but we can know what He is like. Look at Exod. 33:17-34:7.

    a. What does Moses want to see?

    b. According to Exod. 33:20, can anyone see the full, personal manifestation of God's glory and live?

    c. In 34:6, 7, how does God reveal His glory to Moses?

    d. We can summarize this by saying that God's glory is made known by His name, attributes, and work. This is the second thing we learn about God in Deut. 6:4, His name.

4. What are the two names used for God in Deut. 6:4?

    a. Gen. 1 introduces us to the name "God" (the Hebrew "Elohim"). As you read this chapter, list some things you learn about "God."

    b. Therefore, when you come across the name "God" in the Bible what are some truths that this name should bring to mind?

    c. The name "Lord" (the Hebrew "Yahweh") is explained in Exod. 3:1-15. In verse 14 God calls Himself ___________________.

    d. We get the title "Yahweh" (English "Jehovah") from these words. How does the burning bush illustrate this name?

    e. What does this name teach us about the existence and sufficiency of God?

    f. In verse 15 God says that this name is His memorial name. What do you think He means? (Look at Exod. 6:2-8 as you answer this question.)

    g. What then are some things that you should think about God when you read His name "Jehovah" in the Bible?

5. Another way God reveals His name is by His attributes (personal characteristics). List some of the attributes found in Exod. 34:6, 7.

6. In S.C. 4 we find a more complete list. We learn here that God is a spiritual being who may be known by nine attributes. Look up the verses and write a definition for each attribute.

   a. Infinite – Job 11:7-9.

      (1) Ps. 139:1-6 relates God's infinity to God's knowledge. How would you describe God's infinite knowledge? (Theologians call this omniscience.)

      (2) How does the Psalmist in Ps. 139:7-12 describe God's infinite presence? (This is called omnipresence.)

   b. Eternal – Ps. 90:2.

   c. Unchangeable – James 1:17; Mal. 3:6.

   d. Wisdom – Rom. 11:33; Ps. 147:5.

   e. Power – Jer. 32:17; Dan. 4:35.

   f. Holiness – two aspects:

      (1) Isa. 6:2, 3; 57:15.

      (2) Hab. 1:12, 13; 1 John 1:5.

   g. Justice – Exod. 34:7; Rom. 3:23-26.

   h. Goodness – Exod. 34:6, 7; Ps. 103:1-14.

   i. Truth – Exod. 34:6; Titus 1:2.

7. As you think about these attributes you will know God better. Why not begin your times of private and public worship by meditating on at least one of these attributes?

LESSON 4:

THE THREE IN ONE

Assignment:

Read:

W.C.F. 2:3; L.C. 8-11; S.C. 5, 6; B.C. articles 8-11;
H.C. 17, 18, 24, 25, 33, 53; C.D. II article 4.
Complete this study.

Memorize:

S.C. 5, 6.

The truth in this lesson is one of the most profound in the Bible. Ask God to enable you to understand it.

1. In lesson three we talked about two of the three things revealed in Deut. 6:4 about God: He is a personal God who may be known and that we know Him by His names and titles. What is the third thing we learn in this verse about God?
2. What, according to Deut. 4:35, is the implication of the truth that God is one? (Compare your answer with S.C. 5.)
3. What does God forbid in Exod. 20:3?
    a. The worship of false gods is called idolatry. What does Isa. 44:9-17 say about the absurdity of idolatry?
    b. What are some false gods people used to worship?
    c. What are some false gods people worship today?
    d. Are you worshiping any false gods?

4. Even though God is one, the Bible teaches that He exists in three persons: the Father, the Son, and the Holy Spirit. We call this the doctrine of the trinity: God is the three in one. This doctrine is summarized in S.C. 6. What three things do we learn in S.C. 6 about the trinity?

5. The first thing we learn here is that the Father, Son, and Holy Spirit are three distinct and separate persons.

   a. Read John 15:26. Who is speaking here?

   b. Whom does He promise to send?

   c. From whom is the Spirit sent?

   d. Now look at Matt. 3:16, 17. Who is being baptized?

   e. Who comes down on Jesus?

   f. Who speaks?

   g. How do these passages teach that the Father, Son, and Holy Spirit are three distinct persons?

6. The second thing we learn from S.C. 6 is that each person is fully divine. The following exercise will help you to see this. We know God by His titles, attributes, work, and as the only object of our worship. Match the verses listed under the Son and the Holy Spirit with the four ways God is known.

The Son	**God**	**The Holy Spirit**
Heb. 13:8	Titles	John 3:5, 6; 6:63
Rev. 5:12-14	Attributes	Matt. 12:31, 32; Rom. 9:1; 2 Cor. 13:14
John 1:1	Works	Acts 5:3, 4; 2 Cor. 13:17, 18
Luke 5:17-26	Worship	1 Cor. 2:10

From this exercise what conclusion must we derive concerning the deity of the Son and the Spirit?

7. The third thing the catechism teaches is that even though the Father, Son, and Holy Spirit are three equally divine persons, they are not three Gods. Read Matt. 28:19.

a. Into how many names are we baptized?

b. How many persons does this one name embrace?

8. In summary write the doctrine of the trinity in your own words.

9. Because God is triune, we must always think of Him in this way. What does Jesus claim in John 14:6-9?

   a. If this is so, can the Father be known apart from the Son?

   b. What does this say about the gods worshiped by Jews, Muslims, Jehovah's Witnesses, and Mormons?

   c. Is belief in the doctrine of the trinity necessary, if one is to be a Christian?

10. Fodder for meditation. Why is the doctrine of the trinity important?

LESSON 5:

THE DECREE OF GOD

Assignment:

Read:

W.C.F. 3:1, 2; L.C. 12; S.C. 7.
Complete this study.

Memorize:

Ps. 33:11; Isa. 45:7; S.C. 7.

We have learned a little about the person of God, His names and attributes. It remains for us to learn about His work. The first aspect of His work to be considered is His decree. This is another difficult truth; pray for a humble heart as you search the Scriptures.

1. Read the definition of the decree in S.C. 7 and list the things this definition says about the decree:
2. Read Ps. 33:10-11.
   a. What is being contrasted in these two verses?
   b. What does the word "counsel" mean? (Compare with S.C. 7.)
   c. Who controls the plans of men?
   d. Who can thwart the plans of God?
3. According to Isa. 46:10, when did God make His plan?
4. If the decree of God is eternal and God is unchangeable, do you think God's plan can be changed?

a. Read what Heb. 6:13-18 says about God's plan and promise, noting particularly verse 17. Write verse 17 in your own words.

b. If God's plan does not change, how do we explain verses like 1 Sam. 15:11 and Gen. 6:6? Let's look more closely at 1 Sam. 15:11 in order to answer this question. As we do so, we need to keep in mind some of the principles of Bible study we learned in Lesson Two. The only way we can properly understand this verse is to examine it in light of its immediate context and what the Bible teaches elsewhere.

(1) We have seen that the Bible teaches that God's plan is eternal and unchangeable. May we then interpret this verse to mean that God changes His mind?

(2) Now read 1 Sam. 15:10-31. Is there anything in the immediate context that we should keep in mind as we interpret verse 11?

(3) In light of what we have learned, how would you interpret 1 Sam. 15:1 and Gen. 6:6? (Keep in mind that God frequently speaks as if He were a man to help us better to understand what He means.)

5. According to Rom. 9:11, 13; and 11:34, is God's decree dependent on what He knew men would do? (Compare your answer with W.C.F. 3.2.)

6. Pause now and write a summary what you have learned thus far about the decree of God.

7. Now we need to consider what all the decree of God embraces. In order to do so, read the verses for each section and circle (or underline) the phrase that best summarizes the meaning of the verses.

a. Matt. 10:29, 30.	a. God's decree only includes the major events of life. God's decree includes all events, even small things.
b. 1 Kings 22:1-40; Prov. 16:33.	b. God's plan embraces things that appear to be accidental. God's plan does not take into account accidents and chance occurrences.
c. Isa. 45:6, 7; Acts 2:23; 4:27, 28 Job 42:11	c. God's decree includes evil as well as good things. God's decree does not include evil things.

8. Two cautions:
   a. Read 1 John 1:5; James 1:13. Does God's decreeing sin mean that He tempts people to sin?
   b. If God decrees all things, can man still be responsible?
      (1) Read Acts 1:16. Was it prophesied that Judas would betray Christ?
      (2) Why do you think Jesus warns him in Matt. 26:24?
      (3) We learn that, although it was prophesied, Judas was responsible for what he did. Read W.C.F. 3:1. Even though God has decreed all things, He is not the tempter to sin nor is man a puppet who is not responsible for his actions.

9. Thus we have learned that from eternity God has decreed everything that will come to pass. What practical lessons can you learn from the truth of this lesson?

LESSON 6:

CREATION

Assignment:

Read:

W.C.F. 4:1; L.C. 14, 15; S.C. 8, 9; B.C. article 12; H.C. 6.
Complete this study.

Memorize:

Gen. 1:1; Heb. 11:3; S.C. 8, 9.

As you begin this study pray that the Holy Spirit will enable you to understand the Bible and its message.

1. According to S.C. 8, what are the two ways God executes His decree?

   We may compare the decree to the work of an architect, creation to the work of a contractor, and providence to a building/maintenance manager. In this study we will look at the work of creation.

2. Heb. 11:3 gives a summary of the work of creation.
   a. What does this verse tell us about the origin of the universe?
   b. On what basis does one accept this record of origins?
      (1) Write a definition of faith as it is used here.
      (2) Whose testimony are we accepting?
   c. How do many modern scientists explain the origin and development of the universe and our present world?

(1) Can they prove their theories on the basis of observation and experimentation?

(2) On what basis then do they accept their theories of origin?

d. Thus the knowledge of origins is accepted primarily on the basis of faith. Whose testimony should the Christian accept?

3. Now read Gen. 1. As you read, list the phrases that are repeated.

In the repetition of certain words and phrases we note a structure or formula that is used to describe God's work of creation. One way to think of this formula is: the act of creation; the declaration of fulfillment; the statement of name and purpose; the expression of delight; and the indicator of time.

4. The Act of Creation

a. Read Gen. 1:1, 2.

(1) What was the first act of creation?

(2) What did God create by this act? (Compare Heb. 11:3; S.C. 9.)

(3) What was the condition of the original creation?

(4) The rest of Gen. 1 explains how God developed this original dark, unformed, uninhabitable mass.

b. What terms describe the subsequent acts of creation (vv. 6, 7, 27)?

c. What does Heb. 11:3 tell us about the phrase, "God said"?

(1) According to John 1:1-3, who is the one speaking at creation?

(2) How was Christ the agent of creation?

d. What do we learn from the second phrase of the creative act, "and God made" (vv. 21, 27 use the term "create")?

(1) According to Gen. 1:2; Job 26:13; 33:4; and Ps. 104:30, who executed the command of God the Son in the actual execution of creation?

(2) From this we learn that every member of the Trinity was involved in creation.

e. In Gen. 1 the various actions of creation are assigned to specific days. List the things created on each day:

DAY 1

DAY 2

DAY 3

DAY 4

DAY 5

DAY 6

f. What do we learn from the phrase "according to its kind" (vv. 11, 21, 24, 25)? Does this have anything to say about evolution?

5. Declaration of Fulfillment

a. What phrase does God use to declare fulfillment (vv. 7, 9, 15)?

b. Why do you think God makes this declaration?

c. What does this declaration teach us about the perfection of each creative act and how does this relate to the theory of evolution?

6. Statement of Name and Purpose
   a. What does God demonstrate by giving names to the created things (vv. 5, 8, 10)?
   b. God also expresses purpose with purpose statements (vv. 14, 15, 29, 30). What purpose is expressed for vegetation, heavenly bodies, and man?
   c. God blesses sea creatures and man (vv. 22, 28). In these passages how does God's blessing express purpose?
7. Expression of Delight
   a. How does God express His delight (vv. 4, 10, 12, 18, 21, 25, 31)?
   b. What does this tell us about the results and purposes of creation?
   c. How do the various created things glorify and praise God?
   d. How does man glorify God?
8. Indicators of Time
   a. In what two ways does God indicate time (vv. 5, 8, 13, 19, 23, 31)?
   b. What should we assume about the nature and order of the days of creation?
9. What practical benefits may be derived from knowing God as creator (Isa. 40:26; 45:18; Rev. 4:11)?

LESSON 7:

GOD'S PROVIDENCE AND YOUR LIFE

Assignment:

Read:

W.C.F. 5; L.C. 18, 19; S.C. 11;B.C. article 13; H.C. 26-28.
Complete this lesson.

Memorize:

S.C. 11; Ps. 25:12, 14.

As you begin this study pray that the Holy Spirit will enable you to understand the Bible and its message.

God's Providential Rule

1. Introduction.
   a. What are the two ways God executes His decrees?
   b. The second way, providence, is comparable to the work of a building manager. For a definition of providence look at S.C. 11. We may summarize: providence is God's working out in time those things He has decreed from eternity.
2. Providence and Creation.
   a. Read Ps. 104:1-30. List some of the things that God does by His providence.
   b. According to verse 30, do you think that the laws of creation operate apart from providence?

3. Providence and History.

   a. Read Dan. 4:17 and then write it in your own words.

   b. Can any army win a battle or any person be placed into rule apart from providence?

4. Providence and the Church.

   a. Read Eph. 1:20-23. According to these verses, what has been given to the resurrected Christ?

      (1) As Christ rules over all things, what is His special relationship to the Church?

      (2) What does this relationship suggest about the relation of Christ's purposes for the Church to the occurrences of history?

   b. We may say that God directs all things in the world to accomplish His purposes for the Church. Compare Luke 2:1-7 with Micah 5:2. How do these verses illustrate this principle?

Providence and Discerning the Will of God

5. Providence and You.

   a. What does Rom. 8:28 promise about God's providence as it relates to the things that happen to a believer?

      (1) Is there any circumstance beyond the scope of this promise?

      (2) What may you conclude about God's will in your difficult circumstances and afflictions?

   b. Providence and knowing God's will for my life. If God has an eternal plan that includes all things, then He has a plan for our lives. This plan unfolds through God's providence. There are five biblical principles that will help one to discern God's will for one's life.

      (1) First we must consult the Bible. According to Deut. 29:29, what is the purpose of the Bible?

(a) List some things concerning which you believe the Bible gives you guidance.

(b) But there are areas that the Bible does not speak to directly such as what job should I take or whom should I marry. The Bible also helps here. According to Ps. 119:98-100, what does God give to guide us?

(c) Wisdom enables us to apply God's principles to personal situations. List some ways the Bible can help you make decisions.

(2) The second principle is prayer. What does God promise in Ps. 25:12, 14 and Prov. 3:5, 6?

(a) According to John 14:13, 14, what is promised to those who pray according to God's will?

(b) How does this promise relate to praying for guidance?

(3) A third principle is stated in Ps. 139:23, 24. What is the Psalmist directing us to do?

(a) Why is it important to ask God to search our hearts and make our motives known to us?

(b) How would you relate this to seeking to know God's will?

(4) A fourth principle is to weigh the pros and cons and to consider the consequences. Look at Phil. 1:21-25. What two things is Paul contrasting?

(a) What conclusion does he reach?

(b) What do we learn here about weighing the pros and cons?

(5) According to Prov. 11:14, what is the last principle?

c. When we examine God's providence in using these five principles, He will lead us and we may act confidently.

6. What about obstacles? What should we think when God by His providence puts hindrances in the way of our decision?

    a. Look at Exod. 13:21–14:14. Did the obstacle of the Red Sea mean that God was not leading the children of Israel to leave Egypt?

    b. Why did God give this obstacle?

    c. Obstacles should cause us to reflect on our decision and check our principles. They might mean that God would not have us to go in that direction, but they might just be a test.

    d. What about the times we make wrong decisions? What does God promise in 1 John 1:9 and Rom. 8:28?

    e. How would you apply this to making a wrong decision?

LESSON 8:

MAN AND SIN

Assignment:

Read:

W.C.F. 4:2; 6:1-6; 9:1-5; 7:2; L.C. 20, 21-29, 149;
S.C. 10, 12-19, 82; B.C. articles 14, 15; H.C. 5, 7-14;
C.D. I, article 1; II, articles 1, 2 with rejections 3, 6; III, IV, articles 1-3 with rejections.
Complete this lesson.

Memorize:

Gen. 1:26; S.C. 10, 14.

As you begin this study pray that the Holy Spirit will enable you to understand the Bible and its message.

In order to know God rightly we must know ourselves. The purpose of this lesson is that we might know the dignity of man created in the image of God and His plight having fallen into sin.

Man's Created Nature

1. Read Gen. 1:26-30 and 2:7. List some of the ways these verses express man's uniqueness.
    a. What are some of the things entailed in man's being created in the image of God? (Compare your answer with W.C.F. 4:2.)
    b. According to S.C. 10, what three things are involved spiritually in man's being in God's image?

c. From these three things the Bible develops the offices of prophet, priest, and king. In the following verses match the distinctive element with the appropriate passage and then write a definition of each.

(1) 1 John 3:7-10	Knowledge/Prophet
(2) Lev. 11:44,45	Righteousness/Priest
(3) 1 Cor. 2:10, 11	Holiness/King

2. Read Gen. 1:26-28; 2:1-3, 15-25.
   a. List the responsibilities God gave to Adam.
   b. What test did God give man?
   c. What did God say would happen to Adam if he disobeyed?
   d. What may we infer would have happened if he had obeyed?
   e. According to W.C.F. 7.2 what do we call this relationship with its responsibilities?
   f. What name do L.C. 20 and S.C. 12 give to this covenant? We will look at the Covenant of Works in more detail in the next lesson.
3. Write a summary of what you have learned about man's created nature and the responsibilities given to him in that nature.
4. What are things men do today because they are made in the image of God?

Man's Fallen Nature

5. Gen. 3:1-19 describes how Adam and Eve responded to the test and the consequences of their actions.
   a. What did they do? (Compare with S.C. 13, 15.)
   b. What happened to them physically because they disobeyed?
   c. They also died spiritually, which means they lost their original knowledge, righteousness, and

holiness. Illustrate the loss of these three things from verses 7-13.

d. Compare Rom. 6:23 with S.C. 19. What is the third aspect of death that Adam and Eve suffered?

e. By sinning they became sinners. According to S.C. 14 what are the two aspects of sin?

    (1) What is "want of conformity"?

    (2) What is "transgression?"

6. According to Rom. 5:17-19, what three things happened to the human race because of Adam's sin?

    a. This is called original sin. According to S.C. 18, what does original sin entail?

    b. S.C. 16 says that these things happened to the human race because of the covenant of works, which is the contract that God had made with Adam. Can you think of arrangements in our society in which one person acts legally on behalf of many?

    c. Because Adam was the head of the human race he acted on behalf of all. In what ways do you think Adam was the head of the human race?

7. According to Ps. 51:5; 58:3; Job 14:4, at what point do people receive their sinful natures?

    a. Is any person born of a human father and mother exempt from this nature?

    b. How was Christ exempt from original sin?

8. Now look at Rom. 3:10-18; 8:6,7; 1 Cor. 2:14; Eph. 2:1-3 and list the practical effects of being born a sinner?

9. According to S.C. 19 what are the consequences of being sinners who practice sin?

10. In summary describe the condition and need of every person born of a human father and mother.

LESSON 9:

GOD'S COVENANT

Assignment:

Read:

W.C.F. 7 L.C. 30-35; S.C. 12, 20; B.C. article 17;
C.D. II, rejection 2.
Complete this lesson.

Memorize:

Gen. 3:15; Rom. 8:3; S.C. 12, 20.

At the conclusion of our last lesson we left man in a terrible strait – dead in sins and under God's condemnation. This lesson will help us understand the general framework by which God extricates man from His sin and its consequences.

The Nature and Necessity of the Covenant

1. Look up the term "covenant" in a dictionary and write a definition.
2. A good example of a covenant between man and man is Gen. 21:27-31.
    a. What was the difficulty between Abraham and Abimelech?
    b. What was the role of a covenant in settling the difficulty?
    c. Who initiated the idea of a covenant and set the terms?

d. What were the parts of this covenant?
   (1)
   (2)
   (3)

e. From this passage what may we conclude that a Biblical covenant is?

3. The necessity for a covenant is seen in Isa. 40:12-17 and Job 9:32. According to these verses and W.C.F. 7:1, why do you think God uses a covenant to relate to man?

4. According to Hab. 1:13, can you think of another reason God uses a covenant to relate to us?

The Covenant of Works

5. We learned in the previous lesson that all mankind were brought into sin by Adam's fall, because he acted on behalf of all. This arrangement is called the Covenant of Works. In light of what we have said about covenants in general look at Gen. 2:15-17.

   a. Who takes the initiative?

   b. What responsibility was placed on man?

   c. What did God threaten and promise?

6. This covenant transaction is summarized by S.C. 12. There was no sacrifice in this covenant, because man had not yet sinned.

The Covenant of Grace

7. When Adam broke the covenant of works the penalty was in effect for him and the entire human race. Furthermore, the demands of the covenant were still in effect, if man were to be right with God. According to Gal. 3:10,12; James 2:10 what requirement is placed on man and what happens if he does not meet this requirement?

   a. Therefore, if man were to be saved what two things would he have to be able to do?

8. Since none can keep the law perfectly or satisfy its penalty, if anyone is to be saved, God must do these things for him. This is what the Bible means by grace: God's doing for man what man does not deserve and cannot do for himself. This grace is administered through what we call the covenant of grace. According to S.C. 20 what does God promise to do in the covenant of grace?

9. This covenant was first established in Gen. 3:15.

   a. Who initiated and established this arrangement?

   b. Who are the parties involved in this transaction (the serpent represents Satan (Rev. 20:2))?

   c. What does God promise to do?

   d. By whom will God defeat the serpent?

   e. This is the first gospel promise. God says that on the basis of a deliverer who suffers He will destroy Satan and restore His people to Himself. The rest of the Bible is the unfolding of this promise. We might say that the covenant with its promise is the framework that ties the entire Bible together. This is called covenant theology. The covenant of grace was revealed in the Old Testament to Noah, Abraham, Moses, and David. These various administrations are called the Old Covenant. The New Covenant is revealed in Christ. According to covenant theology, all the various covenant administrations were the progressive and unified revelation of God's saving grace. God's people were saved in the Old Testament times in exactly the same way they are now.

      (1) The promises of the Old Covenant and the New Covenant are the same.

         (a) What is the great covenant promise that runs straight through Scripture (Gen. 17:7; Exod. 19:5, 6; Jer. 31:33; Heb. 8:10; Rev. 21:3)?

         (b) This promise is worked out in two more specific promises by which God accomplishes this relationship. According to

Gen. 12:3; cf. Gal. 3:8; Isa. 59:21; Deut. 30:6; Ps. 32:1, 2, what does God promise in the Old Covenant.

(c) Compare Acts 2:38, 39 with Jer. 31:31-34 and Joel 2:28, 29. What two things were promised on the day of Pentecost?

(2) According to Acts 16:31, how does a person receive these benefits?

(3) Look at Rom. 4:1-9. How did David and Abraham receive the benefits of the covenant?

(4) On the basis of the same promises received in the same way we must conclude that it is one covenant.

10. This is not to say there are no differences. We recognize that there must be some differences, because we refer to the Old Covenant or Testament and the New Covenant or Testament. This distinction is based on Heb. 8:13. Read Heb. 8 and put an "o" by the things that are part of the Old Covenant and an "n" by those in the New Covenant.

Description	**Ans.**	**Description**	**Ans.**
Earthly Sanctuary		The Real Thing	
Heavenly Sanctuary		Earthly Priests	
Copies and Shadows		Heavenly Priests	

From this exercise we learn that basically the old was preparatory for the new and the new fulfilled the old. Yet both the old and the new are the covenant of grace. This truth is summarized in W.C.F. 7:5, 6. This is an important principle to keep in mind as you read and study the Bible.

LESSON 10:

THE ATONEMENT

Assignment:

Read:

W.C.F. 8; L.C. 36-50; S.C. 21-27; B.C. articles 17-21, 26; H.C. 11, 12, 15-19, 29, 37, 38, 46-49, 51.

Complete this lesson.

Memorize:

S.C. 21, 22; Phil. 2:6-8.

We have learned that Jesus Christ is the eternal son of God, the same in substance and equal in power and glory with the Father and the Holy Spirit. It remains for us to see how He became our Savior and what He accomplished on our behalf.

How He Became Our Savior

1. We saw in Gen. 3:15 that God promised salvation by a deliverer. According to Isa. 42:1 and John 3:16, who was the deliverer to be?
2. According to John 1:1, 14 what did the eternal son of God have to do in order to become our Savior?
   a. This is called the incarnation (God in the flesh). Read Luke 1:26-38. How did the incarnation take place? (Note carefully the phrase "shall conceive in your womb.")
   b. This is normally called the virgin birth.

3. It is important to understand that Jesus truly became man. To help you understand this truth, look up each verse and write the particular human characteristic, aspect, or infirmity after it.

Verse	Human Characteristic	Human Aspect	Human Infirmity
a. Matt. 26:38			
b. John 4:4-8			
c. Luke 2:52			
d. Luke 19:41			
e. Mark 3:5			
f. Luke 23:46			

4. According to John 8:46 and Heb. 4:15, what human infirmity did Jesus not have?
5. S.C. 22 summarizes what we have learned about the human nature of Jesus. Write the answer in your own words.
6. Now look at Matt. 16:16 and John 20:28. Did Jesus cease being God when He became man?
    a. Paul instructs us in Phil. 2:6, 7 what Jesus did when He took on a human nature. Write these two verses in your own words.
    b. According to S.C. 21, how then did God's Son become our Savior?

What He Accomplished on our Behalf

7. In 1 Tim. 2:5 what word describes the work of Jesus as Savior?
    a. What does a mediator do?

b. What two parties need to be reconciled?

c. According to Rom. 3:25, 26; 6:23; and John 3:18, 36, what do you think had to be done if God is to be reconciled to sinners?

d. What do Rom. 2:13 and Lev. 18:5 tell us must be man's position if he is to be accepted by God?

e. Is any mere man able to fulfill the demands of the law?

f. What is the ultimate penalty man must pay (Rom. 6:23, cf. S.C. 19)?

g. Thus as mediator, Jesus had to fulfill the perfect demands of the law and to satisfy God's punishment of sinners.

8. According to Heb. 10:5-9 what was one of the primary purposes the son of God became a man?

a. How does Christ express this purpose in Matt. 3:15; 5:17; and John 4:34?

b. This is what Paul means in Gal. 4:4 that Christ was made under the law. According to Rom. 10:4 did Christ fulfill this purpose?

c. What does Paul say in Rom. 3:21, 22 God gives to us when we believe in Jesus Christ?

d. Thus we learn that by His obedience Christ purchased righteousness so that we can be accepted by God.

9. According to Gal. 3:13, what did God do to Christ on the cross?

a. According to 2 Cor. 5:21, what did God place on Christ?

b. According to Isa. 53:4-9, what happened to Christ because our sins were placed on Him?

c. This is called the substitutionary atonement. Christ on the cross took the place of His people and suffered the punishment due to their sin. Compare S.C. 25.

10. According to John 10:15, 16; 17:9; and Rev. 5:9, 10, did Christ pay the penalty for all people or for His people?

    It is important to understand this distinction. If Christ suffered hell on the cross, then everyone whose place He took must be released from the punishment of hell. Therefore either He died for all and all must be saved or He died for His people and everyone for whom He died will be saved. When we realize that He died in a special way for the people the Father gave Him, we see that our salvation has fully been accomplished. To be saved we receive what Christ has done for us.

11. In summary write a definition of the doctrine of substitutionary atonement.

LESSON 11:

THE AGENT OF SALVATION

Assignment:

Read:

W.C.F. 2:3; L.C. 9-11, 57-59, 66; S.C. 6, 29, 30; H.C. 53.
Complete this lesson.

Memorize:

John 14:26; 15:26

Having studied man's need, God's covenant, and the work of Christ, we now turn our attention to the application of God's salvation to the individual sinner. Before considering the discrete parts of the application of salvation, we want to study about the agent of salvation, the Holy Spirit. In chapter four we studied the Trinity and learned that the Spirit is the third person of the Godhead. Read S.C. 6 to review what you have learned about the Holy Spirit.

The Names and Relations of the Third Person

1. The third person of the Godhead is given many names in the Bible. After each reference write the name given to the third person of the Godhead and what that name tells you about Him:

   a. Matt. 3:16; 1 Cor. 2:11, 12.

   b. Ps. 51:11

   c. Gal. 4:6; Phil. 1:19

   d. 2 Cor. 3:17, 18

   e. John 14:15, 26; 15:26

   f. Ps. 33:6

2. The names Spirit and breath teach us also about the Spirit's relationship to the other two members of the Godhead. According to John 15:26 what is His relation to the Father?

   a. Comparing John 15:26; Gal. 4:6; Phil. 1:19 with John 20:22, what would you say is the Son's role in the procession of the Spirit?

   b. How does L.C. 10 summarize this relationship?

   c. According to Matt. 28:19 and 2 Cor. 13:14, does this relationship suggest any subordination (see W.C.F. 2:3; L.C. 9, 11)?

3. This relationship within the Godhead teaches us how God operates. As the Spirit completes the Trinity, He completes the work of the Trinity. As the Holy Spirit He is the perfecting and sanctifying agent.

The Work of the Holy Spirit

4. According to Gen. 1:2; Job 26:13; Gen. 1:26, 27; 2:7, what were the Spirit's various activities in the work of creation?

5. We have seen that "God's works of providence are, His most holy, wise, and powerful preserving and governing all His creatures and all their actions (S.C. 11, Lesson Seven)." Match each reference with the work of providence performed by the Holy Spirit:

Ps. 104:30	a. Imparting gifts and talents
Gen. 6:3; Heb. 6:4	b. Preserving and sustaining life
Exod. 31:2ff; 1 Sam. 16:13	c. Providential alterations
Prov. 21:1; Zech. 4:6, 7	d. Preserving moral life

6. Another work of the Spirit was to inspire the men who wrote the Bible. After each reference describe the Spirit's role in revelation and inspiration.

    a. 2 Sam. 23:2

    b. Ezek. 8:3; 11:1

    c. John 14:26

    d. 2 Tim. 3:16; 2 Peter 1:21

7. In Lesson Two we referred to the Spirit's role in the illumination of Scripture. Look up Ps. 119:18; 1 Cor. 2:14; Eph. 1:17, 18 and write out the Spirit's role in illumination.

8. The Spirit was also involved in the work of Christ. After each reference describe the Spirit's role:

    a. Luke 1:35; Matt. 1:18, 20

    b. Matt. 3:16, 17; Isa. 61:13; Luke 4:18, 19

    c. Acts 2:22; Matt. 12:28

    d. Heb. 9:14

    e. 1 Peter 3:18; Rom. 8:11

    f. John 7:39; Acts 2:33

9. The Spirit is the primary agent in our conversion, sanctification, and preservation. We will study these works in greater detail in subsequent lessons. Simply note now how these works are ascribed to the Spirit by listing each work after the reference:

    a. John 3:3-7

    b. 1 Cor. 2:4; 1 Thess. 2:13

    c. Rom. 8:13

    d. Eph. 3:16-19

    e. Rom. 8:16

    f. Rom. 8:10, 11; Eph. 1:13, 14

10. According to Rom. 8:9, what is the Spirit's relation to each believer?

    a. List the terms Paul uses in Rom. 8:1-14 to describe the effects of this indwelling.

    b. By whose power do we live the Christian life?

    c. Match the effects of this indwelling with the appropriate reference:

Uniting us to Christ	a.	Gal. 4:6, 7; 1 John 2:27-29; Rom. 8; 15-16
Seal or earnest of inheritance	b.	Rom. 6:3, 4
Grants assurance	c.	Rom. 8:26; Eph.6:18
Enables us to pray	d.	Rom. 8:14; Gal. 5:1, 16, 18
Leads and guides us in obedience	e.	Eph. 1:13, 14

    d. According to Acts 4:31; Gal. 5:16ff; Eph. 5:18 ff, what are the consequences of being filled with the Spirit?

11. The Spirit also gives gifts to the Church. Some of these gifts were extraordinary for the New Testament age as the Bible was being completed, others are ordinary for our age.

    a. Read 1 Cor. 12:8-10 and list the extraordinary gifts.

    b. According to 2 Cor. 12:12 and Heb. 2:1-4 what was the primary purpose of these gifts.

    c. List the ordinary gifts enumerated in Rom. 12:6-8 and write a definition after each one.

    d. These gifts are for the Church today. Which do you think you have? In Lesson Twenty-Three we will use a Personal Information Sheet to help you determine your gifts.

LESSON 12:

THE SOURCE OF SALVATION

Assignment:

Read:

W.C.F. 3:3-8; 10; L.C. 57-60, 68; S.C. 20, 29-31;
B.C. articles 14, 16; H.C. 54; C.D. I, articles 6-18; II, articles 8, 9 with rejections; II, IV articles 6, 8-16, rejections 6-9.
Complete this lesson.

Memorize:

Eph. 1:3; John 6:44; S.C. 31.

Having studied the work of the Holy Spirit, we now turn our attention to the application of salvation. The first step in the application is the source of salvation.

The Immediate Source

1. Read Matt. 27:44 and Luke 23:39-43.
    a. What happened to one of the robbers who were mocking Christ?
    b. Why do you think this thief turned from mocking to believing in Christ?
2. The full answer to this question is spelled out in John 6:44.
    a. According to this verse what is necessary if a person is to believe in Jesus Christ for salvation?
    b. What does Jesus promise to do to each one who is drawn to Him by the Father?

c. If all who are drawn will be raised on the last day, can any drawn by the Father not believe in the Son?

d. According to S.C. 29 what is this work called? It is called effectual because it always works.

3. According to 1 Peter 1:23 and 2 Cor. 3:3, what are the two instruments involved in effectual calling?

a. On the basis of 2 Tim. 3:15-16 and Rom. 10:14, what would you say is the role of the Word in salvation (Look also at Heb. 4:12-13)?

b. How is the work of the Holy Spirit described in John 3:3-8?

c. What are the three parts of this work described in S.C. 31?

d. After each verse, write what element of the Spirit's work is being described and then match that element with its illustration in the book of Acts.

		Ans.
1. Zech. 12:10	Acts 22:4-10	
2. 1 Cor. 2:12-14	Acts 16:14	
3. Ezek. 36:26-27	Acts 2:37	

The Ultimate Source

4. If God calls some effectually and not others, on what basis is the decision made whom He will call and whom He will pass by? The answer to this question is found in Rom. 8:29-30.

a. List the five elements of salvation found here.

b. According to these verses, what happens to the person who has been called?

c. This demonstrates that Paul is talking about effectual calling. Everyone who is called is justified and glorified.

d. Now go back one step before calling. According to these verses, who are called?

5. The word predestined means foreordained. We have already learned that God by His decree has foreordained all things that come to pass. Eph. 1:3-6 applies this foreordination to salvation.

   a. When did God choose those whom He would save?

   b. For what purpose did God choose them to salvation?

   c. Now look at Acts 13:48. How does this verse relate eternal choice to effectual calling?

   d. Write a summary of what you have learned up to this point.

6. It remains for us to discover on what basis God chooses to save certain people.

   a. The answer is found in the first element of our salvation mentioned in Rom. 8:29. Who are the ones God predestined to salvation?

   b. To understand the word "foreknowledge" or "foreknow," we need to determine how the Bible uses the word "know." Look at Gen. 4:1 (the margin of the New American Standard Bible); Amos 3:2 (again the margin of the NASB); and Ps. 1:6. Keeping these references in mind, write a definition of the idea of "know."

   c. The prefix "fore" means to know before time. Look at Acts 2:23 and 1 Peter 1:20. What do the words "foreknow" and "foreknowledge" mean in these verses?

   d. On the basis of what you have found, write a definition of "foreknew" as it is used in Rom. 8:29, 30.

   e. Compare your definition with what Paul says in Eph. 1:4, 5. What does Paul mean that God chose us according to the kind intention of His will?

f. This doctrine is called unconditional election. It is stated in W.C.F. 3:3-5.

LESSON 13:

JUSTIFICATION

Assignment:

Read:

W.C.F. 11, 14 and 15; L.C. 70, 72, 73, 76, 153;
S.C. 32, 33, 85, 86, 87; B.C. articles 22, 23;
H.C. 1, 20-23, 39, 45, 56, 59-61, 84, 87, 88, 126;
C.D. I, articles 2-4; II,
articles 3, 6, 7 with rejections; III, IV, article 13.
Complete this lesson.

Memorize:

S.C. 32, 33; Rom. 5:1, 2.

In Rom. 8:29, 30, we read that the direct consequence of calling is justification. Luther called this truth the doctrine of a standing or falling church. In this lesson we will consider what the Bible teaches about justification.

The Act of Justification

1. According to Deut. 25:1, in what context is the term "justification" used?
   a. In this verse, what act is considered the opposite of to justify? (Compare Rom. 8:33, 34.)
   b. Who is to be justified?
   c. When a judge justifies an accused criminal, what is He saying about him?

2. When we apply this judicial action to God, what do we mean when we say God justifies us?

   a. We find a dramatization of this in Zech. 3:1-5.

      (1) What was Joshua's problem (relate to what we learned in Lesson 10 about man's responsibility)?

      (2) What two things did God do for him?

3. In other words, justification deals with man's sin problem – it cancels the debt of sin, declares us not guilty and enables God to accept us as righteous.

The Ground of Justification

4. What does Prov. 17:15 say about the judge who justifies the wicked?

   a. Yet is this not what God does in justification? How can God do this and still be a just God?

5. Rom. 3:24-26 helps us understand how God can be just and justify a sinner. According to this passage, what has been done so God can be just and declare sinners not guilty? If you do not know the meaning of the word "propitiation" look it up in a dictionary.

   a. This, of course, relates to what we learned in Lesson 10 about the work of Christ. In Lesson 10, what two things did we learn that Christ did for us?

   b. This purpose and result of Christ's sacrifice is explained in 2 Cor. 5:21. What is the two-fold imputation described here? (You might need to look up imputation in a dictionary.)

   c. Thus we say that the ground or the basis of our justification is the work of the Lord Jesus Christ (W.C.F. 11:1, 3; L.C. 71).

The Means of Justification

6. According to Rom. 4:1-9, how did Abraham receive the righteousness of justification?

7. According to Rom. 3:28 and Gal. 2:16, what is the role of works in our justification?

8. Compare Gal. 2:16 with John 1:12. What is it that faith does in receiving justification? Compare your answer with S.C. 86.

    a. According to Acts 2:38 and 11:18, what other act does faith include?

    b. On the basis of Jer. 31:18, 19, write a definition of repentance. Check your answer by S.C. 87.

9. Now read James 2:14-26.

    a. By what you have learned from the principles of the interpretation of the Bible, could James be contradicting Paul?

    b. The use of cross-references helps clarify the answer to the apparent contradiction. In verse 23 James quotes Gen. 15:6. The occasion referred to in verse 21 is found in Gen. 22. In which of these instances did Abraham receive justification by believing?

    c. About how many years later did he obey God in offering up Isaac?

    d. Thus it appears that when James speaks of justification he is not thinking of justification in the Pauline sense of pardoned sin and free acceptance with God. Look up justify in the dictionary. Is there another meaning to the term that would help explain how James uses the term?

    e. How does Jesus use the term in Matt. 11:19 (some Bibles translate the term vindicated)?

    f. On the basis of what you have learned, how do you think James is using the term in James 2?

    g. Write a paraphrase of James 2:21-24.

The Relationship of Justification to Daily Confession of Sins

10. If God has pardoned all our sins and accepts us as righteous in His sight, why do we need daily to confess our sins? We will answer this question in the next lesson.

LESSON 14:

ADOPTION AND ASSURANCE

Assignment:

Read:

W.C.F. 12, 18; L.C. 74, 80, 81; S.C. 34; H.C. 1, 33;
C.D. I article 12 with rejection 8; V, articles 6, 9-13
with rejections 5, 6.
Complete this lesson.

Memorize:

S.C. 34; Rom. 8:16; 1 John 5:13.

THE ACT OF ADOPTION

1. Give a definition of adoption as it is used in human relationships.

   a. What benefits do parents give to their adopted children?

   b. According to John 1:12, what right does God give to those who believe in the Lord Jesus Christ?

   c. According to Rom. 8:16, 17, what privileges do God's adopted children receive? Compare you answer with S.C. 34.

2. Read John 1:12, 13. When does adoption take place?

   a. On the basis of Eph. 1:4-8 and Gal. 4:4, 5, how does adoption relate to election?

   b. How does it relate to Christ's work of atonement and justification?

The Benefits of Adoption

3. Listed below are a number of verses. Look up the verses and after each group write what benefit of adoption is described in the verses (Check your answers with W.C.F. 12.):

   a. Gal. 4:6, Rom. 8:15

   b. Heb. 4:16; Eph. 3:12; 1 John 5:14; Rom. 8:26, 27

   c. Ps. 103:13, 14

   d. Ps. 34:7; 27:1-3; Prov. 14:26

   e. Heb. 12:6-12

   f. Heb. 13:5; Eph. 4:30

   g. Heb. 6:12

   h. 1 Peter 1:4; Rom. 8:17, 32

4. Explain how you think an understanding of adoption and its benefits can help a person in the following areas:

   a. Problem with self-image and insecurity.

   b. A Christian who has a certain sin in his life that he does not want to give up or recognizes a commandment from God that he does not want to obey.

   c. A person who has a difficulty establishing regular habits of prayer.

The Relationship of Adoption to Daily Confession of Sins

5. Even though God has pardoned all our sins, we still are to make daily confession of sin. Part of the reason is given in 1 John 1:5-10.

   a. What does sin do to our fellowship with God?

   b. Look at Prov. 28:13. What does God say about the person who doesn't confess sin?

   c. Thus if we are to enjoy the presence of God, His fellowship, and His blessing, what must we do?

d. Therefore confession of sin does not maintain our relationship to God, but our fellowship. In justification our sins are freely forgiven once and for all. God as judge has cleared us. As adopted children we are not judicially obligated to confess sin, but rather it is a family responsibility. We ought to confess sins as we commit them, but in addition, we ought to have a time each day during which we take spiritual inventory and ask God to forgive us of our sins. Be sure this is part of your daily time of Bible study and prayer.

The Relation of Adoption to Assurance

6. One of the great practical benefits of the doctrine of adoption is the promotion of assurance of salvation.

   a. According to Gal. 4:6 and Rom. 8:16, what is one of the results of adoption?

   b. What kind of attitude or disposition does the Holy Spirit give the believer?

   c. What testimony does He bear to the believer?

   d. According to Heb. 6:17, 18; 2 Peter 1:4-11; and 2 Cor. 1:12, what two things does the Holy Spirit use to testify to us that God has saved us?

   e. Write a summary statement of how adoption relates assurance. (Compare W.C.F. 18:2.)

7. It remains to us to test our adoption. What does John say in 1 John 5:13 about those who believe?

   a. The phrase "these things" points back to certain marks of sonship that John has given in this letter. Look up the following verses and list some of the things that will be developing in your life if you have been converted: 1 John 5:1; 3:14; 4:7; 5:3, 4; 2:29; 3:9.

   b. Look at Matt. 7:20-23 and James 2:14-26. Do you think a person who has no growth in faith and holiness has any right to assurance of salvation?

8. Therefore, if God has adopted us, He is working changes in us (Phil. 2:12, 13). This, too, is of grace.

LESSON 15:

PERSEVERANCE AND SANCTIFICATION

Assignment:

Read:

W.C.F. 13; 17; L.C. 75, 77, 78, 79; S.C. 35, 36;
B.C. article 24; H.C. 1, 32, 43, 62-64; 86-90;
C.D. I, articles 11, 13 with rejection 6; II, article 9;
V, articles 1-15 with rejections 1-9.
Complete this lesson.

Memorize:

S.C. 35; Heb. 12:14; Rom. 13:4

We read in Eph. 1:4 that God's great purpose in choosing and saving His people is that we be holy and blameless. This work begins with our justification in which God declares us righteous and ends in our glorification that perfects us in righteousness. In this lesson we are concerned with the process that takes place between justification and glorification.

Perseverance

1. What is the fifth link of the chain in Rom. 8:29, 30?
   a. According to John 17:24 and 1 John 3:2, what is glorification?
   b. Why do you think that Paul speaks of glorification in the past tense in Rom. 8:30?

c. According to this verse can any justified person not be glorified?

d. This is the great truth of eternal security, frequently expressed as once saved, always saved. Scripture affirms this truth in a number of ways. After each of the following verses, write what you learn about this truth:

	Verse	Answers
(1)	Phil. 1:6	
(2)	John 6:44	
(3)	John 10:28, 29	

e. Now write a statement of this truth in your own words. (Compare you answer with W.C.F. 17 and L.C. 79.)

2. 2 Tim. 2:19 teaches, however, that there are two sides to the coin of eternal security.

a. How does Paul express the fact of God's preservation of the Christian?

b. What duty does Paul command in this verse?

c. This is the second side of the coin: the one who is preserved perseveres in the faith. Thus we may not sit back and say, "Once saved, always saved, so it does not matter what I do." If we are saved, we will be putting off sin.

d. The two things are put together in Phil. 2:12, 13. How does Paul express perseverance in these verses?

e. How does he express preservation?

SANTIFICATION

3. The responsibility of perseverance is worked out in the process the Bible calls sanctification. Look up in a dictionary the terms "sanctify" and "sanctification" and write a definition of what you think the Bible means when it speaks of sanctification. Compare your answer with S.C. 35.

4. On the basis of 2 Thess. 2:13 and Heb. 12:14, how important to God and to the believer is sanctification?

5. According to Rom. 6:1-10, what act took place when you were converted?

   a. According to Rom. 6:11-14, what should you be doing because you are dead to sin and alive to righteousness?

   b. We call this definitive sanctification. At the moment of conversion we become slaves to Christ and not to sin. This definitive sanctification is the basis of our progressive sanctification.

6. Progressive sanctification is the process between justification and glorification in which a believer becomes more God- like. According to S.C. 35, what are the two aspects of sanctification?

   a. The positive aspect is stated in Eph. 4:23, 24 and Col. 3:10. In what areas are we being renewed?

   b. According to Rom. 8:29, what is the pattern for our renewal?

   c. The negative aspect is set forth in Col. 3:5-9. What must we be putting off in order to be renewed in righteousness?

7. In order to accomplish this putting off and putting on, the Bible teaches us to use certain things God has given us. After each set of verses, write the means described there:

	Verse	Answer
a.	John 17:17; Ps. 119:9	
b.	Eph. 6:18, 19; 1 Thess. 5:17	
c.	Heb. 10:24, 25	
d.	1 Cor. 11:23-26; 12:13	
e.	Rom. 15:14	

f. Are there any of these that you are not using? If so, why? Make plans to implement these things in your life.

8. We also need to learn how to deal with temptation, if we are to grow. According to Ps. 139:23, 24, where do we need to begin in dealing with temptation?

   a. What must we know about our hearts?

   b. According to the Bible, we are attacked by lust from within our hearts, by Satan, and by temptations from the world. In light of Matt. 26:41, what two things should we be doing?

   c. On the basis of 1 Cor. 16:13 and 1 Peter 4:7, what do you think Jesus means by "watch"?

   d. According to Matt. 6:13, for what should we be praying?

   e. What do Gen. 39:10, 15 and 1 Cor. 15:33 tell us about avoiding occasions of temptation?

   f. On the basis of Heb. 10:24, what help should we be getting from Christian friends?

   g. Another thing we must do is develop proper habits. In Eph. 4:25-32, what four things are contrasted?

   h. What four patterns of behavior are we to put off?

   i. With what do we replace them?

j. Here is the principle that you put off by replacing with biblical patterns. Summarize the principles involved in dealing with temptation and then choose one sin with which you have a problem and develop a plan of attack.

LESSON 16:

COMMUNICATING THE GOSPEL

Assignment:

Review the first fifteen lessons.
Complete this lesson.
Memorize your gospel outline.

In the first fifteen lessons we have covered the basic doctrines of God and the Gospel. We must have a grasp of these things in order to communicate the Gospel in its fullness. In this lesson we will work on how to communicate the Gospel. It is a good time to review the first fifteen lessons.

Read:

Matt. 28:19, 20.

In these verses Christ gives the Church the responsibility to make disciples of the nations. Part of this task, we call evangelism and witnessing. Each of us in the Church has a role to play in this task of evangelism. Our roles will vary according to the gifts that God has given us, but each must do his part and each one ought to be able to tell others what Christ means to him and certainly everyone can invite others to worship services and Bible studies. The purpose of this lesson is to equip us to do our part in the Church's task.

Background

1. According to Matt. 5:13-16 and Phil. 2:12-15, what is the Christian's great responsibility?

a. As we saw in the last lesson, our great responsibility is to be holy. As we seek to fulfill this responsibility, men will see our works and want to learn about our faith. Some call this lifestyle or friendship evangelism. As we live a Christian lifestyle, we will seek to develop relationships with those around us and to be sensitive to opportunities to share what Christ means to us by communicating the gospel, and inviting our friends and acquaintances to social events (both in our homes and with other Christians), Bible studies, and worship services.

2. Ideally, evangelism is a dialogue. Look at 1 Peter 3:15, 16 and Col. 4:5, 6. According to these passages, what ought we as Christians always be prepared to do?

   a. What are we to be sensitive to, according to Col. 4:5, 6?

   b. Where should we begin with a person?

   c. We can summarize: We need to be sensitive to where a person is and what his needs are, as well as alert to the opportunities God in his providence gives us to speak. Furthermore, we need to be prepared to try to answer a person's questions or to take him to see someone who can. In John 1:45, 46, how does Philip deal with Nathaniel's question?

3. This means we must not force a memorized gospel presentation on someone, but begin with a person where he is. Look at the following passages and describe the approach used by the person witnessing:

   a. John 3:1-15

   b. John 4:1-30

   c. Acts 13:16-41

   d. Acts 17:22-31

      (1) According to these examples, how should we approach a person with the gospel?

(2) How are we going to know where a person is and what his needs are?

(3) What form of speech is particularly useful in determining where a person is and in getting him to think about the gospel?

Sharing a Testimony

4. What does the Samaritan woman do in John 4:29?

5. In the context of lifestyle evangelism, we need to be prepared to share what Christ means to us. Write out your testimony. Your testimony should be a brief explanation of how God saved you and what He is doing in your life. (Remember that those reared in Christian homes and who never know a day they were not trusting in Christ may testify to God's saving and sanctifying grace.) You may want to divide into pairs and give your testimony.

Gospel Outline

6. It is also important that we have in mind the basic facts of the Gospel. If a person is to be saved, he needs to know who God is, who man is and what is the penalty of his sin, who Christ is and what He has done, how a person must respond, and what are the demands of the Christian life. Using these headings, make an outline, using Scripture from previous lessons, that communicates what you want a person to know about the Gospel.

   a. Who God is:

   b. Who man is and what is the penalty of his sin:

   c. Who Christ is and what He has done:

   d. How a person must respond to the gospel:

   e. What God demands of the Christian life:

LESSON 17:

WORSHIP PART I

Assignment:

Read:

W.C.F. 19, 21; L.C. 91-110; S.C. 39-52; B.C. 25;
H.C. 3, 4, 92-98; C.D. III, IV, article 5.
Complete this lesson.

Memorize:

Exod. 20:1-6; S.C. 41.

We saw earlier in S.C. 3 that Scripture principally teaches two things: what man is to believe concerning God and what duty God requires of man. We have been examining some of the things we are to believe; now we turn our attention to some of our duties. These duties are summarized in the Ten Commandments. In this lesson we look at the importance of the law of God in the life of the believer and at the first two commandments.

The Guide to our Duty

1. According to John 14:15, 21, 23, what does Christ expect the Christian to do?
2. Comparing Matt. 22:37-40 with Deut. 6:1-9 and Lev. 19:11-18; looking also at Rom. 13:8-10, where do we find Jesus' commandments that we are to keep if we love Him?
   a. This truth is summarized for us in S.C. 39-42. The law of God, which is found in the Ten Commandments,

is the primary place that God reveals His will for our duty. The Ten Commandments cover the major areas of relationship between us and God and between us and our fellows.

b. According to L.C. 97 what is the role of law for the Christian?

The Duty of Worship

3. The law and worship. One of the first things the law teaches us is about worship. In fact the duty of worship is the primary focus of the first four commandments. The first commandment teaches us about the duty of worship; the second, the way of worship; the third, the attitude in worship; and the fourth, the day of worship. In this lesson, we shall consider the duty and way of worship.

4. The first commandment is found in Exod. 20:3. What is God forbidding in this commandment? (Compare your answers S.C. 47. Also look back at Lesson 4, # 3.)

5. According to L.C. 99, # 4, what is an important principle of biblical interpretation to keep in mind when one interprets the law?

   a. We may call this the principle of opposites. Keeping this principle in mind, look at Deut. 6:4, 5, 13, 17 and write what positive duty is required by the first commandment.

   b. According to Rom. 12:1, 2, what area of life does the positive duty to love, worship, and fear God embrace?

6. Even though worship embraces all that a Christian should do, the Bible also deals with worship in the more formal capacity of adoring God, learning His Word, and praying. There are three types of formal worship. After each of the following passages, describe the type of formal worship that is required:

	Verses	Answer
a.	Exod. 34:8 Ps. 42:8 Ps. 119:54-56 Dan. 6:10 Matt. 6:6	
b.	Gen. 18:19 2 Tim. 3:15 Ps. 78:1-4	
c.	Neh. 8:1-8 Acts 20:7 Heb. 10:25	

7. On the basis of the first commandment, what types of worship ought you to be involved in?

The Way of Worship

8. The second commandment is found in Exod. 20:4-6. What two things does God forbid by this commandment? (Compare Deut. 4:15-19; 5:8, 9.)

9. God forbids making physical representations of Him.

   a. According to L.C. 109, how should we apply this prohibition to make images of God to visual representations of the person of the Lord Jesus Christ?

   b. What does Paul say about knowledge of Christ in the flesh in 2 Cor. 5:14-16?

   c. According to 1 Peter 1:8, do we worship a visible or an invisible Christ?

   d. What visual representation has Christ given us of Himself?

10. The second prohibition is against worshiping God through images.

    a. In Exod. 32:4, 5 how did Israel violate the second commandment?

b. What are some ways people today violate this commandment?

c. We learn that we may not worship God according to our imaginations. He reserves the right to reveal how we are to think about Him.

11. If we are not to worship God according to our imaginations, what must guide us in our worship?

 a. According to Deut. 12:31, 32, what positive duty is being taught by this commandment? (Compare L.C. 108 and S.C. 50.)

 b. This duty is called the regulative principle.

 c. This principle is stated in W.C.F. 1:6 and 21:1. Write the principle in your own words.

12. If we are only to worship God according to His revelation (commandment or inference from doctrine or example), we must determine from the Bible the elements of worship. Look up the following passages and list after each what element of worship is required by that passage:

 a. Neh. 8:1-8

 b. 1 Tim. 4:13

 c. Ps. 65:2

 d. Eph. 5:19

 e. 1 Cor. 16:1, 2

 f. 2 Tim. 1:13, 14; 1 Tim. 3:16

 g. Num. 6:23-27; 2 Cor. 13:14

 h. Ps. 95:1-3; 147:1

13. Now take a bulletin and see if you can match the things we do in our worship service with these elements taught in Scripture.

14. In Exod. 20:5, 6 what is God's attitude to proper worship?

 a. What does God threaten?

b. In Lev. 10:1-3 and Deut. 4:3, what does He do to those who violate this commandment?

c. What does God promise?

d. We learn that we must be very careful how we approach God in worship.

In the next study, we shall consider the attitude of the worshiper and the day of worship.

LESSON 18:

WORSHIP PART II

Assignment:

Read:

W.C.F. 19, 21; L.C. 111-121; S.C. 53-62; H.C. 99-103.
Complete this lesson.

Memorize:

Exod. 20:7-11.

In the last lesson we established the role of the law for the believer and looked specifically at the first two commandments as they relate to worship. In this lesson we want to learn what the third and fourth commandments say about worship.

The Manner of Worship (Exod. 20:7)

1. The third commandment addresses the use of God's name. We shall consider how this commandment applies generally and then apply it specifically to worship.
   a. What is forbidden by the third commandment? (Compare your answer to S.C. 55.)
   b. We saw in Lesson 3 that God reveals Himself by His name, word, works, and attributes. If all these things make God known to us, how should we then speak of these things?
   c. List some of God's attributes.
   d. Can you think of ways we commonly profane God's attributes by speaking lightly of them?

e. In light of this, what do you think of phrases like "holy cow" or "goodness gracious"?

f. The third commandment also forbids what we call minced oaths. The word minced means to minimize. These are words and phrases that were contractions of the divine name in order to get around this prohibition. Can you think of any examples?

2. The positive teaching of the third commandment applies directly to our worship.

a. How does Eccles. 5:1-5 relate the third commandment to worship?

b. According to Matt. 15:8, what attitude is required?

c. How does Jesus apply this attitude of reverence in John 4:23, 24?

d. What do you think it means to worship God in spirit?

e. Where does such spiritual worship originate?

f. Write a summary of what our attitude and demeanor ought to be in worship and apply it to the parts of worship we noted in the last lesson.

The Day of Worship (Exod. 20:8-11)

3. According to the fourth commandment, when did God institute the observance of the Sabbath?

a. Look at Gen. 2:1-3. What did God do after the six days of creation?

b. What did He say about the day?

c. For whose sake do you think God blessed and sanctified the day?

4. According to the fourth commandment, what was forbidden on the Sabbath day?

a. What things does the prophet Isaiah include in his interpretation of the fourth commandment in Isa. 58:13? (Compare S.C. 61.)

b. What works and activities do you think are forbidden in the fourth commandment?

c. What exception does Jesus make in Matt. 12:1-14? (Compare your answer to the last part of S.C. 60.)

d. Give some examples of things you think are exceptions.

5. According to S.C. 59, what day is to be observed as the Christian Sabbath?

a. This change is established by a number of things:

b. On what day did Christ arise from the dead? In Rev. 1:10, what is the day called? Why do you think it is called the Lord's Day?

c. According to Col. 2:16, 17, what happened to the seventh day Sabbath and other Old Testament holy days?

d. According to 1 Cor. 16:1, 2 and Acts 20:7, on what day of the week did the early church worship?

e. On the basis of these things we say the day is changed to the first day of the week.

6. The purpose of the Sabbath. Compare Exod. 20:8-11 and Deut. 5:12-15. For what two reasons are we to remember and observe the Sabbath?

a. Why then ought we to keep the Sabbath?

b. According to Isa. 58:13, what positive duty does this entail?

c. What does Lev. 23:3 state to be the great work of the Sabbath?

d. Thus this day has been given to us that in acts of private and public worship we may remember God's mighty deeds of creation and redemption and praise Him accordingly. According to L.C. 117, what then are some of the positive things we ought to be doing?

7. In Isa. 58:14, what three things does God promise to do for those who keep the Sabbath?

8. Preparing for public worship. Look at L.C. 117 and 160. List what activities you ought to be doing in preparing for and participating in Sabbath worship.

LESSON 19:

MARRIAGE AND FAMILY

Assignment:

Read:

W.C.F. 24; L.C. 123-133; 137-139;
S.C. 63-66; 70-72; H.C. 104-109.
Complete this lesson.

Memorize:

Exod. 20:12, 14.

Having looked somewhat at man's duty to God, we now look at man's duty to man. In this lesson we consider particularly how the seventh and fifth commandments apply to marriage and family.

Marriage

1. What are some things forbidden by the seventh commandment? (Look at Heb. 13:4; Gal. 5:19; Rom. 1:24-27 as you answer this question. Compare your answer with L.C. 139.)
    a. According to Eph. 5:3, 4 and Matt. 5:28, in addition to immoral actions, what else is forbidden by this commandment?
    b. Why do you think that the sin of adultery is chosen to represent the various sins of immorality?
2. God forbids adultery in order to teach that all sexual sins are a violation of the marriage relationship. Thus,

in forbidding sexual immorality, God is promoting and protecting the sanctity of marriage. We find the institution of marriage in Gen. 2:18-24.

a. What did Adam need?

b. How did God bring Adam to understand his need?

c. What was God's solution?

d. In verses 22, 24, we find the first wedding ceremony. Who gives away the bride?

   (1) What is God establishing in this action?

   (2) What is Adam's response?

   (3) In this response we find the concept of commitment. What does God declare in verse 24?

3. The purpose of marriage. The purpose of marriage is expressed in the concept of woman being a helper corresponding to man's needs and in their being one flesh (see W.C.F. 24.1, 2).

   a. According to Mal. 2:14, what is the primary purpose of marriage?

      (1) What does the concept of companion include?

      (2) What are some aspects of companionship in marriage?

   b. In 1 Cor. 7:1-6 and Prov. 5:18, 19, we learn a second purpose that is expressed in the concept of one flesh. What is this purpose?

      (1) We learn here that sex is a good gift of God that is to be enjoyed only in the bonds of marriage. But we should emphasize that it is a gift to be enjoyed.

      (2) This helps us to understand why all sexual relationships outside the marriage are wrong.

   c. A third purpose is expressed in Gen. 1:28; Ps. 127:3; and Mal. 2:15. What is this purpose?

4. Marriage roles. Read Eph. 5:21-33 and 1 Peter 3:1-7. What is the husband's role in marriage?

   a. What do you think it means to love the wife as Christ loved the Church and gave Himself for it?

   b. How would you relate the command in Eph. 5:21 to the husband's responsibility to love his wife sacrificially?

   c. How would you relate 1 Peter 3:7 to the husband's responsibility to love his wife sacrificially?

   d. Give some examples.

5. What is the wife's role?

   a. Look at John 14:15 and Eph. 5:24 and explain why Paul does not command wives to love their husbands.

   b. According to 1 Peter 3:1-6, what kind of spirit should the wife exhibit in submission?

   c. How should the wife respond when she is convinced that her idea is better than her husband's?

   d. Applying Acts 4:19 to the marriage relationship, how should a wife respond when her husband tells her to do something contrary to scripture?

Family Life

6. We have noted that one of the purposes of marriage is to raise a godly seed. The framework for this responsibility is given us in the fifth commandment. What is required by the term honor? (Compare L.C. 128.)

   a. According to Prov. 30:11; Exod. 21:15, 17; and Prov. 20:20, how important is it that children show proper respect to their parents?

   b. In Eph. 6:1-3 how does Paul apply the commandment to children?

   c. According to Prov. 4:1; 6:20, what does this obedience entail?

7. According to Eph. 6:4, what does this commandment require of parents? (We understand on the basis of Prov. 6:20; 10:1 that mothers are included. Compare L.C. 129.)
    a. What are some ways parents provoke their children to wrath?
    b. According to Prov. 19:18, how important is discipline?
    c. What do 13:24; 22:15; 23:13, 14; 29:15 teach about physical discipline?
    d. How should we in the New Testament church apply Deut. 21:18-21 to incorrigible children?
8. Paul also demands instruction. In Gen. 18:19, what is one of the purposes for which God saved Abraham?
    a. What does Deut. 6:4-9 tell us about the times and places in which we teach our children?
    b. List ways that parents ought to be fulfilling this injunction.
    c. Are you practicing regular family worship and teaching your children in this manner?
    d. How would you relate this commandment to the responsibility of general education?

LESSON 20:

LIFE AND TRUTH

Assignment:

Read:

L.C. 134-136; 143-145; S.C. 67-69; 76-78; H.C. 105-107, 112.

Complete this lesson.

Memorize:

Exod. 20:13, 16.

Having considered God's principles for marriage and home, we now consider two things that are of great importance to God: life and truth. God has declared both of these things sacred, thus we speak of the sanctity of life and truth.

THE SANCTITY OF LIFE (EXOD. 20:13)

1. Comparing Exod. 20:13 with Acts 16:28 and Gen. 9:6, list the things prohibited by the sixth commandment. (Compare your answer with L.C. 136.)
2. According to Gen. 9:5, 6; Num. 35:31, 33; Deut. 20:1, 10-18; Exod. 22:2, 3; and Rom. 13:4, does this commandment prohibit all killing?
   a. List the situations in which it is not wrong to take another person's life.
   b. According to Gen. 9:5, 6; Deut. 21:1, 9; and Lev. 24:17, what is the reason for capital punishment in the case of murder?
   c. Does this reason still have force today?

   d. What then should the Christian's position be on capital punishment?

3. Following the principle that the opposite of that which is forbidden is required, what would be some positive duties required by this commandment? (Look at Eph. 5:28, 29; 1 Kings 18:4, compare your answer with L.C. 135.)

   a. Since life is important and because we are in the image of God and the Christian who is being renewed in that image is indwelt by the Holy Spirit as the temple of God (1 Cor. 6:19, 20), we are responsible to take care of our bodies. Look at Prov. 24:13; 25:16; 1 Tim. 4:8; and 5:23 and list some things required by this commandment in terms of caring for our bodies.

   b. On the basis of Prov. 24:11, 12; Ps. 82:4; and Prov. 31:8, 9, how would you apply this commandment to the matter of abortion?

   c. In light of this commandment, may a Christian remain neutral in the area of abortion?

4. According to Matt. 5:21, 22, this commandment goes beyond actions to thoughts, attitudes, and words. On the basis of 1 John 3:15; Lev. 19:17; Rom. 12:19; and Eph. 4:31, what are some other things prohibited by this commandment?

   a. Ought a Christian to have racial or social prejudice?

   b. According to Exod. 32:15-35; Matt. 21:12, 13; and Eph. 4:26 is all anger a violation of the sixth commandment?

   c. What are some appropriate causes of anger?

The Sanctity of Truth (Exod. 20:16)

5. In addition to the sanctity of life, God teaches a high regard for truth. On the basis of Heb. 6:18; Num. 23:19; Lev. 19:11, 12; and 2 Cor. 1:18, why do you think God places such a high premium on truth?

6. In addition to Exod. 20:16, read Prov. 6:16, 17, 19; 12:22; Acts 5:1-9; Ps. 50:20; James 4:11; Lev. 19:16; Ps. 15:3; and Eph. 4:25 and list some of the things forbidden by the ninth commandment? (Compare your answer with L.C. 145.)
7. What does this commandment have to say about "little white lies"?
8. Read3 John 12;Prov. 14:5,25;Lev. 5:1;Prov. 29:24;1 Cor. 13:7; and Prov. 17:9 and list some of the things required by this commandment. (Compare your answer with L.C. 144.)
9. According to Eph. 4:29 and Col. 4:6, what ought to be one of the great purposes of our speech?
    a. As Christians, what is the great witness to truth that we ought to bear (1 Peter 3:15)?
    b. What are ways we can do this?
10. Now read Exod. 1:15-21 and Josh. 2:1-4. What did the Hebrew midwives and Rahab do?
    a. Why did they do this?
    b. What was God's response?
    c. On the basis of these things, do you think that it is right or wrong to tell lies in order to defend life?
    d. Be prepared to defend your answer.

LESSON 21:

GOD'S VIEW OF WORK AND PROPERTY

Assignment:

Read:

L.C. 140-142; 146-148; S.C. 73-75; 79-81; H.C. 110, 113-115.
Complete this lesson.

Memorize:

Exod. 20:15, 17.

Having examined what God's Word says about marriage, family, life, and truth, it remains for us to see what God teaches in the eighth and tenth commandments concerning work and property.

A Christian View of Work and Property (Exod. 20:15)

1. In Eph. 4:28 what duty does Paul derive from the eighth commandment? (Compare S.C. 74.)
   a. What do you think about work? Circle the appropriate answer after each statement.
      (1) Work is a result of man's fall into sin.
      (a) TRUE (b) FALSE
      (2) The main reason for working is to earn money.
      (a) TRUE (b) FALSE
      (3) Work is not as important in serving God as Bible study, witnessing, and other church activities.
      (a) TRUE (b) FALSE

(4) Career decisions should be made primarily on the basis of where the most jobs will be available and how much money one can earn.
(a) TRUE (b) FALSE

b. The answer to the first statement is found in Gen. 1:28 and 2:15. According to Gen. 1:28, what is part of man's responsibility as one made in the image of God?

(1) According to Gen. 2:15, what type of activity did Adam perform before the fall?

(2) What are some things this might have involved?

(3) We see that work is a positive duty that God has placed on man. How is this implied in Exod. 20:8, 9?

(4) From Gen. 3:17-19 describe what happened to man's work because of the fall.

(5) Thus not work, but the toil, difficulty, and frustration, involved in work, are a result of the fall. Work is a duty placed on man from the very time of his creation.

c. The correct answer to the next two statements is found in Col. 3:22-24. Whom do we really serve in our work?

(1) What should be our attitude in our work?

(2) What are some ways we do work externally to please men?

(3) What do Prov. 10:4, 24:30-34 and 28:19 teach about diligence in our work?

(4) Thus we learn that when we do our work diligently and faithfully we serve God and our primary motivation ought to be God's glory. But according to 1 Tim. 5:8 and 2 Thess. 3:6-12 does this rule out working in order to earn money to care for ourselves and our families?

d. The answer to the last true or false statement is found in 1 Cor. 7:20, "Let each man remain in that condition (calling) in which he was called."
   (1) When Paul refers to work as a calling what is he teaching?
   (2) What then should be our primary consideration in seeking a career?
   (3) Review the principles in Lesson 7 on discerning God's will and apply them in making career decisions. In addition to the principles listed there, you need to consider aptitude and interest. In light of this and if they are not given undue weight, aptitude tests may be helpful.

2. When God forbids stealing, what does He teach us about possessions and private property? (Compare L.C. 141.)
   a. What does Prov. 31:13-24 teach about the believer's procuring property and making a profit?
   b. What does Prov. 20:14 teach about undue or unfair profit?
   c. According to 1 Tim. 6:17 and 4:4, 5, is it wrong to be rich and to enjoy our possessions?
   d. On the basis of Prov. 30:7-9; 1 Tim. 6:9; Prov. 23:4; and 28:20, what should be the believer's attitude about seeking wealth?
   e. What does Prov. 27:23-27 teach about the care of our property?
   f. What do Exod. 23:4, 5; Deut. 22:1-4; and Exod. 22:14, 15 teach us about our responsibility with respect to our neighbor's property?
   g. According to Lev. 25:25 and Deut. 15:11, does the right of private property free us from a responsibility to give to the poor (cf. Gal. 6:10)?

3. Look at Prov. 28:8; Lev. 19:35, 36; and Prov. 11:1; 20:10, 14, 17, 23 and list ways that violate the commandment not to steal. (Compare your answer with L.C. 142.)

A Christian View of Contentment (Exod. 20:17)

4. What positive duty is required by the tenth commandment? (Compare your answer with L.C. 147.)
5. How do 1 Tim. 6:6-10 and Heb. 13:5 relate this duty to our attitude about our possessions and circumstances in life?
6. According to Ps. 16:5, 6 what is the Christian's greatest "possession"?
7. According to Ps. 4:7 and 73:25, 26, relate the possession of God as your greatest good to contentment.
8. Relate the lack of contentment to people's incurring great indebtedness. What does Prov. 18:23 and 22:7 warn about debt?
9. According to Matt. 6:25-34; Phil. 2:14; and 4:6, what are some other ways we violate the tenth commandment?
10. Are there some attitudes or improper dealing with problems you need to address?

LESSON 22:

THE CHURCH

Assignment:

Read:

W.C.F. 25; L.C. 61-66; B.C. articles 27-32; H.C. 54, 82-85.
Complete this lesson.

Memorize:

Matt. 28:19, 20; 1 Tim. 3:15.

Up to this point we have surveyed the major doctrines of the Bible and examined some aspects of the Christian life and worship. Now we turn our attention to the church and its life. In this lesson we shall consider what the church is, what it does, and how it ought to be governed.

What is the Church?

1. In the Bible the term "church" is used in a number of ways. Look at the following passages and after each describe how you think it is using the term "church."

	Verse	Answer
a.	Acts 13:1	
b.	Acts 9:31	
c.	Col. 1:18	

2. Col. 1:18 uses the term in the most general sense the entire people of God. In Eph. 1:22, 23 and 5:23 what two figures are used to describe the church in this sense?

    a. Both of these figures suggests union. To be the body and bride of Christ implies being in union with Him. Thus the church in this sense is all those who belong to Christ; who are in Him. According to Eph. 1:4-8 how does one get to be in Christ?

    b. Thus we may say that the church in this general sense consists of all those whom God has chosen in Christ and for whom Christ has died. In W.C.F. 25:1 and L.C. 64 what terms are used to describe the church in this larger sense?

3. Although the Bible refers to the church as the perfect body of Christ, the primary usage of the term in the New Testament refers to local, visible bodies of God's people. How is the term "church" used in Acts 13:1?

    a. Therefore, even though one is in Christ by election and redemption, according to Eph. 1:13, Matt. 10:32, 33, and 1 Cor. 12:12, 13, how does one enter into the realization and enjoyment of being a part of the body of Christ? (Compare your answer with L.C. 62, 83.)

    b. We find an example of this in Acts 2:41, 47. How are the new converts described?

    c. What do W.C.F. 25:2 and L.C. 62 call this expression of the church? What are some of the figures the Bible uses to describe the visible church?

    d. This language suggests that baptism and profession of faith must take place where?

    e. Thus we see that we ought to join a particular congregation. The way for one to know that he is a part of the body of Christ is to belong to a visible expression of that body? (Compare with W.C.F. 25:2.)

f. That the Bible requires church membership is further seen in 1 Thess. 5:12 and Heb. 13:17. What do these verses require?

g. According to L.C. 62 who are members of the visible church.

4. But if membership in a local church is important, one needs to be able to determine if a group is indeed a church. Read Eph. 4:11-16; 1 Tim. 4:15; Matt. 28:19; 1 Cor. 11:23-26; and Matt. 18:15-17 and list some marks that are the distinguishing characteristics of a church if it is a true church. (Compare your answer with W.C.F. 25:4.)

5. Now, write a definition of the church.

What the Church does

6. The basic outline of the task of the church is set out in Matt. 28:19, 20.

   a. What is the church's task with respect to the unconverted?

   b. What is the church's responsibility to the Christian?

7. According to Eph. 4:11-16 what are some of the things the church ought to be doing to equip the saints?

8. What is the church's purpose in equipping the saints?

9. According to Acts 6:1-7 and Gal. 6:6-10 what other responsibility does the church have?

How the Church should be Governed

10. The Bible is not silent about the government of the church. It tells us what kind of officers the church should have and how they should govern.

    a. Although in the apostolic church there were a number of special officers (Apostles, prophets, and evangelists), what two permanent officers are described in Acts 14:23; 20:28-31 (elder and bishop are used synonymously, Titus 1:5, 7); and Phil. 1:1?

b. According to 1 Tim. 5:17 and Acts 20:28, what tasks are assigned to elders?

   (1) On the basis of this division of labor a distinction is made between ruling elders and teaching or preaching elders.

   (2) In addition to the work of ruling and pastoring, the teaching elder (minister) has the responsibility of preaching and administering the sacraments.

c. According to Acts 6:-6 what is the task of the deacons?

11. In addition to describing the officers of the church, the Bible reveals the outline for a form of government. In the history of the church there have arisen three types of church government:

    a. Episcopal – the authority comes from the top down in a hierarchy of bishops with one bishop (archbishop or pope) as the head of the church. A bishop who is appointed by the other bishops is over a geographical division of the church with a number of ministers under his authority. Congregations have only a limited say in who is to be their pastor. This form of government is found in the Roman Catholic, Greek Orthodox, Anglican/Episcopalian churches, and to some degree in Lutheran and Methodist churches.

    b. Congregational – the authority lies in the people of the congregation who have the final word in all decisions. Each congregation is entirely independent; it may join an association, but the decisions of the association are not binding. In some instances (particularly Baptists) there is only one elder, the minister (there may be assistant ministers), and a group of deacons who along with the minister make decisions subject to the approval of the congregation. Other congregational churches have a plurality of elders. This form of government is found in Baptist and Congregational churches.

c. Presbyterian – the authority rests in Jesus Christ alone as the head of the church. Christ rules in the church through elders elected by the people. It is a representative government and the churches are joined together with other churches in a geographical group called a presbytery or classis. All churches and presbyteries may be further joined together in what is called a General Assembly or Synod. This form of government is found in Presbyterian and Reformed churches.

12. Of the three forms Presbyterianism seems to be most in accord with biblical principles of church government. Let us test the three types of government. Listed below are six principles. After each principle write letter for the group to which the principle applies. A principle may be found in more than one group.

	Principle	Answer
		E C P
a.	Office bearers are chosen by the people. (Acts 1:23; 14:23; 6:1-6)	
b.	The terms "bishop" and "elder" are synonymous. (Acts 20:28; Titus 1:5-7)	
c.	In the New Testament there is a plurality of elders in every congregation. (Acts 14:23; 20:17; Phil. 1:1)	
d.	Ordination was the act of a plurality of elders called a presbytery.(Acts 13:1-3; 1 Tim. 4:14)	
e.	The church is governed by an assembly of elders and there is privilege of appeal from a local assembly to a geographical one. (Acts 15; 16:4)	
f.	Christ alone is the head over all things in his church. (Eph. 1:20-23; 5:23; Col. 1:18)	

13. Which of the three above types of government has the least conformity?

    a. Which has the most?

    b. How is the term "church" used in Acts 9:31?

    c. It is on this basis that we say Presbyterianism is the most biblical form of church government. This is not to say that the others are not churches. As long as a church has the marks noted above it is a true church.

LESSON 23:

LIFE IN THE CONGREGATION

Assignment:

Read

W.C.F. 26; L.C. 65, 66, 82; H.C. 32, 52-55.
Complete this lesson and the Personal Information sheet.

Memorize

Acts 2:42; Heb. 10:24, 25.

Having seen that church membership is not an option, let us examine the responsibility involved in church membership.

The Purpose of Life in the Congregation

1. List what you would consider some wrong reasons for joining the church.
2. List some proper reasons for belonging to a church.
3. Look at Acts 2:42 and list the four things to which early Christians were devoted.
4. Below are some verses that define each of the four things. Look up the verses and write what you think each activity involved.
   a. Doctrine: 2 Tim. 1:13; 2:1, 2; 3:14-17; 4:1, 2.
   b. Fellowship: Acts 2:44-46; Heb. 10:24, 25; Mal. 3:16.

c. Breaking of Bread: Luke 24:30; Acts 20:7.

d. Prayer: Acts 1:14; 2:46, 47; 4:23, 24.

e. All of these elements are important in the Christian life and, if we expect to grow as Christians, we must be committed to them. Thus we should join a church that takes these things seriously and as members of the congregation we ought to avail ourselves of every possible opportunity in these areas. At a minimum we ought to be involved in the stated activities of the Lord's Day: Sunday School, Morning Worship, and Evening Worship. Furthermore, we ought to be involved in weekly prayer meeting and regular service and fellowship.

Service in the Life of the Congregation

5. Paul gives an interesting picture of congregational life in Eph. 4:7-16.

   a. What gifts does the exalted Christ give to the church? We noted in the last lesson that Apostles, prophets, and evangelists were special officers for the early church. The abiding office is that of pastor and teacher or pastor-teacher.

   b. According to verse 13 what is Christ's goal for the church?

   c. In verses 14-16 what are the consequences when this goal is met?

   d. Verse 12 tells us how the officers are used to meet this goal. What is the chief purpose of the pastor teacher?

   e. Who then is responsible for the work of ministry?

   f. Some translations take the phrase "for the work of service" to refer to the pastor-teacher. Even so, we may rightly conclude from other places in the Bible that every member of the congregation has service and ministry to fulfill in the congregation. What duties does the W.C.F. 26:1, 2 assign to members of the church?

6. According to Rom. 12:3-8 and 1 Peter 4:10, 11, what does God give to His people to enable them to serve in the church?

   Note that a gift is not some mysterious thing. It is whatever God has given you naturally by birth as well as supernaturally by grace to aid the church in the full scope of its ministry.

7. Each of us has talents and gifts the church needs. What does Matt. 25:14-30 teach about the use of our gifts and talents?

8. List and define the gifts Paul delineates in Rom. 12:3-8.

   a. Which of these do you think you have?

   b. List some services and functions the church needs.

   c. It is important that each of us understands what he can do to help. One of the best ways to determine your gifts is by considering what you are able and like to do and what activities in the church interest you. Take time now to fill out the Personal Information Sheet. The purpose of this survey is to help you see areas in which you can serve the church and to inform the church of those areas. Ask others as well what they think your gifts are.

9. One very practical service one should participate in is Christian giving.

   a. According to Mal. 3:8-12, what sin are we committing, if we do not tithe?

   b. A tithe is ten percent of our gross income. God uses the giving of His people to support the work and ministry of the church. God promises to bless those who honor Him with the tithe. Our giving, however, should go beyond the tithe. We may give God offerings over and above the tithe (see number 13 below).

Fellowship in the Life of the Congregation

10. Another thing mentioned in Acts 2:42 is fellowship. How did this fellowship manifest itself in Acts 2:44-46?

11. One of the things the people were doing was fellowshipping in one another's homes. We call this hospitality. According to Heb. 13:2; 1 Peter 4:9; and Rom. 12:13, how important is hospitality?

    Note that hospitality is using your home to facilitate getting to know other people and meeting their needs. Biblical fellowship does not need nice things and elaborate meals. Peanut butter and jelly sandwiches served on paper plates do just fine. Have you recently had another Christian in your home? If not, why not plan on doing so within the next two weeks.

12. We also learn from Acts 2 that the people were together with one mind. This phrase expresses the real purpose of fellowship. According to Heb. 10:24, 25 and Eph. 5:19 what are the most important elements in fellowship?

    Note: This does not mean that playing together is not fellowship. It simply reminds us that true fellowship must go much deeper.

13. In Rom. 12:13, what activity in addition to hospitality is mentioned?

    a. The tithe is to be the basis of our giving. According to Rom. 15:26, 27, what other contributions did the early Christians make? We refer to these as offerings to distinguish them from the tithe.

    b. How did the early church do this in Acts 2?

    c. Note the last phrase in verse 45. The key to their selling their possessions was need. This was not "Christian communism." It was the church responding sacrificially to the needs of its own. Moreover, Christ had told them that in a few years Jerusalem would be destroyed (Matt. 24:2).

d. According to Matt. 25:31-40, to whom do we give when we give to needy Christians?

Summary

14. We have seen that church membership demands commitment, service, and fellowship. This concept of church membership is set forth in the membership vows. When one joins the church he takes vows similar to those used by the Presbyterian Church in America. These vows are promises to God. Note particularly the fourth vow.

    a. Do you acknowledge yourselves to be sinners in the sight of God, justly deserving His displeasure, and without hope save in His sovereign mercy?

    b. Do you believe in the Lord Jesus Christ as the Son of God, and Savior of sinners, and do you receive and rest upon Him alone for salvation as He is offered in the Gospel?

    c. Do you now resolve and promise, in humble reliance upon the grace of the Holy Spirit, that you will endeavor to live as becometh the followers of Christ?

    d. Do you promise to support the church in its worship and work to the best of your ability?

    e. Do you submit yourselves to the government and discipline of the church, and promise to study its purity and peace?

LESSON 24:

BAPTISM

Assignment:

Read:

W.C.F. 27, 28; L.C. 161-167; S.C. 91-95;
B.C. articles 33, 34; H.C. 65-74;
C.D. III, IV, article 17; V, article 14.
Complete this lesson.

Memorize:

S.C. 92, 94.

Having discussed the nature of the church and the importance of being a member of the church, we now want to consider two aspects of church life that relate directly to church membership – Baptism and the Lord's Supper.

The Nature of Baptism

1. According to Matt. 28:19, what is to be done to every individual who is brought into the church?
2. This act of baptism is called a sacrament. The term is defined in S.C. 92. Write out this definition in your own words.
    a. Write a definition of ordinance (look up in a dictionary if necessary).
    b. What is the purpose of these ordinances?
    c. According to Matt. 28:19 and 1 Cor. 11:23-26, what two sacraments did Christ institute?

3. According to W.C.F. 27:1, what two terms are used to describe what a sacrament does?

   a. What does a sign or symbol do? Give an example.

   b. What does a seal do (use a dictionary)?

4. According to S.C. 94, what is baptism?

5. Baptism is a sign. After the following verses, write what is signified by baptism.

	Verse	Answer
(1)	Matt. 28:19	
(2)	Gal. 3:27	
(3)	Titus 3:5	
(4)	1 Cor. 12:13	
(5)	Rom. 6:5	
(6)	Mark 1:4; Acts 2:38	

In W.C.F. 28:1 and L.C. 165 there is a summary of what baptism signifies. Check your answer with this list.

6. One of the purposes of baptism is to signify cleansing. According to Ezek. 36:25-27 and John 3:5, what element is used to describe this cleansing of the heart?

   a. In Acts 8:37, 38, what element is used for baptism?

   b. From this we learn that water is used, since it is a sign of cleansing.

7. This aspect of cleansing also teaches us about the mode of the administration of baptism. There are primarily two modes: immersion and pouring or sprinkling.

   a. In Heb. 9:9, 10, the writer is describing some of the Old Testament ceremonial cleansings. The word translated "washings" in verse 10 is the word "baptism." Read verses 11-22. In these verses, what mode is used to describe these ceremonial washings?

b. Look at Ezek. 36:25. What term is used to describe the cleansing of regeneration?

c. In Acts 2:17 (compare Matt. 3:11) what term is used to describe the work of the Holy Spirit in the cleansing of regeneration?

d. It is for these reasons that we believe the best mode is pouring or sprinkling.

8. Baptism is also a seal. In 1 Peter 3:21, what is the function of baptism?

   a. Compare this function with what you wrote about the function of a seal. We see that baptism is used of the Holy Spirit to assure us of the reality in our lives of the things signified by baptism. It is for this reason that the Bible often speaks of the sign as if it were the spiritual reality. Look at Acts 2:38; Rom. 6:3, 4; and Gal. 3:27. What spiritual realities are described in these verses by baptism?

   b. If baptism is to seal to us these spiritual realities, we must have the reality already in our lives and must reflect on the purposes of our baptism in connection with the promises of scripture and our own baptism. As we do so the Holy Spirit will give us assurance and strength. L.C. 167 gives a number of practical things to help us do this. Write a list of things you can do to derive benefit from your baptism.

9. Yet we must ask the question: does baptism guarantee these realities? Read Acts 8:13-23.

   a. When was Simon baptized?

   b. Was Simon converted?

   c. Thus baptism does not convert nor can it do its work as a seal in one who has not been converted.

10. Furthermore, we need to note that the efficacy of the sealing benefits of baptism is not tied to the moment of administration (W.C.F. 28:6). Baptism does this work all through our lives.

The Recipients of Baptism

11. In Acts 8:13 and 36-38, on what occasion were Simon and the Ethiopian Eunuch baptized?

12. Should a person who professes faith and has not been properly baptized seek baptism?

13. According to the W.C.F. 28:4, who else should be baptized?

    a. The biblical basis for including the children of believers becomes clear when we examine the relationship between circumcision and baptism. According to Gen. 17:7-14, when was circumcision instituted?

    b. Circumcision was the sign of the covenant between God and Abraham. After each of the following references write what you think circumcision would have meant.

Verse	Answer
(1) Gen. 17:7-10	
(2) Rom. 4:11	
(3) Deut. 10:16;30:6	
(4) Jer. 4:4	

    c. Now read Col. 2:9-14. How does Paul relate circumcision to the Christian?

    d. With what was circumcision replaced (verse 12)?

    e. Go back now and compare the purposes of baptism with what you said circumcision would have meant to Abraham. Are there any differences between the two?

    f. Do you think that when Abraham circumcised Ishmael (Gen. 17:26) and Isaac circumcised Esau and Jacob (Gen. 25) circumcision meant the same thing for the children that it meant to Abraham (particularly Ishmael and Esau who were unconverted)?

    g. Why then do you think these boys were circumcised?

h. In the New Testament there are four important things to note about the children of believers. After each verse write what you think it is saying about covenant children.

Verse	Answer
(1) Luke 1:41-44	
(cf. 2 Sam. 12:22,23)	
(2) 1 Cor. 7:14	
(3) Matt. 19:13, 14; Luke 18:15-17	
(4) Eph. 6:1, cf. 1:1	

i. In light of these verses and what we have learned about circumcision and its relation to baptism, what ought we to think when we read verses like Acts 16:15, 33; and 1 Cor. 1:16?

j. We then have the right and responsibility to have our children baptized.

LESSON 25:

THE LORD'S SUPPER

Assignment:

Read:

W.C.F. 29; L.C. 168-177; S.C. 96, 97;
B.C. article 35; H.C. 75-82.
Complete this lesson.

Memorize:

1 Cor. 10:16, 17; S.C.96.

We have seen that Christ instituted the sacraments of Baptism and the Lord's Supper. Having studied the first, we now turn our attention to the second.

THE INSTITUTION OF THE LORD'S SUPPER

1. Read 1 Cor. 11:23-26. By whose authority did Paul give the institution of the Lord's Supper?
   a. When did Jesus institute the Lord's Supper (cf. Matt. 26:17-28)?
   b. What is the relationship between the Lord's Supper and the Passover?
2. According to 1 Cor. 11:26, how long should the church practice the observance of the Lord's Supper?
   a. Would you say that it is an option or a duty?

b. What should be your attitude toward partaking of the Lord's Supper?

3. What two elements did Christ take from the Passover and use as the elements of the Lord's Supper? The significance of these elements is seen in the next section.

The Purpose of the Lord's Supper

4. We have seen that the sacraments are signs and seals of the covenant of grace. As a sign, the Lord's Supper pictures three things for us.

   a. A picture of what Christ did. According to 1 Cor. 11:24-26, what is the Lord's Supper to help us to remember?

      (1) It is for this purpose that the elements of bread and wine are used. What do you think Jesus means by the language "this is my body" and "this cup is the New Covenant in my blood"?

      (2) Some teach that this language means that Jesus' real body and blood are present in the sacrament and that He is re-sacrificed each time the sacrament is observed. Such a doctrine is contrary to the simple meaning of the words and to what the Bible says about the sacrifice of Christ (W.C.F. 29.:2, 6).

      (3) Look at John 10:7. Is Jesus saying that the door to the sheepfold is He or that it is a picture of Him?

      (4) What then would you expect Him to mean when He uses the same type of language in the institution of the Lord's Supper?

      (5) What then would be another way to render the phrases about the bread and wine being His body and blood?

      (6) Thus we conclude that Jesus is using a very common metaphor. According to W.C.F. 29:5, what else is signified by the language "this is My body…"?

(7) What does Heb. 9:22-28 say about the once and for all character of the sacrifice of the Lord Jesus?

(8) If Christ has been sacrificed once and for all and Jesus teaches us to observe the Lord's Supper in remembrance of that sacrifice, is there any way that the Lord's Supper can be a re-sacrifice? (Compare W.C.F. 29:2.)

(9) What then should the bread wine remind us of when we observe the Lord's Supper? (See W.C.F. 29:1.)

b. A picture of what we must do. Look at John 6:35,47-51, 53-57. What figure does Jesus use here to picture faith?

(1) How do food and drink become one with our body?

(2) How do we become one with Christ?

(3) How then does the Lord's Supper picture for us the action of faith?

c. A picture of the people of God. According to 1 Cor. 10:16, 17; 12:13; and Luke 22:17, what else is pictured by the Lord's Supper?

(1) According to 1 Cor. 12:13, what appears to be the relationship between Baptism and the Lord's Supper?

(2) Since baptism is the mark of our union with Christ and His people, should an un-baptized person partake of the Lord's Supper?

5. As a seal of the covenant, the Lord's Supper communicates a number of blessings to those who partake by faith.

a. According to Matt. 26:27, 28 and Luke 22:20, what benefit is guaranteed to us as we by faith partake of the Lord's Supper?

(1) Look back at Lesson 9 and review the things promised to us in the covenant of grace.

(2) What do you think God is saying to you as a Christian when you come to the Lord's Table? (Compare L.C. 168.)

b. Another thing food does is nourish us. According to 1 Cor. 10:16, what do we partake of when we eat the Lord's Supper?

(1) We have already noted that we do not literally eat Jesus' body and blood, but He is spiritually present; and as we see in 1 Cor. 10:16, we partake of Him. If eating food gives physical strength, what should the spiritual partaking of Christ do for us spiritually?

(2) The W.C.F. 29:7 gives a summary of this benefit.

c. According to 1 Cor. 10:16-21 compared with 2 Cor. 6:14-16, what should the Lord's Supper motivate us to do?

6. In conclusion, write a summary of what the Lord's Supper should do for you.

The Right Way to Partake of the Lord's Supper

7. What does Paul warn about in 1 Cor. 11:27-31?

a. According to L.C. 173, who ought not to come to the Lord's Table?

b. According to L.C. 172, may a person who is weak in faith and doubts His salvation come to the Lord's Table?

c. What does this teach us about the importance of self examination as we come to the Lord's Table?

d. L.C. 171 gives a number of areas that such examination should cover. List the things that we should do in preparing to come to the Lord's Table. Use this list in the future as you prepare to come.

8. According to L.C. 174, on what things should we be thinking and meditating as we partake of the Lord's Supper?

9. On the basis of L.C. 175, what should we do after we partake of the Lord's Supper? This is a good thing to do on Sunday afternoon.

LESSON 26:

THE END

Assignment:

Read:

W.C.F. 32, 33;
L.C. 29, 56, 84-90; S.C.28, 37, 38;
B.C. article 37; H.C. 57, 58, 123.
Complete this lesson.

Memorize:

1 Thess. 4:14; S.C. 37, 38.

Having surveyed the basic doctrines and practices of the Christian life, it remains for us to draw this work to a close by studying what the Bible teaches about the end (death, the intermediate state, and the final return of Christ).This lesson sets the final hope of the Christian before us. Pray that you will grasp these truths and be greatly comforted by them.

Death

1. According to Heb. 9:27, is death inevitable before the return of Christ?
2. Read Rom. 6:23. Why do people die (review Lesson 8)?
3. According to L.C. 85, why does God allow Christians to die?

The Intermediate State

4. According to 2 Cor. 5:1, 6, 8; Phil. 1:23; and Heb. 12:23, when a Christian dies what happens to his soul?
5. What are we told in Gen. 3:19; Job 19:26; and Acts 13:36 happens to the body at death?
6. According to 1 Thess. 4:14, what is the dead body's relation to the Lord Jesus Christ? (Compare your answer with S.C. 37.)
7. Read Luke 16:23, 24; Acts 1:25; Jude 6, 7. According to these verses what happens to the souls of the wicked when they die? (Compare your answer with L.C. 86.)

The Return of Christ

8. According to 1 Cor. 15:23-28, what will be Christ's final mediatorial act?
9. When, according to Acts 1:11; Luke 9:26; and Matt 25:31, shall Christ destroy death?
10. Although there is controversy over the time of Christ's return, according to Matt. 24:36 can anyone predict the time or generation in which Christ will return?
11. According to 2 Peter 3:11; Rom. 8:23-25; and Matt. 24:37-44, why has He left the time unknown? (Compare your answer with W.C.F. 33:3; L.C. 88.)
12. Read 1 Thess. 4:12-18; 1 Cor. 15:50-52; John 5:27-29; and 2 Peter 2:4 and list the events connected with the return of the Lord Jesus Christ? (Compare your answer with L.C. 56.)
13. What happens to the righteous at the time of Christ's return, according to Job 19:26, 27; 1 Cor. 15:42-44, 51; Phil. 3:21; and 1 John 3:2? (Compare your answer to W.C.F. 33:2, 3.)
14. How does Jesus describe the resurrection of the wicked in John 5:29? What do you think a resurrection to judgment entails? (Compare your answer to L.C. 87, 89.)

15. According to Matt. 25:31-46; Eccl. 12:14; 2 Cor. 5:10; and Matt. 12:36, 37, what shall be the basis of judgment?

16. On the basis of John 5:28, 29; Matt. 10: 32; 12:37; 25:1-23; 31-40, what is the purpose of the judgment of the righteous? (Compare W.C.F. 33:2; L.C. 90.)

17. According to 1 Cor. 6:2, 3; Matt. 25:34, 46; Eph. 5:27; Rev. 14:13; Ps. 16:11; Heb. 12:22, 23, what shall be the state of the righteous (L.C. 90)?

18. What, according to Rom. 2: 15, 16; Matt. 7:23; 25:41-43, will be the purpose of the judgment of the wicked (L.C. 89)?

19. What will be the punishment of the wicked, according to Matt. 25:41; 2 Thess. 1:8, 9 (W.C.F. 33:2; L.C. 89)?

20. According to Rom. 8:18; 1 Thess. 4:18; and 2 Peter 3:14, what should be our response to these great truths of the end times?

TEACHER'S GUIDE

LESSON 1:

GOD'S WORD OUR RULE

Assignment:

Read:

W.C.F. 1; L.C. 1-6; S.C. 1-3;
B.C. 2-7; H.C. 19;
C.D. I, article 3; II, article 5; III, IV,
articles 6, 7, 8, 17; V, article 14.
Complete this study.

Memorize:

2 Tim. 3:16, 17 and S.C. 1-3.

Really encourage those whom you lead to memorize the Scripture and Catechism. Teach them how to memorize and review. Hold them accountable.

As you begin this study pray that the Holy Spirit will enable you to understand the Bible and it message.

General Revelation

1. Read Ps. 19:1-6.

   Q. What physical activity is David describing in verses 1-6?

   A. David is describing the creation, particularly the heavenly bodies and the rising and setting of the sun.

2. Q. Who is speaking through these activities?

   A. God, the Creator, is speaking to mankind and revealing Himself.

3. Compare Rom. 1:19-21 and 2:14, 15 with Ps. 19:1, 2.

   a. Q. What can people learn from the creation? (Compare your answer with W.C.F. 1:1.)

      A. From the creation one knows that God exists. One knows His eternal power and divine nature.

   b. Q. According to Rom. 2:14, 15 what do we know innately?

      A. All have a remnant of the law of God written on their hearts and have an innate ability in our consciences to know good from evil.

   c. This is called General or Natural Revelation. General Revelation encompasses all the creation and providence.

4. Read Rom. 1:32; 2:1, 2, 14, 15.

   Q. Of what use is General or Natural Revelation to man?

   A. Natural Revelation tells man that God will judge him for sins that he commits. It leaves all without excuse, even those who have never heard the gospel.

5. Read Rom. 10:13, 14; Acts 4:12.

   Q. What does the creation not reveal to man?

   A. Creation does not reveal to man God's plan of salvation.

Special Revelation

6. Go back to Ps. 19:7-9.

   Q. According to verses 7-9 in what other way does God speak to men?

   A. God speaks to men by His law, testimony, and judgments; namely, the Word of God. We call this Special Revelation.

7. Read Num. 12:6-8.

   a. Q. What are three ways prophets received God's message?

A. Prophets received God's message in visions, dreams, and face to face (mouth to mouth).

b. Read Heb. 1: 1, 2, cf. John 1:1, 2.

Q. According to these verses, what is the ultimate face to face revelation?

A. The ultimate face to face revelation is the spoken word of the Son, Jesus Christ.

8. Q. If these revelations were to be preserved, what needed to be done? Look at Deut. 31:24; Jer. 36: 1, 2; Luke 1:1-4.

A. To preserve God's revelations they had to been written down.

9. Q. Where do we find God's Word today?

A. Today we find God's Word in the Scriptures, the Bible.

10. Now read 2 Tim. 3:16, 17. (Compare with the last sentence in W.C.F. 1:2.)

a. Q. According to verse 16, how was Scripture given?

A. All Scripture was given by inspiration of God.

b. Look up "inspiration" in a dictionary.

Q. What are some possible meanings of the word "inspiration"?

A. "Inspire" means to inhale; to stimulate or impel, as to some creative effort; to motivate by divine influence; to arouse (a thought or feeling) in (someone).

"Inspiration" means an inhaling; an inspiring or being inspired mentally or emotionally; a) any stimulus to creative thought or action b) an inspired idea, action, etc.

Webster's New World Dictionary, July 1983. Warner Books

c. Q. What do you think "inspiration" means here?

A. It means that God, the Holy Spirit, breathed the words that the men wrote down; they are as much God's Word as if He were audibly speaking them.

d. Read Rom. 1:2; 15:4; 1 Tim. 5:18; 2 Peter 3:15, 16.

Q. According to these verses, what does the term "Scripture' include?

A. *The term "Scripture" includes the books of the Old and New Testament. See the list in W.C.F. 1.2.*

11. Look at 2 Peter 1:20, 21. Write this verse in your own words (Note: in this verse, the word "interpretation" means initiative).

The initiative to write the words contained in Scripture did not originate with the writers, but by the inspiration of the Holy Ghost. Holy men of God wrote as they were moved by the Holy Ghost.

12. Read 2 Sam. 23:1-3.

Q. When David wrote the Psalms, who spoke through him?

A. *The Spirit of God.*

13. Read Gal. 1:1, 11, 12.

Q. What claim does Paul make in these verses?

A. *Paul claimed that the words that he spoke or wrote were given to him by the revelation of the Lord Jesus Christ and not from any man.*

Q. Do you think Paul knew he was writing God's Word?

A. *Yes. Paul knew.*

14. Read 2 Peter 3:15, 16.

Q. What term does Peter use to describe Paul's letters in these verses?

A. *Peter says that Paul's letters are Scripture. Although they contain hard sayings, men should obey them or suffer the consequences.*

Authority of the Bible

15. Q. Whose Word is the Bible?

A. *The Bible is the Word of God.*

16. Q. From whom then does the Bible derive its authority (Look at 1 Thess. 2:13; .W.C.F. 1:4; L.C. 4)?

A. *From God.*

17. Q. According to W.C.F. 1:5 and L.C. 4, what are some of the evidences that the Bible is the Word of God?

A. *Some of the evidences that the Bible is the Word of God are the following: Efficacy of content; majesty of style; consent of the parts; the purpose of the whole (to give glory to God); the ability to convince and convert, the power to build up and comfort believers; the testimony of the Church; and many other incomparable excellencies.*

18. Q. According to John 16:13-14; 1 John 2:20; and W.C.F. :5, what ultimately persuades men that the Bible is the Word of God?

A. *The Holy Spirit bearing witness with and in the Scripture in the heart of man.*

19. Go back to 2 Tim. 3:16.

Q. What are the things for which the Bible is useful or profitable?

A. *The Bible is useful or profitable for doctrine, for reproof, for correction, for instruction in righteousness.*

20. These things are summarized by W.C.F. 1:6; L.C. 3, 5; S.C. 2, 3.

Q. According to these references what does the Bible teach?

A. *The whole counsel of God; the Bible is our only rule of faith and practice.*

21. Read 2 Tim. 3:17 and Ps. 19: 11-14.

Q. According to these verses, why should we study the Bible?

A. *According to these verses we should study the Bible to be adequate, equipped for every good work; to know what sin is and to receive aid in resisting and overcoming sin; and to be in closer communion with God.*

22. All Presbyterian and Reformed churches have a secondary authority based on the Scriptures. Presbyterian Churches have The Westminster Confession of Faith, The Larger and Shorter Catechisms. Churches from the Dutch and German tradition have the Three Forms of Unity: The Belgic Confession, The Heidelberg Catechism, and The Canons of Dordt. Presbyterian and Reformed Churches also have a book or manual of Church Order. The Confession and Catechism are the doctrinal standards of the church. The Book of Church Order gives procedures for the proper government, discipline, and worship of the Church. All officers must take an oath that they believe that the things taught in these documents are scriptural and that they believe them. Furthermore, the doctrines summarized in these documents are the standard for the preaching, teaching, and ordering of the church. In the Presbyterian Church, members do not have to hold to all the doctrines as they are set forth in these standards, but they may in no way work against these truths and practices. In the Reformed Churches, officers and members must hold to the doctrines set forth in the standards.

Matthew Henry in volume V of his commentary wrote on the usefulness of Creeds: "Brief summaries of Christian doctrine are of great use to young beginners. The principles of the oracles of God brought into a little compass in creeds and catechisms have, like the beams of the sun contracted in a burning glass, conveyed divine light and heat with a wonderful power" (p. 1146).

LESSON 2:

THE STUDY OF GOD'S WORD

Assignment:

Read:

W.C.F. 1:7, 9; L.C. 156, 157, 160, 178-196;
S.C. 98-107; H.C. 118-129.
Complete this study.

Memorize:

the titles of the books of the Bible;
review S.C. 1-3 and begin to learn S.C. 4-6.

Background for Bible Study

1. Read Ps. 119:105,130.

   a. Q. What figure is used in these verses to describe the Bible?

      A. Light is used in these verses to describe the Bible.

   b. Q. To what kind of person does the Bible give understanding?

      A. The Bible gives understanding to the simple.

   c. Q. What does "simple" mean in Ps. 119:130?

      A. Those in the covenant who are beginners; those of the weakest capacity.

d. Q. If the Bible is compared to light and if it gives understanding to the simple, do you think that a Christian ought to be able to understand the Bible for himself?

A. *Yes. Read W.C.F. 1:7.*

2. Read Ps. 119:18 and Acts 17:11, 12.

Q. According to these verses what two things are necessary to gain a correct understanding of God's Word?

A. *In order to gain a correct understanding of God's Word a person must have the enlightenment of the Holy Spirit to enable him to understand the Bible and its message. Also, a person should devote a part of each day to reading and studying Scripture.*

3. Q. According to Ps. 119:18, how do you think one receives enlightenment of the Holy Spirit?

A. *One receives enlightenment of the Holy Spirit by requesting it in prayer.*

a. Q. What then should we do every time we begin to study the Bible or to listen to a sermon or Bible lesson?

A. *We shou1d pray for enlightenment of the Holy Spirit.*

b. Did you do this as you began this study? If not, pause now and seek the illumination of the Holy Spirit.

4. Q. What does it mean to examine the Scriptures? (Compare your answer with L.C. 157.)

A. *To examine the Scriptures one must carefully study the Scriptures for an understanding of its contents.*

5. For profitable Bible study, it is helpful to have a good Bible. The Bible preferably should be a modern translation (we recommend the New American Standard Version). It also should have a thorough cross-reference system and maps. An English language dictionary is

needed as well. You need to know the meaning of all words in a verse before you can expect to understand what the verse means. It is also helpful to makes notes in a notebook or the Daily Bible Study Log.

Some other useful reference tools are a concordance, a Bible Dictionary, commentaries and a Bible Atlas.

One of the greatest difficulties in effective Bible Study is consistency. You will need to seek God's grace in order to be consistent, but there are some practical things that help. First, have a time planned in your daily schedule (If you have not been regular, start about twenty minutes a day, ten for Bible study and ten for prayer). Second, set aside a regular place for daily study and prayer. Third, have a plan. Basically, there are four approaches to Bible Study: survey, in-depth book study, thematic study, or work through a commentary like Matthew Henry. We recommend that you use a Bible Reading Calendar and begin with the survey approach.

Principles for Bible Study

6. The goal is to be able to answer three questions about the verse or passage you read:

    a. What is going on in this passage? This is observation. What kind of literature is it (prose, poetry, narrative, didactic, figurative, prophetic, etc.)? Does it contain promises or doctrines? Who is speaking? To whom is the writer speaking?

    b. What does it mean? This is interpretation. What is God communicating in this passage? Be able to state the truth in your own words.

    c. What does it mean to me? This is application. What lessons, promises, commandments, truths, are here for me? This should include meditation. Meditation is explained in Ps. 143:5. Read it. To muse is to talk to oneself, to mull over something. Meditation is mulling over who God is, what He does and what that means to us. Read Ps. 145:5.

7. There are four basic principles of interpretation to be used in accomplishing our goal:

   a. The context – How does this verse or passage fit with what was written before and after it? What is there in the context that will help me to understand the passage I am studying?

   b. Linguistic analysis – Identify the type of literature; know the meaning of the words and the basic sentence structure (Is it a statement of fact, a command or a question? Is the verb tense past, present or future?).

   c. Cross references – Use the footnotes to look at parallel passages and other uses of words, phrases and concepts.

   d. Analogy of faith, W.C.F. 1:9 – The Bible does not contradict itself. An individual passage must be interpreted in light of what the Bible teaches throughout. The Westminster Confession and Catechisms are very helpful at this point.

Practice of Bible Study

8. Bible study on Matt. 6:9-15.

   a. Read verses 1-18 to get the context.

   (1) Q. What is Jesus' purpose in verses 1-18?

   A. In these verses He is teaching the multitudes, as well as us, some elements of personal religion.

   (2) Q. What are the three elements of personal religion that He discusses?

   A. The three elements of personal religion that Jesus discusses are: giving, praying, and fasting.

   (3) Q. In verses 5-8, what principles does He lay down concerning prayer?

   A. In these verses, Jesus is teaching us that prayer should be a private matter between a person (or a group) and God; should be thoughtful and not the vain repetition of words; pray with faith and confidence.

(4) Q. What do you think was His purpose in giving the prayer we are studying in verses 9-13?

A. Jesus gave us this prayer so that we would have a pattern to follow: adoration, confession, thanksgiving, and supplication.

b. Now let us look at linguistic analysis.

(1) Q. What type of literature is this in verses 9-15?

A. In these verses, the type of literature is didactic; it includes instructions and commands.

(2) Look up in a dictionary any words in verses 9-13 that you do not know.

(3) List the main verbs. Beside each write if it is a statement, commandment or a question.

A. Verb	*Type*
pray ye	*commandment*
Hallowed be	*commandment*
come	*commandment*
be done	*commandment*
give us	*commandment*
forgive us	*commandment*
lead us not	*commandment*
deliver us	*commandment*

Note that petitions in prayer are often in the form of commands. We are not commanding God, but using this form of speech to frame our petitions.

c. Next, study cross references.

(1) Look at the parallel passage in Luke 11:2-4.

(a) Q. Are there any major differences?

A. Different occasion; answers a request; is a form of prayer to be used; omits phrase "who art in heaven"; omits the petition about God's will; omits the petition "but deliver us from evil"; omits the closing doxology (You will note in modern versions that some earlier manuscripts omit the doxology in Matthew's account as well.).

(b) Q. Is there anything in the Luke passage that will help you understand Matthew better?

A. No. Luke's account is a shorter version of the Matt. 6 passage. Each time Christ said the prayer the words that He used were not identical, although the meaning was the same.

(2) Some cross references for the word "kingdom" are found in Matt. 3:2; 4:17 and John 3:5.

Q. How do these verses help you to define what Jesus means by "kingdom come?"

A. Matt. speaks of the kingdom of heaven. John speaks of the kingdom of God. Both are speaking of God's rule in and among men by the Lord Jesus Christ.

(3) Look at Ps. 103:20.

(a) Q. How do angels perform God's will?

A. Angels perform God's will the instant that God commands them to.

(b) Q. On the basis of this verse what does Jesus mean when He says, "Thy will be done on earth as it is in heaven"?

A. Jesus is saying pray that men would obey God without hesitation just as the angels do, cf. S.C. 103.

d. Now let us look at analogy of faith.

(1) Verses 14, 15 of Matthew could be interpreted to mean that our salvation can be earned by our works.

Q. In light of what the Bible says of salvation being of grace alone, can this be a proper interpretation (Eph. 2:8, 9)?

A. *No.*

(2) Q. What do you think, then, Jesus means here? (Compare Matt. 18: 21-35 and S.C. 105.)

A. *Jesus is saying that if you are a child of God, then you will evidence this by the way that you act to others. If you have experienced forgiveness, you will forgive.*

e. Finally, look now at answering the three questions.

(1) What is going on?

(a) Q. Why does Jesus give this prayer?

A. *Jesus wanted to provide God's people with a format for speaking to God in a reverent manner that would allow each person to speak from his heart his own words.*

Q. To whom does He give the prayer?

A. *Jesus' gives the prayer to His Church, His disciples.*

(2) What does that mean?

(a) List the petitions found here.

A. *Petitions*

Hallowed be thy name

Thy kingdom come

Thy will be done in earth, as it is in heaven

Give us this day our daily bread

Forgive us our debts, as we forgive our debtors

Lead us not into temptation, but deliver us from evil

(b) List the four elements of prayer with a brief explanation of each (Look at S.C. 98-107).

A. *Elements*

Adoration – worshiping and showing a great love or devotion to God

Confession – admitting or acknowledging one's sins to God and asking for pardon

Thanksgiving – expressing gratitude to God for His many gifts

Supplication – asking God for certain things for ourselves and others

(3) What does it mean to me?

(a) Q. Do you have a regular time of prayer and Bible study each day?

A. *If not, take time now to schedule a time. As teacher help those whom you are discipling to set aside a daily time. As you meet each week hold them accountable. If you are teaching a group, encourage them to be accountable to another person.*

(b) Q. Do your prayers include the four elements taught by Christ?

A. *If not, keep these four things (adoration, confession, thanksgiving, and supplication) in mind as you pray.*

(c) Note: It is very useful to use a prayer journal. Write down daily, weekly, and monthly prayer items. Keep a list of answered prayers.

How to Listen to a Sermon

9. Read L.C. 160.

a. Q. What is required of those that hear the Word preached?

A. *It is required of those that hear the Word preached, that they attend upon it with diligence, preparation, and prayer; examine what they hear by the scriptures; receive the truth with faith, love, and meekness, and readiness of mind, as the Word of God; meditate, and confer of it; hide it in their hearts, and bring forth the fruit of it in their lives.*

b. Q. How should you approach listening to a sermon?

A. *You should approach listening to a sermon by attending upon it with diligence—approach the sermon as you would approach any important task (W.C.F. 21:5 says we are to be conscionable hearers of the word preached); preparation—careful physical and spiritual preparation; and prayer, praying for the service, the preaching, and yourself and the congregation as you listen.*

c. Q. How should you listen?

A. *You should listen attentively so that you can examine what is heard by the scriptures.*

d. Q. What four things should mark how we receive the Word preached?

A. *Faith, love, meekness, and readiness of mind.*

e. Q. What should your response be?

A. *Your response should be that you meditate and confer of the sermon and that you hide it in your heart and bring forth the fruit of it in your life.*

f. "Confer" means to talk about the sermon.

Q. How do you do this with your family? With others?

A. *Spend time after the worship service discussing the sermon with your children. Help them to get the main point. Discuss the truth you learned. Discuss the points of application. Do the same with others in the congregation.*

g. Q. What are you to do with the content of the sermon during the following week?

A. *Meditate on it and seek its fruit in your life.*

10. Keep a record of both Sunday sermons. Include Scripture; main theme; the outline; a paragraph that tells about the passage or doctrine explained; and the lessons and applications you received through the sermons.

    As you work to disciple people, review their Bible study notes and sermon records. Your aim is to help them be consistent and to see them developing in their ability to profit from private Bible study and sermons. Also hold them accountable with respect to having a time of prayer.

11. If you are the head of a household you also should be practicing regular family worship. Have a set time with your wife and children (mothers who are heads of family should do so as well). Sing a psalm or hymn, read and discuss a portion of Scripture, and pray.

    Also, although we have not dealt with family worship in this section, if you are dealing with a head of household, help him (or her) to begin regular family worship. You might need to talk to your pastor about resources. We recommend the Directory for Family Worship, published with annotations by Southern Presbyterian Press. You may also invite those whom you are seeking to disciple into your home to observe family worship.

LESSON 3:

THE NATURE OF GOD

Assignment:

Read:

W.C.F. 2:1, 2; L.C. 6, 7; S.C. 4; B.C. article 1.
Complete this study.

Memorize:

Deut. 6:4; Exod. 34:6, 7; S.C. 4.

As you begin, read Heb. 11:6. Ask God to bless you with knowledge of Himself as you seek to know Him through His Bible.

1. Read Deut. 6:4.

   Q. What three things does this verse tell us about God?

   A. a. He is personal – He is our God.

   b. His name – He is the Lord God.

   c. His unity – He is one.

2. The first thing we learn about God is that He is "our God."

Q. What does this phrase teach us about God?

A. This phrase teaches us that God is personal.

Since God is personal, we must be able to know Him.

a. Q. If you are to know someone personally what are some things that you need to know about him?

   A. If we wish to know someone personally, we want to know such things as: name, birthplace, education, occupation, marital status, interests, church affiliation, etc.

b. However, God is an infinite spirit and not a human being, we must seek the answer in His self revelation.

3. Because God is a spirit we do not know what He looks like, but we can know what He is like. Look at Exod. 33:17–34:7.

   a. Q. What does Moses want to see?

      A. Moses wants to see God's glory.

   b. Q. According to Exod. 33:20, can anyone see the full, personal manifestation of God's glory and live?

      A. According to this verse, no.

   c. Q. How then in 34:6, 7, does God reveal His glory to Moses?

      A. God reveals His glory to Moses by saying who He is (His names and attributes) and what He is capable of doing that no human can do.

   d. We can summarize this by saying that God's glory is made known by His name, attributes, and work. This is the second thing we learn about God in Deut. 6:4, His name.

4. In Exod. 34:6 and Deut. 6:4, we learn two of God's titles: "God," which is the Hebrew word "Elohim," and "Lord," which is the Hebrew word "Jehovah."

a. Gen. 1 introduces us to the name "God" (the Hebrew "Elohim"). As you read this chapter, list some things you learn about "God."

A. God is the Sovereign creator of the heavens and earth, the oceans, trees and grass, all living things, and man.
God created everything with His spoken word without matter.
God is in complete command and nothing or no one can thwart His plan.

b. Q. Therefore, when you come across the name "God" in the Bible, what are some truths that this name should bring to mind?

A. The name "God" teaches us that He is the sovereign maker and ruler of all things. He is to be feared and we are His subjects.

c. The name "Lord" (the Hebrew "Yahweh") is explained in Exod. 3:1-15.
In verse 14, God calls Himself I am.

d. We get the title "Yahweh" (English "Jehovah") from these words.

Q. How does the burning bush illustrate this name?

A. The burning bush illustrates this name, "Jehovah" because the bush does not get consumed. It burns endlessly. God is eternally self-sufficient. He does not have a beginning or an end.

e. Q. What does this name teach us about the existence and sufficiency of God?

A. God is totally self-sufficient and He is eternal.

f. Q. What do you think God means, in verse 15, when He says that this name is His memorial name (Look at Exod. 6:2-8 as you answer this question)?

A. *God tells Moses that His name is "I AM." This name is in remembrance of His relationship with the children of Israel over generations. He has been the Lord God of their fathers, Abraham, Isaac, and Jacob. He is the God of the covenant.*

g. Q. What then are some things that you should think about God when you read His name "Jehovah" in the Bible?

A. *He is the eternal, self-sufficient God. He is a covenant God. He is Lord of all, and yet, He is concerned about the well-being of His chosen ones. He has entered into a unilateral covenant (contract) to be their God. He is the God of Abraham, Isaac, and Jacob.*

5. Another way God reveals His name is by His attributes (personal characteristics). List some attributes found in Exod. 34:6, 7.

   A. *Some of God's attributes found in Exod. 34:6, 7 are as follows:*

   - *merciful and gracious*
   - *long-suffering and abounding in goodness and truth, forgives iniquity and transgression and sin, slow to anger*
   - *compassionate*
   - *punishes the guilty, visiting the iniquity of the fathers upon the children and the children's children to the third and the fourth generation*

6. In S.C. 4 we find a more complete list. We learn here that God is a spiritual being who may be known by nine attributes. Look up the verses and write a definition for each attribute.

   a. Infinite – Job 11:7-9.

   A. *God is perfect. No limits of time, place, or power can be placed on Him. This attribute God does not share with humans. Ps. 139:1-12 relates God's infinity to His presence and knowledge.*

Q. According to Ps. 139:1-6, how would you describe God's infinite knowledge?

A. God knows all things. Nothing can be hid from Him. This is His omniscience.

Q. According to Ps. 139:7-12, describe God's infinite presence.

A. From eternity past until the end of time God has no bounds or limits. He is omnipresent; He is personally present in all places.

b. Eternal – Ps. 90:2.

A. God is not limited by time. He has no beginning or end. From everlasting to everlasting He is God. He exists outside time. This attribute God does not share with humans.

c. Unchangeable – James 1:17; Mal. 3:6.

A. God is immutable. He never changes. All of His attributes are perfect and they will never change. This attribute God does not share with humans.

d. Wisdom – Rom. 11:33; Ps. 147:5.

A. God is all-wise. Whatever He does is marked by His perfect wisdom. God's ability to think and to make judgments and His understanding cannot be comprehended by humans.

e. Power – Jer. 32:17; Dan. 4:35.

A. God is all powerful, omnipotent. He has the ability to perform whatever He wishes without the use of energy or effort. By His own volition He can do whatever He wants. His power is always consistent with His nature.

f. Holiness – two aspects:

(1) Isa. 6:2, 3; 57:15.

A. God's holiness is His transcendence. He is above all creation and above all sin.

(2) Hab. 1:12, 13; 1 John 1:5.

A. God's holiness is absolute freedom from moral evil. He cannot look on iniquity. He is absolutely pure.

g. Justice – Exod. 34:7; Rom. 3:23-26.

A. God is a righteous ruler and a just judge. All His judgments are perfect.

h. Goodness – Exod. 34:6, 7; Ps. 103:1-14.

A. God is a good God as shown by His acts to His chosen ones. He is merciful and gracious, slow to anger and abounding in mercy. He has not dealt with us according to our sins, nor punished us according to our iniquities.

i. Truth – Exod. 34:6; Titus 1:2.

A. God cannot lie. He abounds in truth. Lying is against His nature. Thus He is faithful and keeps His word. All His promises and threats are true.

7. As you think about these attributes you will know God better. Why not begin your times of private and public worship by meditating on at least one of these attributes?

LESSON 4:

THE THREE IN ONE

Assignment:

Read:

W.C.F. 2:3; L.C. 8-11; S.C. 5, 6;
B.C. articles 8-11; H.C. 17, 18, 24, 25, 33, 53;
C.D. II article 4.
Complete this study.

Memorize:

S.C. 5, 6.

The truth in this lesson is one of the most profound in the Bible. Ask God to enable you to understand it.

1. In Lesson 3, we talked about two of the three things revealed in Deut. 6:4 about God: He is a personal God who may be known and that we know Him by His names and titles.

   Q. What is the third thing we learn in this verse about God?

   A. *The third thing we learn from Deut. 6:4 is that God is one.*

2. Q. What, according to Deut. 4:35, is the implication of the truth that God is one? (Compare your answer with S.C. 5.)

A. According to Deut. 4:35, there is none else beside Him. There is but One only, the living and true God, S.C. 5).

3. Q. What does God forbid in Exod. 20:3?

   A. God tells man that he shall have no other gods. He shall not worship any other god.

   a. The worship of false gods is called idolatry.

      Q. What does Isa. 44:9-17 say about the absurdity of idolatry?

      A. Idolatry is foolishness. Those who make a graven image, all of them are useless, and their precious things shall not profit. A man will take a piece of wood and use part to warm himself, part to cook his food, and part to carve an image. He falls down and worships his god and does not see how absurd it is to pray and worship this piece of wood.

   b. Q. What are some false gods people used to worship?

      A. In the past, people worshipped other humans, objects made of materials, such as gold and silver, precious stones, wood, heavenly bodies, and material possessions, etc.

   c. Q. What are some false gods people worship today?

      A. People today worship the same kinds of things. We should also point out that some people today worship one or more of the following: their jobs, hobbies, recreation, and children.

   d. Q. Are you worshiping any false gods?

      A. In discipleship you will want to help those whom you teach identify their idols and hold them accountable in rejecting them.

4. Even though God is one, the Bible teaches that He exists in three persons: the Father, the Son, and the Holy Spirit. We call this the doctrine of the trinity: God is the three in one. This doctrine is summarized in S.C. 6.

Q. What three things do we learn here (in S.C. 6) about the trinity?

A. a. God is three distinct persons.
b. Each person is fully divine.
c. He is one God not three gods.

5. The first thing we learn here is that the Father, Son, and Holy Spirit are three distinct and separate persons. Read John 15:26.

a. Q. Who is speaking here?

A. The Son is speaking here.

b. Q. Whom does He promise to send?

A. He promises to send the Holy Spirit.

c. Q. From whom is the Holy Spirit sent?

A. The Holy Spirit is sent from the Father.

Now look at Matt. 3:16, 17.

d. Q. Who is being baptized?

A. The Son is being baptized.

e. Q. Who comes down on Jesus (the Son)?

A. The Holy Spirit comes down on Jesus (the Son).

f. Q. Who speaks?

A. God (the Father) speaks.

g. Q. How do these passages teach that the Father, Son, and Holy Spirit are three distinct beings?

A. These passages teach us that the Father, Son, and Holy Spirit are three distinct beings because God who cannot lie is revealing to us this truth that there are three persons in the Godhead: the Father (God), the Son (Jesus), and the Holy Spirit. We see all three acting distinctly and personally in the same event.

6. The second thing we learn from S.C. 6 is that each person is fully divine. The following exercise will help you to

see this. We know God by His titles, attributes, work, and as the only object of our worship. Match the verses listed under the Son and the Holy Spirit with the four ways God is known.

The Son	**God**	**The Holy Spirit**
Heb. 13:8	Titles	John 3:5, 6; 6:63
Rev. 5:12-14	Attributes	Matt. 12:31, 32; Rom. 9:1; 2 Cor. 13:14
John 1:1	Works	Acts 5:3, 4; 2 Cor. 13:17, 18
Luke 5:17-26	Worship	1 Cor. 2:10

The Son	*God*	*The Holy Spirit*
Heb. 13:8	*Attributes*	*1 Cor. 2:10*
Rev. 5:12-14	*Worship*	*Matt. 12:31, 32; Rom. 9:1; 2 Cor. 13:14*
John 1:1	*Titles*	*Acts 5:3, 4; 2 Cor. 3:17, 18*
Luke 5:17-26	*Works*	*John 3:5, 6; 6:63*

Q. From this exercise what conclusion must we derive concerning the deity of the Son and the Holy Spirit?

A. *From this exercise, we must conclude that the Son and the Holy Spirit are fully divine.*

7. The third thing the catechism teaches is that even though the Father, Son, and Holy Spirit are three equally divine persons, they are not three gods. Read Matt. 28:19.

   a. Q. Into how many names are we baptized?

      A. *We are baptized into one name.*

   b. Q. How many persons does this one name embrace?

      A. *This one name embraces three equally divine persons. Thus God is one God not three gods.*

8. In summary, write the doctrine of the trinity in your own words.

   The doctrine of the trinity states that there is one God only, not three gods. The one and only true God exists as three separate, fully divine persons: the Father, the Son, and the Holy Spirit. Each person of the Godhead can be known by His titles, attributes, works, and worship.

9. Because God is triune, we must always think of Him in this way.

Q. What does Jesus claim in John 14:6-9?

A. *Jesus claims to be God. He is telling them that whatever they attributed to God, the Father, they can attribute to Him (God, the Son). If they have seen Him, they have seen the Father. Jesus says that "I am the way, the truth, and the life". He is saying that He is "I AM" (Jehovah).*

a. Q. If this is so, can the Father be known apart from the Son?

A. *No.*

b. Q. What does this say about the gods worshiped by Jews, Muslims, Jehovah's Witnesses, and Mormons?

A. *To worship their gods would be idolatry.*

c. Q. Is belief in the doctrine of the trinity necessary, if one is to be a Christian?

A. *Yes. A belief in the doctrine of the trinity is an absolute necessity for one to be a Christian.*

10. Fodder for meditation.

Q. Why is the doctrine of the trinity important?

A. *The doctrine of the trinity is important because of Jesus Christ. He claimed to be the Son of God, and, if He is not God and man, He could not satisfy God's (the Father) justice. For God (the Father) had said, "The soul that sins must die" and "Without the shedding of blood there is no remission of sin". Jesus had to be a man so that He could obey and die in the place of men. He had to be God (the Son) in order to live a sinless life so He could be an acceptable sacrifice and in order for His obedience and sacrifice to have an infinite and eternal value. Moreover*

His work needed to be offered to the Father, who justifies. The Spirit needs to be a distinct divine persons so He can indwell us as the Spirit of Christ.

The doctrine of the trinity is revealed to us in the Bible. If this doctrine were in error, then the Bible would contain serious errors. We know that the Bible is inerrant.

LESSON 5:

THE DECREE OF GOD

Assignment:

Read

W.C.F. 3:1, 2; L.C. 12; S.C. 7.
Complete this study.

Memorize

Ps. 33:11; Isa. 45:7; S.C. 7.

We have learned a little about the person of God, His names, and attributes. It remains for us to learn about His work. The first aspect of His work to be considered is His decree. This is another difficult truth; pray for a humble heart as you search the Scriptures.

1. Read the definition of the decree in S.C. 7 and list the things this definition says about the decree:

   A. The decrees of God are (1) His eternal purpose, (2) according to the counsel of His will, whereby, (3) for His own glory, (4) He hath foreordained whatsoever comes to pass.

2. Read Ps. 33:10-11.

   a. Q. What is being contrasted in these two verses?

      A. In these two verses the counsel and plans of men are being contrasted with those of God.

b. Q. What does the word "counsel" mean? (Compare with S.C. 7.)

A. *The word "counsel" means a purpose, a plan of action.*

c. Q. Who controls the plans of men?

A. *God controls the plans of men.*

d. Q. Who can thwart the plans of God?

A. *No one can thwart the plans of God.*

3. Q. According to Isa. 46:10, when did God make His plan?

A. *According to Isa. 46:10, God made His plan in ancient times, in eternity past.*

4. Q. If the decree of God is eternal and God is unchangeable, do you think God's plan can be changed?

A *No. God's plan cannot be changed.*

a. Read what Heb. 6:13-18 says about God's plan and promise, noting particularly verse 17. Write verse 17 in your own words.

A. *God's plan is eternal and unchangeable. God's promise is certain for He swore by Himself and it is impossible for God to lie.*

b. Q. If God's plan does not change, how do we explain verses like 1 Sam. 15:11 and Gen. 6:6?

Let's look more closely at 1 Sam. 15:11 in order to answer this question. As we do so, we need to keep in mind some of the principles of Bible study we learned in Lesson Two. The only way we can properly understand this verse is to examine it in light of its immediate context and what the Bible teaches elsewhere.

(1) Q. We have seen that the Bible teaches that God's plan is eternal and unchangeable. May we then interpret this verse

(1 Sam. 15:11) to mean that God changes His mind?

A. *No. we may not interpret this verse to mean that God changes His mind.*

(2) Now read 1 Sam. 15:10-31.

Q. Is there anything in the immediate context that we should keep in mind as we interpret verse 11?

A. *As we attempt to interpret verse 11, we should keep in mind verse 29 which tells us that God will not lie or change His mind for He is not a man.*

(3) Q. Now, in light of what we have learned, how do we explain or interpret verses like 1 Sam. 15:11 and Gen. 6:6? (Keep in mind that God frequently speaks as if He were a man to help us better to understand what He means.)

A. *Verses such as these must be interpreted in light of their immediate context and what the Bible teaches elsewhere, bearing in mind that God frequently speaks as if He were a man (anthropomorphically) to help us better to understand what He means.*

In 1 Sam. 15:11, the verse should be explained by interpreting the verse to say:

'Samuel, speaking to you as though I were a man, let me say that I regret making Saul king for he has turned back from following Me and has not carried out My commands. However, you know that I am God and I do not make any mistakes. Saul knows that he has sinned and I have just told you what he has done so that you can carry My message to him. He is no longer fit to rule My people.'

Gen. 6:6 may be interpreted to say:

'God wants us to know how grieved He is over man's corruption. If God were a man, and considering what has happened thus far, He would say that He was sorry that He had made man and was grieved in His heart. God, however, is an infinite spirit, not a human; God does not make any mistakes.'

5. Q. According to Rom. 9:11, 13; and 11:34, is God's decree dependent on what He knew men would do? (Compare your answer with W.C.F. 3.2.)

   A. *No. God's decree is of His own purpose, not on the basis of what He foresaw would happen.*

6. Pause now and write a summary of what you have learned thus far about the decree of God.

   A. *The decree of God is His eternal purpose, according to His own will and not according to what He saw men would do. His decree cannot be thwarted and it is unchangeable.*

7. Now we need to consider what all the decree of God embraces. In order to do so, read the verses for each section and circle (or underline) the phrase that best summarizes the meaning of the verses.

a. Matt. 10:29, 30.	a. God's decree only includes the major events of life.
	a. God's decree includes all events, even small things
b. 1 Kings 22:1-40; Prov. 16:33.	b. God's plan embraces things that appear to be accidental.
	b. God's plan does not take into account accidents and chance occurrences
c. Isa. 45:6, 7; Acts 2:23; 4:27, 28; Job 42:11.	c. God's decree includes evil as well as good things
	c. God's decree does not include evil things.

8. Two cautions:

   a. Read 1 John 1:5 and James 1:13.

      Q. Does God's decreeing sin mean that He tempts people to sin?

      A. No. According to these verses, God is infinite goodness and He cannot be tempted to evil and He does not tempt anyone to sin.

   b. Q. If God decrees all things, can man still be responsible?

      Let's look at the following verses in order to answer this question.

      (1) Read Acts 1:16.

         Q. Was it prophesied that Judas would betray Christ?

         A. Yes. In Acts 1:16, Luke tells us that the Holy Spirit by the mouth of David prophesied that Judas would betray Christ. See Ps. 41:9.

      (2) Q. Why do you think Jesus warns him in Matt. 26:24?

         A. Jesus warns Judas so as to let him know that he would be responsible for his own acts.

      (3) We learn that although it was prophesied, Judas was responsible for what he did. Read W.C.F. 3:1.

         Even though God has decreed all things, He is not the tempter to sin nor is man a puppet who is not responsible for his actions.

9. Thus we have learned that from eternity God has decreed everything that will come to pass.

   Q. What practical lessons can you learn from the truth of this lesson?

A. *God's plan was made in eternity past, before the foundation of the world. Nothing can alter His plan. He planned every act that would be done; however, because God is infinite goodness, He cannot be tempted to sin, nor will He tempt anyone to sin.*

Man is responsible for his own acts, and he cannot blame God for his sinful acts. Man is not a robot. He acts willfully and is held accountable for whatever he does.

We may have great comfort in all that happens in our lives. We know that all things work together for our good (Rom. 8:28).

LESSON 6:

CREATION

Assignment:

Read:

W.C.F. 4:1; L.C. 14, 15; S.C. 8, 9; B.C. article 12; H.C. 6.
Complete this study.

Memorize:

Gen. 1:1; Heb. 11:3; S.C. 8, 9.

As you begin this study pray that the Holy Spirit will enable you to understand the Bible and its message.

1. We may compare the decree to the work of an architect, creation to the work of a contractor, and providence to a building maintenance manager. In this study we will look at the work of creation.

   Q. According to S. C. 8, what are the two ways God executes His decree?

   A. God executes His decree in the works of creation and providence.

2. Heb. 11:3 gives a summary of the work of creation.

   a. Q. What does this verse tell us about the origin of the universe?

A. *God made all things of nothing by the power of His Word.*

b. Q. On what basis does one accept this record of origins?

A. *By faith alone one accepts this record of origins.*

(1) Write a definition of faith as it is used here.

A. *Faith is the conviction of things not seen. It is the reception of information on the basis of reliable testimony.*

(2) Q. Whose testimony is the Christian to accept?

A. *We accept God's testimony about the origin of the universe.*

c. Q. How do many modern scientists explain the origin and development of the universe and our present world?

A. *Many modern scientists explain the origin and development of the universe and our present world through an evolution process.*

(1) Q. Can they prove their theories on the basis of observation and experimentation?

A. *No. These scientists cannot prove their theories on the basis of observation and experimentation.*

(2) Q. On what basis then do they accept their theories of origin?

A. *The scientists accept their theories of origin on the basis of their faith in science and their presuppositions.*

d. Thus the knowledge of origins is accepted primarily on the basis of faith.

Q. Whose testimony should the Christian accept?

A. *The Christian should accept God's testimony.*

3. Now read Gen. 1. As you read list any words and phrases that are repeated.

   A. *The words that are repeated are as follows:*

   God created; God called; God made; God said, "Let" and it was so; God saw that ... was good; There was evening and there was morning, nth day.

   In the repetition of certain words and phrases we note a structure or formula that is used to describe God's work of creation. One way to think of this formula is: the act of creation; the declaration of fulfillment; the statement of name and purpose; expression of delight; and the indicator of time.

4. The Act of Creation

   a. Read Gen. 1:1, 2.

      (1) Q. What was the first act of creation?

         A. *God created the heavens and the earth.*

      (2) Q. What did God create by this act? (Compare Heb. 11:3; S.C. 9.)

         A. *He brought into existence from nothing the original created mass.*

      (3) Q. What was the condition of this original created mass?

         A. *Dark, unformed, and uninhabitable.*

      (4) The rest of Gen. 1 explains how God developed this original dark, unformed, uninhabitable mass.

   b. Read Gen. 1:6, 7, 27.

      Q. What two terms describe the act of creation?

      A. *The two terms that describe the act of creation are: "God said" and "God made" ("Created" is used in two verses for made. 21, 27)*

   c. Read Heb. 11:3.

Q. What does this verse tell us about the phrase, "God said"?

A. *In Heb. 11:3 we are told that the worlds were prepared (created) by the Word of God. God brought each thing into existence by His Word.*

(1) Read John 1:1-3.

Q. According to these verses, who is the one speaking at creation?

A. *Jesus Christ, God the Son, is speaking at creation.*

(2) Q. How was Christ the agent of creation?

A. *He was the executor of the work of creation; He spoke all things into existence.*

d. Q. What do we learn from the second phrase of the creative act, "and God made/created"?

A. *From this second phrase of the creative act we learn that when God spoke He made/created each thing He commanded into existence.*

(1) Read Gen. 1:2; Job 26:13; 33:4; and Ps. 104:30.

Q. According to these verses, who executed the command of God the Son in the actual execution of creation?

A. *According to these verses God the Spirit executed the command of God the Son.*

(2) From this we learn that every member of the Trinity was involved in creation.

e. In Gen. 1, we learn that the various actions of creation are assigned to specific days. List the things created on each day:

A. *DAY 1* *light/darkness; day/night*

DAY 2 *the heavens*

DAY 3 *sea/dry land; vegetation*

DAY 4	*heavenly bodies*
DAY 5	*sea creatures; birds and flying creatures*
DAY 6	*living creatures on earth (cattle, creeping things, beasts); man*

f. (1) Q. According to Gen. 1: 11, 21, 24, 25, what do we learn from the phrase "according to its kind"?

A. *We learn that God created every thing and that He created distinct kinds that belong uniquely to their own category.*

(2) Q. Does this have anything to say about evolution?

A. *Yes. In evolution, all life comes from one source and one species evolves into another. We learn here that there was no evolution from one kind (species of some sort) to another.*

5. Declaration of Fulfillment

a. Read Gen. 1:7, 9, 15.

Q. What phrase does God use to declare fulfillment?

A. *God uses the phrase "and it was so" to declare fulfillment.*

b. Q. Why do you think God makes this declara-tion?

A. *God makes this declaration to let us know that the creative act was completed at that time. By His power and His creative ability the creative act was accomplished once for all.*

c. Q. What does this declaration teach us about the perfection of each creative act and how does this relate to the theory of evolution?

A. *God's declaration of fulfillment tells us that each creative act was done perfectly. God is all wise and all powerful; whatever He does is perfect.*

These individual creative acts tell us that the theory of evolution is incorrect, because it denies that God was involved in creation.

6. Statement of Name and Purpose

   a. Q. What does God demonstrate by giving names to the created things (vv. 5, 8, 10)?

      A. *By giving names to the created things God demonstrates ownership and assigns purpose.*

   b. Q. God also expresses purpose with purpose statements (vv. 14, 15, 29, 30).What purpose is expressed for vegetation, heavenly bodies, and man?

      A. *The purposes expressed are as follows:*
      For vegetation – food for man and animals (v. 29, 30);
      For heavenly bodies – to regulate day and night, to separate light from darkness, to produce the pattern of varied signs and seasons, to regulate years (v. 14);
      For man – to fill the earth and to have dominion over all living creatures (v.28).

   c. God blesses sea creatures and man (vv. 22, 28).

      Q. How does God's blessing express purpose?

      A. *God's blessing assigns purpose and endows with the ability to fulfill that purpose.*

7. Expression of Delight

   a. Read Gen. 1:4, 10, 12, 18, 21, 25, 31.

      Q. According to these verses, how does God express His delight?

      A. *God expresses His delight by telling us that what He saw after He had created each part pleased Him. It was good or very good.*

   b. Q. What does this express about the results and purposes of creation?

      A. *These expressions of delight tell us that the results from each creative act were accomplished exactly the way God had purposed. Every thing was completed and would serve the purposes for which*

God had intended it. The creation would glorify God (Ps. 148:1-10).

c. Q. How do the various created things glorify and praise God?

A. *The various created things glorify and praise God by being and doing what God intended them to do.*

d. Q. How does man glorify God?

A. *Man glorifies God by being and doing what God intended him to do. Man was created to live his life in obedience to God, not as though God did not exist. Also, he was to live in peace and harmony with his fellow man.*

As our Lord Jesus said, "You shall love the Lord with all your heart, and with all your soul, and with all your mind. This is the great and foremost commandment. The second is like unto it. You shall love your neighbor as yourself." (Matt. 22:37-39)

8. Indicators of Time

a. Q. In what two ways does God indicate time (verses 5, 8, 13, 19, 23, 31)?

A. *"And there was evening and there was morning"; first day, second day, third day, etc.*

b. Q. What should we assume about the nature and order of the days of creation?

A. *They were normal days in sequential order.*

9. Read Isa. 40:26; 45:18; Rev. 4:11.

Q. What practical benefits may be derived from knowing God as creator?

A. *God alone is the true God. He has the ability to give power to the weak. Look to Him for your salvation. He alone can give you righteousness and strength. God is able to do whatever thing He has ordained. To Him belongs all praise and worship.*

LESSON 7:

GOD'S PROVIDENCE AND YOUR LIFE

Assignment:

Read:

W.C.F. 5; L.C. 18, 19; S.C. 11; B.C. article 13; H.C. 26-28.
Complete this study.

Memorize:

S.C. 11; Ps. 25:12, 14.

As you begin this study pray that the Holy Spirit will enable you to understand the Bible and its message.

God's Providential Rule

1. Introduction.

   a. Q. What are two ways God executes His decrees?

      A. God executes His decrees (1) in the works of creation and (2) in His works of providence.

   b. The second way, providence, is comparable to the work of a building manager. For a definition of providence look at S.C. 11.

      We may summarize: providence is the temporal working out of what we have already noted about the decree of God.

2. Providence and Creation.

    a. Read Ps. 104:1-30.
    List some of the things that God does by His providence.

    A. Some of the things that God does by His providence are as follows:

    Keeps the waters in their place (v. 9); gives water to the animals (vv. 10-12); waters the earth (v. 13); provides food for animals and man (vv. 14-18, 27); governs the seasons and day and night (vv. 19-23); controls life and death (vv. 29, 30); renews the earth in the spring (v. 30).

    b. Q. According to verse 30, do you think that the laws of creation operate apart from providence?

    A. No. In this verse we see that the laws of creation are carried out by God the Holy Spirit.

3. Providence and History.

    a. Read Dan. 4:17 and then write it in your own words.

    A. God providentially controls the rulers of men. As He wills, He chooses those that are the lowliest and humblest and sets them over the kingdom to rule over men.

    b. Q. Can any army win a battle or any person be placed into rule apart from providence?

    A. No. God controls all acts, both small and great.

4. Providence and the Church.

    a. Read Eph. 1:20-23.

    Q. According to these verses, what has been given to the resurrected Christ?

    A. Christ has been given authority over all things and is head of the Church.

    (1) Q. As Christ rules, what is His special relationship to the Church?

A. *Christ's special relationship to the Church is that He is head of the church, which is His body, the fullness of Him who fills all in all.*

(2) Q. What does this suggest about the relation of Christ's purposes for the Church to the occurrences of history?

A. *The occurrences of history are directed toward Christ's purposes for the Church.*

b. We may say that God directs all things in the world to accomplish His purposes for the Church.

Q. Compare Luke 2:1-7 with Micah 5:2. How do these passages illustrate this principle?

A. *The Old Testament (Micah 5:2) prophesied that the Messiah would be born in Bethlehem. From that time on the actual events (history) led to the final fulfillment – the birth of Jesus in Bethlehem. God used the decree of a Roman Emperor to help fulfill that prophecy.*

Providence and Discerning the Will of God

5. Providence and You.

a. Read Rom. 8:28.

Q. What does this verse promise about God's providence as it relates to the things that happen to a believer?

A. *A believer is promised that God causes all things to work together for good to those who love God, to those who are called according to His purpose.*

(1) Q. Is there any circumstance beyond the scope of this promise?

A. *No.*

(2) Q. What may you conclude about God's will in your difficult circumstances and afflictions?

A. *No person or thing can do me harm. God will bless everything in my life to my good.*

b. Providence and knowing God's will for your life. If God has an eternal plan that includes all things, then He has a plan for our lives. This plan unfolds through God's providence. There are five biblical principles that will help one to discern God's will for one's life.

(1) First, you must consult the Bible.

Q. According to Deut. 29:29, what is the purpose of the Bible?

A. *According to this verse, the purpose of the Bible is that we may know and do God's will.*

(a) Q. List some things you believe the Bible can give you guidance in.

A. *Some things that the Bible can give guidance in are as follows:*

How to be saved; how to obey God; how to worship God; the kind of person I should marry; how I should conduct my marriage; how I should rear my children; how to use my time; and what vocations are appropriate for a Christian.

(b) But there are areas that the Bible does not speak to directly such as what job should I take or whom should I marry. The Bible also helps here.

Q. According to Ps. 119:98-100, what does God give to guide us?

A. *According to these verses God has given us wisdom through His Word to guide us.*

(c) Wisdom enables us to apply God's principles to personal situations. List some ways the Bible can help you make decisions.

A. *Some ways the Bible can help me make personal decisions are as follows: My heart and mind are trained by God's Word to think His thoughts and make wise decisions. The parameters in which I operate. For example I ought not to marry a non-Christian or spiritually immature person. My vocation should be something that I enjoy and am competent to do. I must be able to keep a balance between work, family, and church. I need to do good for people and not just make money. I ought not to be involved in work that will cause me to break the Sabbath or others of God's commandments. I must do all for God's glory.*

(2) The second principle is prayer.

Read Ps. 25:12, 14 and Prov. 3:5, 6.

Q. According to these verses, what does God promise?

A. *To those who acknowledge God and pray, God promises to instruct them, to make them know His covenant, to make their paths straight, and to lead them*

(a) Read John 14:13, 14.

Q. According to these verses, what is promised to those who pray according to God's will?

A. *To those who pray according to God's will, they are promised that whatever they ask will be done.*

(b) Q. How does this relate to praying for guidance?

A. *A believer, who honestly requests guidance in the name of Jesus, will receive it.*

(3) A third principle is stated in Ps. 139:23, 24.

Q. What is the Psalmist asking God to do?

A. *The Psalmist is asking God to search his heart in order to reveal his thoughts and motives and to guide him in the everlasting way.*

(a) Q. Why is it important to ask God to search our hearts and make our motives known to us?

A. *When God makes known to us our motives we can discern if we really desire God's purposes in our lives and God's glory.*

(b) Q. How would you relate this to seeking to know God's will?

A. *We will be kept from making selfish and harmful decisions.*

(4) A fourth principle is to weigh the pros and cons and to consider the consequences. Look at Phil. 1:21-25.

Q. What two things is Paul contrasting?

A. *Paul is contrasting (1) to die and be with Christ with (2) to remain on in the flesh.*

Q. What conclusion does he reach?

A. *Paul decides it is better to remain alive for the sake of ministry.*

Q. What do we learn here about weighing the pros and cons?

A. *We should consider the advantages and disadvantages of each decision.*

(5) Look at Prov. 11:14.

Q. According to this verse what is the last principle?

A. *The last principle is to seek wise counsel. The more the better.*

c. When we examine God's providence using these five principles, He will lead us and we may act confidently.

6. Obstacles and Mistakes
Sometimes God by His providence puts hindrances in the way of our decision.

a. Read Exod. 13:21–14:14.

Q. Did the obstacle of the Red Sea mean that God was not leading the children of Israel to leave Egypt?

A. No.

b. Q. Why did God give this obstacle?

A. It was given to teach the Israelites to fear God and to believe in the Lord and in His servant Moses.

c. Obstacles should cause us to reflect on our decision and check our principles. They might mean that God would not have us to go in that direction, but they might just be a test.

d. Sometimes we make mistakes and sinful decisions. Look at 1 John 1:9 and Rom. 8:28.

Q. What does God promise when we make mistakes or sinful decisions?

A. According to this verse God promises to forgive us of our sins and to cleanse us from all unrighteousness. He also promises that all things will work out for our good.

e. Q. How would you apply this to making a wrong decision?

A. If we make sinful decisions and ask God's forgiveness, He will forgive us. We may though live with difficult consequences. But He also promises that He will work out even our mistakes and sins to our own good as we seek Him.

LESSON 8:

MAN AND SIN

Assignment:

Read:

W.C.F. 4:2; 6:1-6; 9:1-5; 7:.2; L.C. 20, 21-29, 149;
S.C. 10, 12-19, 82; B.C. articles 14, 15; H.C. 5, 7-14;
C.D. I, article1; II, articles 1, 2 with rejections 3, 6; III, IV,
articles 1-3 with rejections.
Complete this lesson.

Memorize:

Gen. 1:26; S.C. 10, 14.

As you begin this study pray that the Holy Spirit will enable you to understand the Bible and its message.

In order to know God rightly we must know ourselves. The purpose of this lesson is that we might know the dignity of man created in the image of God and his plight having fallen into sin.

Man's Created Nature

1. Read Gen. 1:26-30 and 2:7.

List some of the ways these verses express man's uniqueness.

A. *Some of the ways these verses express man's uniqueness are as follows: created in the image of God after God's likeness, given dominion over all living things on earth, created from the dust of the ground by God who breathed into his nostrils, created with a soul.*

a. Q. What are some of the things entailed in man's being created in the image of God? (Compare your answer with W.C.F. 4:2.)

A. *Some of the things entailed in man's being created in the image of God are as follows: knowledge, righteousness, holiness, communion with God, dominion over the creatures.*

b. Read S.C. 10.

Q. According to S.C. 10, what three things are involved spiritually in man's being in God's image?

A. *The three things are: knowledge, righteousness, and holiness.*

c. From these three things the Bible develops the offices of prophet, priest and king.
Read 1 John 3:7-10; Lev. 11:44, 45; 1 Cor. 2:10, 11.

From these verses match the distinctive element with the appropriate passage and then write a definition of each.

Distinctive Element	**Distinctive Element**
(1) 1 John 3:7-10	(a) Knowledge/ Prophet
(2) Lev.. 11:44, 45	(b) Righteousness/ Priest
(3) 1 Cor. 2:10, 11	(c) Holiness/ King

A. *(1) and (b) – A righteous man is one who obeys God. A priest is a minister for God to His people; makes atonement for the sins of the people (unrighteousness); and intercedes on their behalf.*

(2) and (c) – A holy man is one who is separated unto God. A king is who is separated to rule over God's people and creation.

(3) and (a) –The man with knowledge knows God and His will. A prophet reveals the will of God to His people.

2. Read Gen. 1:26-28; 2:1-3, 15-25.

   a. List the responsibilities God gave to Adam.

      A. *The responsibilities that God gave to Adam were as follows: to rule over the creation, to till the soil for food, to procreate, to keep the Sabbath, to work, and to marry.*

   b. Q. What test did God give man?

      A. *God gave man the test of obedience. He must not eat of the fruit of the tree of the knowledge of good and evil.*

   c. Q. What did God say would happen to Adam if he disobeyed?

      A. *God said that if Adam disobeyed he would die.*

   d. Q. What may we infer would have happened if he had obeyed?

      A. *We may infer that had Adam obeyed God's test, he would not have died, but would have lived in eternal communion with God.*

   e. Q. According to W.C.F. 7.2 what do we call this relationship with its responsibilities?

      A. *The Covenant of Works.*

   f. Q. What name do L.C. 20 and S.C. 12 give to this covenant? We will look at the Covenant of Works in more detail in the next lesson.

      A. *The Covenant of Life.*

3. Write a summary of what you have learned about man's created nature and the responsibilities given to him in that nature.

   A. *Of all God's creation, man was unique. He was created in the image of God, and spiritually, he was God's prophet, priest, and king. He alone was endowed with knowledge, righteousness, and holiness.*

Man was put to the test by God; he was told by God that if he disobeyed, he would die.

4. Q. What are things men can do today because they are in the image of God?

   A. *Today men can carry out the responsibilities God gave to Adam, but not perfectly. They like Adam can think, plan, construct, and create.*
   As we will see next, Adam died spiritually.

Man's Fallen Nature

5. Read Gen. 3:1-19.
   These verses describe how Adam and Eve responded to the test and the consequences of their actions.

   a. Q. What did they do? (Compare with S.C. 13, 15.)

      A. *Adam and Eve failed the test. Being left to their own free wills, they sinned against God by eating the fruit from the tree which is in the midst of the garden.*

   b. Q. What happened to them physically because they disobeyed?

      A. *Because they disobeyed they died physically.*

   c. They also died spiritually, which means they lost their original knowledge, righteousness, and holiness. Illustrate the loss of these three things from verses 7-13.

      A. *The illustrations of the loss of Adam and Eve's original knowledge, righteousness, and holiness are as follows:*

      They lost their knowledge. Their eyes were opened, and they knew that they were naked. They foolishly thought they could cover themselves and hide from God.

      They lost their righteousness. Because of their guilt they were ashamed. They sought to blame others for their sin

They lost their holiness. They did not want to commune with God. They made excuses and blamed others for their sin.

d. Q. Compare Rom. 6:23 with S.C. 19. What is the third aspect of death that Adam and Eve suffered?

A. *Pains of hell, eternal death.*

e. By sinning they became sinners. Read S.C. 14.

Q. According to S.C. 14 what are the two aspects of sin?

A. *The two aspects of sin are as follows: want of conformity to the law of God and transgression of the law of God.*

(1) Q. What is "want of conformity?"

A. *Falling short of the demands of God's law.*

(2) Q. What is transgression?

A. *To disobey God's commandments.*

6. Sin and the human race, Rom. 5:17-19.

Q. According to these verses what three things happened to the human race because of Adam's sin?

A. *The three things that happened to the human race because of Adam's sin were: death, condemnation, and judgment.*

a. This is called original sin.

(1) Q. According to S.C. 18, what does original sin entail?

A. *The guilt of Adam's first sin, the lack of original righteousness, and the corruption of our natures.*

b. Q. S.C. 16 says that these things happened to the human race because of the covenant or contract that God made with Adam. Can you think of arrangements in our society in which one person acts legally on behalf of many?

A. *In representative government, each branch of government acts legally on behalf of its citizens.*

In corporations, the Board of Directors acts legally for the stockholders.

In the Presbyterian and Reformed churches, the Session, Presbytery and General Assembly act legally for the various churches and/or church members.

Parents are the legal guardians of their children.

c. Because Adam was the head of the human race he acted on behalf of all.

Q. In what ways do you think Adam was the head of the human race?

A. *Adam was the head of the human race in the following ways:*

He was the physical head and covenantal head.

7. Q. According to Ps. 51:5; 58:3; Job 14:4, at what point do people receive their sinful natures?

A. *According to these verses people receive their sinful natures at the point of conception.*

a. Q. Is there any person born of a human father and mother exempt from this nature?

A. *No.*

b. Q. How was Christ exempt from original sin?

A. *By being born of a virgin.*

8. Now look at Rom. 3:10-18; 8:6, 7; 1 Cor. 2:14; Eph. 2:1-3.

Q. List the practical effects of being born a sinner.

A. *The practical effects of being born a sinner are as follows:*

You are not righteous, you do not seek God, you cannot submit to God's law, you cannot understand the Spirit, all of your faculties are perverted, and you are depraved.

9. Q. According to S.C. 19, what are the consequences of being sinners?

   A. *Sinners have lost their communion with God, are under His wrath and curse, and so made liable to all the miseries of this life, to death itself, and to the pains of hell forever.*

LESSON 9:

GOD'S COVENANT

Assignment:

Read:

W.C.F. 7; L.C. 30-35; S.C. 12, 20;
B.C. article 17; C.D. II, rejection 2.
Complete this lesson.

Memorize:

Gen. 3:15, Rom. 8:3; S.C. 12, 20.

As you begin this study pray that the Holy Spirit will enable you to understand the Bible and its message.

At the conclusion of our last lesson we left man in a terrible strait – dead in sins and under God's condemnation. This lesson will help us understand the general framework by which God extricates man from his sin and its consequences.

The Nature and Necessity of the Covenant

1. Q. Look up the term "covenant" in a dictionary and write a definition.

   A. A covenant is an agreement; compact (contract).

2. A good example of a covenant between man and man is found in Gen. 21:27-31.

Explain the scripture and include in your explanation the answers to a. through d; and then state the conclusion from e.

a. Q. What was the difficulty between Abraham and Abimelech?

   A. *Abraham complained to Abimelech because Abimelech's servants had seized his water well.*

b. Q. What was the role of a covenant in settling the difficulty?

   A. *The covenant was to assure that Abraham's ownership of the well would be acknowledged by Abimelech.*

c. Q. Who initiated the idea of a covenant and set the terms?

   A. *Abraham initiated the idea of the covenant and set the terms.*

d. Q. What were the parts of this covenant?

   A. *There were three parts to this covenant:*

   (1) It was initiated by one party, Abraham,

   (2) setting forth the obligations which both parties swear to perform, and

   (3) it is normally sealed by a sacrifice, the seven ewe lambs.

e. Q. From this passage what may we conclude that a Biblical covenant is?

   A. *From this passage we may conclude that a Biblical covenant is a compact or contract initiated by one party that sets forth obligations which both parties swear to perform and is normally sealed by a sacrifice. We may infer from the animals that it is normally sealed by a sacrifice.*

3. The necessity for a covenant is seen in Isa. 40:12-17 and Job 9:32. Read these verses and W.C.F. 7:1.

Q. According to these verses and W.C.F. 7:1, why do you think God uses a covenant to relate to man?

A. "The distance between God and the creature is so great, that although reasonable creatures do owe obedience unto Him as their Creator, yet they could never have any fruition of Him as their blessedness and reward, but by some voluntary condescension on God's part, which He hath been pleased to express by way of covenant.

(W.C.F. 7:1)

4. Q. According to Hab. 1:13, can you think of another reason God uses a covenant to relate to us?

   A. God uses a covenant to relate to us because we know that they are legally binding between men. Therefore, when the covenant is between us and God, who is infinitely good, just, and merciful, we know that the covenant will be fulfilled by God.

The Covenant of Works

5. We learned in the previous lesson that all mankind were brought into sin by Adam's fall, because he acted on behalf of all. This arrangement is called the Covenant of Works. In light of what we have said about covenants in general look at Gen. 2:15-17.

   a. Q. Who takes the initiative?

      A. God takes the initiative.

   b. Q. What responsibility was placed on man?

      A. The responsibility that was placed on man was to cultivate and keep the garden of Eden and not to eat of the fruit of the tree of the knowledge of good and evil.

   c. Q. What did God threaten and promise?

      A. God threatened death if man ate from the tree of good and evil. God promised life to Adam and his posterity if he obeyed.

6. This covenant transaction is summarized by S.C. 12. There was no sacrifice in this covenant because man had not yet sinned.

The Covenant of Grace

7. When Adam broke the covenant of works the penalty was in effect for him and the entire human race. Furthermore, the demands of the covenant were still in effect, if man were to be right with God.

   Look at Gal. 3:10, 12 and James 2:10.

   Q. According to these verses what requirement is placed on man and what happens if he does not meet that requirement?

   A. According to these verses, man must keep the Law in all points. If man fails to do so, he is guilty of all points and is condemned.

   a. Q. Therefore, if man were to be saved what two things would he have to be able to do?

      A. If man were to be saved, he had to do the following two things:

      (1) Keep the Law perfectly, or

      (2) Satisfy its penalty.

8. Since none can keep the law perfectly or satisfy its penalty, if anyone is to be saved God must do these things for him. This is what the Bible means by grace – God's doing for man what man does not deserve and cannot do for himself. This grace is administered through what we call the covenant of grace. Read S.C. 20.

   Q. According to S.C. 20, what does God promise to do in the covenant of grace?

   A. According to S.C. 20, God promises to save some and give them everlasting life, to deliver them out of the estate of sin and misery and to bring them into the estate of salvation by a Redeemer.

9. This covenant was first established in Gen. 3:15.

   a. Q. Who initiated and established this arrangement?

      A. God initiated and established this arrangement.

   b. Q. Who are the parties involved in this transaction?

      A. The parties involved in this transaction are as follows:
      The serpent who represents Satan (Rev. 20:2),
      The woman, Eve, and
      The man, Adam.

   c. Q. What does God promise to do?

      A. God promised to put enmity between the serpent (Satan) and the woman and between the serpent's seed and Eve's seed (all mankind).

   d. Q. By whom will God defeat the serpent?

      A. God will defeat the serpent (Satan) by Jesus Christ, the deliverer.

   e. This is the first gospel promise. God says that on the basis of a deliverer who suffers He will destroy Satan and restore His people to Himself. The rest of the Bible is the unfolding of this promise. We might say that the covenant with its promise is the framework that ties the entire Bible together. This is called covenant theology. The covenant of grace was revealed in the Old Testament to Noah, Abraham, Moses and David. These various administrations are called the Old Covenant. The New Covenant is revealed in Christ. According to covenant theology, God's people were saved in the Old Testament times in exactly the same way they are now.

      (1) The promises of the Old Covenant and the New Covenant are the same.

         (a). Q. What is the great covenant promise that runs straight through Scripture (Gen. 17:7; Exod. 19:5, 6; Jer. 31:33; Heb. 8:10; Rev. 21:3)?

A. *I will be your God and you will be my people.*

(b) Q. This promise is worked out in two more specific promises by which God accomplishes this relationship. According to Gen. 12:3; Gal. 3:8; Isa. 59:21; Deut. 30:6; Ps. 32:1, 2, what does God promise in the Old Covenant?

A. *According to these verses God has made the following promises: to forgive sins and give the gift of the Holy Spirit.*

(c) Q. Compare Acts 2:38, 39 with Jer. 31:31-34 and Joel 2:28, 29. What two things were promised on the day of Pentecost?

A. *The two things that were promised on the day of Pentecost were forgiveness of sins and the gift of the Holy Spirit.*

(2) Q. According to Acts 16:31, how does a person receive these benefits?

A. *According to this verse, if a person believes in the Lord Jesus, he will be saved and receive these benefits..*

(3) Look at Rom. 4:1-9.

Q. How did David and Abraham receive the benefits of the covenant?

A. *According to these verses, they received the benefits of the covenant when they believed God.*

(4) On the basis of the same promises received in the same way we must conclude that it is one covenant.

10. This is not to say there are no differences. We recognize that there must be some differences, because we refer to the Old Covenant or Testament and the New Covenant or Testament. This distinction is based on Heb. 8:13. Read Heb. 8:13.

Now complete the following exercise. Put an "o" by the things that are part of the Old Covenant and an "n" by those in the New Covenant.

Description	**Ans.**	**Description**	**Ans.**
Earthly Sanctuary	o	The Real Thing	n
Heavenly Sanctuary	n	Earthly Priests	o
Copies and Shadows	o	Heavenly Priests	n

From this exercise we learn that basically the old was preparatory for the new and the new fulfilled the old. Yet both the old and the new are the covenant of grace. This is summarized in W.C.F. 7:5, 6.

This is an important principle to keep in mind as you read and study the Bible.

LESSON 10:

THE ATONEMENT

Assignment:

Read:

W.C.F. 8; L.C. 36-50; S.C. 21-27; B.C. articles 17-21, 26; H.C. 11, 12, 15-19, 29, 37, 38, 46-49, 51.

Complete this lesson.

Memorize:

S.C. 21, 22; Phil. 2:6-8.

We have learned that Jesus Christ is the eternal son of God, the same in substance and equal in power and glory with the Father and the Holy Spirit. It remains for us to see how He became our Savior and what He accomplished on our behalf.

How He Became Our Savior

1. Q. We saw in Gen. 3:15 that God promised salvation by a deliverer. According to Isa. 42:1 and John 3:16, who was the deliverer to be?

   A. According to Isa. 42:1 and John 3:16, the deliverer was to be God's servant, the Son of God, Jesus Christ.

2. Q. According to John 1:1, 14 what did the eternal son of God have to do in order to become our Savior?

   A. *He had to become a man.*

   a. Q. This is called the incarnation (God in the flesh). Read Luke 1:26-38. How did the incarnation take place (Note carefully the phrase "shall conceive in your womb.")?

      A. *The Holy Spirit (God the Spirit) fertilized Mary's egg and she conceived a son that she had carried in her womb for nine months. The second person of the Godhead joined Himself to that fertilized egg so that Jesus was man and God.*

   b. This is normally called the virgin birth.

3. It is important to understand that Jesus truly became man. To help you understand this truth, look up each verse and write the particular human characteristic, aspect, or infirmity after it.

Verse	Human Characteristic	Human Aspect	Human Infirmity
a. Matt. 26:38	Agony		
b. John 4:4-8	Weary, Thirsty	Physical	
c. Luke 2:52	Wisdom		
d. Luke 19:41	Wept	Emotional	
e. Mark 3:5	Anger, Grief	Emotional	
f. Luke 23:46	Cried Out		Pain

4. Q. According to John 8:46 and Heb. 4:15, what human infirmity did Jesus not have?

   A. *According to John 8:46 and Heb. 4:15, Jesus did not have the human infirmity of sin.*

5. Q. S.C. 22 summarizes what we have learned about the human nature of Jesus. Write the answer in your own words.

A. *The second person of the Godhead took to Himself a true human nature, body and soul. This human nature was conceived in the womb of the Virgin Mary. In her womb He became the God-man.*

6. Q. Now look at Matt. 16:16 and John 20:28. Did Jesus cease being God when He became man?

A. *No.*

a. Q. Paul instructs us in Phil. 2:6, 7 what Jesus did when He took on a human nature. Write these two verses in your own words.

A. *Jesus who was both God and man set aside His privileges of being recognized as God by taking upon Himself the nature of man, even a servant. He became obedient as a man to God the Father's command even to the point of death by crucifixion.*

b. Q. According to S.C. 21, how then did God's Son become our Savior?

A. *Jesus became our Savior by continuing to be the eternal Son of God while He became a man. He was and continued to be, God and man in two distinct natures, and one person, forever.*

What He Accomplished on our Behalf

7. Q. In 1 Tim. 2:5 what word describes the work of Jesus as Savior?

A. *Mediator*

a. Q. What does a mediator do?

A. *The mediator attempts to reconcile two parties in a dispute in order to bring about a settlement.*

b. Q. What two parties need to be reconciled?

A. *According to 1 Tim. 2:5, God and man are the two parties that need to be reconciled.*

c. Q. According to Rom. 3:25, 26; 6:23; and John 3:18, 36, what do you think had to be done if God is to be reconciled to sinners?

A. *God's wrath and justice had to be satisfied.*

d. Q. What do Rom. 2:13 and Lev. 18:5 tell us must be man's position if he is to be accepted by God?

A. *One must obey the law of God perfectly.*

e. Q. Is any mere man able to fulfill the demands of the law?

A. *No.*

f. Q. What is the ultimate penalty man must pay (Rom. 6:23, cf. S.C. 19)?

A. *Eternal damnation in hell.*

g. Thus as mediator, Jesus had to fulfill the perfect demands of the law and to satisfy God's punishment of sinners.

8. Q. According to Heb. 10:5-9 what was one of the primary purposes the son of God became a man?

A. *According to these verses, Jesus became a man in order to satisfy the demands of the law. He always did everything that was required; and He never did anything that was prohibited.*

a. Q. How does Christ express this purpose in Matt. 3:15; 5:17; and John 4:34?

A. *According to these verses, Christ satisfied the law by fulfilling all righteousness, fulfilling all requirements of the Law or Prophets and by doing the will of God, the Father, and accomplishing His work.*

b. Q. This is what Paul means in Gal. 4:4 that Christ was made under the law. According to Rom. 10:4 did Christ fulfill this purpose?

A. *Yes. "Christ is the end of the law for righteousness to everyone who believes."*

c. Q. What does Paul say in Rom. 3:21, 22 God gives to us when we believe in Jesus Christ?

A. God gives us righteousness.

d. Thus we learn that by His obedience Christ purchased righteousness so that we can be accepted by God.

9. Q. According to Gal. 3:13, what did God do to Christ on the cross?

A. God made Christ cursed for us.

a. Q. According to 2 Cor. 5:21, what did God place on Christ?

A. The guilt of the sins of His people was placed on Him. Our sins were imputed to Him.

b. Q. According to Isa. 53:4-9, what happened to Christ because our sins were placed on Him?

A. He bore them suffering in our place. He satisfied the justice of God.

c. This is called the substitutionary atonement. Christ on the cross took the place of His people and suffered the punishment due to their sin. Compare S.C. 25.

10. Q. According to John 10:15, 16; 17:9; and Rev. 5:9, 10, did Christ pay the penalty for all people or for His people?

A. Christ full paid the penalty for His people.

It is important to understand this distinction. If Christ suffered hell on the cross, then everyone whose place He took must be released from the punishment of hell. Therefore either He died for all and all must be saved or He died for His people and everyone for whom He died will be saved. When we realize that He died in a special way for the people the Father gave Him, we see that our salvation has fully been accomplished. To be saved we receive what Christ has done for us.

11. Q. In summary write a definition of the doctrine of substitutionary atonement.

A. *God has said that all have sinned, that there is not one who is righteous. He has said that the penalty for sin is death, that is eternal separation from God. Before the foundation of the world God chose those whom He would save. In His plan of salvation, He sent forth His only begotten Son, Jesus Christ, to be the mediator. In this role of mediator, Christ obeyed the law of God perfectly and died to pay the penalty that God required for those whom God had chosen. Christ who knew no sin bore the sins of all those the Father chose and thus became the substitute to atone for their sins.*

LESSON 11:

THE AGENT OF SALVATION

Assignment:

Read:

W.C.F. 2:3; L.C. 9-11, 57-59, 66;
S.C. 6, 29, 30; H.C. 53.
Complete this lesson.

Memorize:

John 14:26; 15:26

Having studied man's need, God's covenant, and the work of Christ, we now turn our attention to the application of God's salvation to the individual sinner. Before considering the discrete parts of the application of salvation, we want to study about the agent of salvation, the Holy Spirit. In chapter four we studied the Trinity and learned that the Spirit is the third person of the Godhead. Read S.C. 6 to review what you have learned about the Holy Spirit.

The Names and Relations of the Third Person

1. The third person of the Godhead is given many names in the Bible. After each reference write the name given to the third person of the Godhead and what that name tells you about Him:

a. Q. Matt. 3:16; 1 Cor. 2:11, 12.

A. *Spirit of God. He is a spirit who is divine. God the Spirit.*

b. Q. Ps. 51:11

A. *Holy Spirit. He is absolutely holy.*

c. Q. Gal. 4:6; Phil. 1:19

A. *Spirit of the Son, of the Lord Jesus Christ. Spirit relates to God the Son in the same way as to the Father.*

d. Q. 2 Cor. 3:17, 18

A. *Spirit of the Lord; the Lord who is the Spirit. The Spirit is Jehovah, the Lord.*

e. Q. John 14:15, 26; 15:26

A. *Another Helper, helper, counselor, comforter, Spirit of truth. He comes in Christ's place to comfort and help His people. He is the communicator of truth.*

f. Q. Ps. 33:6

A. *The breath of the Lord. God reveals Himself and power through the Holy Spirit.*

2. Q. The names Spirit and breath teach us also about the Spirit's relationship to the other two members of the Godhead. According to John 15:26 what is His relation to the Father?

A. *He proceeds from the Father.*

a. Q. Comparing John 15:26; Gal. 4:6; Phil. 1:19 with John 20:22, what would you say is the Son's role in the procession of the Spirit?

A. *He proceeds from the Son as well.*

b. Q. How does L.C. 10 summarize this relationship?

A. *The Son is eternally begotten, and the Spirit eternally proceeds from the Father and Son; hence, His name Spirit, spiration.*

c. Q. According to Matt. 28:19 and 2 Cor. 13:14, does this relationship suggest any subordination (see W.C.F. 2:3; L.C.9, 11)?

A. No. They are the same in substance, equal in power and glory.

3. This relationship within the Godhead teaches us how God operates. As the Spirit completes the Trinity, He completes the work of the Trinity. As the Holy Spirit He is the perfecting and sanctifying agent.

The Work of the Holy Spirit

4. Q. According to Gen. 1:2; Job 26:13; Gen. 1:26, 27; 2:7, what were the Spirit's various activities in the work of creation?

A. Preserving, forming, animating man, making the heavens, perfecting the creation.

5. We have seen that "God's works of providence are, His most holy, wise, and powerful preserving and governing all His creatures and all their actions (S.C. 11, Lesson Seven)." Match each reference with the work of providence performed by the Holy Spirit:

Ps. 104:30 *b*	a. Imparting gifts and talents
Gen. 6:3; Heb. 6:4 *d*	b. Preserving and sustaining life
Exod. 31:2ff; 1 Sam. 16:13 *a*	c. Providential alterations
Prov. 21:1; Zech. 4:6, 7 *c*	d. Preserving moral life

6. Another work of the Spirit was to inspire the men who wrote the Bible. After each reference describe the Spirit's role in revelation and inspiration.

a. Q. 2 Sam. 23:2

A. Gave David the words of the Psalms.

b. Q. Ezek. 8:3; 11:1

A. *Gave visions to the Prophets.*

c. Q. John 14:26

A. *Give the disciples Christ's infallible message.*

d. Q. 2 Tim. 3:16; 2 Peter 1:21

A. *Inspired all Scripture writers.*

7. Q. In Lesson Two we referred to the Spirit's role in the illumination of Scripture. Look up Ps. 119:18; 1 Cor. 2:14; Eph. 1:17, 18 and write out the Spirit's role in illumination.

A. *Giving understanding of the Bible; giving understanding of the gospel and spiritual truth; giving wisdom and understanding.*

8. The Spirit was also involved in the work of Christ. After each reference describe the Spirit's role:

a. Q. Luke 1:35; Matt. 1:18, 20

A. *Preparing His human nature in the womb of the Virgin Mary.*

b. Q. Matt. 3:16, 17; Isa. 61:13; Luke 4:18, 19

A. *Anointing for ministry.*

c. Q. Acts 2:22; Matt. 12:28

A. *Power to work miracles.*

d. Q. Heb. 9:14

A. *Enabled Christ to offer Himself as perfect sacrifice.*

e. Q. 1 Peter 3:18; Rom. 8:11

A. *Raised Him from the dead.*

f. Q. John 7:39; Acts 2:33

A. *Spirit given by Christ to the Church.*

9. The Spirit is the primary agent in our conversion, sanctification, and preservation. We will study these works

in greater detail in subsequent lessons. Simply note now how these works are ascribed to the Spirit by listing each work after the reference:

a. Q. John 3:3-7

   A. *Being born again; regeneration.*

b. Q. 1 Cor. 2:4; 1 Thess. 2:13

   A. *Empowers the preaching of the Word.*

c. Q. Rom. 8:13

   A. *Enables us to die to sin.*

d. Q. Eph. 3:16-19

   A. *Strengthens, assures.*

e. Q. Rom. 8:16

   A. *Seals our adoption.*

f. Q. Rom. 8:10, 11; Eph. 1:13, 14

   A. *Resurrect and glorify us.*

10. Q. According to Rom. 8:9, what is the Spirit's relation to each believer?

    A. *Indwells each believer. Christ indwells us by His Spirit.*

a. Q. List the terms Paul uses in Rom. 8:1-14 to describe the effects of this indwelling.

   A. *No condemnation; walking according to the Spirit; in the Spirit; Christ in you; Sprit indwells; give life to your spirits at resurrection; live by the Spirit; led by the Spirit.*

b. Q. By whose power do we live the Christian life?

   A. *The Holy Spirit.*

c. Q. Match the effects of this indwelling with the appropriate reference:

Uniting us to Christ *b*	a.	Gal. 4:6, 7; 1 John 2:27-29; Rom. 8; 15-16
Seal or earnest of inheritance *e*	b.	Rom. 6:3, 4
Grants assurance *a*	c.	Rom. 8:26; Eph. 6:18
Enables us to pray *c*	d.	Rom. 8:14; Gal. 5:1, 16, 18
Leads and guides us in obedience *d*	e.	Eph. 1:13, 14

d. Q. According to Acts 4:31; Gal. 5:16ff; Eph. 5:18ff, what are the consequences of being filled with the Spirit?

A. Speaking the gospel with power; walk in holiness, exhibiting the fruit of the Spirit; worshipping; living in proper biblical relationships.

11. The Spirit also gives gifts to the Church. Some of these gifts were extraordinary for the New Testament age as the Bible was being completed, others are ordinary for our age.

a. Q. Read 1 Cor. 12:8-10 and list the extraordinary gifts.

A. Word of wisdom and knowledge (Revelation); healing; miracles; prophecy; distinguishing the spirits (recognizing false prophets); tongues; interpretation of tongues.

b. Q. According to 2 Cor. 12:12 and Heb. 2:1-4 what was the primary purpose of these gifts.

A. Confirms the Apostolic message.

c. Q. List the ordinary gifts enumerated in Rom. 12:6-8 and write a definition after each one.

A. Prophecy—preaching.
Service—diaconal ministry.
Teaching—ability to explain the truths of God's Word privately and publicly.

Exhortation—admonition, encouragement, particularly in counseling and evangelism.
Giving—ability to give sacrificially of one's time and money and encourage others to do so.
Leading—administration, delegating, and governing.
Mercy—Compassion to empathize and minister to those in need.

d. These gifts are for the Church today. Which do you think you have? In Lesson Twenty-Three we will use a Personal Information Sheet to help you determine your gifts.

Teacher's Edition

LESSON 12:

THE SOURCE OF SALVATION

Assignment:

Read:

W.C.F. 3:3-8; 10; L.C. 57-60, 68; S.C. 20, 29-31;
B.C. articles 14, 16; H.C. 54; C.D. I, articles 6-18; II, articles 8, 9 with rejections; II, IV articles 6, 8-16, rejections 6-9.
Complete this lesson.

Memorize:

Eph. 1:3; John 6:44; S.C. 31.

Having studied the work of the Holy Spirit, we now turn our attention to the application of God's salvation to the individual sinner. The first step is the source of salvation.

The Immediate Source

1. Read Matt. 27:44 and Luke 23:39-43.

a. Q. What happened to one of the robbers who was mocking Christ?

A. He was saved. Jesus said, "Today you will be with me in Paradise."

b. Q. Why do you think this thief turned from mocking to believing in Christ?

A. *The thief turned from mocking to believing in Christ because God moved in his heart to bring him to faith.*

2. The full answer to this question is spelled out in John 6:44.

   a. Q. According to this verse what is necessary if a person is to believe in Jesus Christ for salvation?

      A. *God, the Father, must draw that person to Jesus.*

   b. Q. What does Jesus promise to do to each one who is drawn to Him by the Father?

      A. *Jesus has promised that He will raise that person up (glorify him) at the last day.*

   c. Q. If all who are drawn will be raised on the last day, can any drawn by the Father not believe in the Son?

      A. *No, if the Father draws someone, that person must believe in the Son and he will persevere.*

   d. According to S.C. 29, it is called the effectual application of salvation. It is called effectual because it always works.

3. Look at 1 Peter 1:23 and 2 Cor. 3:3.

   Q. According to these verses what are the two instruments involved in effectual calling?

   A. *According to these verses the two instruments involved in effectual calling are: God's Word (the Bible) and God's Spirit (the Holy Spirit).*

   a. Look at 2 Tim. 3:15-16; Rom. 10:14; and Heb. 4:12-13.

      Q. On the basis of these verses, what would you say is the role of the Word in salvation?

      A. *The role of the Word in salvation is to reveal to the person that he is a lost sinner without hope outside of the finished work of Christ, convict him of sin, reveal God's plan of salvation, and show the duty of faith and repentance.*

b. Look at John 3:3-8.

Q. In these verses how is the work of the Holy Spirit described?

A. According to John 3:3-8, the Holy Spirit gives the believer second birth/regeneration.

c. These things are summarized in S.C. 31.

Q. What are the three parts of this work described in S.C. 31?

A. Conviction of sin; enlightening our minds; renewing our wills.

d. The work of the Holy Spirit in the new birth is broken down into three parts. After each verse, write what element of the Spirit's work is being described and then match that element with its illustration in the book of Acts.

			Ans.
1.	Zech. 12:10 convincing us of our sin and misery	Acts 22:4-10	3
2.	1 Cor. 2:12-14 enlightening our minds in the knowledge of Christ	Acts 16:14	2
3.	Ezek. 36:26-27 renewing our wills	Acts 2:37	1

The Ultimate Source

4. Q. If God calls some effectually and not others, on what basis is the decision made whom He will call and whom He will pass by?

A. The answer to this question is found in Rom. 8:29-30. Those He calls have been predestined.

a. Q. List the five elements of salvation found in these verses.

A. 1. *Foreknew* 4. *Justified*
2. *Predestined* 5. *Glorified*
3. *Called*

b. Q. According to these verses, what happens to the person who has been called?

A. *The person is justified and glorified.*

c. This demonstrates that Paul is talking about effectual calling. Everyone who is called is justified and glorified.

d. Now go back one step before calling.

Q. According to these verses, who are called?

A. *Those whom He predestined.*

5. The word predestined means foreordained. We have already learned that God by His decree has foreordained all things that come to pass. Eph. 1:3-6 applies this foreordination to salvation.

a. Q. When did God choose those whom He would save?

A. *God chose those whom He would save before the foundation of the world.*

b. Q. For what purpose did God choose them to salvation?

A. *That they may be holy and blameless (conformed to the image of Jesus Christ).*

c. Now look at Acts 13:48.

Q. How does this verse relate eternal choice to effectual calling?

A. *All who were chosen for eternal life believed when called.*

d. Write a summary of what you have learned up to this point.

A. *Before the foundation of the world God chose those whom He would save, according to the good pleasure of His will. A series of events would then occur. Those who were chosen (foreordained) to eternal life were effectually called so that when they heard the Word they were caused to believe. Those called were justified and ultimately will be glorified.*

6. It remains for us to discover on what basis God chooses to save certain people.

   a. The answer is found in the first element of our salvation mentioned in Rom. 8:29.

      Q. Who are the ones God predestined to salvation?

      A. *Those whom God foreknew are the ones predestined to salvation.*

   b. To understand the word "foreknowledge" or "foreknow," we need to determine how the Bible uses the word "know". Look at Gen. 4:1 (the margin of the New American Standard Bible); Amos 3:2 (again the margin of the NASB); and Ps. 1:6.

      Keeping these references in mind, write a definition of "know."

      A. *The Bible uses the word "know" to mean love and approve.*

   c. The prefix "fore" means to know before time. Look at Acts 2:23 and 1 Peter 1:20.

      Q. What do the words "foreknow" and "foreknowledge" mean in these verses?

      A. *According to these verses, these words mean that before the foundation of the world God knew, loved, the Lord Jesus Christ and ordained that He would be born and crucified to save His elect.*

   d. On the basis of what you have found, write a definition of "foreknew" as it is used in Rom. 8:29, 30.

      A. *"Foreknew" means that God before the foundation of the world loved and placed His favor on those whom*

He elected, not because of anything found in them, but according to His own good pleasure.

e. Compare your definition with what Paul says in Eph. 1:4, 5.

Q. What does Paul mean that God chose in love and according to the kind intention of His will?

A. Paul means that God chose us according to the good pleasure of His will, not because of anything in us, but because He sovereignly loved us.

f. This doctrine is called unconditional election. It is stated in W.C.F. 3:3-5.

LESSON 13:

JUSTIFICATION

Assignment:

Read:

W.C.F. 11, 14, and 15; L.C. 70, 72, 73, 76, 153;
S.C. 32, 33, 85, 86, 87; B.C. articles 22, 23;
H.C. 1, 20-23, 39, 45, 56, 59-61, 84, 87, 88, 126;
C.D. I, articles 2-4; II, articles 3, 6, 7 with rejections; III, IV, article 13.
Complete this lesson.

Memorize:

S.C. 32, 33; Rom. 5:1, 2.

In Rom. 8:29, 30, we read that the direct consequence of calling is justification. Luther called this truth the doctrine of a standing or falling church. In this lesson we will consider what the Bible teaches about justification.

The Act of Justification

1. Read Deut. 25:1.

   Q. According to this verse, in what context is the term "justification" used?

   A. In this verse a dispute has been taken to court to acquit the innocent, to justify the righteous.

a. Q. In this verse, what act is considered the opposite of to justify? (Compare Rom. 8:33, 34.)

A. The act that is considered the opposite of to justify is to condemn the wicked or guilty.

b. Q. Who is to be justified?

A. The innocent, the righteous is to be justified.

c. Q. When a judge justifies an accused criminal, what is he saying about him?

A. The judge is saying that the accused criminal has been declared innocent of the charge and that in the eyes of the law he has been exonerated of the charges.

2. Q. When we apply this judicial action to God, what do we mean when we say God justifies us?

A. When we apply this judicial action to God, we mean to say that God declares someone not guilty, innocent.

We find a dramatization of this in Zech. 3:1-5.

a. (1) Q. What was Joshua's problem (relate to what we learned in Lesson 10 about man's responsibility)?

A. Joshua's problem was sin.

(2) Q. What two things did God do for him?

A. First, God had his filthy garments removed. God took away his iniquity, his sin.
Second, God declared him righteous and God clothed him in festal robes.

3. In other words, justification deals with man's sin problem – it cancels the debt of sin, declares us not guilty, and enables God to accept us as righteous.

The Ground of Justification

4. Look at Prov. 17:15.

Q. What does this verse say about the judge who justifies the wicked?

A. *Prov. 17:15 says that the judge who justifies the wicked is an abomination (exceedingly disgusting and hateful) to the Lord.*

a. Q. Yet is this not what God does in justification?

A. *Yes.*

Q. How can God do this and still be a just God?

A. *God can justify the wicked (the sinner) and still be a just God only by making provision for the satisfaction of justice.*

5. Rom. 3:24-26 helps us understand how God can be just and justify a sinner.

Q. According to this passage, what has been done so that God can be just and declare sinners not guilty?

A. *According to Rom. 3:24-26, God has provided for His elect righteousness as a gift by His grace through the redemption which is in Christ Jesus. Christ purchased our salvation by being a propitiatory sacrifice. He bore God's wrath in our place that God's justice against us might be satisfied.*

a. This, of course, relates to what we learned in Lesson 10 about the work of Christ.

Q. In Lesson 10, what two things did we learn that Christ did for us?

A. *We learned that Christ obeyed the law perfectly and that He died for our sins.*

b. The purpose and result of Christ's sacrifice is explained in 2 Cor. 5:21.

Q. What is the two-fold imputation described here? (You might need to look up "imputation" in a dictionary.)

A. *The two-fold imputation described here is as follows:*

(1) God (the Father) made Christ who knew no sin to be sin on our (the elect sinners) behalf,

(2) *that we (the elect sinners) might be righteousness in the sight of God (the Father) in Him (Christ).*

c. Thus we say that the ground or the basis of our justification is the work of the Lord Jesus Christ (W.C.F. 11:1, 3; L.C. 71).

The Means of Justification

6. Read Rom. 4:1-9.

Q. How did Abraham receive the righteousness of justification?

A. According to Rom. 4:1-9, Abraham believed God and faith was reckoned to him as righteousness.

7. Read Rom. 3:28 and Gal. 2:16.

Q. What is the role of works in our justification?

A. According to this verse, no one will be justified by works of the Law.

8. Look again at Gal. 2:16 and compare that with John 1:12. Look at S.C. 86.

Q. What is it that faith does in receiving justification?

A. Faith in Christ Jesus is a saving grace, whereby we receive and rest upon Him alone for salvation. As many as received (by faith alone) Him (Christ Jesus), to them He (Christ Jesus) gave the right (the privilege) to become children of God, even to those who believe in His (Christ Jesus') name.

a. Look at Acts 2:38 and 11:18.

Q. According to these verses, what other act does faith include?

A. According to Acts 2:28 and 11:18, faith also includes the act of repentance.

b. Read Jer. 31:18, 19.

Q. On the basis of these verses, write a definition of repentance.

A. *The act of repentance involves a sinner's confessing his disobedient behavior to God and a promising to make a sincere effort to live one's life in obedience to God's Law.*

Look at S.C. 87.

9. Now read James 2:14-26.

a. Q. By what you have learned from the principles of the interpretation of the Bible, could James be contradicting Paul?

A. *No. James is concerned with the demonstration of faith). These verses pick out the ways that your faith can be tested. James is describing how true faith responds in obedience.*

b. The use of cross-references helps clarify the answer to the apparent contradiction. The reference James quotes in verse 23 is Gen. 15:6. The occasion referred to in verse 21 is found in Gen. 22.

Q. In which of these instances did Abraham receive justification by believing?

A. *In Gen. 15:6 Abraham received justification by believing.*

c. Q. About how many years later did he obey God in offering up Isaac?

A. *It was about forty years later.*

d. Thus it appears that when James speaks of justification he is not thinking of justification in the Pauline sense of pardoned sin and free acceptance with God. Look up justify in the dictionary.

Q. Is there another meaning to the term that would explain how James uses the term?

A. *James could have used the term to mean to demonstrate or to prove right.*

e. Look at Matt. 11:19.

Q. How does Jesus use the term in this verse (some Bibles translate the term vindicated)?

A. In this verse, Jesus uses the term to mean proved right.

f. Q. On the basis of what you have learned, how do you think James is using the term in James 2?

A. In James 2, James is using the term to mean that the genuine nature of faith is proven by works.

g. Write a paraphrase of James 2:21-24.

A. Was not Abraham our father tested and proved faithful by his works when he offered up Isaac his son on the altar?

You see that saving faith, God's gift to Abraham almost forty years before, was working with his works (of offering up Isaac his son on the altar), and as a result of the works, the testing of faith was accomplished;

and the Scripture was fulfilled which early declared that God reckoned Abraham righteous on the basis of faith.

You see that the genuine nature of a man's faith is proven by his works.

The Relationship of Justification to Daily Confession of Sins

10. Even though God pardoned all our sins, we still are to make daily confession of sin. We will discuss this in the next lesson. We confess sin in order to maintain fellowship with God.

LESSON 14:

ADOPTION AND ASSURANCE

Assignment:

Read:

W.C.F. 12, 18; L.C. 74, 80, 81; S.C. 34; H.C. 1, 33;
C.D. I article 12 with rejection 8; V, articles 6, 9-13
with rejections 5, 6.
Complete this lesson.

Memorize:

S.C. 34; Rom. 8:16; 1 John 5:13.

The Act of Adoption

1. Give a definition of adoption as it is used in human relationships.

   A. Adoption is a legal act by which an individual is incorporated into a family of which he was not naturally a part by birth.

   a. Q. What benefits do parents give to their adopted children?

      A. Legally, parents give the adopted children the same rights and privileges as natural born children: their name, possessions, food, clothing, shelter, culture, values, status, and membership in God's covenant.

b. Look at John 1:12.

Q. According to this verse, what right does God give those who believe in the Lord Jesus Christ?

A. According to John 1:12, God gives those who believe in the Lord Jesus Christ the right or authority to become the sons of God.

c. Look at Rom. 8:16, 17.

Q. According to these verses, what privileges do God's adopted children receive?

A. According to Rom. 8:16, 17, God's adopted children become heirs, heirs of God and fellow heirs with Christ, if indeed the adopted children suffer with Him (Christ) in order that they may also be glorified with Him (Christ).

Adoption is summarized in S.C. 34.

2. Read John 1:12, 13.

Q. According to these verses, when does adoption take place?

A. According to John 1:12, 13, adoption takes place at the time a person savingly believes in the Lord Jesus Christ.

a. On the basis of Eph. 1:4-8 and Gal. 4:4, 5, how does adoption relate to election?

A. God predestined (elected) us to adoption as sons through Jesus Christ to Himself (God). (Eph.1:5).

b. How does it relate to Christ's work of atonement and justification?

A. God sent forth His (God) Son (Christ), born of a woman, born under the Law, in order that He (Christ) might redeem (atone for) those who were under the Law, that they might receive the adoption as sons. (Gal. 4:4, 5).

Because God has pardoned our sins and declared us to be righteous, He may freely adopt us into His family. (Eph. 1:7).

The Benefits of Adoption

3. Listed below are a number of verses. Look up the verses and after each group write what benefit of adoption is described in that verse:

   A. The answers are as follows:

   a. Gal. 4:6 and Rom. 8:15 – the believer receives the Holy Spirit and assurance.

   b. Heb. 4:16; Eph. 3:12; 1 John 5:14; Rom. 8:26, 27 – the believer gains confidence that he can approach God in prayer.

   c. Ps. 103:13, 14 – receives God's compassion and condescension.

   d. Ps. 34:7; 27:1-3; Prov. 14:26 – the believer receives God's protection.

   e. Heb. 12:6-12 – receives God's discipline.

   f. Heb. 13:5; Eph. 4:30 – has God's consistent presence.

   g. Heb. 6:12 – inherits the promises of God.

   h. 1 Peter 1:4; Rom. 8:17, 32 – as an heir shares in God's and Christ's glory.

   Check your answers with W.C.F. 12.

4. Explain how you think an understanding of adoption and its benefits can help a person in the following areas:

   a. Problem with self-image and insecurity.

   A. An understanding of adoption and its benefits can help a person who has a problem with self-image and insecurity by reminding the person that he is a child of God and joint-heir with the Lord Jesus Christ.

   b. A Christian who has a certain sin in his life that he does not want to give up or recognizes a commandment from God that he does not want to obey.

A. *An understanding of adoption and its benefits can help a Christian who has a certain sin in his life that he does not want to give up or who recognizes a commandment from God that he does not want to obey by reminding him of the great privileges that belong to him in his adoption and that it would be the height of ingratitude not to obey.*

c. A person who has difficulty establishing regular habits of prayer.

A. *An understanding of adoption and its benefits can help a person who has difficulty establishing regular habits of prayer by reminding himself what it cost Christ to procure the privilege of prayer and that he may have sure access into the very presence of God.*

The Relationship of Adoption to Daily Confession of Sins

5. Even though God has pardoned all our sins, we still are to make daily confession of sin. Part of the reason is given in 1 John 1:5-10.

a. Q. What does sin do to our fellowship with God?

A. *Sin hinders our fellowship and communion with God. We must confess our sins in order to maintain fellowship.*

b. Q. Look at Prov. 28:13. What does God say about the person who doesn't confess sin?

A. *His way will not prosper. He will not enjoy God's blessing.*

c. Q. Thus if we are to enjoy the presence of God, His fellowship, and His blessing, what must we do?

A. *We must regularly confess our sins and hide none.*

d. Therefore confession of sin does not maintain our relationship to God, but our fellowship. In justification our sins are freely forgiven once and for all. God as judge has cleared us. As adopted children we are not judicially obligated to confess sin, but rather it is a family responsibility. We ought to confess sins as we commit them, but in addition, we ought to have a time each day during which we take spiritual inventory and ask God to forgive us of our sins. Be sure this is part of your daily time of Bible study and prayer.

The Relation of Adoption to Assurance

6. One of the great practical benefits of the doctrine of adoption is the promotion of assurance of salvation.

   a. Read Gal. 4:6 and Rom. 8:16.

      Q. According to these verses, what is one of the results of adoption?

      A. According to Gal. 4:6 and Rom. 8:16, one of the results of adoption is that the Holy Spirit bears witness to us that we are children of God.

   b. Q. What kind of attitude or disposition does the Holy Spirit give the believer?

      A. When the Holy Spirit comes into the heart of the believer, that person is given a hungering childlike disposition. He now regards God as his father, not his enemy.

   c. Q. What testimony does He (the Holy Spirit) bear to the believer?

      A. The Holy Spirit bears witness with the believer's spirit that he is a child of God, and that God is his father.

   d. Now look at Heb. 6:17, 18; 2 Peter 1:4-11; 2 Cor. 1:12.

      Q. According to these verses, what two things does the Holy Spirit use to testify to us that God has saved us?

      A. The promises of God and the sanctification of our lives.

e. Q. Write a summary statement of how adoption relates to assurance. (Compare W.C.F. 18:2.)

A. *Because the Holy Spirit has been given to us, He points us to the promises of Scripture and the inward evidence of those graces to which the promise are made, teaching us that the promises belong to us.. Moreover, He bears witness within our hearts that we are the children of God.*

7. It remains for us to test our adoption. Read 1 John 5:13.

Q. According to this verse, what does John say about those who have believed?

A. *John says he has written these things so that all who believe may know that they have eternal life.*

a. Q. The phrase "these things" points back to certain marks of sonship that John has given in this letter. Look up the following verses: 1 John 5:1; 3:14; 4:7; 5:3, 4; 2:29; 3:9. List some of the things, according to these verses, that will be developing in your life if you have been converted.

A. *According to these verses, some of the things that will be developing in my life if I have been converted are as follows:*

Love for God the Father

Love for other Christians

Keep His commandments

Overcomes the world

Practices righteousness

Does not practice sin

b. Look at Matt. 7:20-23 and James 2:14-26.

Q. According to these verses, do you think a person who has no growth in faith and holiness has any right to assurance of salvation?

A. *According to Matt. 7:20-23 and James 2:14-26, works are an evidence that a person has been saved. If the evidences are lacking, a person does not have any right to assurance of salvation.*

8. Therefore, if God has adopted us, He is working changes in us (Phil. 2:12, 13). This, too, is of grace.

LESSON 15:

PERSEVERANCE AND SANCTIFICATION

Assignment:

Read:

W.C.F. 13; 17; L.C. 75, 77, 78, 79; S.C. 35, 36;
B.C. article 24; H.C. 1, 32, 43, 62-64; 86-90;
C.D. I, articles 11, 13 with rejection 6; II, article 9; V,articles 1-15 with rejections 1-9.
Complete this lesson.

Memorize:

S.C. 35; Heb. 12:14; Rom. 13:4.

We read in Eph. 1:4 that God's great purpose in choosing and saving His people is that we be holy and blameless. This work begins with our justification in which God declares us righteous and ends in our glorification that perfects us in righteousness. In this lesson we are concerned with the process that takes place between justification and glorification.

Perseverance

1. Read Rom. 8:29, 30.

Q. What is the fifth link of the chain in Rom. 8:29, 30?

A. The fifth link of the chain is glorification.

a. Look at John 17:24 and 1 John 3:2.

Q. According to these verses, what is glorification?

A. The glorification of the believer is his perfect conformity, body and soul, to the Lord Jesus Christ, accomplished at the second coming. The believer shall dwell with God forever more in this perfect condition.

b. Q. Why do you think that Paul speaks of glorification in the past tense in Rom. 8:30?

A. It is certain to happen.

c. Q. According to this verse can any justified person not be glorified?

A. No. According to Rom. 8:30, everyone who is justified will be glorified.

d. This is the great truth of eternal security, frequently expressed as once saved, always saved. Scripture affirms this truth in a number of ways. After each of the following verses, write what you learn about this truth:

Verse		**Answers**
(1)	Phil. 1:6	God began a good work (conversion) in the believer and He will perfect it until the Last Day.
(2)	John 6:44	Those called by God will be raised up at the Last Day.
(3)	John 10:28, 29	Jesus says that a person saved has been given eternal life. God has chosen him and Christ gives him eternal life. He cannot lose it. No one can take it away.

e. Q. Now write a statement of this truth in your own words. (Compare your answer with W.C.F. 17 and L.C. 79.)

A. *All whom the Father has chosen and Christ has redeemed shall believe on the Lord Jesus Christ and shall be kept by God and raised to perfection when Christ returns.*

2. 2 Tim. 2:19 teaches, however, that there are two sides to the coin of eternal security.

   a. Q. How does Paul express the fact of God's preservation of the Christian?

      A. *The firm foundation of God stands, having this seal, "The Lord knows those who are His." All those chosen are loved and kept by God.*

   b. Q. What duty is commanded here?

      A. *The believer is to abstain from wickedness. He is to put off sin. He is to persevere.*

   c. This is the second side of the coin: the one who is preserved perseveres in the faith. Thus we may not sit back and say, "Once saved always saved, so it does not matter what I do." If we are saved, we will be putting off sin.

   d. The two things are put together in Phil. 2:12, 13.

      Q. How does Paul express perseverance in these verses?

      A. *In these verses Paul expresses perseverance by telling the believer to work out his salvation with fear and trembling.*

   e. Q. How does he express preservation?

      A. *He expresses preservation by telling the believer that God is working in him, both to will and work for His good pleasure.*

Sanctification

3. The responsibility of perseverance is worked out in the process the Bible calls sanctification.

Q. Look up in a dictionary the terms "sanctify" and "sanctification" and write a definition of what you think the Bible means when it speaks of sanctification.

A. *To "sanctify" is to set apart. "Sanctification" is the process of setting apart. When the Bible speaks of sanctification it means that someone (or something) has been set apart as holy. When the Bible speaks of a person, it means that he has been made free from sin and will grow in conformity to the Lord Jesus Christ.*

Q. Compare your answer with S.C. 35.

A. *In the S.C. 35 we read that sanctification is a work of God's grace by which a person is enabled more and more to die unto sin, and live unto righteousness.*

4. Look at 2 Thess. 2:13 and Heb. 12:14.

Q. On the basis of these verses, how important would you say sanctification is to God?

A. *On the basis of 2 Thess. 2:13 and Heb. 12:14, I would say that sanctification is very important to God. God has chosen the believer for salvation through sanctification. The believer is told to pursue sanctification without which he will not see the Lord.*

Q. How important, then, should it be to the Christian?

A. *The pursuit of sanctification is absolutely necessary for the Christian.*

5. Q. According to Rom. 6:1-10, what act took place when you were converted?

A. *I died to sin and was raised to holiness.*

a. Q. According to Rom. 6:11-14, what should you be doing because you are dead to sin and alive to righteousness?

A. *Reckoning myself dead to sin. Not giving myself to sin, but to godliness. Not letting sin be my master, because I am dead to it.*

b. We call this definitive sanctification. At the moment of conversion we become slaves to Christ and not to sin. This definitive sanctification is the basis of our progressive sanctification.

6. Progressive sanctification is the process between justification and glorification in which a believer becomes more God-like.

Q. According to S.C. 35, what are the two aspects of sanctification?

A. According to S.C. 35, the two aspects of sanctification are as follows: the believer should die unto sin ("put off") the believer should live unto righteousness ("put on").

a. The positive aspect is stated in Eph. 4:23, 24 and Col. 3:10.

Q. According to these verses, in what areas are we being renewed?

A. According to Eph. 4:23, 24 and Col. 3:10, the believer is being renewed in knowledge, righteousness, and holiness.

b. Q. According to Rom. 8:29, what is the pattern for our renewal?

A. According to Rom. 8:29, the believer's pattern should be Christ. God predestined us to become conformed to the image of His Son.

This is stated as living unto righteousness.

c. The negative aspect is set forth in Col. 3:5-9.

Q. According to these verses, what must we be putting off in order to be renewed in righteousness?

A. According to Col. 3:5-9, the believer should be putting off sin. Sins such as immorality, impurity, passion, evil desire, greed, idolatry, anger, wrath, malice, slander, abusive speech, and lying are given as examples.

7. In order to accomplish this putting off and putting on, the Bible teaches us to use certain things God has given us. After each verse, write the means described there:

	Verse	Answer
a.	John 17:17; Ps. 119:9	The Word of God.
b.	Eph. 6:18, 19; 1 Thess. 5:17	Prayer.
c.	Heb. 10:24, 25	Public worship.
d.	1 Cor. 11:23-26; 12:13	The sacraments of the Lord's table and baptism.
e.	Rom. 15:14	Admonition and exhortation.

f. Q. Are there any of these you are not using? If so, why? Will you make plans to implement these things in your life?

A. *Work with those you are discipling to help them make a plan and to hold them accountable.*

8. We also need to learn how to deal with temptation, if we are to grow.

Q. According to Ps. 139:23, 24, where do we need to begin in dealing with temptation?

A. *Searching our hearts under the scrutiny of the Holy Spirit by the Word of God.*

a. Q. What must we know about our hearts?

A. *The hidden and destructive ways of our hearts and thoughts.*

b. Q. According to the Bible, we are attacked by lust from within our hearts, by Satan and by temptations from the world. In light of Matt. 26:41, what two things should we be doing?

A. *Watching and praying.*

c. Q. On the basis of 1 Cor. 16:13 and 1 Peter 4:7, what do you think Jesus means by "watch"?

A. *Guard oneself against temptation and the wiles of Satan. Stay spiritually alert for prayer.*

d. Q. According to Matt. 6:13, for what should we be praying?

A. *That God would keep us from temptation and when we are tempted He would keep us from sin.*

e. Q. What do Gen. 39:10, 15 and 1 Cor. 15:33 tell us about avoiding occasions of temptation?

A. *Avoid people and occasions that tempt us. Flee temptation when it comes.*

f. Q. On the basis of Heb. 10:24, what help should we be getting from Christian friends?

A. *Be accountable to friends for exhortation.*

g. Q. Another thing we must do is develop proper habits. In Eph. 4:25-32, what four things are contrasted?

A. *Lying/truth telling; anger/proper dealing with strife; stealing/work; destructive speech/edifying speech.*

h. Q. What four patterns of behavior are we to put off?

A. *Put off lying, improper anger, stealing, destructive speech.*

i. Q. With what do we replace them?

A. *Truth telling, proper dealing with strife, work, edifying speech*

j. Here is the principle that you put off by replacing with biblical patterns. Summarize the principles involved in dealing with temptation and then choose one sin with which you have a problem and develop a plan of attack. Review the principles and work with the people you are training on how to develop a plan and to hold them accountable.

Teacher's Edition

LESSON 16:

COMMUNICATING THE GOSPEL

Assignment:

Review the first fifteen lessons.
Complete this lesson.
Memorize your gospel outline

In the first fifteen lessons we have covered the basic doctrines of God and the Gospel. We must have a grasp of these things in order to communicate the Gospel in its fullness. In this lesson we will work on how to communicate the Gospel. It is a good time to review the first fifteen lessons.

Read:

Matt. 28:19, 20.

In these verses Christ gives the Church the responsibility to make disciples of the nations. Part of this task, we call evangelism and witnessing. Each of us in the Church has a role to play in this task of evangelism. Our roles will vary according to the gifts that God has given us, but each must do his part and each one ought to be able to tell others what Christ means to him and certainly everyone can invite others to worship services and Bible studies. The purpose of this lesson is to equip us to do our part in the Church's task.

Background

1. Look at Matt. 5:13-16 and Phil. 2:12-15.

   Q. According to these verses, what is the Christian's great responsibility?

   A. According to Matt. 5:13-16 and Phil. 2:12-15, the Christian's great responsibility is to be holy.

   a. As we saw in the last lesson, our great responsibility is to be holy. As we seek to fulfill this responsibility, men will see our works and want to learn about our faith. Some call this lifestyle or friendship evangelism. As we live a Christian lifestyle we seek to develop relationships with those around us and to be sensitive to opportunities to share what Christ means to us, to communicate the gospel, and to invite our friends and acquaintances to social events (both in our homes and with other Christians), Bible studies, and worship services.

2. Ideally, evangelism is a dialogue. Look at 1 Peter 3:15, 16 and Col. 4:5, 6.

   Q. According to these passages, what ought we as Christians always be prepared to do?

   A. The Christian ought to live and speak in a such way that provokes questions and be able to give an answer to those who inquire about his faith.

   a. Q. What are we to be sensitive to according to Col. 4:5, 6?

      A. The opportunities God provides each day to speak naturally of God and our faith in Him.

   b. Q. Where should we begin with a person?

      A. We need to begin with a person where he is in terms of his knowledge, interest, condition, and questions. We seek to determine what the Spirit is doing in that person.

   c. We can summarize: We need to be sensitive to where a person is and what his needs are, as well as alert to the opportunities God in His providence gives us to speak. Furthermore, we need to be prepared to try to answer a person's questions or to take him to see someone who can. Look at John 1:45, 46.

Q. How does Philip deal with Nathaniel's question?

A. Knowing that he is seeking God and His Messiah he tells him that they have found Him. He is Jesus of Nazareth. He takes seriously his objection and suggests that he come and see for himself.

3. This means we must not force a memorized gospel presentation on someone, but begin with a person where he is. Look at the following passages and describe the approach used by the person witnessing:

    a. John 3:1-15: Jesus, knowing that Nicodemus belongs to a group that is proud and self-righteous, begins with the necessity of being born again. After that He calls him to faith.

    b. John 4:1-30: Jesus asks a favor and then begins with the women's felt needs, but quickly moves to her restlessness expressed in sexual promiscuity. As He exposes her sin, He directs her attention unto Himself as the Messiah. He takes seriously her questions about the place of worship, because salvation is found where God reveals Himself.

    c. Acts 13:16-41: With the Jews and God-fearers, Paul begins with covenant history leading up to the advent of the Messiah. He points out that although the Old Testament clearly prophesied His person and the events of His life they put Him to death. God raised Him from the dead on the third day. By His death and resurrection there is remission of sins for all who believe in Him. He Paul covers the essential facts of the Gospel. Compare this sermon with 1 Cor. 15:1-9.

    d. Acts 17:22-31: Paul begins here with the basic facts of God as a divine spirit who made and upholds all things by His power. He is just. He has been forbearing with sinners, but will judge them by Jesus Christ whom He raised from the dead.

(1) Q. According to these examples, how should we approach a person with the gospel?

A. *We need to discern where he is and what he knows.*

(2) Q. How are we going to know where a person is and what his needs are?

A. *We need to be in conversation with him, seeking to determine where he is and what are his needs. The use of questions is a very good tool to determine interest, knowledge, and spiritual condition.*

(3) Q. What form of speech is particularly useful in determining where a person is and in getting him to think about the gospel.

A. *The use of questions is very helpful in learning where a person is and in getting him to think about the gospel.*

Sharing a Testimony

4. Look at John 4:29.

   Q. What does the Samaritan woman do?

   A. *She gives her testimony and invites people to meet Christ.*

5. In the context of lifestyle evangelism, we need to be prepared to share what Christ means to us. Write out your testimony. Your testimony should be a brief explanation of how God saved you and what He is doing in your life (remember that those reared in Christian homes and who never know a day they were not trusting in Christ may testify to God's saving and sanctifying grace). Write your own testimony as a model for those you are training. You may want to divide into pairs to practice giving your testimony one to the other.

Gospel Outline

6. It is also important that we have in mind the basic facts of the Gospel. If a person is to be saved, he needs to know who God is, who man is and what is the penalty of his sin, who Christ is and what He has done, how a person must respond, and what are the demands of the Christian life. Using these headings, make an outline, using Scripture from previous lessons, that communicate what you want a person to know about the Gospel.

   a. *Who God Is: Acts 17:24-31; Gen. 1:1;*

      1. *Trinity.*
      2. *Basic attributes.*
      3. *Work—creator and ruler.*
      4. *Owed all honor and obedience.*

   b. *Who Man Is:*

      1. *Created in God's image.*
      2. *Fallen into sin; refusing to give homage.*
      3. *Dead in sins and trespasses, living selfishly, rebelling; unable and unwilling to come to God (use of law of God to convince of sin).*
      4. *Penalty of death spiritually, physically, and eternally.*

   c. *What Christ Has Done For Me:*

      1. *Person – who He is (incarnate Son of God; three offices).*
      2. *Work—perfect obedience, suffering, sacrificial sin – bearing death, resurrection, exaltation, intercession, second coming as Savior and judge.*

   d. *How Do I Respond:*

      1. *Repent.*
      2. *Believe on the Lord Jesus Christ (three parts of faith—knowledge, assent, and trust).*

e. *What Are The Demands Of The Christian Life:*

1. *Be examined and accepted into church membership (including being baptized if not been properly baptized).*

2. *Strive to live godly life according to the law of God.*

LESSON 17:

WORSHIP PART I

Assignment:

Read:

W.C.F. 19, 21; L.C. 91-110; S.C. 39-52; B.C. 25;
H.C. 3, 4, 92-98; C.D. III, IV, article 5.
Complete this lesson.

Memorize:

Exod. 20:1-6; S.C. 41.

We saw earlier in S.C. 3 that Scripture principally teaches two things: what man is to believe concerning God and what duty God requires of man. We have been examining some of the things we are to believe; now we turn our attention to some of our duties. These duties are summarized in the Ten Commandments. We will look at the importance of the law in the life of the believer and the first two commandments.

The Guide to our Duty

1. Look at John 14:15, 21, 23.

   Q. According to these verses, what does Christ expect the Christian to do?

   A. Keep His commandments.

2. Look at Matt. 22:37-40; Deut. 6:1-9; Lev. 19:11-18; and Rom. 13:8-10.

Q. Comparing the Matthew verses with the Deuteronomy and Leviticus verses, looking also at the Romans verses, where do we find Jesus' commandments that we are to keep if we love Him?

A. *In the law of God, particularly as it is summarized in the Ten Commandments.*

a. This truth is summarized for us in S.C. 39-42. The law of God, which is found in the Ten Commandments, is the primary place that God reveals His will for our duty. The Ten Commandments cover the major areas of relationship between us and God and between us and our fellows.

b. Q. According to L.C. 97, what is the role of the law for the Christian?

A. *God did not give His law that we might earn salvation by law-keeping. This is what Paul means in Rom. 6:14 when he says we are under grace and not under the law. The law is not a means of salvation. But the law does reveal how we are to serve God in gratitude. It reminds us of what God has done for us.*

The Duty of Worship

3. The law and worship. One of the first things the law teaches us is worship. In fact the duty of worship is the primary focus of the first four commandments. The first commandment teaches us about the duty of worship; the second the way of worship; the third the attitude in worship; and the fourth the day of worship. In this lesson, we shall consider the duty of worship and the way.

4. The first commandment is found in Exod. 20:3.

Q. What is God forbidding in this commandment? (Compare your answer with S.C. 47. Also look back at Lesson 4, # 3.)

A. *That we have the Lord God only as our God.*

5. Q. According to L.C. 99, # 4, what is an important principle of biblical interpretation to keep in mind when one interprets the law?

A. *An important principle of biblical interpretation is that the opposite of whatever is forbidden is required and the opposite of whatever is required is forbidden.*

a. Q. We may call this the principle of opposites. Keeping this principle in mind, look at Deut. 6:4, 5, 13, and 17 and write what positive duty is required by the first commandment.

A. *We are to love, fear, worship, and serve God; swear by Him; and keep all His commandments.*

b. Read Rom. 12:1, 2.

Q. According to these verses, what area of life does the positive duty to love, worship and fear God embrace?

A. *It embraces the totality of life.*

6. Even though worship embraces all that a Christian should do, the Bible also deals with worship in a more formal capacity of adoring God, learning His Word and praying. There are three types of formal worship. After each of the following passages, describe the type of formal worship that is required:

	Verses	**Answer:**
a.	Exod. 34:8;Ps. 42:8;Ps. 119:54-56; Dan. 6:10; Matt. 6:6	Private worship
b	Gen. 18:19; 2 Tim. 3:15; Ps. 78:1-4	Family worship
c.	Neh. 8:1-8; Acts 20:7; Heb. 10:25	Corporate worship

7. Q. On the basis of the first commandment, what types of worship ought you to be involved in (of course, family worship is required only of families)?

A. *We should be involved in formal worship privately, with spouses and children, and corporately. (Of course if one is not married, one is not obligated to be involved in family worship. Those, however, living with room-mates would benefit by having family worship together.)*

The Way of Worship

8. The second commandment is found in Exod. 20:4-6.

   Q. What two things does God forbid by this commandment? (Compare Deut. 4:15-19; 5:8, 9.)

   A. Making images of God and worshipping God through images.

9. God forbids making any physical representation of Him.

   a. Q. According to L.C. 109, how should we apply this commandment to Jesus Christ?

      A. We are not to make physical images of Christ.

   b. Q. What does Paul say about knowledge of Christ in the flesh in 2 Cor. 5:14-16?

      A. Those who once knew Him according to the flesh do not know Him in that manner any longer.

   c. Q. According to 1 Peter 1:8, do we worship a visible or an invisible Christ?

      A. An invisible Christ.

   d. Q. What visual representation has Christ given us of Himself?

      A. The Lord's Supper.

10. The second prohibition is against worshiping God through images.

    a. Q. In Exod. 32:4, 5 how did Israel violate the second commandment in worshiping the golden calf ?

       A. They claimed to be worshiping the Lord (Jehovah) who delivered them from Egypt.

    b. Q. What are some ways people violate this commandment today?

       A. Praying to statues of Christ; praying to images of Mary the mother of the Lord, and to saints; attaching sacredness to a place rather than to God who is worshiped.

c. We learn that we may not worship God according to our imaginations. He reserves the right to reveal how we are to think about Him.

11. Q. If we are not to worship God according to our imaginations, what must guide us in our worship?

A. *His revealed will found in the Bible.*

a. Q. According to Deut. 12:31, 32, what positive duty is being taught by this commandment? (Compare L.C. 108 and S.C. 50.)

A. *We are to worship God according to His revelation.*

b. This duty is called the regulative principle.

c. Q. This principle is stated in W.C.F. 1:6 and 21:1. Write the principle in your own words.

A. *We are only to do in worship those things commanded by the Word of God directly or by good and necessary inference (a deduction based on a teaching or example found in the Bible). Moreover, we must do all that the Bible requires.*

12. Look up the following passages and list after each what element of worship is required by that passage:

	Verse	Answer
a.	Neh. 8:1-8	Preaching
b.	1 Tim. 4:13	Public reading of God's Word and preaching
c.	Ps. 65:2	Prayer
d.	Eph. 5:19	Singing
e.	1 Cor. 16:1, 2	Offering
f.	2 Tim. 1:13, 14; 1 Tim.. 3:16	Creeds
g.	Num. 6:22:27; 2 Cor. 13:14	Benediction
h.	Ps. 95:1-3; 147:1	Call to worship

13. Now take a bulletin and see if you can match the things we do in our worship service with these elements taught in Scripture.

14. Q. In Exod. 20:5 what is God's attitude to proper worship?

    A. *He declares that He is a jealous God. He is jealous of His worship.*

    a. Q. What does God threaten?

       A. *To punish to the fourth generation those who violate the commandment.*

    b. Q. In Leviticus 10:1-3 and Deut. 4:3, what does He do to those who violate the commandment?

       A. *He destroys them. We remember that God does not in this life punish every sin as it deserves, but He reveals occasions like these to teach us the seriousness of sin.*

    c. Q. What does God promise?

       A. *To show lovingkindness to thousands of generations of those who keep it.*

    d. We learn that we must be very careful how we approach God in worship.

In the next study, we shall consider the attitude of the worshiper and the day of worship.

LESSON 18:

WORSHIP PART II

Assignment:

Read:

W.C.F. 19, 21; L.C. 111-121;
S.C. 53-62; H.C. 99-103.
Complete this lesson.

Memorize:

Exod. 20:7-11.

In the last lesson we established the role of the law for the believer and looked specifically at the first two commandments as they relate to worship. In this lesson we want to learn what the third and fourth commandments say about worship.

The Manner of Worship (Exod. 20:7)

1. The third commandment addresses the use of God's name. We shall consider how this commandment applies generally and then apply it specifically to worship.

   a. Q. What is forbidden by the third commandment? (Compare your answer to S.C. 55.)

      A. Any irreverent or improper use of God's name.

   b. Q. We saw in Lesson 3 that God reveals Himself by His name, word, works, and attributes. If all these things make God known to us, how should we then speak of these things?

A. *We must reverently speak and deal with all of these ways by which God reveals Himself.*

c. Q. List some of God's attributes.

A. *Goodness, mercy, grace, holiness.*

d. Q. Can you think of ways we commonly profane God's attributes by speaking lightly of them?

A. *Using them in expressions that have nothing to do with God or His work.*

e. Q. In light of this, what do you think of phrases like "holy cow" or "goodness gracious"?

A. *Such phrases would be taking God's name in vain.*

f. Q The third commandment also forbids what we call minced oaths. The word minced means to minimize. These are words and phrases that are contractions of the divine name in order to get around the prohibition of the third commandment. Can you think of any examples?

A *Gee whiz; golly*

2. The positive teaching of the third commandment applies directly to our worship.

a. Q. How does Eccles. 5:1-5 relate the third commandment to worship?

A. *We are to approach God in worship with great reverence.*

b. Q. According to Matt. 15:8, what attitude is required?

A. *Our hearts must be engaged so that what we do and say comes from the heart.*

c. Q. How does Jesus apply this attitude of reverence in John 4:23, 24?

A. *We are to worship in spirit.*

d. Q. What do you think it means to worship God in spirit?

A. *We are to offer to God spiritual worship in sincerity and simplicity.*

e. Q. Where does such spiritual worship originate?

A. *From the work of the Holy Spirit in our hearts.*

f. Q. Write a summary of what our attitude and demeanor ought to be in worship and apply it to the parts of worship we noted in the last lesson.

A. *We are to worship in dependence on the Holy Spirit from our hearts in sincerity and simplicity. We must guard our minds from wandering in prayer, singing, reading, preaching. We need to be sure our affections are engaged. We are offering spiritual sacrifices to God. We consciously are expressing love to God in praise and dependence on Him in prayer. We are actively to exercise faith in each part of the service.*

THE DAY OF WORSHIP (EXOD. 20:8-11)

3. Q. According to the fourth commandment, when did God institute the observance of the Sabbath?

A. *On the seventh day of creation.*

a. Q. Look at Gen. 2:1-3. What did God do after the six days of creation?

A. *He rested and set aside His day of rest for mankind.*

b. Q. What did He say about the day?

A. *He blessed and sanctified it.*

c. Q. For whose sake do you think God blessed and sanctified the day?

A. *For man's sake.*

4. Q. According to the fourth commandment, what was forbidden on the Sabbath day?

A. *All unnecessary work.*

a. Q. What things does the prophet Isaiah include in his interpretation of the fourth commandment in Isa. 58:13? (Compare S.C. 61.)

A. *Work, recreation, and unnecessary thoughts and conversation about our work and recreation.*

b. Q. What works and activities do you think are forbidden in the fourth commandment?

A. *All regular work and recreation. Also causing others to work.*

c. Q. What exception does Jesus make in Matt. 12:1-14? (Compare you answer to the last part of S.C. 60.)

A. *Works of necessity and mercy. Those things are for the well-being and safety of ourselves and others and for the necessary pursuits of worship.*

d. Q. Give some examples of things you think are exceptions.

A. *Doctors, policemen, emergency electrical or plumbing, military operations, opening the church, shoveling snow if necessary, preaching and teaching, visiting sick and shut-ins, and certain types of factories that if they shut down people would not be able to pursue their work on Monday.*

5. Q. According to S.C. 59, what day is to be observed as the Christian Sabbath?

A. *The first day of the week.*

a. This change is established by a number of things:

b. Q. On what day did Christ arise from the dead? In Rev. 1:10, what is the day called? Why do you think it is called the Lord's Day?

A. *Christ was raised on the first day of the week. The day belongs to Him for His worship. Just as all food belongs to Him and is to be eaten for His glory, but the Lord's Supper is a meal devoted to His worship, all days belong to Him, but the Lord's Day is devoted to His worship.*

c. Q. According to Col. 2:16, 17, what happened to the seventh day Sabbath and other Old Testament holy days?

A. *They were types and shadows of the work of Christ and have been done away with.*

d. Q. According to 1 Cor. 16:1, 2 and Acts 20:7, on what day of the week did the early church worship?

A. *The first day of the week.*

e. On the basis of these things we say the day is changed to the first day of the week.

6. Q. The purpose of the Sabbath. Compare Exod. 20:8-11 and Deut. 5:12-15. For what two reasons are we to remember and observe the Sabbath?

A. *To remember God's works of creation and redemption.*

a. Q. Why then ought we to keep the Sabbath?

A. *Because God is our maker and our Savior.*

b. Q. According to Isa. 58:13, what positive duty does this entail?

A. *Delighting in it and honoring it. Using it in a reverent manner.*

c. Q. What does Lev. 23:3 state to be the great work of the Sabbath?

A. *Holy convocation—corporate worship.*

d. Q. Thus this day has been given to us that in acts of private and public worship we may remember God's mighty deeds of creation and redemption and praise Him accordingly. According to L.C. 117, what then are some of the positive things we ought to be doing?

A. *Public and private exercises of worship—attending worship with God's people, extended times of private and family worship, preparing for public worship, Christian fellowship, evangelism, visitation.*

7. Q. In Isa. 58:14, what three things does God promise to do for those who keep the Sabbath?

   A. *Give them increased delight in Him; give them spiritual victory; give them delight in their privileges as God's sons and daughters.*

8. Q. Preparing for public worship. Look at L.C. 117 and 160. List what activities you ought to be doing in preparing for and participating in Sabbath worship.

   A. *Get all our business out of the way (both weekday and Saturday), make physical preparations for Sunday (food, clothing, gas in the car), get proper physical rest, prepare heart and mind by prayer and meditation.*

LESSON 19:

MARRIAGE AND FAMILY

Assignment:

Read

W.C.F. 24; L.C. 123-133; 137-139;
S.C. 63-66; 70-72; H.C. 104-109.
Complete this lesson.

Memorize

Exod. 20:12, 14.

Having looked somewhat at man's duty to God we now look at man's duty to man. In this lesson we consider particularly how the seventh and fifth commandments apply to marriage and family.

Marriage

1. Q. What are some things forbidden by the seventh commandment (look at Heb. 13:4; Gal. 5:19; Rom. 1:24-27 as you answer this question. Compare your answer with L.C. 139.)?

   A. *Adultery, fornication, homosexuality, pornography, immodesty, polygamy, improper divorce, and other things that promote sexual promiscuity.*

   a. Q. According to Eph. 5:3, 4 and Matt. 5:28, in addition to immoral actions, what else is forbidden by this commandment?

A. *Corrupt speech, jesting and entertainment, as well as lust.*

c. Q. Why do you think that the sin of adultery is chosen to represent the various sins of immorality?

A. *It is the most grievous violation, breaking the marriage covenant. All other violations of the commandment not only would be sin in and of themselves, but would also be a violation of the marriage covenant.*

2. God forbids adultery in order to teach that all sexual sins are a violation of the marriage relationship. Thus, in forbidding sexual immorality, God is promoting and protecting the sanctity of marriage. We find the institution of marriage in Gen. 2:18-24.

a. Q. What did Adam need?

A. *A helper corresponding to his need.*

b. Q. How did God bring Adam to understand his need?

A. *He had him name the animals in order to teach him that all animals had partners and that none of them would be a compatible partner for him.*

c. Q. What was God's solution?

A. *Made Eve from the side of Adam to be a helper corresponding to his need. In doing this He instituted marriage.*

d. Q. In verses 22 24, we find the first wedding ceremony. Who gives away the bride?

A. *God.*

(1) Q. What is God establishing in this action?

A. *The institution of marriage.*

(2) Q. What is Adam's response?

A. *Joyful reception of God's gift and commitment to her for life.*

(3) Q. In this response we find the concept of commitment. What does God declare in verse 24?

A. *Monogamous, heterosexual marriage that is the primary relationship in society.*

3. The purpose of marriage. The purpose of marriage is expressed in the concept of woman being a helper corresponding to man's needs and in their being one flesh (see W.C.F. 24.1, 2).

a. Q. According to Mal. 2:14, what is the primary purpose of marriage?

A. *Companionship*

(1) Q. What does the concept of companion include?

A. *Friendship, encouragement, support, counsel.*

(2) Q. What are some aspects of companionship in marriage?

A. *Friendship, encouragement, support, counsel, mutual fulfillment spiritually, physically, mentally, and emotionally.*

b. Q. In 1 Cor. 7:1-6 and Prov. 5:18, 19, we learn a second purpose that is expressed in the concept of one flesh. What is this purpose?

A. *Sexual enjoyment.*

(1) We learn here that sex is a good gift of God that is to be enjoyed only in the bonds of marriage. But we should emphasize that it is a gift to be enjoyed.

(2) This helps us to understand why all sexual relationships outside the marriage are wrong.

c. Q. A third purpose is expressed in Gen. 1:28; Ps. 27:3; and Mal. 2:15. What is this purpose?

A. *To have children to rear for the Lord.*

4. Q. Marriage roles. Read Eph. 5:21-33 and 1 Peter 3:1-7. What is the husband's role in marriage?

   A. *To love his wife as Christ loves the Church, to nurture and cherish her, to bear with her weaknesses and infirmities, to seek her sanctification.*

   a. Q. What do you think it means to love the wife as Christ loved the Church and gave Himself for it?

      A. *To love her sacrificially, putting her and her needs before Himself and his needs.*

   b. Q. How would you relate the command in Eph. 5:21 to the husband's responsibility to love his wife sacrificially?

      A. *If he does not love her this way, he is sinning and cannot expect God's purposes for marriage to be fulfilled.*

   c. Q. How would you relate 1 Peter 3:7 to the husband's responsibility to love his wife sacrificially?

      A. *The husband's sanctification and prayers will be hindered if he does not love his wife in this manner.*

   d. Q. Give some examples of sacrificial love.

      A. *Even though the husband has had a difficult day, seeing his wife is tired he does the dishes for her or puts the children to bed. Taking her to do things she enjoys, even if he does not enjoy them. Listening to her, encouraging and building her up. Expressing appreciation for her and what she does for him and the family.*

5. Q. What is the wife's role?

   A. *She is to be submissive, subjecting her will to his in everything that does not cause her to sin.*

a. Q. Look at John 14:15 and Eph. 5:24 and explain why Paul does not command wives to love their husbands.

A. *Jesus says that if we love Him we will keep His commandments. So if a wife loves her husband that will manifest itself in obedience.*

b. Q. According to 1 Peter 3:1-6, what kind of spirit should the wife exhibit in submission?

A. *A quiet and gentle spirit.*

c. Q. How should the wife respond when she is convinced that her idea is better than her husband's?

A. *She may explain her idea, but if he does not accept it, she is to submit.*

d. Q. Applying Acts 4:19 to the marriage relationship, how should a wife respond when her husband tells her to do something contrary to scripture?

A. *She humbly must refuse.*

Family Life

6. Q. We have noted that one of the purposes of marriage is to raise a godly seed. The framework for this responsibility is given us in the fifth commandment. What is required by the term honor? (Compare L.C. 128.)

A. *To respect and obey.*

a. Q. According to Prov. 30:11; Exod. 21:15, 17; and Prov. 20:20, how important is it that children show proper respect to their parents?

A. *The failure to show respect is the height of impiety. Such a failure will bring covenant curses and in the old covenant persistent disrespect could incur the death penalty.*

b. Q. In Eph. 6:1-3 how does Paul apply the commandment to children?

A. *They are to obey their parents.*

c. Q. According to Prov. 4:1; 6:20, what does this obedience entail?

A. *Heeding their commands and listening to their instruction.*

7. Q. According to Eph. 6:4, what does this commandment require of parents? (We understand on the basis of Prov. 6:20; 10:1 that mothers are included. Compare L.C. 129.)

A. *Do not provoke them to anger, but teach and discipline them according to the Word of God.*

a. Q. What are some ways parents provoke their children to wrath?

A. *Permissiveness, inconsistency, wrath and impatience, hypocrisy, lack of affection, lack of encouragement, and inattention.*

b. Q. According to Prov. 19:18, how important is discipline?

A. *It can save his life physically and spiritually.*

c. Q. What do Prov. 13:24; 22:15; 23:13, 14; 29:15 teach about physical discipline?

A. *It is instituted by God. If one loves one's child he will use the rod. Such discipline will remove foolishness from his heart and may deliver him from hell. Accompanied with instruction it will give wisdom. The undisciplined child will bring great reproach to his parents.*

d. Q. How should we in the New Testament church apply Deut. 21:18-21 to incorrigible children?

A. *They should be brought to the elders for church discipline.*

8. Q. Paul also demands instruction. In Gen. 18:19, what is one of the purposes for which God saved Abraham?

   A. *To teach his children how to walk in the way of the Lord.*

   a. Q. What does Deut. 6:4-9 tell us about the times and places in which we teach our children?

      A. *In addition to formal instruction, we should use all the circumstances of life.*

   b. Q. List ways that parents ought to be fulfilling this injunction.

      A. *Regular family worship; catechizing our children and teaching them the truths of the Bible; teaching them to think biblically about every aspect of life; carefully answering their questions in ways that will enable them to relate God and His Word to everything in life; discuss current events, books, movies, music.*

   c. Q. Are you practicing regular family worship and teaching your children in this manner?

      A. *Again seek to hold the one whom you are discipling. You may want to review with the principles studied in Lesson 2.*

   d. Q. How would you relate this commandment to the responsibility of general education?

      A. *The parents are ultimately responsible for the education of their children. Such an education needs to be from a biblical world-view and not a secular one. The best way to accomplish this is by sending your child to a good Christian school or by home schooling.*

LESSON 20:

LIFE AND TRUTH

Assignment:

Read:

L.C. 134-136; 143-145; S.C. 67-69; 76-78;
H.C. 105-107, 112.
Complete this lesson.

Memorize:

Exod. 20:13, 16.

Having considered God's principles for marriage and home, we now consider two things that are of great importance to God: life and truth. God has declared both of these things sacred, thus we speak of the sanctity of life and truth.

The Sanctity of Life – Exod. 20:13

1. Q. Comparing Exod. 20:13 with Acts 16:28 and Gen. 9:6, list the things prohibited by the sixth commandment. (Compare your answer with L.C. 136.)

   A. Unlawful shedding of human blood: murder, suicide.

2. Q. According to Gen. 9:5, 6; Num. 35:31,33; Deut. 20:1, 10, 18; Exod. 22:2, 3; and Rom. 13:4, does this commandment prohibit all killing?

   A. No.

a. Q. List the situations in which it is not wrong to take another person's life.

A. *Lawful warfare, self-defense or defense of another, capital punishment.*

b. Q. According to Gen. 9:5, 6; Deut. 21:1-9; and Lev. 24:17, what is the reason for capital punishment in the case of murder?

A. *Because man is in the image of God. He who sheds man's blood must die.*

c. Q. Does this reason still have force today?

A. *By all means.*

d. Q. What then should the Christian's position be on capital punishment?

A. *The Christian position on capital punishment is that when there are two witnesses (finger prints or DNA could serve as a witness) a murderer should be executed.*

3. Q. Following the principle that the opposite of that which is forbidden is required, what would be some positive duties required by this commandment? (Look at Eph. 5:28, 29; 1 Kings 18:4. Compare your answer with L.C. 135.)

A. *Moderate care for one's life and protection of life of others.*

a. Q. Because life is important, people are in the image of God, and the Christian who is being renewed in that image is indwelt by the Holy Spirit as the temple of God (1 Cor. 6:19, 20), we are responsible to take care of our bodies. Look at Prov. 24:13; 25:16; 1 Tim. 4:8; and 5:23 and list some things required by this commandment in terms of caring for our bodies.

A. *Eat carefully and in moderation, give attention to moderate, physical discipline, be willing to use those things that are good for the body.*

b. Q. On the basis of Prov. 24:11, 12; Ps. 82:4; and Prov. 31:8,9, how would you apply this commandment to the matter of abortion?

A. *Abortion is murder.*

c. Q. In light of this commandment, may a Christian remain neutral in the area of abortion?

A. *No, he must oppose it, teach against it, and pray against it. There are many avenues for involvement: pregnancy centers and counseling, political activity, having an unwed mother in the home, etc. No one is required to do all of these things. Each should do what is consistent with other obligations and ministries.*

4. Q. According to Matt. 5:21, 22, this commandment goes beyond actions to thoughts, attitudes, and words. On the basis of 1 John 3:15; Lev. 19:17; Rom. 12:19; and Eph. 4:31, what are some other things prohibited by this commandment?

A. *Hatred, vindictiveness, malice, anger, slander, and gossip.*

a. Q. Ought a Christian to have racial or social prejudice?

A. *No.*

b. Q. According to Exod. 32:15-35; Matt. 21:12, 13; and Eph. 4:26 is all anger a violation of the sixth commandment?

A. *No, there is a righteous anger.*

c. Q. What are some appropriate causes of anger?

A. *Injustice, blasphemy, abuse, persecution.*

The Sanctity of Truth – Exod. 20:16

5. Q. In addition to the sanctity of life, God teaches a high regard for truth. On the basis of Heb. 6:18; Num. 23:19; Lev. 19:11, 12; and 2 Cor. 1:18, why do you think God places such a high premium on truth?

A. *God is faithful and true; He cannot lie, it is contrary to His nature; lying profanes His name.*

6. Q. In addition to Exod. 20:16, read Prov. 6:16, 17, 19; 12:22; Acts 5:1-9; Ps. 50:20; James 4:11; Lev. 19:16; Ps. 15:3; and Eph. 4:25 and list some of the things forbidden by the ninth commandment.

   A. *A false witness, a slanderer who spreads strife, lying lips, hypocrisy, improper judgment; and breaking oaths and vows. (Compare your answer with L.C. 145.)*

7. Q. What does this commandment have to say about "little white lies"?

   A. *Even such apparently innocent lies are a violation of God's law.*

8. Q. Read 3 John 12; Prov. 14:5, 25; Lev. 5:1; Prov. 29:24; 1 Cor. 13:7; and Prov. 17:9 and list some of the things required by this commandment. (Compare your answer with L.C. 144.)

   A. *Faithful witness bearing; speaking the truth under an oath; cover over sins of others in love.*

9. Q. According to Eph. 4:29 and Col. 4:6, what ought to be one of the great purposes of our speech?

   A. *To edify and show the glory of the Gospel.*

   a. Q. As Christians, what is the great witness to truth that we ought to bear (1 Peter 3:15)?

      A. *To give a testimony of our Christian hope, an answer to those who inquire.*

   b. Q. What are ways we can do this?

      A. *Bearing witness to God through current events; bearing witness to God in midst of trial and affliction; speaking kindly and gently; not responding angrily to those who insult us.*

10. Q. Now read Exod. 1:15-21 and Josh. 2:1-4. What did the Hebrew midwives and Rahab do?

A. They deceived the enemies of God's people.

a. Q. Why did they do this?

A. To save life.

b. Q. What was God's response?

A. He blessed them.

c. Q. On the basis of these things, do you think that it is right or wrong to tell lies in order to defend life?

A. Some will say that the women were wrong to lie; they should have trusted the providence of God. His blessing was not on their lie, but their desire to honor Him. Others say that as all killing is not a violation of the sixth commandment, all falsehood is not a violation of the ninth commandment. If a murderer or oppressor has forfeited his right to life, he has forfeited his right to truth.

d. Be prepared to defend your answer.

LESSON 21:

GOD'S VIEW OF WORK AND PROPERTY

Assignment:

Read:

L.C. 140-142, 146-148; S.C. 73-75, 79-81;
H.C. 110, 113-115.
Complete this lesson.

Memorize:

Exod. 20:15, 17.

Having examined what God's Word says about marriage, family, life, and truth it remains for us to see what God teaches in the eighth and tenth commandments concerning work and property.

A Christian View of Work (Exod. 20:15)

1. Read Eph. 4:28.

   Q. According to this verse, what duty does Paul derive from the eighth commandment? (Compare S.C. 74.)

   A. We are to work in order to do good and to be useful to others.

   a. What do you think about work? Underline the appropriate answer after each statement.

	Statement	Answer
(1)	Work is a result of man's fall into sin.	F
(2)	The main reason for working is to earn money.	F
(3)	Work is not as important in serving God as Bible study, witnessing and other church activities.	F
(4)	Career decisions should be made primarily on the basis of where the most jobs will be available and how much money one can earn.	F

b. The answer to the first statement is found in Gen. 1:28 and 2:15.

Q. According to Gen. 1:28, what is part of man's responsibility as one made in the image of God?

A. *To exercise dominion over all the rest of creation.*

(1) Q. According to Gen. 2:15, what type of activity did Adam perform before the fall?

A. *He cultivated the garden.*

(2) Q. What are some things this might have involved?

A. *Pruning, ordering, planting, and harvesting.*

(3) We see that work is a positive duty that God has placed on man.

Look at Exod. 20:8, 9.

Q. According to these verses, how is this implied

A. *It is God's gift that we have six days to do all our work.*

(4) Look at Gen. 3:17-19.

Q. Now describe what happened to man's work because of the fall.

A. It was marked by frustration and toil.

(5) Thus not work, but the toil, difficulty, and frustration, involved in work, are a result of the fall. Work is a duty placed on man from the very time of his creation.

c. The correct answer to the next two statements is found in Col. 3:22-24.

Q. Whom ought we to serve in our work?

A. We are to serve God.

(1) Q. What should be our attitude in our work?

A. We should do it for God's glory and pleasure.

(2) Q. What are some ways we do work with external service and to please men?

A. Time watching, doing a better job when people see us, not doing a better job than others around us, working for praise of men or primarily for income.

(3) Look at Prov. 10:4, 24:30-34 and 28:19.

Q. What do theses verses teach about diligence in our work?

A. If we are not diligent, our work will reflect and we can be impoverished. God will use our work to provide for us.

(4) Thus we learn that to do our work diligently and faithfully is service to God and our primary motivation ought to be God's glory.

Now look at 1 Tim. 5:8 and 2 Thess. 3:6-12.

Q. According to these verses, does this rule out working in order to earn money to care for ourselves and our families?

A. Now we have the responsibility to care for ourselves and our families.

d. The answer to the last true or false statement is found in 1 Cor. 7:20, "Let each man remain in that condition (calling) in which he is called."

(1) Q. When Paul refers to work as a calling what is he teaching?

A. *Our work is to be viewed as a calling; a vocation received from God.*

(2) Q. What then should be our primary consideration in seeking a career?

A. *Has God called me to do this.*

(3) Review the principles in Lesson 7 on discerning God's will for you and apply them in making career decisions. In addition, you need to consider aptitude and interest. In light of this, and if they are not given undue weight, aptitude tests may be helpful.

A Christian View of Property (Exod. 20:15)

2. Q. When God forbids stealing, what does He teach us about possessions and private property?(Compare L.C. 141.)

A. *We are to respect the property rights of all people.*

Read Prov. 31:13-24.

a. Q. What do these verses teach about the believer's procuring property and making a profit?

A. *It is not wrong to buy, sell, invest, and make a profit.*

b. Look at Prov. 20:14.

Q. What does this verse teach about undue or unfair profit?

A. *We are not to make a profit at the expense of the seller or buyer.*

c. Look at 1 Tim. 6:17 and 4:4, 5.

Q. According to these verses, is it wrong to be rich and to enjoy our possessions?

A. *No.*

d. Now read Prov. 30:7-9; 1 Tim. 6:9; Prov. 23:4; and 28:20.

Q. On the basis of these verses, what should be the believer's attitude about seeking wealth and prosperity?

A. *Although we are to seek to provide adequately for ourselves and our families, we are not to pursue wealth as an end in itself. There are those who seek to develop wealth from their resources for the sake of the work of God. These are not seeking wealth as an end in itself.*

e. Read Prov. 27:23-27.

Q. What do these verses teach about the care of property?

A. *The wise man is a careful steward of his property.*

f. Look at Exod. 23:4, 5, Deut. 22:1-4 and Exod. 22:14, 15.

Q. What do these verses teach us about our responsibility with respect to our neighbor's property?

A. *We are to assist our neighbor when it is in our ability. If we borrow his property we are responsible for its well-being. Lost property belongs to the owner not the finder.*

g. Read Lev. 25:25 and Deut. 15:11.

Q According to these verses, does the right of private property free us from a responsibility to give to the poor (cf. Gal. 6:10)?

A. *No, we are to help the poor as we are able, beginning with those in the Church who have need.*

3. Look at Prov. 28:8; Lev. 19:35, 36; Prov. 11:1; 20:10, 14, 17, 23.

Q. According to these verses, what are some of the ways that we violate God's commandment not to steal? (Compare your answer with L.C. 142.)

A. *Charging interest (above inflation), to the needy in the church; unjust business practices; misleading buyer or seller; seeking to defraud one of a lawful profit; and getting property deceitfully.*

A Christian View of Contentment (Exod. 20:17)

4. Q. What positive duty is required by the tenth commandment? (Compare your answer with L.C. 147.)

   A. *Contentment in all circumstances and rejoicing in our neighbor's blessings.*

5. Look at 1 Tim. 6:6-10 and Heb. 13:5.

   Q. How do these verses relate this to our attitude about our possessions and circumstances in life?

   A. *Contentment with what we have is a mark of godliness. Avoid the love of money.*

6. Read Ps. 16:5, 6.

   Q. According to these verses, what is the Christian's greatest possession?

   A. *God is the Christian's greatest possession.*

7. According to Ps. 4:7 and 73:25, 26, relate this contentment.

   A. *When we recognize that God is our greatest good then we can be content and joyful in all circumstances.*

8. Q. Relate the lack of contentment to people's incurring great indebtedness.

   A. *Discontent motivates people to live and buy beyond their means and thus incurring great debt.*

   Look at Prov. 18:23 and 22:7.

   Q. What do these verses warn about debt?

A. *The debtor is a slave to the creditor. Many financial advisors recommend that aside from a house mortgage a Christian should avoid all debt. This is a good time to discuss with the one you are discipling the importance of living by a budget. You may offer help in preparing a budget and accountability in living by a budget.*

9. Read Matt. 6:25-34; Phil. 2:14; and 4:6.

Q. According to these verses, what are some of the ways we violate the tenth commandment?

A. *Worry and anxiety; murmuring and complaining.*

10. Q. Are there some attitudes or improper dealing with problems you need to address?

A. *Help the person you are discipling to sort through these things. Again seek to hold them accountable.*

LESSON 22:

THE CHURCH

Assignment:

Read:

W.C.F. 25; L.C. 61-66; B.C. articles 27-32;
H.C. 54, 82-85.
Complete this lesson.

Memorize:

Matt. 28:19, 20; 1 Tim. 3:15.

Up to this point we have surveyed the major doctrines of the Bible and examined some aspects of the Christian life and worship. Now we turn our attention to the church and its life. In this lesson we shall consider what the church is, what it does, and how it ought to be governed.

What is the Church?

1. In the Bible the term "church" is used in a number of ways.

   Look at the following passages and after each describe how you think it is using the term "church."

	Verse	**Answer**
a.	Acts 13:1	As a local congregation of believers
b.	Acts 9:31	As all local congregations in a geographical area.

c. Col. 1:18 As all believers that have ever existed or will exist, the invisible church

2. Col. 1:18 uses the term in the most general sense – the entire people of God.

Look at Eph. 1:22, 23 and 5:23.

Q. In these verses what two figures are used to describe the church in this most general sense?

A. According to Eph. 1:22, 23 and 5:23 the two figures used to describe the church in this most general sense are the body of Christ and the bride of Christ.

a. Both of these figures suggest union. To be the body and bride of Christ implies being in union with Him. Thus the church in this sense is all those who belong to Christ; who are in Him.

Look at Eph. 1:4-8.

Q. According to these verses, how does one get to be in Christ?

A. According to Eph. 1:4-8, we got to be in Christ when God chose us before the foundation of the world. He predestined us to adoption as sons through Jesus Christ to Himself.

b. Thus we may say that the church in this general sense consists of all those whom God has chosen in Christ and for whom Christ has died. In Christ we have redemption through His blood, the forgiveness of our trespasses.

Q. What terms are used in W.C.F. 25:1 and L.C. 64 to describe the church in this larger sense?

A. The terms that are used are the catholic or universal church and the invisible church.

3. Although the church in the largest sense of the term is the body of Christ, the primary usage of the term in the New Testament refers to local, visible bodies of God's people. How is the term "church" used in Acts 13:1?

a. Q. Now look at Eph. 1:13, Matt. 10:32, 33, and 1 Cor. 12:12, 13. Therefore, even though one is in Christ by election and redemption, according to these verses, how does one enter into the realization and enjoyment of being a part of the body of Christ? (Compare your answer with L.C. 62, 83.)

A. *By being born again by the Holy Spirit, believing in Christ and confessing Christ before men.*

b. We find an example of this in Acts 2:41, 47.

Q. How are the new converts described?

A. *They were baptized and added to the number of those who believed.*

c. Q. What do W.C.F. 25:2 and L.C. 62 call this expression of the church? What are some of the figures the Bible uses to describe the visible church?

A. *Catholic, universal, visible church; society of professors and their children; the kingdom of the Lord Jesus Christ; the house and family of God.*

d. Q. This suggests that baptism and profession of faith must take place where?

A. *Baptism and profession of faith must take place in the Church.*

e. Thus we see that we ought to join a particular congregation. The way for one to know that he is a part of the body of Christ is to belong to a visible expression of that body. (Compare with W.C.F. 25:2).

f. That the Bible requires church membership is further seen in 1 Thess. 5:12 and Heb. 13:17.

Q. What do these verses require?

A. *According to 1 Thess. 5:12 and Heb. 13:17, believers must be in a local church, because they are to obey and submit to their church leaders.*

g. Q. According to L.C. 62 who are members of the visible church?

A. *Professors of faith and their children.*

4. But if membership in a local church is important, one needs to be able to determine if a group is indeed a church. Read Eph. 4:11-16; 1 Tim. 4:15; Matt. 28:19; 1 Cor. 11:23-26; Matt. 18:15-17 and list some marks that are the distinguishing characteristics of a group if it is a church. (Compare your answer with W.C.F. 25:4.)

A. *A list of some of the marks that are the distinguishing characteristics of a group if it is a church are as follows:*

Doctrine of the gospel is taught and embraced,

Ordinances of baptism and the Lord's Supper are administered,

Public worship is performed, and

Discipline is practiced.

5. Q. Now, write a definition of the church.

A. *A church may be defined as a congregation of believers who believe and teach the gospel, worship God, observe the sacraments, and practice church discipline.*

What the Church Does

6. The basic outline of the task of the church is set out in Matt. 28:19, 20.

a. Q. What is the church's task with respect to the unconverted?

A. *According to Matt. 28:19, 20 the church's task with respect to the unconverted is to teach them the gospel; and when they make a creditable profession of faith, the church is to baptize them and make them members of the church.*

b. Q. What is the church's responsibility to the Christian?

A. *The church's responsibility is to equip the saints, teaching them to observe all that Christ commands.*

7. Look at Eph. 4:11-16.

Q. According to these verses, what are some of the things the church ought to be doing to equip the saints?

A. *The church equips the saints by giving them a place to worship God and to receive the sacraments, to comprehend the Bible, to share their God-given gifts with others, and to grow in grace.*

8. Q. What is the church's purpose in equipping the saints?

A. *The church's purpose in equipping the saints is to glorify God. God is glorified in many ways, but He is glorified the most when the saints are mature, well-grounded in doctrine, serving Him and speaking the truth in love.*

9. Q. According to Acts 6:1-7 and Gal. 6:6-10 what other responsibility does the church have?

A. *Ministering to the material needs of the congregation.*

How the Church Should be Governed

10. The Bible is not silent about the government of the church. It tells us what kind of officers the church should have and how they should govern.

a. Q. Although in the apostolic church there were a number of special officers (Apostles, prophets, and evangelists), what two permanent officers are described in Acts 14:23, 20:28-31 (elder and bishop are used synonymously in Titus 1:5, 7); and Phil. 1:1?

A. *The two permanent officers of the church are the deacons and elders.*

b. Q. According to 1 Tim. 5:17 and Acts 20:28, what tasks are assigned to elders?

A. *According to 1 Tim. 5:17 and Acts 20:28, the elders are assigned the task of being the spiritual rulers, the overseers who shepherd and rule the flock and those who preach and teach.*

(1) *On the basis of this division of labor a distinction is made between ruling elders and teaching or preaching elders.*

(2) *In addition to the work of ruling and pastoring, the teaching elder (minister) has the responsibility of preaching and administering the sacraments. The ruling elder does not have the authority to preach or to administer the sacraments.*

c. Look at Acts 6:1-6.

Q. According to these verses, what is the task of the deacons?

A. *According to Acts 6:1-6, the task of the deacons is to minister to the physical needs of the congregation.*

11. In addition to describing the officers of the church, the Bible reveals the outline for a form of government. In the history of the church there have arisen three types of church government:

a. Episcopal – the authority comes from the top down in a hierarchy of bishops with one bishop (archbishop or pope) as the head of the church. A bishop who is appointed by the other bishops is over a geographical division of the church with a number of ministers under his authority. Congregations have only a limited say in who is to be their pastor. This is found in the Roman Catholic, Greek Orthodox, Anglican/Episcopalian churches, and to some degree in Lutheran and Methodist churches.

b. Congregational – the authority lies in the people of the congregation who have the final word in all decisions. Each congregation is entirely independent; it may join an association, but the decisions of the association are not binding. In some instances (particularly Baptists) there is only one elder, the minister (there may be assistant ministers), and a group of deacons who along with the minister make decisions subject to the approval of the congregation. Other congregational churches would have a plurality of elders. This form of government is found in Baptist and Congregational churches.

c. Presbyterian – the authority rests in Jesus Christ alone as the head of the church. Christ rules in the church through elders elected by the people. It is a representative government and the churches are joined together with other churches in geographical groups called presbyteries. All churches and presbyteries are further joined together in what is called a General Assembly. This is found in Presbyterian and Reformed churches.

12. Of the three forms Presbyterianism seems to be the most in accord with biblical principles of church government. Let us test the three types of government.

    Listed below are six principles of church government. After each principle write the letter for the group to which the principle applies. A principle may be found in more than one group.

Principle	*Answer*
a. Office bearers are chosen by the people. (Acts 1:23; 14:23; 6:1-6)	x C P
b. The terms "bishop" and "elder" are synonymous. (Acts 20:28; Titus 1:5-7)	x ? P
c. In the New Testament there is a plurality of elders in every congregation. (Acts 14:23; 20:17; Phil. 1:1)	x ? P
d. Ordination was the act of a plurality of elders called a presbytery. (Acts 13:1-3; 1 Tim. 4:14)	? ? P

e. *The church is governed by an assembly of elders and there is privilege of appeal from a local assembly to a geographical one. (Acts 15; 16:4)* ? x P

f. *Christ alone is the head over all things in His church. (Eph. 1:20-23; 5:23; Col. 1:18)* x ? P

13. Q. Which of the three above types of government has the least conformity?

    A. *The Episcopal type of church government has the least conformity.*

    a. Q. Which has the most?

       A. *The Presbyterian type of church government has the most conformity.*

    b. Q. How is the term "church" used in Acts 9:31?

       A. *It is used of a number of congregations in a geographic location. We call this a presbytery or classis.*

    c. It is on this basis that we say Presbyterianism is the most biblical form of church government. This is not to say that the others are not churches. As long as a church has the marks noted above it is a true church.

LESSON 23:

LIFE IN THE CONGREGATION

Assignment:

Read:

W.C.F. 26; L.C. 65, 66, 82; H.C. 32, 52-55.

Complete this lesson and the Personal Information Sheet.

Memorize:

Acts 2:42; Heb. 10:24, 25.

Having seen that church membership is not an option, let us examine the responsibility involved in church membership.

The Purpose of Life in the Congregation

1. Q. List what you would consider some wrong reasons for joining the church.

   A. *Family expectations, social standing, job advancement.*

2. Q. List some proper reasons for belonging to a church.

   A. *Doctrinal integrity, biblical worship, sound preaching, good pastoral oversight, commitment to prayer meeting.*

3. Look at Acts 2:42.

   Q. List the four things to which early Christians were devoted.

A. a. Apostles' doctrine

b. Fellowship

c. Breaking of bread

d. Prayer

4. Below are some verses that define each of the four things. Look up the verses and write what you think each activity involved.

a. Q. Doctrine: 2 Tim. 1:13; 2:1, 2; 3:14-17; 4:1, 2.

A. Summary of Apostolic teaching; the content of the Bible. The Christian must know the truth of the Bible.

b. Q. Fellowship: Acts 2:44-46; Heb. 10:24, 25; Mal. 3:16.

A. Sharing with one another; encouraging and exhorting one another; spiritual conversation.

c. Q. Breaking of Bread: Luke 24:30; Acts 20:7.

A. The Lord's Supper. We have already noted that baptism was the sign of entrance. Thus the sacraments were part of the life of the early church.

d. Q. Prayer: Acts 1:14; 2:46, 47; 4:23, 24.

A. The prayer meeting and corporate worship.

e. All of these elements are important in the Christian life and, if we expect to grow as Christians, we must be committed to them. Thus we should join a church that takes these things seriously and as members of the congregation we ought to avail ourselves of every possible opportunity in these areas. At a minimum we ought to be involved in the stated activities of the Lord's Day: Sunday School, Morning Worship, and Evening Worship. Furthermore, we ought to be involved in a weekly prayer meeting and regular service and fellowship.

Service in the Life in the Congregation

5. Paul gives an interesting picture of congregational life in Eph. 4:7-16.

   a. Q. What gifts does the exalted Christ give to the church?

      A. *Office bearers.*

      We noted in the last lesson that Apostles, prophets, and evangelists were special officers for the early church. The abiding office is that of pastor and teacher or better rendered, pastor-teacher.

   b. Q. According to verse 13, what is Christ's goal for the church?

      A. *For all her members to be built up in the unity of faith as mature and godly people.*

   c. Q. In verses 14-16 what are the consequences when this goal is met?

      A. *God's people will be firm, discerning, speaking the truth in love, growing and maturing, all being used by Christ for the building up of the whole.*

   d. Verse 12 tells us how the officers are used to meet this goal.

      Q. What is the chief purpose of the pastor-teacher?

      A. *To equip the saints for work.*

   e. Q. Who then is responsible for the work of ministry?

      A. *The members of the church.*

   f. Some translations take the phrase "for the work of service" to refer to the pastor-teacher. Even so, we may rightly conclude from other places in the Bible that every member of the congregation has service and ministry to fulfill in the congregation.

Q. What duties does the W.C.F. 26:1, 2 assign to members of the church?

A. *Obliged to do those things publicly and privately, according to their gifts and resources, that promote the mutual good of their brethren. These things include worship, fellowship, and service.*

We may rightly conclude that every member of the congregation has service and ministry to fulfill in the congregation.

6. Look at Rom. 12:3-8 and 1 Peter 4:10, 11.

   Q. According to these verses, what does God give to His people to enable them to serve in the church?

   A. *Gifts.*

Note that a gift is not some mysterious thing. It is whatever God has given you naturally by birth as well as supernaturally by grace to aid the church in the full scope of its ministry.

7. Each of us has talents and gifts the church needs. Look at Matt. 25:14-30.

   Q. What do these verses teach about the use of our gifts and talents?

   A. *We have a stewardship from God and are accountable to Him for what we do with what He has entrusted to us.*

8. Q. List and define the gifts Paul delineates in Rom. 12:3-8.

   A. a. *Prophecy – the ability to expound and apply God's Word (preaching). It belongs to those called to the ministry.*

   b. *Service – the ability to serve others in a way that is helpful and edifying.*

   c. *Teaching – the ability publicly and privately to explain God's Word to others.*

   d. *Exhorting – the ability to encourage and admonish, to counsel, to call to repentance and faith.*

e. *Giving – the ability to give of oneself, time, and possessions in an extraordinary manner.*

f. *Leading – the ability to anticipate, plan, delegate, motivate, and see things through.*

g. *Mercy – the ability to show kindness and sympathy by word and deed to those in need.*

a. Q. Which of these do you think you have?

A.

b. Q. List below some services and functions the church needs.

A. Some of the services and functions that the church needs are as follows: Teaching, discipleship, planning, cleaning, repairing, serving, evangelism, counseling, visiting shut-ins and those in the hospital, etc.

c. It is important that each of us understands what he can do to help. One of the best ways to determine your gifts is by considering what you are able and like to do and what activities in the church interest you. Take time now to fill out the Personal Information Sheet. The purpose of this survey is to help you see areas in which you can serve the church and to inform the church of those areas. Ask others as well what they think your gifts are. Discuss this with the one who you are teaching and help him to determine what some of his gifts are.

9. One very practical service one should participate in is Christian giving.

a. Look at Mal. 3:8-12.

Q. According to these verses, what sin are we committing, if we do not tithe?

A. We are robbing God.

b. A tithe is ten percent of our gross income. God uses the giving of His people to support the work and ministry of the church. God promises to bless those who honor Him with the tithe. Our giving, however, should go beyond a tithe. We may give God offerings over and above the tithe (see number 13 below).

Fellowship in the Life of the Congregation

10. Look at Acts 2:42-46.

Another thing mentioned in Acts 2:42 is fellowship.

Q. How did this fellowship manifest itself in Acts 2:44-46?

A. *They enjoyed being together, taking meals together.*

11. One of the things the people were doing was fellowshipping in one another's homes. We call this hospitality.

Now look at Heb. 13:2; 1 Peter 4:9; and Rom. 12:13.

Q. According to these verses, how important is hospitality?

A. *It is an essential part of Christian piety.*

Note that hospitality is using your home to facilitate getting to know other people and meeting their needs. Biblical fellowship does not need nice things and elaborate meals. Peanut butter and jelly sandwiches served on paper plates do just fine. Have you recently had another Christian in your home? If not, why not plan on doing so within the next two weeks. Again you may want to help the one you are teaching. If you have not done so, have him in your home. Perhaps later host a meal with him.

12. We also learn from Acts 2 that the people were together with one mind. This phrase expresses the real purpose of fellowship.

Look at Heb. 10:24, 25 and Eph. 5:19.

Q. According to these verses, what are the most important elements in fellowship?

A. *Mutual encouragement and edification.*

This does not mean that playing together is not fellowship. It simply reminds us that true fellowship must go much deeper.

13. Look at Rom. 12:13.

Q. According to this verse, what activity in addition to hospitality is mentioned?

A. Contributing to the needs of the saints.

a. Q. The tithe is to be the basis of our giving. According to Rom. 15:26, 27, what other contributions did the early Christians make?

A. Contributions for the poor. We refer to these as offerings to distinguish them from the tithe.

b. Read Acts 2.

Q. How did the early church do this in Acts 2?

A. Sold property and gave the proceeds to the church to use for the poor.

c. Note the last phrase in verse 45. The key to their selling their possessions was need. This was not "Christian communism." It was the church responding sacrificially to the needs of its own. Moreover, Christ had told them that in a few years Jerusalem would be destroyed (Matt. 24:2).

d. Look at Matt. 25:31-40.

Q. According to these verses, to whom do we give when we give to needy Christians?

A. We give to Christ Himself.

Summary

14. We have seen that church membership demands commitment, service, and fellowship. This concept of church membership is set forth in the membership vows. When one joins the church he takes vows similar to those used by the Presbyterian Church in America. These vows are promises to God. Note particularly the fourth vow.

a. Do you acknowledge yourselves to be sinners in the sight of God, justly deserving His displeasure, and without hope save in His sovereign mercy?

b. Do you believe in the Lord Jesus Christ as the Son of God, and Savior of sinners, and do you receive and rest upon Him alone for salvation as He is offered in the Gospel?

c. Do you resolve and promise, in humble reliance upon the grace of the Holy Spirit, that you will endeavor to live as becometh the followers of Christ?

d. Do you promise to support the church in its worship and work to the best of your ability?

e. Do you submit yourselves to the government and discipline of the church, and promise to study its purity and peace?

LESSON 24:

BAPTISM

Assignment:

Read:

W.C.F. 27, 28; L.C. 161-167; S.C. 91-95; B.C. articles 33, 34; H.C. 65-74; C.D. III, IV, article 17; V, article 14. Complete this lesson.

Memorize:

S.C. 92, 94.

Having discussed the nature of the church and the importance of being a member of the church, we now want to consider two aspects of church life that relate directly to church membership – Baptism and the Lord's Supper.

The Nature of Baptism

1. Read Matt. 28:19.

   Q. According to this verse, what is to be done to every individual who is brought into the church?

   A. He is to be baptized.

2. Q. This act of baptism is called a sacrament. The term is defined in S.C. 92. Write out this definition in your own words.

A. *Baptism is a holy ordinance appointed by Christ as a sign and seal of belonging to Christ and of the benefits of the new covenant.*

a. Q. Write a definition of ordinance (look up in a dictionary if necessary).

A. *An ordinance is a sacred order to be observed by the church.*

b. Q. What is the purpose of these ordinances?

A. *They are means of grace for the people of God, like preaching and the sacraments.*

c. Look at Matt. 28:19 and 1 Cor. 11:23-26.

Q. According to these verses, what two sacraments did Christ institute?

A. *Baptism and the Lord's Supper.*

3. Q. According to W.C.F. 27:1, what two terms are used to describe what a sacrament does?

A. *A sacrament serves as a sign and seal.*

a Q. What does a sign do? Give an example.

A. *A sign is a symbolic representation of a specific reality: the picture of a gas pump on a sign on the Interstate Highway.*

b. Q. What does a seal do (use a dictionary)?

A. *A seal confirms and authenticates: like a seal of a Notary Public or a special stamp on a contract.*

4. Q. According to S.C. 94, what is baptism?

A. *A sacrament in which by the application of water in the name of the triune God we have signified and sealed our union with Christ, our partaking of the benefits of the New Covenant, and our commitment to serve the Lord.*

5. Q. Baptism is a sign. After the following verses, write what is signified by baptism.

A.

	Verse	*Answer*
(1)	Matt. 28:19	Being a disciple of Christ
(2)	Gal. 3:27	Being in union with Christ
(3)	Titus 3:5	Regeneration and renewing of the Holy Spirit
(4)	1 Cor. 12:13	Spiritual baptism into the body of Christ
(5)	Rom. 6:5	Union with Christ in His death, burial, and resurrection
(6)	Mark 1:4; Acts 2:38	Remission of sins

In W.C.F. 28:1 and L.C. 165 there is a summary of what baptism signifies. Check your answer with this list.

6. One of the purposes of baptism is to signify cleansing. Look at Ezek. 36:25-27 and John 3:5.

   Q. What element is used to describe this cleansing of the heart?

   A. Water

   a. Look at Acts 8:37, 38.

      Q. According to these verses, what element is used for baptism?

      A. Water

   b. From this we learn that water is used, since it is a sign of cleansing.

7. This aspect of cleansing also teaches us about the mode of the administration of baptism. There are primarily two modes: immersion and pouring or sprinkling. In Heb. 9:9, 10, the writer is describing some of the Old Testament ceremonial cleansings. The word translated "washings" in verse 10 is the word "baptism."

   a. Read verses 11-22.

Q. In these verses, what mode is used to describe these ceremonial washings?

A. *Sprinkling.*

b. Look at Ezek. 36:25.

Q. What term is used to describe the cleansing of regeneration?

A. *Sprinkling.*

c. Look at Acts 2:17 (cf. Matt. 3:11).

Q. What term is used to describe the cleansing of regeneration?

A. *Pouring out.*

It is for these reasons that we believe the best mode is pouring or sprinkling.

8. Baptism is also a seal.

Look at 1 Peter 3:21.

Q. According to this verse, what is the function of baptism?

A. *An appeal to God for a good conscience.*

a. Q. Compare this function with what you wrote about the function of a seal. We see that baptism is used of the Holy Spirit to assure us of the reality in our lives of the things signified by baptism. It is for this reason that the Bible often speaks of the sign as if it were the spiritual reality. Look at Acts 2:38; Rom. 6:3, 4; and Gal. 3:27. What spiritual realities are described in these verses by baptism?

A. *Remission of sin, baptized into Christ's death, burial, and resurrection, putting on Christ as a garment.*

b. Q. If baptism is to seal to us spiritual realities, we must have the reality already in our lives and must reflect on the purposes of our baptism in connection with the promises of scripture and our baptism. As we do so the Holy Spirit will give us assurance and strength. L.C. 167 gives a number of practical things to help us do this. Write a list of things you can do to derive benefit from your baptism.

A. *Think on its nature and purpose; think on your vows; be humbled for your sin and falling short of your baptism; seek assurance; drawing strength for mortification and sanctification from the death and resurrection of Christ; endeavor to live by faith in godliness; remember you have been baptized into the one body of Christ, so love your brethren.*

9. Yet we must ask the question: does baptism guarantee these realities? Read Acts 8:13-23.

   a. Q. According to Acts 8:13-23, when was Simon baptized?

      A. *Upon his profession of faith.*

   b. Q. Was Simon converted?

      A. *No*

   c. Thus baptism does not convert nor can it do its work as a seal in one who has not been converted.

10. Furthermore, we need to note that the efficacy of the sealing benefits of baptism is not tied to the moment of administration (W.C.F. 28:6). As we make use of our baptism, it does this work all through our lives.

The Recipients of Baptism

11. Read Acts 8:13 and 36-38.

    Q. On what occasion were Simon and the Ethiopian Eunuch baptized?

    A. *Upon profession of faith.*

12. Q. Should a person who professes faith and has not been properly baptized seek baptism?

    A. *By all means.*

13. Look at W.C.F. 28:4.

Q. Who else should be baptized?

A. *Children of professors.*

a. Q. The biblical basis for including children of believers becomes clear when we examine the relationship between circumcision and baptism. According to Gen. 17:7-14, when was circumcision instituted?

A. *When God confirmed the covenant with Abraham.*

b. Q. Circumcision was the sign of the covenant between God and Abraham. After each of the following references write what you think circumcision would have meant.

A.

Verse	*Answer*
(1) Gen. 17:7-10	Abraham and his seed in covenant with God
(2) Rom. 4:11	Seal of justification
(3) Deut. 10:16; 30:6	Mark of regeneration
(4) Jer. 4:4	Mortification and repentance

c. Now read Col. 2:9-14.

Q. How does Paul relate circumcision to the Christian?

A. *Physical circumcision points to the spiritual circumcision by which we are born again because of our union with Christ in His death and resurrection.*

d. Q. By what was circumcision replaced (verse 12)?

A. *Baptism.*

e. Q. Go back now and compare the purposes of baptism with what you said circumcision would have meant to Abraham. Are there any differences between the two?

A. *No.*

f. Q. Do you think that when Abraham circumcised Ishmael (Gen. 17:26) and Isaac circumcised Esau and Jacob (Gen. 25) circumcision sealed the same spiritual reality to the children that it sealed to Abraham (particularly Ishmael and Esau who were unconverted)?

A. No.

g. Q. Why then do you think these boys were circumcised?

A. Abraham and his descendants circumcised their children because they belonged to the covenant community and were in a sense heirs to the promises. Furthermore, God had told them to circumcise their sons. There was no guarantee that all those circumcised would receive the reality.

h. Q. In the New Testament there are four important things to note about the children of believers. After each verse write what you think it is saying about covenant children.

A.

	Verse	*Answer*
(1)	Luke 1:41-44; (cf. 2 Sam. 12:22, 23)	May be regenerate from the womb
(2)	1 Cor. 7:14	Are federally holy
(3)	Matt. 19:13, 14; Luke 18:15-17	May receive God's blessing
(4)	Eph. 6:1, cf. 1:1	Addressed as recipients of the letter and members of the church

i Q. In light of the verses in the above table and what we have learned about circumcision and its relation to baptism, what ought we to think when we read verses like Acts 16:15, 33; and 1 Cor. 1:16?

A. *The children of professors received baptism.*

j. We then have the right and responsibility to have our children baptized.

LESSON 25:

THE LORD'S SUPPER

Assignment:

Read:

W.C.F. 29; L.C. 168-177; S.C. 96, 97;
B.C. article 35; H.C. 75-82.
Complete this lesson.

Memorize:

1 Cor. 10:16, 17; S.C. 96.

We have seen that Christ instituted the sacraments of Baptism and the Lord's Supper. Having studied the first, we now turn our attention to the second.

The Institution of the Lord's Supper

1. Read 1 Cor. 11:23-26.

Q. By whose authority did Paul give the institution of the Lord's Supper?

A. By the authority of the Lord Jesus Christ.

a. Q. When did Jesus institute the Lord's Supper (cf. Matt. 26:17-28)?

A. According to Matt. 26:17-28, Jesus instituted the Lord's Supper at the Feast of the Passover the night he was betrayed.

b. Q. What is the relationship between the Lord's Supper and the Passover?

A. *Jesus transformed the Passover into the Lord's Supper. The Passover was a picture of Christ's predicted death. The Lord's Supper looks back at his death.*

2. Q. According to 1 Cor. 11:26, how long should the church practice the observance of the Lord's Supper?

A. *Until Christ returns.*

a. Q. Would you say that it is an option or a duty?

A. *It is a duty and privilege.*

b. Q. What should be your attitude toward partaking of the Lord's Supper?

A. *Eager expectation and joy.*

3. Q. What two elements did Christ take from the Passover and use as the elements of the Lord's Supper?

A. *The two elements that Christ took from the Passover and used as the elements of the Lord's Supper were bread and wine.*

The significance of these elements is seen in the next section.

The Purpose of the Lord's Supper

4. We have seen that the sacraments are signs and seals of the covenant of grace. As a sign, the Lord's Supper pictures three things for us.

a. A picture of what Christ did.

Q. According to 1 Cor. 11:24-26, what is the Lord's Supper to help us to remember?

A. *The Lord's suffering and death on our behalf.*

(1) It is for this purpose that the elements of bread and wine are used.

Q. What do you think Jesus means by the language "this is my body" and "this cup is the New Covenant in my blood"?

A. *The bread represents His body and the wine represents His blood and communicates the benefits of His death and resurrection.*

(2) Some teach that this language means that Jesus' real body and blood are present in the sacrament and that he is re-sacrificed each time the sacrament is observed. Such a doctrine is contrary to the simple meaning of the words and to what the Bible says about the sacrifice of Christ (W.C.F. 29.2, 6).

(3) Look at John 10:7.

Q. Is Jesus saying that the door to the sheepfold is He or that it is a picture of Him?

A. *Jesus is saying the latter.*

(4) Q. What then would you expect Him to mean when he uses the same type of language in the institution of the Lord's Supper?

A. *It is a picture of Him. After all He was reclining with them when He said the bread was His body and the wine His blood. They would have understood that He was speaking figuratively.*

(5) Q. What then would be another way to render the phrases about the bread and wine being his body and blood?

A. *Representations or pictures.*

(6) Q. Thus we conclude that Jesus is using a very common metaphor. According to W.C.F. 29:5, what else is signified by the language "this is My body. . ."?

A. *The close relationship between Christ's death and this sacrament.*

(7) Q. Look at Heb. 9:22-28. What do these verses say about the once and for all character of the sacrifice of the Lord Jesus?

A. *His work was complete and finished. His death was the final sacrifice for sin. By His death He fully accomplished redemption.*

(8) Q. If Christ has been sacrificed once and for all and Jesus now teaches us to observe the Lord's Supper in remembrance of that sacrifice, is there any way that the Lord's Supper can be a re-sacrifice? (Compare W.C.F. 29:2.)

A. *No.*

(9) Q. What then should the bread and wine remind us of when we observe the Lord's Supper (see W.C.F. 29:1)?

A. *It reminds us that He is God incarnate, who gave Himself as the perfect sacrifice for our sin.*

b. A picture of what we must do. Look at John 6:35, 47-51, 53-57.

Q. What does Jesus use here to picture faith?

A. *Taking, eating, and drinking.*

(1) Q. How does food and drink become one with our body?

A. *By eating and drinking.*

(2) Q. How do we become one with Christ?

A. *By faith.*

(3) Q. How then does the Lord's Supper picture for us the action of faith?

A. *Teaches that faith brings us into a living union with Christ.*

c. A picture of the people of God. Read 1 Cor. 10:16, 17; 12:13; and Luke 22:17.

Q. According to these verses, what else is pictured by the Lord's Supper?

A. *Our communion in the body of Christ's people.*

(1) Q. According to 1 Cor. 12:13, what appears to be the relationship between Baptism and the Lord's Supper?

A. *They both picture the reality of our union with Christ and His people through the work of the Holy Spirit.*

(2) Q. Since Baptism is the mark of our union with Christ and His people, should an un-baptized person partake of the Lord's Supper?

A. *No.*

5. As a seal of the covenant, the Lord's Supper communicates a number of blessings to those who partake by faith.

a. Look at Matt. 26:27, 28 and Luke 22:20.

Q. According to these verses, what benefit is guaranteed to us as we by faith partake of the Lord's Supper?

A. *That we enjoy the benefits of the New Covenant and our sins have been forgiven.*

(1) Q. Look back at Lesson 9 and review the things promised to us in the covenant of grace.

A. *We are God's and He is ours. He has forgiven our sins and given us the gift of the Holy Spirit.*

(2) Q. What do you think God is saying to you as a Christian when you come to the Lord's Table? (Compare L.C. 168.)

A. *That my sins are forgiven and I am in communion with the triune God.*

b. Another thing food does is nourish us. Look at 1 Cor. 10:16.

Q. According to this verse, what do we partake of when we eat the Lord's Supper?

A. *The body of Christ.*

(1) We have already noted that we do not literally eat Jesus' body and blood, but he is spiritually present; and as we see in 1 Cor. 10:16, we partake of Him.

Q. If eating food gives physical strength, what should the spiritual partaking of Christ do for us spiritually?

A. *It should strengthen us spiritually.*

(2) The W.C.F. 29:7 gives a summary of this benefit.

c. Look at 1 Cor. 10:16-21 and 2 Cor. 6:14-16.

Q. According to 1 Cor. 10:16-21 compared with 2 Cor. 6:14-16, what should the Lord's Supper motivate us to do?

A. *To cling to Him alone and to avoid idolatry and sin.*

6. Q. In conclusion, write a summary of what the Lord's Supper should do for you.

A. *It should confirm to me my union with Christ in the covenant and the remission of my sin. It should strengthen me to die to sin and grow in conformity to Christ. It should motivate me to serve God.*

The Right Way to Partake of the Lord's Supper

7. Read 1 Cor. 11:27-31.

Q. What does Paul warn about in these verses?

A. *Partaking improperly. Not examining myself.*

a. Look at L.C. 173.

Q. According to L.C. 173, who ought not come to the Lord's Table?

A. *The unconverted, the ignorant, and those living in scandalous sin.*

b. Look at L.C. 172.

Q. According to L.C. 172, may a person who is weak in faith and doubts his salvation come to the Lord's Table?

A. Yes, if he has been examined by the elders and received into the Church as a communicant member.

c. Q. What does this teach us about the importance of self-examination as we come to the Lord's Table?

A. We should examine ourselves often and particularly in preparation of coming to the Lord's Supper.

d. L.C. 171 gives a number of areas that such examination should cover.

Q. List the things that we should do in preparing to come to the Lord's Table. Use this list in the future as you prepare to come.

A. A list of things that we should do in preparing to come to the Lord's Table is as follows: Being in Christ; realization of sin and need; the truth and measure of knowledge, faith, repentance, love of God and the brethren; willingness to forgive others; desires for Christ and obedience; renewal of the exercise of these graces by meditation and prayer.

8. Now read L.C. 174.

Q. According to L.C. 174, on what things should we be thinking and meditating as we partake of the Lord's Supper?

A. Seek God in the ordinance; observe the sacramental actions and elements (W.C.F. 29:3); meditate on how Christ is present and communicated to us; meditate on His death and suffering for us; judge ourselves and sorrow for sin; hunger and thirst for Christ and His benefits; renew our covenant with God and love to the saints.

9. Look at L.C. 175.

Q. On the basis of L.C. 175, what should we do after we partake of the Lord's Supper?

A. *Examine how we behaved and with what success. Bless God for any quickening and comfort. Beg the continuance of blessing. Guard against lapses. Fulfill covenant vows. Commit to frequent attendance. If no present benefit, review preparation and behavior. If failed, be humbled and resolve to participate the next time more carefully. If find no serious fault, wait on God for blessing.*

This is a good thing to do on Sunday afternoon.

LESSON 26:

THE END

Assignment:

Read:

W.C.F. 32, 33; L.C. 29, 56, 84-90;
S.C. 28, 37, 38; B.C. article 37; H.C. 57, 58, 123.
Complete this lesson.

Memorize:

1 Thess. 4:14; S.C. 37, 38.

Having surveyed the basic doctrines and practices of the Christian life, it remains for us to draw this work to a close by studying what the Bible teaches about the end (death, the intermediate state, and the final return of Christ).This lesson sets the final hope of the Christian before us. Pray that you will grasp these truths and be greatly comforted by them.

Death

1. Q. According to Heb. 9:27, is death inevitable before the return of Christ?

   A. *Yes, until Christ returns death is inevitable.*

2. Q. Read Rom. 6:23. Why do people die (review Lesson 8)?

   A. *We die because of Adam's sin and our own.*

3. Q. According to L.C. 85, why does God allow Christians to die?

   A. *Christians die because it is God's wise provision to free them from sin and misery and fit them for further communion with Christ.*

THE INTERMEDIATE STATE

4. Q. According to 2 Cor. 5:1, 6, 8; Phil. 1:23; and Heb. 12:23, when a Christian dies what happens to his soul?

   A. *When a Christian dies his soul immediately goes into the presence of God in heaven and is made perfect.*

5. Q. What are we told in Gen. 3:19; Job 19:26; and Acts 13:36 happens to the body at death?

   A. *The body decays, turning back into dust.*

6. Q. According to 1 Thess. 4:14, what is the dead body's relation to the Lord Jesus Christ? (Compare you answer with S.C. 37.)

   A. *The body remains in union with the Lord Jesus Christ.*

7. Q. Read Luke 16:23, 24; Acts 1:25; Jude 6, 7. According to these verses what happens to the souls of the wicked when they die? (Compare your answer with L.C. 86.)

   A. *They are cast into hell, where they begin to suffer the eternal punishment for their sins.*

THE RETURN OF CHRIST

8. Q. According to 1 Cor. 15:23-28, what will be Christ's final mediatorial act?

   A. *Christ's final mediatorial act will be the destruction of death.*

9. Q. When, according to Acts 1:11; Luke 9:26; and Matt. 25:31, shall Christ destroy death?

   A. *Christ shall destroy death at His second coming.*

10. Q. Although there is controversy over the time of Christ's return, according to Matt. 24:36 can anyone predict the time or generation in which Christ will return?

A. *No man or angel knows the time or the generation of Christ's second coming.*

11. Q. According to 2 Peter 3:11; Rom. 8:23-25; and Matt. 24:37-44, why has He left the time unknown? (Compare your answer with W.C.F. 33:3; L.C. 88.)

A. *He has left the time unknown so that men will not be presumptuous in their sin, that the Christian will be alert, living carefully, and that the Christian may comfort himself with this future hope in the midst of trial and adversity.*

12. Q. Read 1 Thess. 4:12-18; 1 Cor. 15:50-52; John 5:27-29; and 2 Peter 2:4 and list the events connected with the return of the Lord Jesus Christ. (Compare your answer with L.C. 56.)

A. *He shall be accompanied by the angels and the souls of those who died and have been with Him; He shall descend with a shout (cry of command), the voice of the archangel, and the sound of a trumpet; He shall raise the bodies both of His dead saints and of the wicked; all His people who are alive shall be caught up in the air to meet Him; saints shall be glorified in body and soul; and Christ shall judge both the righteous and the wicked.*

13. Q. What happens to the righteous at the time of Christ's return, according to Job 19:26, 27; 1 Cor. 15:42-44, 51; Phil. 3:21; 1 John 3:2? (Compare your answer to W.C.F. 33:2, 3.)

A. *At the return of Christ the righteous dead shall be raised so their perfect souls shall be joined to perfect bodies; those who are alive shall be transformed body and soul, and all shall be perfectly conformed to the glorious human nature of the Lord Jesus Christ.*

14. Q. How does Jesus describe the resurrection of the wicked in John 5:29? What do you think a resurrection to judgment entails? (Compare your answer to L.C. 87, 89.)

    A. *The wicked are raised to a resurrection to judgment. Such language implies that they will be raised so as to receive God's judgment on their bodies as well as in their souls.*

15. Q. According to Matt. 25:31-46, Eccl. 12:14; 2 Cor. 5:10; and Matt. 12:36, 37, what shall be the basis of judgment?

    A. *All thoughts, words, and deeds, both good and bad, shall be judged.*

16. Q. On the basis of John 5:28, 29; Matt. 10:32; 12:37; 25:1-23; 31-40, what is the purpose of the judgment of the righteous? (Compare with W.C.F. 33:2; L.C. 90.)

    A. *The manifestation of God's glory and grace; the open acknowledgment and acquittal of the elect; the manifestation of God's mercy and grace in saving them; and, by God's grace, the assignment of reward. After their judgment they will participate in the judgment of reprobate angels and men.*

17. Q. According to 1 Cor. 6:2, 3; Matt. 25:34, 46; Eph. 5:27; Rev. 14:13; Ps. 16:11; and Heb. 12:22, 23, what shall be the state of the righteous (L.C. 90)?

    A. *They will participate in the judgment of reprobate angels and men; they shall be brought into heaven (which is the renovated earth – 2 Peter 3:13); they shall be free from all sin and misery; they will see God and perfectly enjoy and serve Him for eternity; and they will enjoy the company of the saints and angels, all of which is eternal life.*

18. Q. What, according to Rom. 2: 15, 16; Matt. 7:23; 25:41-43, will be the purpose of the judgment of the wicked (L.C. 89)?

    A. *The purpose of the judgment of the wicked is to pronounce on them the sentence of eternal damnation and to leave them without excuse when they are declared guilty.*

19. Q. What will be the punishment of the wicked, according to Matt. 25:41; 2 Thess. 1:8, 9 (W.C.F. 33:2; L.C. 89)?

A. *They shall be cast out of the favorable presence of God and cast into hell where with reprobate angels they shall suffer the eternal punishment of God in both body and soul, which state is hell.*

20. Q. According to Rom. 8:18; 1 Thess. 4:18; and 2 Peter 3:14, what should be our response to these great truths of the end of the age?

A. *As we await the return of Christ and the end of the age, we should comfort ourselves with the hope of His return, comfort ourselves with the hope of the resurrection, and labor to grow in godliness in order to be found godly by Him when He returns.*

APPENDIX 1

THE WESTMINSTER CONFESSION OF FAITH

CHAPTER I

Of the Holy Scripture

I. Although the light of nature, and the works of creation and providence do so far manifest the goodness, wisdom, and power of God, as to leave men unexcusable;[1] yet are they not sufficient to give that knowledge of God, and of His will, which is necessary unto salvation.[2] Therefore it pleased the Lord, at sundry times, and in divers manners, to reveal Himself, and to declare that His will unto His church;[3] and afterwards, for the better preserving and propagating of the truth, and for the more sure establishment and comfort of the church against the corruption of the flesh, and the malice of Satan and of the world, to commit the same wholly unto writing:[4] which maketh the Holy Scripture to be most necessary;[5] those former ways of God's revealing His will unto His people being now ceased.[6]

II. Under the name of Holy Scripture, or the Word of God written, are now contained all the books of the Old and New Testaments, which are these:

Of the Old Testament:

Genesis	Ecclesiastes
Exodus	The Song of Songs
Leviticus	Isaiah
Numbers	Jeremiah
Deuteronomy	Lamentations
Joshua	Ezekiel
Judges	Daniel
Ruth	Hosea
I Samuel	Joel
II Samuel	Amos
I Kings	Obadiah
II Kings	Jonah
I Chronicles	Micah
II Chronicles	Nahum
Ezra	Habakkuk
Nehemiah	Zephaniah
Esther	Haggai
Job	Zechariah
Psalms	Malachi
Proverbs	

Of the New Testament:

The Gospels according to Matthew	the Thessalonians I
Mark	the Thessalonians II
Luke	Timothy I
John	Timothy II
The Acts of the Apostles	Titus
Paul's Epistles to the Romans	Philemon
the Corinthians I	The Epistle to the Hebrews
the Corinthians II	The Epistle of James
the Galatians	The first and second Epistles of Peter
the Ephesians	The first, second, and third Epistles of John
the Philippians	The Epistle of Jude
the Colossians	The Revelation of John

All which are given by inspiration of God to be the rule of faith and life.[7]

III. The books commonly called Apocrypha, not being of divine inspiration, are no part of the canon of the Scripture, and therefore are of no authority in the church of God, nor to be any otherwise approved, or made use of, than other human writings.[8]

IV. The authority of the Holy Scripture, for which it ought to be believed, and obeyed, dependeth not upon the testimony of any man, or church; but wholly upon God (who is truth itself) the author thereof: and therefore it is to be received, because it is the Word of God.[9]

V. We may be moved and induced by the testimony of the church to an high and reverent esteem of the Holy Scripture.[10] And the heavenliness of the matter, the efficacy of the doctrine, the majesty of the style, the consent of all the parts, the scope of the whole (which is, to give all glory to God), the full discovery it makes of the only way of man's salvation, the many other incomparable excellencies, and the entire perfection thereof, are arguments whereby it doth abundantly evidence itself to be the Word of God: yet notwithstanding, our full persuasion and assurance of the infallible truth and divine authority thereof, is from the inward work of the Holy Spirit bearing witness by and with the Word in our hearts.[11]

VI. The whole counsel of God concerning all things necessary for His own glory, man's salvation, faith and life, is either expressly set down in Scripture, or by good and necessary consequence may be deduced from Scripture: unto which nothing at any time is to be added, whether by new revelations of the Spirit, or traditions of men.[12] Nevertheless, we acknowledge the inward illumination of the Spirit of God to be necessary for the saving understanding of such things as are revealed in the Word:[13] and that there are some circumstances concerning the worship of God, and government of the church, common to human actions and societies, which are to be ordered by the light of nature, and Christian prudence, according to the general rules of the Word, which are always to be observed.[14]

VII. All things in Scripture are not alike plain in themselves, nor alike clear unto all:[15] yet those things which are necessary to be known, believed, and observed for salvation, are so clearly propounded, and opened in some place of Scripture or other, that not only the learned, but the unlearned, in a due use of the ordinary means, may attain unto a sufficient understanding of them.[16]

VIII. The Old Testament in Hebrew (which was the native language of the people of God of old), and the New Testament in Greek (which, at the time of the writing of it, was most generally known to the nations), being immediately inspired by God, and, by His singular care and providence, kept pure in all ages, are therefore authentical;[17] so as, in all controversies of religion, the church is finally to appeal unto them.[18] But, because these original tongues are not known to all the people of God, who have right unto, and interest in the Scriptures, and are commanded, in the fear of God, to read and search them,[19] therefore they are to be translated into the vulgar language of every nation unto which they come,[20] that, the Word of God dwelling plentifully in all, they may worship Him in an acceptable manner;[21] and, through patience and comfort of the Scriptures, may have hope.[22]

IX. The infallible rule of interpretation of Scripture is the Scripture itself: and therefore, when there is a question about the true and full sense of any Scripture (which is not manifold, but one), it must be searched and known by other places that speak more clearly.[23]

X. The supreme judge by which all controversies of religion are to be determined, and all decrees of councils, opinions of ancient writers, doctrines of men, and private spirits, are to be examined, and in whose sentence we are to rest, can be no other but the Holy Spirit speaking in the Scripture.[24]

[1]Rom. 2:14-15, Rom. 1:19-20, Ps. 9:1-3, Rom. 1:32, Rom. 2:1, [2]1 Cor. 1:21, 1 Cor. 2:13-14. [3]Heb. 1:1, [4]Prov. 22:19-21, Luke 1:3-4, Rom. 15:4, Matt. 4:4, 7, 10, Isa. 8:19, 20. [5]2 Tim. 3:15, 2 Peter 1:19. [6]Heb. 1:1-2. [7]Luke 16:29, 31, Eph. 2:20, Rev. 22:18-19. 2 Tim. 3:16. [8]Luke 24:27, 44, Rom. 3:2, 2 Peter 1:21 [9]2 Peter 1:19, 21, 2 Tim. 3:16, 1 John 5:9. 1 Thess. 2:13. [10]1 Tim. 3:15. [11]1 John 2:20, 27, John 16:13-14, 1 Cor. 2:10-12, Isa. 59:21. [12]2 Tim. 3:15-17, Gal. 1:8-9, 2 Thess. 2:2. [13]John 6:45, 1 Cor. 2:9-12. [14]1 Cor. 11:13-14,

1 Cor. 14:26, 40.[15]2 Peter 3:16.[16]Ps. 119:105, 130.[17]Matt. 5:18.[18]Isa. 8:20. Acts 15:15. John 5:39, 46.[19]John 5:39.[20]1 Cor. 14:6, 9, 11-12, 24, 27-28.[21]Col. 3:16.[22]Rom. 15:4. [23]2 Peter 1:20-21, Acts 15:15-16. [24]Matt. 22:29, 31. Eph. 2:20, Acts 28:25.

CHAPTER 2

Of God, and of the Holy Trinity

I. There is but one only,[1] living, and true God,[2] who is infinite in being and perfection,[3] a most pure spirit,[4] invisible,[5] without body, parts,[6] or passions;[7] immutable,[8] immense,[9] eternal,[10] incomprehensible,[11] almighty,[12] most wise,[13] most holy,[14] most free,[15] most absolute;[16] working all things according to the counsel of His own immutable and most righteous will,[17] for His own glory;[18] most loving,[19] gracious, merciful, long-suffering, abundant in goodness and truth, forgiving iniquity, transgression, and sin;[20] the rewarder of them that diligently seek Him;[21] and withal, most just, and terrible in His judgments,[22] hating all sin,[23] and who will by no means clear the guilty.[24]

II. God hath all life,[25] glory,[26] goodness,[27] blessedness,[28] in and of Himself; and is alone in and unto Himself all-sufficient, not standing in need of any creatures which he hath made,[29] nor deriving any glory from them,[30] but only manifesting His own glory in, by, unto, and upon them. He is the alone fountain of all being, of whom, through whom, and to whom are all things;[31] and hath most sovereign dominion over them, to do by them, for them, or upon them whatsoever Himself pleaseth.[32] In His sight all things are open and manifest,[33] His knowledge is infinite, infallible, and independent upon the creature,[34] so as nothing is to Him contingent, or uncertain.[35] He is most holy in all His counsels, in all His works, and in all His commands.[36] To Him is due from angels and men, and every other creature, whatsoever worship, service, or obedience he is pleased to require of them.[37]

III. In the unity of the Godhead there be three persons, of one substance, power, and eternity: God the Father, God the Son, and God the Holy Ghost:[38] the Father is of none, neither begotten, nor proceeding; the Son is eternally begotten of the Father;[39] the Holy Ghost eternally proceeding from the Father and the Son.[40]

[1]Deut. 6:4, 1 Cor. 8:4, 6.[2]1 Thess. 1:9, Jer. 10:10. [3]Job 11:7-9, Job 26:14.[4]John 4:24.[5]1 Tim. 1:17. [6]Deut. 4:15-16, John 4:24. Luke 24:39.[7]Acts 14:11, 15.[8]James 1:17, Mal. 3:6.[9]1 Kings 8:27, Jer. 23:23-24.[10]Ps. 90:2, 1 Tim. 1:17.[11]Ps. 145:3. [12]Gen. 17:1, Rev. 4:8.[13]Rom. 16:27.[14]Isa. 6:3, Rev. 4:8.[15]Ps. 115:3.[16]Exod. 3:14.[17]Eph. 1:11. [18]Prov. 16:4. Rom. 11:36.[19]1 John 4:8, 16. [20]Exod. 34:6-7,[21]Heb. 11:6.[22]Neh. 9:32-33. [23]Ps. 5:5-6.[24]Nahum 1:2-3. Exod. 34:7.[25]John 5:26. [26]Acts 7:2.[27]Ps. 119:68.[28]1 Tim. 6:15. Rom. 9:5. [29]Acts 17:24-25.[30]Job 22:2-3.[31]Rom. 11:36. [32]Rev. 4:11, 1 Tim. 6:15. Dan. 4:25, 35.[33]Heb. 4:13. [34]Rom. 11:33-34. Ps. 147:5.[35]Acts 15:18, Ezek. 11:5.[36]Ps. 145:17. Rom. 7:12.[37]Rev. 5:12-14. [38]1 John 5:7. Matt. 3:16-17. Matt. 28:19. 2 Cor. 13:14.[39]John 1:14, 18.[40]John 15:26. Gal. 4:6.

CHAPTER 3

Of God's Eternal Decree

I. God, from all eternity, did, by the most wise and holy counsel of His own will, freely, and unchangeably ordain whatsoever comes to pass:[1] yet so as thereby neither is God the author of sin,[2] nor is violence offered to the will of the creatures; nor is the liberty or contingency of second causes taken away, but rather established.[3]

II. Although God knows whatsoever may or can come to pass upon all supposed conditions,[4] yet hath he not decreed anything because he foresaw it as future, or as that which would come to pass upon such conditions.[5]

III. By the decree of God, for the manifestation of His glory, some men and angels[6] are predestinated unto everlasting life; and others foreordained to everlasting death.[7]

IV. These angels and men, thus predestinated, and foreordained, are particularly and unchangeably designed, and their number so certain and definite, that it cannot be either increased or diminished.[8]

V. Those of mankind that are predestinated unto life, God, before the foundation of the world was laid, according to His eternal and immutable purpose, and the secret counsel and good pleasure of His will, hath chosen, in Christ, unto everlasting glory,[9] out of His mere free grace and love, without any foresight of faith, or good works, or perseverance in either of them, or any other thing in the creature, as conditions, or causes moving Him thereunto;[10] and all to the praise of His glorious grace.[11]

VI. As God hath appointed the elect unto glory, so hath he, by the eternal and most free purpose of His will, foreordained all the means thereunto.[12] Wherefore, they who are elected, being fallen in Adam, are redeemed by Christ,[13] are effectually called unto faith in Christ by His Spirit working in due season, are justified, adopted, sanctified,[14] and kept by His power, through faith, unto salvation.[15] Neither are any other redeemed by Christ, effectually called, justified, adopted, sanctified, and saved, but the elect only.[16]

VII. The rest of mankind God was pleased, according to the unsearchable counsel of his own will, whereby he extendeth or withholdeth mercy, as he pleaseth, for the glory of his sovereign power over his creatures, to pass by; and to ordain them to dishonor and wrath for their sin, to the praise of his glorious justice.[17]

VIII. The doctrine of this high mystery of predestination is to be handled with special prudence and care,[18] that men, attending the will of God revealed in his Word, and yielding obedience thereunto, may, from the certainty of their effectual vocation, be assured of their eternal election.[19] So shall this doctrine afford matter of praise, reverence, and admiration of God;[20] and of humility, diligence, and abundant consolation to all that sincerely obey the gospel.[21]

[1]Eph. 1:11. Rom. 11:33. Heb. 6:17. Rom. 9:15, 18. [2]James 1:13, 17. 1 John 1:5. [3]Acts 2:23. Matt. 17:12. Acts 4:27-28. John 19:11. Prov. 16:33. [4]Acts 15:18. 1 Sam. 23:11-12. Matt. 11:21, 23. [5]Rom. 9:11, 13, 16, 18. [6]1 Tim. 5:21. Matt. 25:41. [7]Rom. 9:22-23. Eph. 1:5-6. Prov. 16:4. [8]2 Tim. 2:19. John 13:18. [9]Eph. 1:4, 9, 11. Rom. 8:30. 2 Tim. 1:9. 1 Thess. 5:9. [10]Rom. 9:11, 13, 16. Eph. 1:4, 9. [11]Eph. 1:6, 12. [12]1 Peter 1:2. Eph. 1:4, 5. Eph. 2:10. 2 Thess. 2:13. [13]1 Thess. 5:9-10. Titus 2:14. [14]Rom. 8:30. Eph. 1:5. 2 Thess. 2:13. [15]1 Peter 1:5. [16]John 17:9. Rom. 8:28. John 6:64-65. John 10:26. John 8:47. 1 John 2:19. [17]Matt. 11:25-26. Rom. 9:17-18, 21-22. 2 Tim. 2:19-20. Jude 4. 1 Peter 2:8. [18]Rom. 9:20. Rom. 11:33. Deut. 29:29. [19]2 Peter 1:10. [20]Eph. 1:6. Rom. 11:33. [21]Rom. 11:5-6, 20. 2 Peter 1:10. Rom. 8:3. Luke 10:20.

CHAPTER 4
Of Creation

I. It pleased God the Father, Son, and Holy Ghost,[1] for the manifestation of the glory of his eternal power, wisdom, and goodness,[2] in the beginning, to create, or make of nothing, the world, and all things therein whether visible or invisible, in the space of six days; and all very good.[3]

II. After God had made all other creatures, he created man, male and female,[4] with reasonable and immortal souls,[5] endued with knowledge, righteousness, and true holiness, after his own image;[6] having the law of God written in their hearts,[7] and power to fulfill it:[8] and yet under a possibility of transgressing, being left to the liberty of their own will, which was subject unto change.[9] Beside this law written in their hearts, they received a command, not to eat of the tree of the knowledge of good and evil;[10] which while they kept, they were happy in their communion with God, and had dominion over the creatures.[11]

[1]Heb. 1:2. John 1:2-3. Gen. 1:2. Job 26:13. Job 33:4. [2]Rom. 1:20. Jer. 10:12. Ps. 104:24. Ps. 33:5-6. [3]Gen. 1. Heb. 11:3. Col. 1:16. Acts 17:24. [4]Gen. 1:27. [5]Gen. 2:7. Eccles. 12:7. Luke 23:43. Matt. 10:28. [6]Gen. 1:26. Col. 3:10. Eph. 4:24. [7]Rom. 2:14-15. [8]Eccles. 7:29. [9]Gen. 3:6. Eccles. 7:29. [10]Gen. 2:17. Gen. 3:8 11, 23. [11]Gen. 1:26, 28.

CHAPTER 5
Of Providence

I. God the great Creator of all things doth uphold,[1] direct, dispose, and govern all creatures, actions, and things,[2] from the greatest even to the least,[3] by his most wise and holy providence,[4] according to his infallible foreknowledge,[5] and the free and immutable counsel of his own will,[6] to the praise of the glory of his wisdom, power, justice, goodness, and mercy.[7]

II. Although, in relation to the foreknowledge and decree of God, the first Cause, all things come to pass immutably, and infallibly;[8] yet, by the same providence, he ordereth them to fall out, according to the nature of second causes, either necessarily, freely, or contingently.[9]

III. God, in his ordinary providence, maketh use of means,[10] yet is free to work without,[11] above,[12] and against them,[13] at his pleasure.

IV. The almighty power, unsearchable wisdom, and infinite goodness of God so far manifest themselves in his providence, that it extendeth itself even to the first fall, and all other sins of angels and men;[14] and that not by a bare permission,[15] but such as hath joined with it a most wise and powerful bounding,[16] and otherwise ordering, and governing of them, in a manifold dispensation, to his own holy ends;[17] yet so as the sinfulness thereof proceedeth only from the creature, and not from God, who, being most holy and righteous, neither is nor can be the author or approver of sin.[18]

V. The most wise, righteous, and gracious God doth oftentimes leave, for a season, his own children to manifold temptations, and the corruption of their own hearts, to chastise them for their former sins, or to discover unto them the hidden strength of corruption and deceitfulness of their hearts, that they may be humbled;[19] and, to raise them to a more close and constant dependence for their support upon Himself, and to make them more watchful against all future occasions of sin, and for sundry other just and holy ends.[20]

VI. As for those wicked and ungodly men whom God, as a righteous Judge, for former sins, doth blind and harden,[21] from them he not only withholdeth his grace whereby they might have been enlightened in their understandings, and wrought upon in their hearts;[22] but sometimes also withdraweth the gifts which they had,[23] and exposeth them to such objects as their corruption makes occasions of sin;[24] and, withal, gives them over to their own lusts, the temptations of the world, and the power of Satan,[25] whereby it comes to pass that they harden themselves, even under those means which God useth for the softening of others.[26]

VII. As the providence of God doth, in general, reach to all creatures; so, after a most special manner it taketh care of his church, and disposeth all things to the good thereof.[27]

[1]Heb. 1:3. [2]Dan. 4:34-35. Ps. 135:6. Acts 17:25-28. Job 38-41. [3]Matt. 10:29-31. [4]Prov. 15:3. Ps. 104:24. Ps. 145:17. [5]Acts 15:18. Ps. 94:8-11. [6]Eph. 1:11. Ps. 33:10-11. [7]Isa. 63:14. Eph. 3:10. Rom. 9:17. Gen. 45:7. Ps. 145:7. [8]Acts 2:23. [9]Gen. 8:22. Jer. 31:35. Exod. 21:13. Deut. 19:5. 1 Kings 22:28, 34. Isa. 10:6-7. [10]Acts 27:31, 44. Isa. 55:10-11. Hosea 2:21-22. [11]Hosea 1:7. Matt. 4:4. Job 34:10. [12]Rom. 4:19-21. [13]2 Kings 6:6. Dan. 3:27. [14]Rom. 11:32-34. 2 Sam. 24:1. 1 Chron. 21:1. 1 Kings 22:22-23. 1 Chron. 10:4. 2 Sam. 16:10. Acts 2:23. Acts 4:27-28. [15]Acts 14:16. [16]Ps. 76:10. 2 Kings 19:28. [17]Gen. 50:20. Isa. 10:6-7, 12. [18]James 1:13-14, 17. 1 John 2:16. Ps. 50:21. [19]2 Chron. 32:25-26, 31. 2 Sam. 24:1. [20]2 Cor. 12:7-9. Ps. 77:1, 10, 12. Mark 14:66-72. John 21:15-17. [21]Rom. 1:24, 26, 28. Rom. 11:7-8. [22]Deut. 29:4. [23]Matt. 13:12. Matt. 25:29. [24]Deut. 2:30. 2 Kings 8:12-13. [25]Ps. 81:11-12. 2 Thess. 2:10-12. [26]Exod. 7:3. Exod. 8:15, 32. 2 Cor. 2:15-16. Isa. 8:14. 1 Peter 2:7-8. Isa. 6:9-10. Acts 28:26-27. [27]1 Tim. 4:10. Amos 9:8-9. Rom. 8:28. Isa. 43:3-5, 14.

CHAPTER 6

Of the Fall of Man, of Sin, and of the Punishment Thereof

I. Our first parents, being seduced by the subtlety and temptation of Satan, sinned, in eating the forbidden fruit.[1] This their sin, God was pleased, according to his wise and holy counsel, to permit, having purposed to order it to his own glory.[2]

II. By this sin they fell from their original righteousness and communion with God,[3] and so became dead in sin,[4] and wholly defiled in all the parts and faculties of soul and body.[5]

III. They being the root of all mankind, the guilt of this sin was imputed;[6] and the same death in sin, and corrupted nature, conveyed to all their posterity descending from them by ordinary generation.[7]

IV. From this original corruption, whereby we are utterly indisposed, disabled, and made opposite to all good,[8] and wholly inclined to all evil,[9] do proceed all actual transgressions.[10]

V. This corruption of nature, during this life, doth remain in those that are regenerated;[11] and although it be, through Christ, pardoned, and mortified; yet both itself, and all the motions thereof, are truly and properly sin.[12]

VI. Every sin, both original and actual, being a transgression of the righteous law of God, and contrary thereunto,[13] doth, in its own nature, bring guilt upon the sinner,[14] whereby he is bound over to the wrath of God,[15] and curse of the law,[16] and so made subject to death,[17] with all miseries spiritual,[18] temporal,[19] and eternal.[20]

[1]Gen. 3:13. 2 Cor. 11:3. [2]Rom. 11:32. [3]Gen. 3:6-8. Eccles. 7:29. Rom. 3:23. [4]Gen. 2:17. Eph. 2:1. [5]Titus 1:15. Gen. 6:5. Jer. 17:9. Rom. 3:10-18. [6]Gen. 1:27-28. Gen. 2:16-17. Acts 17:26. Rom. 5:12, 15-19. 1 Cor. 15:21-22, 45, 49. [7]Ps. 51:5. Gen. 5:3. Job 14:4. Job 15:14. [8]Rom. 5:6. Rom. 8:7. Rom. 7:18. Col. 1:21. [9]Gen. 6:5. Gen. 8:21. Rom. 3:10-12. [10]James 1:14-15. Eph. 2:2-3. Matt. 15:19. [11]1 John 1:8, 10. Rom. 7:14, 17-18, 23. James 3:2. Prov. 20:9. Eccles. 7:20. [12]Rom. 7:5, 7-8, 25. Gal. 5:17. [13]1 John 3:4. [14]Rom. 2:15. Rom. 3:9, 19. [15]Eph. 2:3. [16]Gal. 3:10. [17]Rom. 6:23. [18]Eph. 4:18. [19]Rom. 8:20. Lam. 3:39. [20]Matt. 25:41. 2 Thess. 1:9.

CHAPTER 7

Of God's Covenant with Man

I. The distance between God and the creature is so great, that although reasonable creatures do owe obedience unto Him as their Creator, yet they could never have any fruition of Him as their blessedness and reward, but by some voluntary condescension on God's part, which he hath been pleased to express by way of covenant.[1]

II. The first covenant made with man was a covenant of works,[2] wherein life was promised to Adam; and in him to his posterity,[3] upon condition of perfect and personal obedience.[4]

III. Man, by his fall, having made himself incapable of life by that covenant, the Lord was pleased to make a second,[5] commonly called the covenant of grace; wherein he freely offereth unto sinners life and salvation by Jesus Christ; requiring of them faith in Him, that they may be saved,[6] and promising to give unto all those that are ordained unto eternal life his Holy Spirit, to make them willing, and able to believe.[7]

IV. This covenant of grace is frequently set forth in Scripture by the name of a testament, in reference to the death of Jesus Christ the Testator, and to the everlasting inheritance, with all things belonging to it, therein bequeathed.[8]

V. This covenant was differently administered in the time of the law, and in the time of the gospel:[9] under the law, it was administered by promises, prophecies, sacrifices, circumcision, the paschal lamb, and other types and ordinances delivered to the people of the Jews, all foresignifying Christ to come;[10] which were, for that time, sufficient and efficacious, through the operation of the Spirit, to instruct and build up the elect in faith in the promised Messiah,[11] by whom they had full remission of sins, and eternal salvation; and is called the old testament.[12]

VI. Under the gospel, when Christ, the substance,[13] was exhibited, the ordinances in which this covenant is dispensed are the preaching of the Word, and the administration of the sacraments of baptism and the Lord's Supper:[14] which, though fewer in number, and administered with more simplicity, and less outward glory, yet, in them, it is held forth in more fullness, evidence and spiritual efficacy,[15] to all nations, both Jews and Gentiles;[16] and is called the new testament.[17] There are not therefore two covenants of grace, differing in substance, but one and the same, under various dispensations.[18]

[1]Isa. 40:13-17. Job 9:32-33. 1 Sam. 2:25. Ps. 113:5-6. Ps. 100:2-3. Job 22:2-3. Job 35:7-8. Luke 17:10 Acts 17:24-25. [2]Gal. 3:12. [3]Rom. 10:5. Rom. 5:12-20. [4]Gen. 2:17. Gal. 3:10. [5]Gal. 3:21. Rom. 8:3. Rom. 3:20-21. Gen. 3:15. Isa. 42:6. [6]Mark 16:15-16. John 3:16. Rom. 10:6,9. Gal. 3:11. [7]Ezek. 36:26-27. John 6:44-45. [8]Heb. 9:15-17. Heb. 7:22. Luke 22:20. 1 Cor. 11:25. [9]2 Cor. 3:6-9. [10]Heb. 8-10. Rom. 4:11. Col. 2:11-12. 1 Cor. 5:7. [11]1 Cor. 10:1-4. Heb. 11:13. John 8:56. [12]Gal. 3:7-9, 14. [13]Col. 2:17. [14]Matt. 28:19-20. 1 Cor. 11:23-25. [15]Heb. 12:22-27. Jer. 31:33-34. [16]Matt. 28:19. Eph. 2:15-19. [17]Luke 22:20. [18]Gal. 3:14, 16. Acts 15:11. Rom. 3:21-23, 30. Ps. 32:1. Rom. 4:3, 6, 16-17, 23-24. Heb. 13:8.

CHAPTER 8

Of Christ the Mediator

I. It pleased God, in his eternal purpose, to choose and ordain the Lord Jesus, his only begotten Son, to be the Mediator between

God and man,[1] the Prophet,[2] Priest,[3] and King,[4] the Head and Savior of his church,[5] the Heir of all things,[6] and Judge of the world:[7] unto whom he did from all eternity give a people, to be his seed,[8] and to be by Him in time redeemed, called, justified, sanctified, and glorified.[9]

II. The Son of God, the second person in the Trinity, being very and eternal God, of one substance and equal with the Father, did, when the fullness of time was come, take upon Him man's nature,[10] with all the essential properties, and common infirmities thereof, yet without sin;[11] being conceived by the power of the Holy Ghost, in the womb of the virgin Mary, of her substance.[12] So that two whole, perfect, and distinct natures, the Godhead and the manhood, were inseparably joined together in one person, without conversion, composition, or confusion.[13] Which person is very God, and very man, yet one Christ, the only Mediator between God and man.[14]

III. The Lord Jesus, in his human nature thus united to the divine, was sanctified, and anointed with the Holy Spirit, above measure,[15] having in Him all the treasures of wisdom and knowledge;[16] in whom it pleased the Father that all fullness should dwell;[17] to the end that, being holy, harmless, undefiled, and full of grace and truth,[18] he might be thoroughly furnished to execute the office of a mediator, and surety. Which office he took not unto Himself, but was thereunto called by his Father,[19] who put all power and judgment into his hand, and gave Him commandment to execute the same.[20]

IV. This office the Lord Jesus did most willingly undertake;[21] which that he might discharge, he was made under the law,[22] and did perfectly fulfill it;[23] endured most grievous torments immediately in his soul,[24] and most painful sufferings in his body;[25] was crucified, and died,[26] was buried, and remained under the power of death, yet saw no corruption.[27] On the third day he arose from the dead,[28] with the same body in which he suffered,[29] with which also he ascended into heaven, and there sitteth at the right hand of his Father,[30] making intercession,[31] and shall return, to judge men and angels, at the end of the world.[32]

V. The Lord Jesus, by his perfect obedience, and sacrifice of Himself, which he, through the eternal Spirit, once offered up unto God, hath fully satisfied the justice of his Father;[33] and purchased, not only reconciliation, but an everlasting inheritance in the kingdom of heaven, for all those whom the Father hath given unto Him.[34]

VI. Although the work of redemption was not actually wrought by Christ till after his incarnation, yet the virtue, efficacy, and benefits thereof were communicated unto the elect, in all ages successively from the beginning of the world, in and by those promises, types, and sacrifices, wherein he was revealed, and signified to be the seed of the woman which should bruise the serpent's head; and the Lamb slain from the beginning of the world; being yesterday and today the same, and forever.[35]

VII. Christ, in the work of mediation, acts according to both natures, by each nature doing that which is proper to itself;[36] yet, by reason of the unity of the person, that which is proper to one nature is sometimes in Scripture attributed to the person denominated by the other nature.[37]

VIII. To all those for whom Christ hath purchased redemption, he doth certainly and effectually apply and communicate the same;[38] making intercession for them,[39] and revealing unto them, in and by the Word, the mysteries of salvation;[40] effectually persuading them by his Spirit to believe and obey, and governing their hearts by his Word and Spirit;[41] overcoming all their enemies by his almighty power and wisdom, in such manner, and ways, as are most consonant to his wonderful and unsearchable dispensation.[42]

[1]Isa. 42:1. 1 Peter 1:19-20. John 3:16. 1 Tim. 2:5. [2]Acts 3:22. [3]Heb. 5:5-6. [4]Ps. 2:6. Luke 1:33. [5]Eph. 5:23. [6]Heb. 1:2. [7]Acts 17:31. [8]John 17:6. Ps. 22:30. Isa. 53:10. [9]1 Tim. 2:6. Isa. 55:4-5. 1 Cor. 1:30. [10]John 1:1, 14. 1 John 5:20. Phil. 2:6. Gal. 4:4. [11]Heb. 2:14, 16-17. Heb. 4:15. [12]Luke 1:27, 31, 35. Gal. 4:4. [13]Luke 1:35. Col. 2:9. Rom. 9:5. 1 Peter 3:18. 1 Tim. 3:16. [14]Rom. 1:3. Rom. 1:4. 1 Tim. 2:5. [15]Ps. 45:7. John 3:34. [16]Col. 2:3. [17]Col. 1:19. [18]Heb. 7:26. John 1:14. [19]Acts 10:38. Heb. 12:24. Heb. 7:22. [20]Heb. 5:4-5. [21]John 5:22, 27. Matt. 28:18.

Acts 2:36. [22]Ps. 40:7-8. Heb. 10:5-10. John 10:18. Phil. 2:8. [23]Gal. 4:4. [24]Matt. 3:15. Matt. 5:17. [25]Matt. 26:37-38. Luke 22:44. Matt. 27:46. [26]Matt. 26-27. [27]Phil. 2:8. [28]Acts 2:23-24, 27. Acts 13:37. Rom. 6:9. [29]1 Cor. 15:3-4. [30]John 20:25, 27. [31]Mark 16:19. [32]Rom. 8:34. Heb. 9:24. Heb. 7:25. [33]Rom. 14:9-10. Acts 1:11. Acts 10:42. Matt. 13:40-42. Jude 6. 2 Peter 2:4. [34]Rom. 5:19. Heb. 9:14, 16. Heb. 10:14. Eph. 5:2. Rom. 3:25-26. [196] Dan. 9:24, 26. Col. 1:19-20. Eph. 1:11, 14. John 17:2. Heb. 9:12, 15. [35]Gal. 4:4-5. Gen. 3:15. Rev. 13:8. Heb. 13:8. [36]Heb. 9:14. 1 Peter 3:18. [37]Acts 20:28. John 3:13. 1 John 3:16. [38]John 6:37, 39. John 10:15-16. [39]1 John 2:1-2. Rom. 8:34. [40]John 15:13, 15. Eph. 1:7-9. John 17:6. [41]John 14:16. Heb. 12:2. 2 Cor. 4:13. Rom. 8:9, 14. Rom. 15:18-19. John 17:17. [42]Ps. 110:1. 1 Cor. 15:25-26. Mal. 4:2-3. Col. 2:15.

CHAPTER 9
Of Free Will

I. God hath endued the will of man with that natural liberty, that it is neither forced, nor, by any absolute necessity of nature, determined to good, or evil.[1]

II. Man, in his state of innocency, had freedom, and power to will and to do that which was good and well pleasing to God;[2] but yet, mutably, so that he might fall from it.[3]

III. Man, by his fall into a state of sin, hath wholly lost all ability of will to any spiritual good accompanying salvation:[4] so, as a natural man, being altogether averse from that good,[5] and dead in sin,[6] is not able, by his own strength, to convert himself, or to prepare himself thereunto.[7]

IV. When God converts a sinner, and translates him into the state of grace, he freeth him from his natural bondage under sin;[8] and, by his grace alone, enables him freely to will and to do that which is spiritually good;[9] yet so as that by reason of his remaining corruption, he doth not perfectly, nor only, will that which is good, but doth also will that which is evil.[10]

V. The will of man is made perfectly and immutably free to good alone, in the state of glory only.[11]

[1]Matt. 17:12. James 1:14. Deut. 30:19. [2]Eccles. 7:29. Gen. 1:26. [3]Gen. 2:16-17. Gen. 3:6. [4]Rom. 5:6. Rom. 8:7. John 15:5. [5]Rom. 3:10, 12. [6]Eph. 2:1, 5. Col. 2:13. [7]John 6:44, 65. Eph. 2:2-5. 1 Cor. 2:14. Titus 3:3-5. [8]Col. 1:13. John 8:34, 36. [9]Phil. 2:13. Rom. 6:18, 22. [10] Gal. 5:17. Rom. 7:15, 18-19, 21, 23. [11]Eph. 4:13. Heb. 12:23. 1 John 3:2. Jude 24.

CHAPTER 10
Of Effectual Calling

I. All those whom God hath predestinated unto life, and those only, he is pleased, in his appointed and accepted time, effectually to call,[1] by his Word and Spirit,[2] out of that state of sin and death, in which they are by nature, to grace and salvation, by Jesus Christ;[3] enlightening their minds spiritually and savingly to understand the things of God,[4] taking away their heart of stone, and giving unto them a heart of flesh;[5] renewing their wills, and, by his almighty power, determining them to that which is good,[6] and effectually drawing them to Jesus Christ:[7] yet so as they come most freely, being made willing by his grace.[8]

II. This effectual call is of God's free and special grace alone, not from anything at all foreseen in man,[9] who is altogether passive therein, until, being quickened and renewed by the Holy Spirit,[10] he is thereby enabled to answer this call, and to embrace the grace offered and conveyed in it.[11]

III. Elect infants, dying in infancy, are regenerated, and saved by Christ, through the Spirit,[12] who worketh when, and where, and how he pleaseth:[13] so also are all other elect persons who are incapable of being outwardly called by the ministry of the Word.[14]

IV. Others, not elected, although they may be called by the ministry of the Word,[15] and may have some common operations of the Spirit,[16] yet they never truly come unto Christ, and therefore cannot be saved:[17] much less can men, not professing the Christian religion, be saved in any other way whatsoever, be they never so diligent to frame their lives according to the light of nature, and the laws of that religion they do profess.[18] And, to assert and maintain that they may, is very pernicious, and to be detested.[19]

[1]Rom. 8:30. Rom. 11:7. Eph. 1:10-11. [2]2 Thess. 2:13-14. 2 Cor. 3:3, 6. [3]Rom. 8:2. Eph. 2:1-5. 2 Tim. 1:9-10. [4]Acts 26:18. 1 Cor. 2:10, 12. Eph. 1:17-18. [5]Ezek. 36:26. [6]Ezek. 11:19. Phil. 2:13. Deut. 30:6. Ezek. 36:27. [7]Eph. 1:19. John 6:44-45. [8]Song of Solomon 1:4. Ps. 110:3. John 6:37. Rom. 6:16-18. [9]2 Tim. 1:9. Titus 3:4-5. Eph. 2:4-5, 8-9. Rom. 9:11. [10]1 Cor. 2:14. Rom. 8:7. Eph. 2:5. [11]John 6:37. Ezek. 36:37. John 5:25. [12]Luke 18:15-16. Acts 2:38-39. John 3:3, 5. 1 John 5:12. Rom. 8:9. [13]John 3:8. [14]1 John 5:12. Acts 4:12. [15]Matt. 22:14. [16]Matt. 7:22. Matt. 13:20-21. Heb. 6:4-5. [17]John 6:64-66. John 8:24. [18]Acts 4:12. John 14:6. Eph. 2:12. John 4:22. John 17:3. [19]2 John 9-11. 1 Cor. 16:22. Gal. 1:6-8.

CHAPTER 11
Of Justification

I. Those whom God effectually calleth, he also freely justifieth:[1] not by infusing righteousness into them, but by pardoning their sins, and by accounting and accepting their persons as righteous; not for anything wrought in them, or done by them, but for Christ's sake alone; nor by imputing faith itself, the act of believing, or any other evangelical obedience to them, as their righteousness; but by imputing the obedience and satisfaction of Christ unto them,[2] they receiving and resting on Him and his righteousness, by faith; which faith they have not of themselves, it is the gift of God.[3]

II. Faith, thus receiving and resting on Christ and his righteousness, is the alone instrument of justification:[4] yet is it not alone in the person justified, but is ever accompanied with all other saving graces, and is no dead faith, but worketh by love.[5]

III. Christ, by his obedience and death, did fully discharge the debt of all those that are thus justified, and did make a proper, real, and full satisfaction to his Father's justice in their behalf.[6] Yet, inasmuch as he was given by the Father for them;[7] and his obedience and satisfaction accepted in their stead;[8] and both, freely, not for anything in them; their justification is only of free grace;[9] that both the exact justice and rich grace of God might be glorified in the justification of sinners.[10]

IV. God did, from all eternity, decree to justify all the elect,[11] and Christ did, in the fullness of time, die for their sins, and rise again for their justification:[12] nevertheless, they are not justified, until the Holy Spirit doth, in due time, actually apply Christ unto them.[13]

V. God doth continue to forgive the sins of those that are justified;[14] and, although they can never fall from the state of justification,[15] yet they may, by their sins, fall under God's fatherly displeasure, and not have the light of his countenance restored unto them, until they humble themselves, confess their sins, beg pardon, and renew their faith and repentance.[16]

VI. The justification of believers under the old testament was, in all these respects, one and the same with the justification of believers under the new testament.[17]

[1]Rom. 8:30. Rom. 3:24. [2]Rom. 4:5-8. 2 Cor. 5:19, 21. Rom. 3:22, 24-25, 27-28. Titus 3:5, 7. Eph. 1:7. Jer. 23:6. 1 Cor. 1:30-31. Rom. 5:17-19. [3]Acts 10:44. Gal. 2:16. Phil. 3:9. Acts 13:38-39. Eph. 2:7-8. [4]John 1:12. Rom. 3:28. Rom. 5:1. [5]James 2:17, 22, 26. Gal. 5:6. [6]Rom. 5:8-10, 19. 1 Tim. 2:5-6. Heb. 10:10, 14. Dan. 9:24, 26. Isa. 53:4-6, 10-12. [7]Rom. 8:32. [8]2 Cor. 5:21. Matt. 3:17. Eph. 5:2. [9]Rom. 3:24. Eph. 1:7. [10]Rom. 3:26. Eph. 2:7. [11]Gal. 3:8. 1 Peter 1:2, 19-20. Rom. 8:30. [12]Gal. 4:4. 1 Tim. 2:6. Rom. 4:25. [13]Col. 1:21-22. Gal. 2:16. Titus 3:4-7. [14]Matt. 6:12. 1 John 1:7, 9. 1 John 2:1-2. [15]Luke 22:32. John 10:28. Heb. 10:14. [16]Ps. 89:31-33. Ps. 51:7-12. Ps. 32:5. Matt. 26:75. 1 Cor. 11:30, 32. Luke 1:20. [17]Gal. 3:9, 13-14. Rom. 4:22-24. Heb. 13:8.

CHAPTER 12
Of Adoption

I. All those that are justified, God vouchsafeth, in and for his only Son Jesus Christ, to make partakers of the grace of adoption,[1] by which they are taken into the number, and enjoy the liberties and privileges of the children of God,[2] have his name put upon them,[3] receive the Spirit of adoption,[4] have access to the throne of grace with boldness,[5] are enabled to cry, Abba, Father,[6] are pitied,[7] protected,[8] provided for,[9] and chastened by Him, as by a father:[10] yet never cast off,[11] but sealed to the day of redemption;[12] and inherit the promises,[13] as heirs of everlasting salvation.[14]

[1]Eph. 1:5. Gal. 4:4-5. [2]Rom. 8:17. John 1:12. [3]Jer. 14:9. 2 Cor. 6:18. Rev. 3:12. [4]Rom. 8:15.

[5]Eph. 3:12. Rom. 5:2. [6]Gal. 4:6. [7]Ps. 103:13. [8]Prov. 14:26. [9]Matt. 6:30, 32. 1 Peter 5:7. [10]Heb. 12:6. [11]Lam. 3:31. [12]Eph. 4:30. [13]Heb. 6:12. [14] Peter 1:3-4. Heb. 1:14.

CHAPTER 13
Of Sanctification

I. They, who are once effectually called, and regenerated, having a new heart, and a new spirit created in them, are further sanctified, really and personally, through the virtue of Christ's death and resurrection,[1] by his Word and Spirit dwelling in them:[2] the dominion of the whole body of sin is destroyed,[3] and the several lusts thereof are more and more weakened and mortified;[4] and they more and more quickened and strengthened in all saving graces,[5] to the practice of true holiness, without which no man shall see the Lord.[6]

II. This sanctification is throughout, in the whole man;[7] yet imperfect in this life, there abiding still some remnants of corruption in every part;[8] whence ariseth a continual and irreconcilable war, the flesh lusting against the Spirit, and the Spirit against the flesh.[9]

III. In which war, although the remaining corruption, for a time, may much prevail;[10] yet, through the continual supply of strength from the sanctifying Spirit of Christ, the regenerate part doth overcome;[11] and so, the saints grow in grace,[12] perfecting holiness in the fear of God.[13]

[1]1 Cor. 6:11. Acts 20:32. Phil. 3:10. Rom. 6:5-6. [2]John 17:17. Eph. 5:26. 2 Thess. 2:13. [3]Rom. 6:6, 14. [4]Gal. 5:24. Rom. 8:13. [5]Col. 1:11. Eph. 3:16-19. [6]2 Cor. 7:1. Heb. 12:14. [7]1 Thess. 5:23. [8]1 John 1:10. Rom. 7:18, 23. Phil. 3:12. [9]Gal. 5:17. 1 Peter 2:11. [10]Rom. 7:23. [11]Rom. 6:14. 1 John 5:4. Eph. 4:15-16. [12]2 Peter 3:18. 2 Cor. 3:18. [13]2 Cor. 7:1.

CHAPTER 14
Of Saving Faith

I. The grace of faith, whereby the elect are enabled to believe to the saving of their souls,[1] is the work of the Spirit of Christ in their hearts,[2] and is ordinarily wrought by the ministry of the Word,[3] by which also, and by the administration of the sacraments, and prayer, it is increased and strengthened.[4]

II. By this faith, a Christian believeth to be true whatsoever is revealed in the Word, for the authority of God Himself speaking therein;[5] and acteth differently upon that which each particular passage thereof containeth; yielding obedience to the commands,[6] trembling at the threatenings,[7] and embracing the promises of God for this life, and that which is to come.[8] But the principal acts of saving faith are accepting, receiving, and resting upon Christ alone for justification, sanctification, and eternal life, by virtue of the covenant of grace.[9]

III. This faith is different in degrees, weak or strong;[10] may be often and many ways assailed, and weakened, but gets the victory:[11] growing up in many to the attainment of a full assurance, through Christ,[12] who is both the author and finisher of our faith.[13]

[1]Heb. 10:39. [2]2 Cor. 4:13. Eph. 1:17-19. Eph. 2:8. [3]Rom. 10:14, 17. [4]1 Peter 2:2. Acts 20:32. Rom. 4:11. Luke 17:5. Rom. 1:16-17. [5]John 4:42. 1 Thess. 2:13. 1 John 5:10. Acts 24:14. [6]Rom. 16:26. [7]Isa. 66:2. [8]Heb. 11:13. 1 Tim. 4:8. [9]John 1:12. Acts 16:31. Gal. 2:20. Acts 15:11. [10]Heb. 5:13-14. Rom. 4:19-20. Matt. 6:30. Matt. 8:10. [11]Luke 22:31-32. Eph. 6:16. 1 John 5:4-5. [12]Heb. 6:11-12. Heb. 10:22. [13]Heb. 12:2.

CHAPTER 15
Of Repentance unto Life

I. Repentance unto life is an evangelical grace,[1] the doctrine whereof is to be preached by every minister of the gospel, as well as that of faith in Christ.[2]

II. By it, a sinner, out of the sight and sense not only of the danger, but also of the filthiness and odiousness of his sins, as contrary to the holy nature, and righteous law of God; and upon the apprehension of his mercy in Christ to such as are penitent, so grieves for, and hates his sins, as to turn from them all unto God,[3] purposing and endeavoring to walk with Him in all the ways of his commandments.[4]

III. Although repentance be not to be rested in, as any satisfaction for sin, or any cause of the pardon thereof,[5] which is the act of God's free grace in Christ;[6] yet it is of such necessity to all sinners, that none may expect pardon without it.[7]

IV. As there is no sin so small, but it deserves damnation;[8] so there is no sin so great, that it can bring damnation upon those who truly repent.[9]

V. Men ought not to content themselves with a general repentance, but it is every man's duty to endeavor to repent of his particular sins, particularly.[10]

VI. As every man is bound to make private confession of his sins to God, praying for the pardon thereof;[11] upon which, and the forsaking of them, he shall find mercy;[12] so, he that scandalizeth his brother, or the church of Christ, ought to be willing, by a private or public confession, and sorrow for his sin, to declare his repentance to those that are offended,[13] who are thereupon to be reconciled to Him, and in love to receive Him.[14]

[1]Zech. 12:10. Acts 11:18. [2]Luke 24:47. Mark 1:15. Acts 20:21. Ezek. 18:30-31. Ezek. 36:31. Isa. 30:22. Ps. 51:4. Jer. 31:18-19. Joel 2:12-13. Amos 5:15. Ps. 119:128. 2 Cor. 7:11. [4]Ps. 119:6, 59, 106. Luke 1:6. 2 Kings 23:25. [5]Ezek. 36:31-32. Ezek. 16:61-63. [6]Hosea 14:2, 4. Rom. 3:24. Eph. 1:7. [7]Luke 13:3, 5. Acts 17:30-31. [8]Rom. 6:23. Rom. 5:12. Matt. 12:36. [9]Isa. 55:7. Rom. 8:1. Isa. 1:16, 18. [10]Ps. 19:13. Luke 19:8. 1 Tim. 1:13, 15. [11]Ps. 51:4-5, 7, 9, 14. Ps. 32:5-6. [12]Prov. 28:13. 1 John 1:9. [13]James 5:16. Luke 17:3-4. Josh. 7:19. Ps. 51. [14]2 Cor. 2:8.

CHAPTER 16
Of Good Works

I. Good works are only such as God hath commanded in his holy Word,[1] and not such as, without the warrant thereof, are devised by men, out of blind zeal, or upon any pretense of good intention.[2]

II. These good works, done in obedience to God's commandments, are the fruits and evidences of a true and lively faith:[3] and by them believers manifest their thankfulness,[4] strengthen their assurance,[5] edify their brethren,[6] adorn the profession of the gospel,[7] stop the mouths of the adversaries,[8] and glorify God,[9] whose workmanship they are, created in Christ Jesus thereunto,[10] that, having their fruit unto holiness, they may have the end, eternal life.[11]

III. Their ability to do good works is not at all of themselves, but wholly from the Spirit of Christ.[12] And that they may be enabled thereunto, beside the graces they have already received, there is required an actual influence of the same Holy Spirit, to work in them to will, and to do, of his good pleasure:[13] yet are they not hereupon to grow negligent, as if they were not bound to perform any duty unless upon a special motion of the Spirit; but they ought to be diligent in stirring up the grace of God that is in them.[14]

IV. They who, in their obedience, attain to the greatest height which is possible in this life, are so far from being able to supererogate, and to do more than God requires, as that they fall short of much which in duty they are bound to do.[15]

V. We cannot by our best works merit pardon of sin, or eternal life at the hand of God, by reason of the great disproportion that is between them and the glory to come; and the infinite distance that is between us and God, whom, by them, we can neither profit, nor satisfy for the debt of our former sins,[16] but when we have done all we can, we have done but our duty, and are unprofitable servants:[17] and because, as they are good, they proceed from his Spirit;[18] and as they are wrought by us, they are defiled, and mixed with so much weakness and imperfection, that they cannot endure the severity of God's judgment.[19]

VI. Notwithstanding, the persons of believers being accepted through Christ, their good works also are accepted in Him;[20] not as though they were in this life wholly unblamable and unreprovable in God's sight;[21] but that he, looking upon them in his Son, is pleased to accept and reward that which is sincere, although accompanied with many weaknesses and imperfections.[22]

VII. Works done by unregenerate men, although for the matter of them they may be things which God commands; and of good use both to themselves and others:[23] yet, because they proceed not from an heart purified by faith;[24] nor are done in a right manner, according to the Word;[25] nor to a right end, the glory of God,[26] they are therefore sinful, and cannot please God, or make a man meet to receive grace from God:[27] and yet, their neglect of them is more sinful and displeasing unto God.[28]

[1]Micah 6:8. Rom. 12:2. Heb. 13:21.
[2]Matt. 15:9. Isa. 29:13. 1 Peter 1:18.
Rom. 10:2. John 16:2. 1 Sam. 15:21-23.
[3]James 2:18, 22. [4]Ps. 116:12-13. 1 Peter 2:9.
[5]1 John 2:3, 5. 2 Peter 1:5-10. [6]2 Cor. 9:2.
Matt. 5:16. [7]Titus 2:5, 9-12. 1 Tim. 6:1.
[8]1 Peter 2:15. [9]1 Peter 2:12. Phil. 1:11.
John 15:8. [10]Eph. 2:10. [11]Rom. 6:22.
[12]John 15:4-6. Ezek. 36:26-27. [13]Phil. 2:13.
Phil. 4:13. 2 Cor. 3:5. [14]Phil. 2:12. Heb. 6:11-12.
2 Peter 1:3, 5, 10-11. Isa. 64:7. 2 Tim. 1:6.
Acts 26:6-7. Jude 20-21. [15]Luke 17:10.
Neh. 13:22. Job 9:2-3. Gal. 5:17. [16]Rom. 3:20.
Rom. 4:2, 4, 6. Eph. 2:8-9. Titus 3:5-7. Rom. 8:18.
Ps. 16:2. Job 22:2-3. Job 35:7-8. [17]Luke 17:10.
[18]Gal. 5:22-23. [19]Isa. 64:6. Gal. 5:17.
Rom. 7:15, 18. Ps. 143:2. Ps. 130:3.
[20]Eph. 1:6. 1 Peter 2:5. Exod. 28:38.
Gen. 4:4. Heb. 11:4. [21]Job 9:20. Ps. 143:2.
[22]Heb. 13:20-21. 2 Cor. 8:12. Heb. 6:10.
Matt. 25:21, 23. [23]2 Kings 10:30-31.
1 Kings 21:27, 29. Phil. 1:15. Phil. 1:16, 18.
[24]Gen. 4:5. Heb. 11:4, 6. [25]1 Cor. 13:3. Isa. 1:12.
[26]Matt. 6:2, 5, 16. [27]Haggai 2:14. Titus 1:15.
Amos 5:21-22. Hosea 1:4. Rom. 9:16.
Titus 3:15. [28]Ps. 14:4. Ps. 36:3. Job 21:14-15.
Matt. 25:41-43, 45. Matt. 23:23.

CHAPTER 17
Of the Perseverance of the Saints

I. They, whom God hath accepted in his Beloved, effectually called, and sanctified by his Spirit, can neither totally nor finally fall away from the state of grace, but shall certainly persevere therein to the end, and be eternally saved.[1]

II. This perseverance of the saints depends not upon their own free will, but upon the immutability of the decree of election, flowing from the free and unchangeable love of God the Father;[2] upon the efficacy of the merit and intercession of Jesus Christ,[3] the abiding of the Spirit, and of the seed of God within them,[4] and the nature of the covenant of grace:[5] from all which ariseth also the certainty and infallibility thereof.[6]

III. Nevertheless, they may, through the temptations of Satan and of the world, the prevalency of corruption remaining in them, and the neglect of the means of their preservation, fall into grievous sins;[7] and, for a time, continue therein:[8] whereby they incur God's displeasure,[9] and grieve his Holy Spirit,[10] come to be deprived of some measure of their graces and comforts,[11] have their hearts hardened,[12] and their consciences wounded;[13] hurt and scandalize others,[14] and bring temporal judgments upon themselves.[15]

[1]Phil. 1:6. 2 Peter 1:10. John 10:28-29.
1 John 3:9. 1 Peter 1:5, 9. [2]2 Tim. 2:18-19.
Jer. 31:3. [3]Heb. 10:10, 14. Heb. 13:20-21.
Heb. 9:12-15. Rom. 8:33-39. John 17:11, 24.
Luke 22:32. Heb. 7:25. [4]John 14:16-17.
1 John 2:27. 1 John 3:9. [5]Jer. 32:40. [6]John 10:28.
2 Thess. 3:3. 1 John 2:19. [7]Matt. 26:70, 72, 74.
[8]Ps. 51 (title). Ps. 51:14. [9]Isa. 64:5, 7, 9.
2 Sam. 11:27. [10]Eph. 4:30. [11]Ps. 51:8, 10, 12.
Rev. 2:4. Song of Solomon 5:2-4, 6. [12]Isa. 63:17.
Mark 6:52. Mark 16:14. [13]Ps. 32:3-4. Ps. 51:8.
[14]2 Sam. 12:14. [15]Ps. 89:31-32. 1 Cor. 11:32.

CHAPTER 18
Of the Assurance of Grace and Salvation

I. Although hypocrites and other unregenerate men may vainly deceive themselves with false hopes and carnal presumptions of being in the favor of God, and estate of salvation[1] (which hope of theirs shall perish):[2] yet such as truly believe in the Lord Jesus, and love Him in sincerity, endeavoring to walk in all good conscience before Him, may, in this life, be certainly assured that they are in the state of grace,[3] and may rejoice in the hope of the glory of God, which hope shall never make them ashamed.[4]

II. This certainty is not a bare conjectural and probable persuasion grounded upon a fallible hope;[5] but an infallible assurance of faith founded upon the divine truth of the promises of salvation,[6] the inward evidence of those graces unto which these promises are made,[7] the testimony of the Spirit of adoption witnessing with our spirits that we are the children of God,[8] which Spirit is the earnest of our inheritance, whereby we are sealed to the day of redemption.[9]

III. This infallible assurance doth not so belong to the essence of faith, but that a true believer may wait long, and conflict with many difficulties before he be partaker of it:[10] yet, being enabled by the Spirit to know the things which are freely given him of God, he may, without extraordinary revelation, in the right use of ordinary means, attain thereunto.[11] And therefore it is the duty of everyone to give all diligence to make his calling and election sure,[12] that thereby his heart may be enlarged in peace and joy in the Holy Ghost, in love and thankfulness to God, and in strength and cheerfulness in the duties of obedience,[13] the proper fruits of this assurance; so far is it from inclining men to looseness.[14]

IV. True believers may have the assurance of their salvation divers ways shaken, diminished, and intermitted; as, by negligence in preserving of it, by falling into some special sin which woundeth the conscience and grieveth the Spirit; by some sudden or vehement temptation, by God's withdrawing the light of his countenance, and suffering even such as fear Him to walk in darkness and to have no light:[15] yet are they never utterly destitute of that seed of God, and life of faith, that love of Christ and the brethren, that sincerity of heart, and conscience of duty, out of which, by the operation of the Spirit, this assurance may, in due time, be revived;[16] and by the which, in the meantime, they are supported from utter despair.[17]

[1]Job 8:13-14. Micah 3:11. Deut. 29:19. John 8:41. [2]Matt. 7:22-23. [3]1 John 2:3. 1 John 3:14, 18-19, 21, 24. 1 John 5:13. [4]Rom. 5:2, 5. [5]Heb. 6:11, 19. [6]Heb. 6:17-18. [7]2 Peter 1:4-5, 10-11. 1 John 2:3. 1 John 3:14. 2 Cor. 1:12. [8]Rom. 8:15-16. Eph. 1:13-14. Eph. 4:30. 2 Cor. 1:21-22. [10]1 John 5:13. Isa. 50:10. Mark 9:24. Ps. 88. Ps. 77:1-12. [11]1 Cor. 2:12. 1 John 4:13. Heb. 6:11-12. Eph. 3:17-19. [12]2 Peter 1:10. [13]Rom. 5:1-2, 5. Rom. 14:17. Rom. 15:13. Eph. 1:3-4. Ps. 4:6-7. Ps. 119:32. [14]1 John 2:1-2. Rom. 6:1-2. Titus 2:11-12, 14. 2 Cor. 7:1. Rom. 8:1, 12. 1 John 3:2-3. Ps. 130:4. 1 John 1:6-7. [15]Song of Solomon 5:2-3, 6. Ps. 51:8, 12, 14. Eph. 4:30-31. Ps. 77:1-10. Matt. 26:69-72. Ps. 31:22. Ps. 88. Isa. 50:10. [16]1 John 3:9. Luke 22:32. Job 13:15. Ps. 73:15. Ps. 51:8, 12. Isa. 50:10. [17]Micah 7:7-9. Jer. 32:40. Isa. 54:7-10. Ps. 22:1. Ps. 88.

CHAPTER 19
Of the Law of God

I. God gave to Adam a law, as a covenant of works, by which he bound him and all his posterity to personal, entire, exact, and perpetual obedience, promised life upon the fulfilling, and threatened death upon the breach of it, and endued him with power and ability to keep it.[1]

II. This law, after his fall, continued to be a perfect rule of righteousness; and, as such, was delivered by God upon Mount Sinai, in ten commandments, and written in two tables:[2] the first four commandments containing our duty towards God; and the other six, our duty to man.[3]

III. Beside this law, commonly called moral, God was pleased to give to the people of Israel, as a church under age, ceremonial laws, containing several typical ordinances, partly of worship, prefiguring Christ, his graces, actions, sufferings, and benefits;[4] and partly, holding forth divers instructions of moral duties.[5] All which ceremonial laws are now abrogated, under the new testament.[6]

IV. To them also, as a body politic, he gave sundry judicial laws, which expired together with the State of that people; not obliging any other now, further than the general equity thereof may require.[7]

V. The moral law doth forever bind all, as well justified persons as others, to the obedience thereof;[8] and that, not only in regard of the matter contained in it, but also in respect of the authority of God the Creator, who gave it.[9] Neither doth Christ, in the gospel, any way dissolve, but much strengthen this obligation.[10]

VI. Although true believers be not under the law, as a covenant of works, to be thereby justified, or condemned;[11] yet is it of great use to them, as well as to others; in that, as a rule of life informing them of the will of God, and their duty, it directs and binds them to walk accordingly;[12] discovering also the sinful pollutions of their nature, hearts, and lives;[13] so as, examining themselves thereby, they may come to further conviction of, humiliation for, and hatred against sin,[14] together with a clearer sight of the need they have of Christ, and the perfection of his obedience.[15] It is likewise of use to the regenerate, to restrain their corruptions, in that it forbids sin:[16] and the threatenings of it serve to show what even their sins deserve; and what afflictions, in this life, they may expect for them, although freed from the curse thereof threatened in the law.[17] The promises of it, in like manner, show them God's approbation of obedience, and what blessings they may expect upon the performance thereof:[18] although not as due to them by the law as a covenant of works.[19] So as, a man's doing good, and refraining from evil, because the law encourageth to the one, and deterreth from the other, is no evidence of his being under the law; and not under grace.[20]

VII. Neither are the forementioned uses of the law contrary to the grace of the gospel, but do sweetly comply with it;[21] the Spirit of Christ subduing and enabling the will of man to do that freely, and cheerfully, which the will of God, revealed in the law, requireth to be done.[22]

[1]Gen. 1:26-27. Gen. 2:17. Rom. 2:14-15. Rom. 10:5. Rom. 5:12, 19. Gal. 3:10, 12. Eccles. 7:29. Job 28:28. [2]James 1:25. James 2:8, 10-12. Rom. 13:8-9. Deut. 5:32. Deut. 10:4. Exod. 24:1. [3]Matt. 22:37-40. [4]Heb. 9. Heb. 10:1. Gal. 4:1-3. Col. 2:17. [5]1 Cor. 5:7. 2 Cor. 6:17. Jude 23. [6]Col. 2:14, 16-17. Dan. 9:27. Eph. 2:15-16. [7]Exod. 21:1–22:29. Gen. 49:10. 1 Peter 2:13-14. Matt. 5:17, 38-39. 1 Cor. 9:8-10. [8]Rom. 13:8-10. Eph. 6:2. 1 John 2:3-4, 7-8. [9]James 2:10-11. [10]Matt. 5:17-19. James 2:8. Rom. 3:31. [11]Rom. 6:14. Gal. 2:16. Gal. 3:13. Gal. 4:4-5. Acts 13:39. Rom. 8:1. [12]Rom. 7:12, 22, 25. Ps. 119:4-6. 1 Cor. 7:19. Gal. 5:14, 16, 18-23. [13]Rom. 7:7. Rom. 3:20. [14]James 1:23-25. Rom. 7:9, 14, 24. [15]Gal. 3:24. Rom. 7:24-25. Rom. 8:3-4. [16]James 2:11. Ps. 119:101, 104, 128. [17]Ezra 9:13-14. Ps. 89:30-34. [18]Lev. 26:1-14. etc. 2 Cor. 6:16. Eph. 6:2-3. Ps. 37:11. Matt. 5:5. Ps. 19:11. [19]Gal. 2:16. Luke 17:10. [20]Rom. 6:12, 14. 1 Peter 3:8-12. Ps. 34:12-16. Heb. 12:28-29. [21]Gal. 3:21. [22]Ezek. 36:27. Heb. 8:10. Jer. 31:33.

CHAPTER 20

Of Christian Liberty, and Liberty of Conscience

I. The liberty which Christ hath purchased for believers under the gospel consists in their freedom from the guilt of sin, the condemning wrath of God, the curse of the moral law;[1] and, in their being delivered from this present evil world, bondage to Satan, and dominion of sin;[2] from the evil of afflictions, the sting of death, the victory of the grave, and everlasting damnation;[3] as also, in their free access to God,[4] and their yielding obedience unto Him, not out of slavish fear, but a childlike love and willing mind.[5] All which were common also to believers under the law.[6] But, under the new testament, the liberty of Christians is further enlarged, in their freedom from the yoke of the ceremonial law, to which the Jewish church was subjected;[7] and in greater boldness of access to the throne of grace,[8] and in fuller communications of the free Spirit of God, than believers under the law did ordinarily partake of.[9]

II. God alone is Lord of the conscience,[10] and hath left it free from the doctrines and commandments of men, which are, in anything, contrary to his Word; or beside it, if matters of faith, or worship.[11] So that, to believe such doctrines, or to obey such commands, out of conscience, is to betray true liberty of conscience:[12] and the requiring of an implicit faith, and an absolute and blind obedience, is to destroy liberty of conscience, and reason also.[13]

III. They who, upon pretense of Christian liberty, do practice any sin, or cherish any lust, do thereby destroy the end of Christian liberty, which is, that being delivered out of the hands of our enemies, we might serve the Lord without fear, in holiness and righteousness before Him, all the days of our life.[14]

IV. And because the powers which God hath ordained, and the liberty which Christ hath purchased, are not intended by God to destroy, but mutually to uphold and preserve one another, they who, upon pretense of Christian liberty, shall oppose any lawful power, or the lawful exercise of it, whether it be civil or ecclesiastical, resist the ordinance of God.[15] And, for their publishing of such opinions, or maintaining of such practices, as are contrary to the light of nature, or to the known principles of Christianity (whether concerning faith, worship, or conversation), or to the power of godliness; or, such erroneous opinions or practices, as either in their own nature, or in the manner of publishing or maintaining them, are destructive to the external peace and order which Christ hath established in the church, they may lawfully be called to account, and proceeded against, by the censures of the church.[16]

[1]Titus 2:14. 1 Thess. 1:10. Gal. 3:13. [2]Gal. 1:4. Col. 1:13. Acts 26:18. Rom. 6:14. [3]Rom. 8:28. Ps. 119:71. 1 Cor. 15:54-57. Rom. 8:1. [4]Rom. 5:1-2. [5]Rom. 8:14-15. 1 John 4:18. [6]Gal. 3:9, 14. [7]Gal. 4:1-3, 6-7. Gal. 5:1. Acts 15:10-11. [8]Heb. 4:14, 16. Heb. 10:19-22. [9]John 7:38-39. 2 Cor. 3:13, 17-18. [10]James 4:12. Rom. 14:4. [11]Acts 4:19. Acts 5:29. 1 Cor. 7:23. Matt. 23:8-10. 2 Cor. 1:24. Matt. 15:9. [12]Col. 2:20, 22-23. Gal. 1:10. Gal. 2:4-5. Gal. 5:1. [13]Rom. 10:17. Rom. 14:23. Isa. 8:20. Acts 17:11. John 4:22. Hosea 5:11. Rev. 13:12, 16-17. Jer. 8:9. [14]Gal. 5:13. 1 Peter 2:16. 2 Peter 2:19. John 8:34. Luke 1:74-75. [15]Matt. 12:25. 1 Peter 2:13-14, 16. Rom. 13:1-8. Heb. 13:17. [16]Rom. 1:32. 1 Cor. 5:1, 5, 11, 13. 2 John 10-11. 2 Thess. 3:14. 1 Tim. 6:3-5. Titus 1:10-11, 13. Titus 3:10. Matt. 18:15-17. 1 Tim. 1:19-20. Rev. 2:2, 14-15, 20. Rev. 3:9.

CHAPTER 21
Of Religious Worship, and the Sabbath Day

I. The light of nature showeth that there is a God, who hath lordship and sovereignty over all, is good, and doth good unto all, and is therefore to be feared, loved, praised, called upon, trusted in, and served, with all the heart, and with all the soul, and with all the might.[1] But the acceptable way of worshiping the true God is instituted by Himself, and so limited by his own revealed will, that he may not be worshiped according to the imaginations and devices of men, or the suggestions of Satan, under any visible representation, or any other way not prescribed in the Holy Scripture.[2]

II. Religious worship is to be given to God, the Father, Son, and Holy Ghost; and to Him alone;[3] not to angels, saints, or any other creature:[4] and, since the fall, not without a Mediator; nor in the mediation of any other but of Christ alone.[5]

III. Prayer, with thanksgiving, being one special part of religious worship,[6] is by God required of all men:[7] and, that it may be accepted, it is to be made in the name of the Son,[8] by the help of his Spirit,[9] according to his will,[10] with understanding, reverence, humility, fervency, faith, love, and perseverance;[11] and, if vocal, in a known tongue.[12]

IV. Prayer is to be made for things lawful;[13] and for all sorts of men living, or that shall live hereafter:[14] but not for the dead,[15] nor for those of whom it may be known that they have sinned the sin unto death.[16]

V. The reading of the Scriptures with godly fear,[17] the sound preaching[18] and conscionable hearing of the Word, in obedience unto God, with understanding, faith, and reverence,[19] singing of psalms with grace in the heart;[20] as also, the due administration and worthy receiving of the sacraments instituted by Christ, are all parts of the ordinary religious worship of God:[21] beside religious oaths,[22] vows,[23] solemn fastings,[24] and thanksgivings upon special occasions,[25] which are, in their several times and seasons, to be used in an holy and religious manner.[26]

VI. Neither prayer, nor any other part of religious worship, is now, under the gospel, either tied unto, or made more acceptable by any place in which it is performed, or towards which it is directed:[27] but God is to be worshiped everywhere,[28] in spirit and truth;[29] as, in private families[30] daily,[31] and in secret, each one by himself;[32] so, more solemnly in the public assemblies, which are not carelessly or willfully to be neglected, or forsaken, when God, by his Word or providence, calleth thereunto.[33]

VII. As it is the law of nature, that, in general, a due proportion of time be set apart for the worship of God; so, in his Word, by a positive, moral, and perpetual commandment binding all men in all ages, he hath particularly appointed one day in seven, for a Sabbath, to be kept holy unto Him:[34] which, from the beginning of the world to the resurrection of Christ, was the last day of the week; and, from the resurrection of Christ, was changed into the first day of the week,[35] which, in Scripture, is called the Lord's day,[36] and is to be continued to the end of the world, as the Christian Sabbath.[37]

VIII. This Sabbath is then kept holy unto the Lord, when men, after a due preparing of their hearts, and ordering of their common affairs beforehand, do not only observe an holy rest, all the day, from their own works, words, and thoughts about their worldly employments and recreations,[38] but also are taken up, the whole time, in the public and private exercises of his worship, and in the duties of necessity and mercy.[39]

[1]Rom. 1:20. Acts 17:24. Ps. 119:68. Jer. 10:7. Ps. 31:23. Ps. 18:3. Rom. 10:12. Ps. 62:8. Josh. 24:14. Mark 12:33. [2]Deut. 12:32. Matt. 15:9. Acts 17:25. Matt. 4:9-10. Deut. 4:15-20. Exod. 20:4-6. Col. 2:23. [3]Matt. 4:10. John 5:23. 2 Cor. 13:14. [4]Col. 2:18. Rev. 19:10. Rom. 1:25. [5]John 14:6. I Tim. 2:5. Eph. 2:18. Col. 3:17. [6]Phil. 4:6. [7]Ps. 65:6. [8]John 14:13-14. I Peter 2:5. [9]Rom. 8:26. [10]I John 5:14. [11]Ps. 47:7. Eccles. 5:1-2. Heb. 12:28. Gen. 17:27. James 5:16. James 1:6-7. Mark 11:24. Matt. 6:12, 14-15. Col. 4:2. Eph. 6:18. [12]I Cor. 14:14. [13]I John 5:14. [14]I Tim. 2:1-2. John 17:20. 2 Sam. 7:29. Ruth 4:12. [15]2 Sam. 12:21-23. Luke 16:25-26. Rev. 14:13. [16]I John 5:16. [17]Acts 15:21. Rev. 1:3. [18]2 Tim. 4:2. [19]James 1:22. Acts 10:33. Matt. 13:19. Heb. 4:2. Isa. 66:2. [20]Col. 3:16. Eph. 5:19. James 5:13. [21]Matt. 28:19. I Cor. 11:23-28. Acts 2:42. [22]Deut. 6:13. Neh. 10:29. [23]Isa. 19:21. Eccles. 5:4-5. [24]Joel 2:12. Esther 4:16. Matt. 9:15. I Cor. 7:5. [25]Ps. 107. Esther 9:22. [26]Heb. 12:28. [27]John 4:21. [28]Mal. 1:11. I Tim. 2:8. [29]John 4:23-24. [30]Jer. 10:25. Deut. 6:6-7. Job 1:5. 2 Sam. 6:18, 20. I Peter 3:7. Acts 10:2. [31]Matt. 6:11. [32]Matt. 6:6. Eph. 6:18. [33] Isa. 56:6-7. Heb. 10:25. Prov. 1:20-21, 24. Prov. 8:34. Acts 13:42. Luke 4:16. Acts 2:42. [34]Exod. 20:8, 10-11. Isa. 56:2, 4, 6-7. [35]Gen. 2:2-3. I Cor. 16:1-2 Acts 20:7. [36]Rev. 1:10. [37]Exod. 20:8, 10. Matt. 5:17-18. [38]Exod. 20:8. Exod. 16:23, 25-26, 29-30. Exod. 31:15-17. Isa. 58:13. Neh. 13:15-19. Neh. 13:21-22. [39]Isa. 58:13. Matt. 12:1-13.

CHAPTER 22
Of Lawful Oaths and Vows

I. A lawful oath is a part of religious worship,[1] wherein, upon just occasion, the person swearing solemnly calleth God to witness what he asserteth, or promiseth, and to judge him according to the truth or falsehood of what he sweareth.[2]

II. The name of God only is that by which men ought to swear, and therein it is to be used with all holy fear and reverence.[3] Therefore, to swear vainly, or rashly, by that glorious and dreadful Name; or, to swear at all by any other thing, is sinful, and to be abhorred.[4] Yet, as in matters of weight and moment, an oath is warranted by the Word of God, under the new testament as well as under the old;[5] so a lawful oath, being imposed by lawful authority, in such matters, ought to be taken.[6]

III. Whosoever taketh an oath ought duly to consider the weightiness of so solemn an act, and therein to avouch nothing but what he is fully persuaded is the truth:[7] neither may any man bind himself by oath to anything but what is good and just, and what he believeth so to be, and what he is able and resolved to perform.[8]

IV. An oath is to be taken in the plain and common sense of the words, without equivocation, or mental reservation.[9] It cannot oblige to sin; but in anything not sinful, being taken, it binds to performance, although to a man's own hurt.[10] Nor is it to be violated, although made to heretics, or infidels.[11]

V. A vow is of the like nature with a promissory oath, and ought to be made with the like religious care, and to be performed with the like faithfulness.[12]

VI. It is not to be made to any creature, but to God alone:[13] and, that it may be accepted, it is to be made voluntarily, out of faith, and conscience of duty, in way of thankfulness for mercy received, or for the obtaining of what we want, whereby we more strictly bind ourselves to necessary duties; or, to other things, so far and so long as they may fitly conduce thereunto.[14]

VII. No man may vow to do anything forbidden in the Word of God, or what would hinder any duty therein commanded, or which is not in his own power, and for the performance whereof he hath no promise of ability from God.[15] In which respects, popish monastical vows of perpetual single life, professed poverty, and regular obedience, are so far from being degrees of higher perfection, that they are superstitious and sinful snares, in which no Christian may entangle himself.[16]

[1]Deut. 10:20. [2]Exod. 20:7. Lev. 19:12. 2 Cor. 1:23. 2 Chron. 6:22-23. [3]Deut. 6:13. [4]Exod. 20:7. Jer. 5:7. Matt. 5:34, 37. James 5:12. [5]Heb. 6:16. 2 Cor. 1:23. Isa. 65:16. [6]I Kings 8:31. Neh. 13:25. Ezra 10:5.

[7]Exod. 20:7. Jer. 4:2. [8]Gen. 24:2-3, 5-6, 8-9. [9]Jer. 4:2. Ps. 24:4. [10]1 Sam. 25:22, 32-34. Ps. 15:4. [11]Ezek. 17:16, 18-19. Joshua 9:18-19. 2 Sam. 21:1. [12]Isa. 19:21. Eccles. 5:4-6. Ps. 61:8. Ps. 66:13-14. [13]Ps. 76:11. Jer. 44:25-26. [14]Deut. 23:21-23. Ps. 50:14. Gen. 28:20-22. 1 Sam. 1:11. Ps. 66:13-14. Ps. 132:2-5. [15] Acts 23:12, 14. Mark 6:26. Num. 30:5, 8, 12-13. [16]Matt. 19:11-12. 1 Cor. 7:2, 9. Eph. 4:28. 1 Peter 4:2. 1 Cor. 7:23.

CHAPTER 23

Of the Civil Magistrate

I. God, the supreme Lord and King of all the world, hath ordained civil magistrates, to be, under Him, over the people, for his own glory, and the public good: and, to this end, hath armed them with the power of the sword, for the defense and encouragement of them that are good, and for the punishment of evildoers.[1]

II. It is lawful for Christians to accept and execute the office of a magistrate, when called thereunto:[2] in the managing whereof, as they ought especially to maintain piety, justice, and peace, according to the wholesome laws of each commonwealth;[3] so, for that end, they may lawfully, now under the new testament, wage war, upon just and necessary occasion.[4]

III. Civil magistrates may not assume to themselves the administration of the Word and sacraments;[5] or the power of the keys of the kingdom of heaven;[6] or, in the least, interfere in matters of faith.[7] Yet, as nursing fathers, it is the duty of civil magistrates to protect the church of our common Lord, without giving the preference to any denomination of Christians above the rest, in such a manner that all ecclesiastical persons whatever shall enjoy the full, free, and unquestioned liberty of discharging every part of their sacred functions, without violence or danger.[8] And, as Jesus Christ hath appointed a regular government and discipline in his church, no law of any commonwealth should interfere with, let, or hinder, the due exercise thereof, among the voluntary members of any denomination of Christians, according to their own profession and belief.[9] It is the duty of civil magistrates to protect the person and good name of all their people, in such an effectual manner as that no person be suffered, either upon pretense of religion or of infidelity, to offer any indignity, violence, abuse, or injury to any other person whatsoever: and to take order, that all religious and ecclesiastical assemblies be held without molestation or disturbance.[10]

IV. It is the duty of people to pray for magistrates,[11] to honor their persons,[12] to pay them tribute or other dues,[13] to obey their lawful commands, and to be subject to their authority, for conscience' sake.[14] Infidelity, or difference in religion, doth not make void the magistrates' just and legal authority, nor free the people from their due obedience to them:[15] from which ecclesiastical persons are not exempted,[16] much less hath the pope any power and jurisdiction over them in their dominions, or over any of their people; and, least of all, to deprive them of their dominions, or lives, if he shall judge them to be heretics, or upon any other pretense whatsoever.[17]

[1]Rom. 13:1-4. 1 Peter 2:13-14. [2]Prov. 8:15-16. Rom. 13:1-2, 4. [3]Ps. 2:10, 12. 1 Tim. 2:2. Ps. 82:3-4. 2 Sam. 23:3. 1 Peter 2:13. [4] Luke 3:14. Rom. 13:4. Matt. 8:9-10. Acts 10:1-2. Rev. 17:14, 16. [5]2 Chron. 26:18. [6]Matt. 18:17. Matt. 16:19. 1 Cor. 12:28-29. Eph. 4:11. 1 Cor. 4:1-2. Rom. 10:15. Heb. 5:4. [7]John 18:36. Acts 5:29. Eph. 4:11-12. [8]Isa. 49:23. Rom. 13:1-6. [9]Ps. 105:15. Acts 18:14-15. [10]Rom. 13:4. 1 Tim. 2:2. [11]1 Tim. 2:1-2. [12]1 Peter 2:17. [13]Rom. 13:6-7. [14]Rom. 13:5. Titus 3:1. [15]1 Peter 2:13-14, 16. [15]Rom. 13:1. 1 Kings 2:35. Acts 25:9-11. 2 Peter 2:1, 10-11. Jude 8-11. [17]2 Thess. 2:4. Rev. 13:15-17.

CHAPTER 24

Of Marriage and Divorce

I. Marriage is to be between one man and one woman: neither is it lawful for any man to have more than one wife, nor for any woman to have more than one husband, at the same time.[1]

II. Marriage was ordained for the mutual help of husband and wife,[2] for the increase of mankind with legitimate issue, and of the church with an holy seed;[3] and for preventing of uncleanness.[4]

III. It is lawful for all sorts of people to marry, who are able with judgment to give their consent.[5] Yet it is the duty of Christians to marry only in the Lord.[6] And therefore such as profess the true reformed religion should not marry with infidels, papists, or other idolaters: neither should such as are godly be unequally yoked, by marrying with such as are notoriously wicked in their life, or maintain damnable heresies.[7]

IV. Marriage ought not to be within the degrees of consanguinity or affinity forbidden by the Word.[8] Nor can such incestuous marriages ever be made lawful by any law of man or consent of parties, so as those persons may live together as man and wife.[9]

V. Adultery or fornication committed after a contract, being detected before marriage, giveth just occasion to the innocent party to dissolve that contract.[10] In the case of adultery after marriage, it is lawful for the innocent party to sue out a divorce:[11] and, after the divorce, to marry another, as if the offending party were dead.[12]

VI. Although the corruption of man be such as is apt to study arguments unduly to put asunder those whom God hath joined together in marriage: yet, nothing but adultery, or such willful desertion as can no way be remedied by the church, or civil magistrate, is cause sufficient of dissolving the bond of marriage:[13] wherein, a public and orderly course of proceeding is to be observed; and the persons concerned in it not left to their own wills, and discretion, in their own case.[14]

[1]Gen. 2:24. Matt. 19:5-6. Prov. 2:17. [2]Gen. 2:18. [3]Mal. 2:15. [4]1 Cor. 7:2, 9. [5]Heb. 13:4. 1 Tim. 4:3. 1 Cor. 7:36-38. Gen. 24:57. [6]1 Cor. 7:39. [7]Gen. 34:14. Exod. 34:16. Deut. 7:3-4. 1 Kings 11:4. Neh. 13:25-27. Mal. 2:11-12. 2 Cor. 6:14. [8]Lev. 18. 1 Cor. 5:1. Amos 2:7. [9]Mark 6:18. Lev. 18:24-28. [10]Matt. 1:18-20. [11]Matt. 5:31-32. [12]Matt. 19:9. Rom. 7:2-3. [13]Matt. 19:8-9. 1 Cor. 7:15. Matt. 19:6. [14]Deut. 24:1-4.

CHAPTER 25
Of the Church

I. The catholic or universal church, which is invisible, consists of the whole number of the elect, that have been, are, or shall be gathered into one, under Christ the Head thereof; and is the spouse, the body, the fullness of Him that filleth all in all.[1]

II. The visible church, which is also catholic or universal under the gospel (not confined to one nation, as before under the law), consists of all those throughout the world that profess the true religion;[2] and of their children:[3] and is the kingdom of the Lord Jesus Christ,[4] the house and family of God,[5] out of which there is no ordinary possibility of salvation.[6]

III. Unto this catholic visible church Christ hath given the ministry, oracles, and ordinances of God, for the gathering and perfecting of the saints, in this life, to the end of the world: and doth, by his own presence and Spirit, according to his promise, make them effectual thereunto.[7]

IV. This catholic church hath been sometimes more, sometimes less visible.[8] And particular churches, which are members thereof, are more or less pure, according as the doctrine of the gospel is taught and embraced, ordinances administered, and public worship performed more or less purely in them.[9]

V. The purest churches under heaven are subject both to mixture and error;[10] and some have so degenerated, as to become no churches of Christ, but synagogues of Satan.[11] Nevertheless, there shall be always a church on earth, to worship God according to his will.[12]

VI. There is no other head of the church but the Lord Jesus Christ.[13] Nor can the pope of Rome, in any sense, be head thereof.[14]

[1]Eph. 1:10, 22-23. Eph. 5:23, 27, 32. Col. 1:18. [2]1 Cor. 1:2. 1 Cor. 12:12-13. Ps. 2:8. Rev. 7:9. Rom. 15:9-12. [3]1 Cor. 7:14. Acts 2:39. Ezek. 16:20-21. Rom. 11:16. Gen. 3:15. Gen. 17:7. [4]Matt. 13:47. Isa. 9:7. [5]Eph. 2:19. Eph. 3:15. [6]Acts 2:47. [7]1 Cor. 12:28. Eph. 4:11-13. Matt. 28:19-20. Isa. 59:21. [8]Rom. 11:3-4. Rev. 12:6, 14. [9]Rev. 2–3. 1 Cor. 5:6-7. [10]1 Cor. 13:12. Matt. 13:24-30, 47. [11]Rev. 18:2. Rom. 11:18-22. [12]Matt. 16:18. Ps. 72:17. Ps. 102:28. Matt. 28:19-20. [13]Col. 1:18. Eph. 1:22. [14]Matt. 23:8-10. 2 Thess. 2:3-4, 8-9. Rev. 13:6.

CHAPTER 26
Of the Communion of Saints

I. All saints, that are united to Jesus Christ their Head, by his Spirit, and by faith, have fellowship with Him in his graces, sufferings, death, resurrection, and glory:[1] and, being united to one another in love, they have communion in each other's gifts and graces,[2] and are obliged to the performance of such duties, public and private, as do conduce to their mutual good, both in the inward and outward man.[3]

II. Saints by profession are bound to maintain an holy fellowship and communion in the worship of God, and in performing such other spiritual services as tend to their mutual edification;[4] as also in relieving each other in outward things, according to their several abilities and necessities. Which communion, as God offereth opportunity, is to be extended unto all those who, in every place, call upon the name of the Lord Jesus.[5]

III. This communion which the saints have with Christ, doth not make them in any wise partakers of the substance of his Godhead; or to be equal with Christ in any respect: either of which to affirm is impious and blasphemous.[6] Nor doth their communion one with another, as saints, take away, or infringe the title or propriety which each man hath in his goods and possessions.[7]

[1] I John 1:3 Eph. 3:16-19, John 1:16. Eph. 2:5-6. Phil. 3:10, Rom. 6:5-6. 2 Tim. 2:12.
[2] Eph. 4:15-16. I Cor. 12:7. I Cor. 3:21-23. Col. 2:19. [3] I Thess. 5:11, 14. Rom. 1:11-12, 14. I John 3:16-18. Gal. 6:10.
[4] Heb. 10:24-25. Acts 2:42, 46. Isa. 2:3. I Cor. 11:20. [5] Acts 2:44-45. I John 3:17. 2 Cor. 8-9. Acts 11:29-30. [6] Col. 1:18-19. I Cor. 8:6. Isa. 42:8. I Tim. 6:15-16. Ps. 45:7. Heb. 1:8-9. [7] Exod. 20:15. Eph. 4:28. Acts 5:4.

CHAPTER 27
Of the Sacraments

I. Sacraments are holy signs and seals of the covenant of grace[1] immediately instituted by God,[2] to represent Christ, and his benefits; and to confirm our interest in Him:[3] as also, to put a visible difference between those that belong unto the church, and the rest of the world;[4] and solemnly to engage them to the service of God in Christ, according to his Word.[5]

II. There is, in every sacrament, a spiritual relation, or sacramental union, between the sign and the thing signified: whence it comes to pass, that the names and effects of the one are attributed to the other.[6]

III. The grace which is exhibited in or by the sacraments rightly used, is not conferred by any power in them; neither doth the efficacy of a sacrament depend upon the piety or intention of him that doth administer it:[7] but upon the work of the Spirit,[8] and the word of institution, which contains, together with a precept authorizing the use thereof, a promise of benefit to worthy receivers.[9]

IV. There be only two sacraments ordained by Christ our Lord in the Gospel; that is to say, baptism, and the Supper of the Lord: neither of which may be dispensed by any, but by a minister of the Word lawfully ordained.[10]

V. The sacraments of the old testament, in regard of the spiritual things thereby signified and exhibited, were, for substance, the same with those of the new.[11]

[1] Rom. 4:11. Gen. 17:7, 10. [2] Matt. 28:19. I Cor. 11:23. [3] I Cor. 10:16. I Cor. 11:25-26. Gal. 3:17. [4] Rom. 15:8. Exod. 12:48. Gen. 34:14.
[5] Rom. 6:3-4. I Cor. 10:16, 21.
[6] Gen. 17:10. Matt. 26:27-28. Titus 3:5.
[7] Rom. 2:28-29. I Peter 3:21. [8] Matt. 3:11. I Cor. 12:13. [9] Matt. 26:27-28. Matt. 28:19-20.
[10] Matt. 28:19. I Cor. 11:20, 23. I Cor. 4:1. Heb. 5:4. [11] I Cor. 10:1-4.

CHAPTER 28
Of Baptism

I. Baptism is a sacrament of the new testament, ordained by Jesus Christ,[1] not only for the solemn admission of the party baptized into the visible church;[2] but also, to be unto him a sign and seal of the covenant of grace,[3] of his ingrafting into Christ,[4] of regeneration,[5] of remission of sins,[6] and of his giving up unto God, through Jesus Christ, to walk in newness of life.[7] Which sacrament is, by Christ's own appointment, to be continued in his church until the end of the world.[8]

II. The outward element to be used in this sacrament is water, wherewith the party is to be baptized, in the name of the Father, and of the Son, and of the Holy Ghost, by a minister of the gospel, lawfully called thereunto.[9]

III. Dipping of the person into the water is not necessary; but baptism is rightly administered by pouring, or sprinkling water upon the person.[10]

IV. Not only those that do actually profess faith in and obedience unto Christ,[11] but also the infants of one, or both, believing parents, are to be baptized.[12]

V. Although it be a great sin to contemn or neglect this ordinance,[13] yet grace and salvation are not so inseparably annexed unto it, as that no person can be regenerated, or saved, without it;[14] or, that all that are baptized are undoubtedly regenerated.[15]

VI. The efficacy of baptism is not tied to that moment of time wherein it is administered;[16] yet, notwithstanding, by the right use of this ordinance, the grace promised is not only offered, but really exhibited, and conferred, by the Holy Ghost, to such (whether of age or infants) as that grace belongeth unto, according to the counsel of God's own will, in his appointed time.[17]

VII. The sacrament of baptism is but once to be administered unto any person.[18]

[1]Matt. 28:19. [2]1 Cor. 12:13.
[3]Rom. 4:11. Col. 2:11-12. [4]Gal. 3:27.
Rom. 6:5. [5]Titus 3:5. [6]Mark 1:4.
[7]Rom. 6:3-4. [8]Matt. 28:19-20. [9]Matt. 3:11.
John 1:33. Matt. 28:19-20. [10]Heb. 9:10,
19-22. Acts 2:41. Acts 16:33. Mark 7:4.
[11]Mark 16:15-16. Acts 8:37-38.
[12]Gen. 17:7, 9. Gal. 3:9, 14. Col. 2:11-12.
Acts 2:38-39. Rom. 4:11-12. 1 Cor. 7:14.
Matt. 28:19. Mark 10:13-16. Luke 18:15.
[13]Luke 7:30. Exod. 4:24-26. [14]Rom. 4:11.
Acts 10:2, 4, 22, 31, 45, 47. [15]Acts 8:13, 23.
[16]John 3:5, 8. [17]Gal. 3:27. Titus 3:5. Eph. 5:25-26.
Acts 2:38, 41. [18]Titus 3:5.

CHAPTER 29
Of the Lord's Supper

I. Our Lord Jesus, in the night wherein he was betrayed, instituted the sacrament of his body and blood, called the Lord's Supper, to be observed in his church, unto the end of the world, for the perpetual remembrance of the sacrifice of Himself in his death; the sealing all benefits thereof unto true believers, their spiritual nourishment and growth in Him, their further engagement in and to all duties which they owe unto Him; and, to be a bond and pledge of their communion with Him, and with each other, as members of his mystical body.[1]

II. In this sacrament, Christ is not offered up to his Father; nor any real sacrifice made at all, for remission of sins of the quick or dead;[2] but only a commemoration of that one offering up of Himself, by Himself, upon the cross, once for all: and a spiritual oblation of all possible praise unto God, for the same:[3] so that the popish sacrifice of the mass (as they call it) is most abominably injurious to Christ's one, only sacrifice, the alone propitiation for all the sins of his elect.[4]

III. The Lord Jesus hath, in this ordinance, appointed his ministers to declare his word of institution to the people; to pray, and bless the elements of bread and wine, and thereby to set them apart from a common to an holy use; and to take and break the bread, to take the cup, and (they communicating also themselves) to give both to the communicants;[5] but to none who are not then present in the congregation.[6]

IV. Private masses, or receiving this sacrament by a priest, or any other, alone;[7] as likewise, the denial of the cup to the people,[8] worshiping the elements, the lifting them up, or carrying them about, for adoration, and the reserving them for any pretended religious use; are all contrary to the nature of this sacrament, and to the institution of Christ.[9]

V. The outward elements in this sacrament, duly set apart to the uses ordained by Christ, have such relation to Him crucified, as that, truly, yet sacramentally only, they are sometimes called by the name of the things they represent, to wit, the body and blood of Christ;[10] albeit, in substance and nature, they still remain truly and only bread and wine, as they were before.[11]

VI. That doctrine which maintains a change of the substance of bread and wine, into the substance of Christ's body and blood (commonly called transubstantiation) by consecration of a priest, or by any other way, is repugnant, not to Scripture alone, but even to common sense, and reason; overthroweth the nature of the sacrament, and hath been, and is, the cause of manifold superstitions; yea, of gross idolatries.[12]

VII. Worthy receivers, outwardly partaking of the visible elements, in this sacrament,[13] do then also, inwardly by faith, really and indeed, yet not carnally and corporally but spiritually, receive, and feed upon, Christ crucified, and all benefits of his death: the body and blood of Christ being then, not corporally or carnally, in, with, or under the bread and wine; yet, as really, but spiritually, present to the faith of believers in that ordinance, as the elements themselves are to their outward senses.[14]

VIII. Although ignorant and wicked men receive the outward elements in this sacrament; yet, they receive not the thing signified thereby; but, by their unworthy coming thereunto, are guilty of the body and blood of the Lord, to their own damnation. Wherefore, all ignorant and ungodly persons, as they are unfit to enjoy communion with Him, so are they unworthy of the Lord's table; and cannot, without great sin against Christ, while they remain such, partake of these holy mysteries,[15] or be admitted thereunto.[16]

[1] I Cor. 11:23-26. I Cor. 10:16-17, 21. I Cor. 12:13. [2]Heb. 9:22, 25-26, 28. [3] I Cor. 11:24-26. Matt. 26:26-27. [4]Heb. 7:23-24, 27. Heb. 10:11-12, 14, 18. [5]Matt. 26:26-28. Mark 14:22-24. Luke 22:19-20. I Cor. 11:23-26. [6]Acts 20:7. I Cor. 11:20. [7] I Cor. 10:6. [8]Mark 14:23. I Cor. 11:25-29. [9]Matt. 15:9. [10]Matt. 26:26-28. [11] I Cor. 11:26-28. Matt. 26:29. [12]Acts 3:21. I Cor. 11:24-26. Luke 24:6, 39. [13] I Cor. 11:28. [14] I Cor. 10:16. [15] I Cor. 11:27-29. 2 Cor. 6:14-16. [16] I Cor. 5:6-7, 13. 2 Thess. 3:6, 14-15. Matt. 7:6.

CHAPTER 30
Of Church Censures

I. The Lord Jesus, as King and Head of his church, hath therein appointed a government, in the hand of church officers, distinct from the civil magistrate.[1]

II. To these officers the keys of the kingdom of heaven are committed; by virtue whereof, they have power, respectively, to retain, and remit sins; to shut that kingdom against the impenitent, both by the Word, and censures; and to open it unto penitent sinners, by the ministry of the gospel; and by absolution from censures, as occasion shall require.[2]

III. Church censures are necessary, for the reclaiming and gaining of offending brethren, for deterring of others from the like offenses, for purging out of that leaven which might infect the whole lump, for vindicating the honor of Christ, and the holy profession of the gospel, and for preventing the wrath of God, which might justly fall upon the church, if they should suffer his covenant, and the seals thereof, to be profaned by notorious and obstinate offenders.[3]

IV. For the better attaining of these ends, the officers of the church are to proceed by admonition; suspension from the sacrament of the Lord's Supper for a season; and by excommunication from the church; according to the nature of the crime, and demerit of the person.[4]

[1]Isa. 9:6-7. I Tim. 5:17. I Thess. 5:12. Acts 20:17-18. Heb. 13:7, 17, 24. I Cor. 12:28. Matt. 28:18-20. [2]Matt. 16:19. Matt. 18:17-18. John 20:21-23. 2 Cor. 2:6-8. [3] I Cor. 5. I Tim. 5:20. Matt. 7:6. I Tim. 1:20. I Cor. 11:27-34. Jude 23. [4] I Thess. 5:12. 2 Thess. 3:6, 14-15. I Cor. 5:4-5, 13. Matt. 18:17. Titus 3:10.

CHAPTER 31
Of Synods and Councils

I. For the better government, and further edification of the church, there ought to be such assemblies as are commonly called synods or councils:[1] and it belongeth to the overseers and other rulers of the particular churches, by virtue of their office, and the power which Christ hath given them for edification and not for destruction, to appoint such assemblies;[2] and to convene together in them, as often as they shall judge it expedient for the good of the church.[3]

II. It belongeth to synods and councils, ministerially to determine controversies of faith, and cases of conscience; to set down rules and directions for the better ordering of the public worship of God, and government of his church; to receive complaints in cases of maladministration, and authoritatively to determine the same: which decrees and determinations, if consonant to the Word of God, are to be received with reverence and submission; not only for their agreement with the Word, but also for the power whereby they are made, as being an ordinance of God appointed thereunto in his Word.[4]

III. All synods or councils, since the Apostles' times, whether general or particular, may err; and many have erred. Therefore they are not to be made the rule of faith, or practice; but to be used as a help in both.[5]

IV. Synods and councils are to handle, or conclude nothing, but that which is ecclesiastical: and are not to intermeddle with civil affairs which concern the commonwealth, unless by way of humble petition in cases extraordinary; or, by way of advice, for satisfaction of conscience, if they be thereunto required by the civil magistrate.[6]

[1]Acts 15:2, 4, 6. [2]Acts 15. [3]Acts 15:22-23, 25. [4]Acts 15:15, 19, 24, 27-31. Acts 16:4. Matt. 18:17-20. [5]Eph. 2:20. Acts 17:11. 1 Cor. 2:5. 2 Cor. 1:24. [6]Luke 12:13-14. John 18:36.

CHAPTER 32

Of the State of Men after Death, and of the Resurrection of the Dead

I. The bodies of men, after death, return to dust, and see corruption:[1] but their souls, which neither die nor sleep, having an immortal subsistence, immediately return to God who gave them:[2] the souls of the righteous, being then made perfect in holiness, are received into the highest heavens, where they behold the face of God, in light and glory, waiting for the full redemption of their bodies.[3] And the souls of the wicked are cast into hell, where they remain in torments and utter darkness, reserved to the judgment of the great day.[4] Besides these two places, for souls separated from their bodies, the Scripture acknowledgeth none.

II. At the last day, such as are found alive shall not die, but be changed:[5] and all the dead shall be raised up, with the selfsame bodies, and none other (although with different qualities), which shall be united again to their souls forever.[6]

III. The bodies of the unjust shall, by the power of Christ, be raised to dishonor: the bodies of the just, by his Spirit, unto honor; and be made conformable to his own glorious body.[7]

[1]Gen. 3:19. Acts 13:36. [2]Luke 23:43. Eccles. 12:7. [3]Heb. 12:23. 2 Cor. 5:1, 6, 8. Phil. 1:23. Acts 3:21. Eph. 4:10. [4]Luke 16:23-24. Acts 1:25. Jude 6-7. 1 Peter 3:19. [5]1 Thess. 4:17. 1 Cor. 15:51-52. [6]Job 19:26-27. 1 Cor. 15:42-44. [7]Acts 24:15. John 5:28-29. 1 Cor. 15:43. Phil. 3:21.

CHAPTER 33

Of the Last Judgment

I. God hath appointed a day, wherein he will judge the world, in righteousness, by Jesus Christ,[1] to whom all power and judgment is given of the Father.[2] In which day, not only the apostate angels shall be judged,[3] but likewise all persons that have lived upon earth shall appear before the tribunal of Christ, to give an account of their thoughts, words, and deeds; and to receive according to what they have done in the body, whether good or evil.[4]

II. The end of God's appointing this day is for the manifestation of the glory of his mercy, in the eternal salvation of the elect; and of his justice, in the damnation of the reprobate, who are wicked and disobedient. For then shall the righteous go into everlasting life, and receive that fullness of joy and refreshing, which shall come from the presence of the Lord; but the wicked who know not God, and obey not the gospel of Jesus Christ, shall be cast into eternal torments, and be punished with everlasting destruction from the presence of the Lord, and from the glory of his power.[5]

III. As Christ would have us to be certainly persuaded that there shall be a day of judgment, both to deter all men from sin; and for the greater consolation of the godly in their adversity:[6] so will he have that day unknown to men, that they may shake off all carnal security, and be always watchful, because they know not at what hour the Lord will come; and may be ever prepared to say, Come Lord Jesus, come quickly, Amen.[7]

[1]Acts 17:31. [2]John 5:22, 27. [3]1 Cor. 6:3. Jude 6. 2 Peter 2:4. [4]2 Cor. 5:10. Eccles. 12:14. Rom. 2:16. Rom. 14:10, 12. Matt. 12:36-37. [5]Matt. 25:31-46. Rom. 2:5-6. Rom. 9:22-23. Matt. 5:21. Acts 3:19. 2 Thess. 1:7-10. [6]2 Peter 3:11, 14. 2 Cor. 5:10-11. 2 Thess. 1:5-7. Luke 21:7, 28. Rom. 8:23-25. [7]Matt. 24:36, 42-44. Mark 13:35-37. Luke 12:35-36. Rev. 22:20.

Finis.

APPENDIX 2

THE LARGER CATECHISM

THE

LARGER CATECHISM;

AGREED UPON BY THE ASSEMBLY OF DIVINES AT WESTMINSTER, WITH THE ASSISTANCE OF COMMISSIONERS FROM THE CHURCH OF SCOTLAND, AS A PART OF THE COVENANTED UNIFORMITY IN RELIGION BETWIXT THE CHURCHES OF CHRIST IN THE KINGDOMS OF SCOTLAND, ENGLAND, AND IRELAND.

AND

APPROVED ANNO 1648, BY THE GENERAL ASSEMBLY OF THE CHURCH OF SCOTLAND, TO BE A DIRECTORY FOR CATECHISING SUCH AS HAVE MADE SOME PROFICIENCY IN THE KNOWLEDGE OF THE GROUNDS OF RELIGION,

WITH

THE PROOFS FROM THE SCRIPTURE.

Assembly at EDINBURGH,
July 2, 1648. Sess. 10.
Act approving the LARGER CATECHISM.

THE General Assembly having exactly examined and seriously considered the LARGER CATECHISM, agreed upon by the Assembly of Divines sitting at Westminister, with assistance of Commissioners from this Kirk, copies thereof being printed, and sent to Presbyteries, for the more exact trial thereof; and publick intimation being frequently made in this Assembly, that every one that had any doubts or objections upon it might put them in; do find, upon due examination thereof, That the said Catechism is agreeable to the Word of God, and in nothing contrary to the received doctrine, worship, discipline, and government of this Kirk; a necessary part of the intended uniformity in religion, and a rich treasure for increasing knowledge among the people of God: and therefore the Assembly, as they bless the Lord that so excellent a Catechism is prepared, so they approve the same, as a part of uniformity; agreeing, for their part, that it be a common Catechism for the three kingdoms, and a Directory for catechising such as have made some proficiency in the knowledge of the grounds of religion.

Q. 1. What is the chief and highest end of man?
A. Man's chief and highest end is to glorify God,[1] and fully to enjoy Him forever.[2]

[1]Rom. 11:36. 1 Cor. 10:31. [2]Ps. 73:24-28. John 17:21-23.

Q. 2. How doth it appear that there is a God?
A. The very light of nature in man, and the works of God, declare plainly that there is a God;[1] but His Word and Spirit only do sufficiently and effectually reveal Him unto men for their salvation.[2]

[1]Rom. 1:19-20. Ps. 19:1-3. Acts 17:28.
[2]1 Cor. 2:9-10. 2 Tim. 3:15-17. Isa. 59:21.

Q. 3. What is the Word of God?
A. The holy Scriptures of the Old and New Testament are the Word of God,[1] the only rule of faith and obedience.[2]

[1]2 Tim. 3:16. 2 Peter 1:19-21. [2]Eph. 2:20. Rev. 22:18-19. Isa. 8:20. Luke 16:29, 31. Gal. 1:8-9. 2 Tim. 3:15-16.

Q. 4. How doth it appear that the Scriptures are of the Word of God?
A. The Scriptures manifest themselves to be the Word of God, by their majesty[1] and purity;[2] by the consent of all the parts,[3] and the scope of the whole, which is to give all glory to God;[4] by their light and power to convince and convert sinners, to comfort and build up believers unto salvation:[5] but the Spirit of God bearing witness by and with the Scriptures in the heart of man, is alone able fully to persuade it that they are the very Word of God.[6]

[1]Hosea 8:12. 1 Cor. 2:6-7, 13. Ps. 119:18, 129. [2]Ps. 12:6. Ps. 119:140. [3]Acts 10:43. Acts 26:22. [4]Rom. 3:19, 27. [5]Acts 18:28. Heb. 4:12. James 1:18. Ps. 19:7-9. Rom. 15:4. Acts 20:32. [6]John 16:13-14. 1 John 2:20, 27. John 20:31.

Q. 5. What do the Scriptures principally teach?
A. The Scriptures principally teach, what man is to believe concerning God, and what duty God requires of man.[1]

[1]2 Tim. 1:13.

WHAT MAN OUGHT TO BELIEVE CONCERNING GOD.

Q. 6. What do the Scriptures make known of God?
A. The Scriptures make known what God is,[1] the persons in the Godhead,[2] His decrees,[3] and the execution of His decrees.[4]

[1]Heb. 11:6. [2]1 John 5:17. [3]Acts 15:14-15, 18. [4]Acts 4:27-28.

Q. 7. What is God?
A. God is a Spirit,[1] in and of Himself infinite in being,[2] glory,[3] blessedness,[4] and perfection;[5] all-sufficient,[6] eternal,[7] unchangeable,[8] incomprehensible,[9] every where present,[10] almighty,[11] knowing all things,[12] most wise,[13] most holy,[14] most just,[15] most merciful and gracious, long-suffering, and abundant in goodness and truth.[16]

[1]John 4:24. [2]Exod. 3:14. Job 11:7-9. [3]Acts 7:2. [4]1 Tim. 6:15. [5]Matt. 5:48. [6]Gen. 17:1. [7]Ps. 90:2. [8]Mal. 3:6. [9]1 Kings 8:27. [10]Ps. 139:1-13. [11]Rev. 4:8. [12]Heb. 4:13. Ps. 147:5. [13]Rom. 16:27. [14]Isa. 6:3. Rev. 15:4. [15]Deut. 32:4. [16]Exod. 34:6.

Q. 8. Are there more Gods than one?
A. There is but one only, the living and true God.[1]

[1]Deut. 6:4. 1 Cor. 8:4, 6. Jer. 10:10.

Q. 9. How many persons are there in the Godhead?
A. There be three persons in the Godhead, the Father, the Son, and the Holy Ghost; and these three are one true, eternal God, the same in substance, equal in power and glory; although distinguished by their personal properties.[1]

[1]1 John 5:7. Matt. 3:16-17. Matt. 28:19. 2 Cor. 13:14. John 10:30.

Q. 10. What are the personal properties of the three persons in the Godhead?
A. It is proper to the Father to beget the Son,[1] and to the Son to be begotten of the Father,[2] and to the Holy Ghost to proceed from the Father and the Son from all eternity.[3]

[1]Heb. 1:5-6, 8. [2]John 1:14, 18. [3]John 15:26. Gal. 4:6.

Q. 11. How doth it appear that the Son and the Holy Ghost are God equal with the Father?
A. The Scriptures manifest that the Son and the Holy Ghost are God equal with the Father, ascribing unto them such names,[1] attributes,[2] works,[3] and worship,[4] as are proper to God only.

[1]Isa. 6:3, 5, 8. John 12:41. Acts 28:25. 1 John 5:20. Acts 5:3-4. [2]John 1:1. Isa. 9:6. John 2:24-25. 1 Cor. 2:10-11. [3]Col. 1:16. Gen. 1:2. [4]Matt. 28:19. 2 Cor. 8:14.

Q. 12. What are the decrees of God?
A. God's decrees are the wise, free, and holy acts of the counsel of His will,[1] whereby, from all eternity, He hath, for His own glory, unchangeably foreordained whatsoever comes to pass in time,[2] especially concerning angels and men.

[1]Eph. 1:11. Rom. 11:33. Rom. 9:14-15, 18. [2]Eph. 1:4, 11. Rom. 9:22-23. Ps. 33:11.

Q. 13. What hath God especially decreed concerning angels and men?
A. God, by an eternal and immutable decree, out of His mere love, for the praise of His glorious grace, to be manifested in due time, hath elected some angels to glory;[1] and in Christ hath chosen some men to eternal life, and the means thereof:[2] and also, according to His sovereign power, and the unsearchable counsel of His own will, (whereby He extendeth or withholdeth favor as He pleaseth,) hath passed by and foreordained the rest to dishonor and wrath, to be for their sin inflicted, to the praise of the glory of His justice.[3]

[1]1 Tim. 5:21. [2]Eph. 1:4-6. 2 Thess. 2:13-14. [3]Rom. 9:17-18, 21-22. Matt. 11:25-26. 2 Tim. 2:20. Jude 4. 1 Peter 2:8.

Q. 14. How doth God execute His decrees?
A. God executeth His decrees in the works of creation and providence, according to His infallible foreknowledge, and the free and immutable counsel of His own will.[1]

[1]Eph. 1:11.

Q. 15. What is the work of creation?
A. The work of creation is that wherein God did in the beginning, by the Word of His power, make of nothing the world, and all things therein, for Himself, within the space of six days, and all very good.[1]

[1]Gen. 1. Heb. 11:3. Prov. 16:4.

Q. 16. How did God create angels?
A. God created all the angels[1] spirits,[2] immortal,[3] holy,[4] excelling in knowledge,[5] mighty in power,[6] to execute His commandments, and to praise His name,[7] yet subject to change.[8]

[1]Col. 1:16. [2]Ps. 104:4. [3]Matt. 22:30. [4]Matt. 25:31. [5]2 Sam. 14:17. Matt. 24:36. [6]2 Thess. 1:7. [7]Ps. 103:20-21. [8]2 Peter 2:4.

Q. 17. How did God create man?
A. After God had made all other creatures, He created man male and female;[1] formed the body of the man of the dust of the ground,[2] and the woman of the rib of the man,[3] endued them with living, reasonable, and immortal souls;[4] made them after His own image,[5] in knowledge,[6] righteousness, and holiness;[7] having the law of God written in their hearts,[8] and power to fulfill it,[9] and dominion over the creatures;[10] yet subject to fall.[11]

[1]Gen. 1:27. [2]Gen. 2:7. [3]Gen. 2:22. [4]Gen. 2:7. Job 35:11. Eccles. 12:7. Matt. 10:28. Luke 23:43. [5]Gen. 1:27. [6]Col. 3:10. [7]Eph. 4:24. [8]Rom. 2:14-15. [9]Eccles. 7:29. [10]Gen. 1:28. [11]Gen. 3:6. Eccles. 7:29.

Q. 18. What are God's works of providence?
A. God's works of providence are His most holy,[1] wise,[2] and powerful preserving[3] and governing[4] all His creatures; ordering them, and all their actions,[5] to His own glory.[6]

[1]Ps. 145:17. [2]Ps. 104:24. Isa. 28:29. [3]Heb. 1:3. [4] Ps. 103:19. [5]Matt. 10:29-31. Gen. 45:7. [6]Rom. 11:36. Isa. 63:14.

Q. 19. What is God's providence towards the angels?
A. God by His providence permitted some of the angels, willfully and irrecoverably, to fall into sin and damnation,[1] limiting and ordering that, and all their sins, to His own glory;[2] and established the rest in holiness and happiness;[3] employing them all,[4] at His pleasure, in the administrations of His power, mercy, and justice.[5]

[1]Jude 6. 2 Peter 2:4. Heb. 2:16. John 8:44. [2]Job 1:12. Matt. 8:31. [3]1 Tim. 5:21. Mark 8:38. Heb. 12:22. [4]Ps. 104:4. [5]2 Kings 19:35. Heb. 1:14.

Q. 20. What was the providence of God toward man in the estate in which he was created?
A. The providence of God toward man in the estate in which he was created, was the placing him in paradise, appointing him to dress it, giving him liberty to eat of the fruit of the earth;[1] putting the creatures under His dominion,[2] and ordaining marriage for His help;[3] affording him communion with Himself;[4] instituting the sabbath;[5] entering into a covenant of life with him, upon condition of personal, perfect, and perpetual obedience,[6] of which the tree of life was a pledge;[7] and forbidding to eat of the tree of knowledge of good and evil, upon the pain of death.[8]

[1]Gen. 2:8, 15-16. [2]Gen. 1:28. [3]Gen. 2:18. [4]Gen. 1:26-29. Gen. 3:8. [5]Gen. 2:3. [6]Gal. 3:12. Rom. 10:5. [7]Gen. 2:9. [8]Gen. 2:17.

Q. 21. Did man continue in that estate wherein God at first created him?
A. Our first parents being left to the freedom of their own will, through the temptation of Satan, transgressed the commandment of God in eating the forbidden fruit; and thereby fell from the estate of innocency wherein they were created.[1]

[1]Gen. 3:6-8, 13. Eccles. 7:29. 2 Cor. 11:3.

Q. 22. Did all mankind fall in that first transgression?
A. The covenant being made with Adam as a public person, not for himself only, but for His posterity, all mankind descending from him by ordinary generation,[1] sinned in him, and fell with him in that first transgression.[2]

[1]Acts 17:26. [2]Gen. 2:16-17. Rom. 5:12-20. 1 Cor. 15:21-22.

Q. 23. Into what estate did the fall bring mankind?
A. The fall brought mankind into an estate of sin and misery.[1]

[1]Rom. 5:12. Rom. 3:23.

Q. 24. What is sin?
A. Sin is any want of conformity unto, or transgression of, any law of God, given as a rule to the reasonable creature.[1]

[1]1 John 3:4. Gal. 3:10, 12.

Q. 25. Wherein consisteth the sinfulness of that estate whereinto man fell?
A. The sinfulness of that estate whereinto man fell, consisteth in the guilt of Adam's first sin,[1] the want of that righteousness wherein he was created, and the corruption of His nature, whereby he is utterly indisposed, disabled, and made opposite unto all that is spiritually good, and wholly inclined to all evil, and that continually;[2] which is commonly called original sin, and from which do proceed all actual transgressions.[3]

[1]Rom. 5:12, 19. [2]Rom. 3:10-19. Eph. 2:1-3. Rom. 5:6. Rom. 8:7-8. Gen. 6:5. [3]James 1:14-15. Matt. 15:19.

Q. 26. How is original sin conveyed from our first parents unto their posterity?
A. Original sin is conveyed from our first parents unto their posterity by natural generation, so as all that proceed from them in that way are conceived and born in sin.[1]

[1]Ps. 51:5. Job 14:4. John 3:6.

Q. 27. What misery did the fall bring upon mankind?
A. The fall brought upon mankind the loss of communion with God,[1] His displeasure and curse; so as we are by nature children of wrath,[2] bond slaves to Satan,[3] and justly liable to all punishments in this world, and that which is to come.[4]

[1]Gen. 3:8, 10, 24. [2]Eph. 2:2-3. [3]2 Tim. 2:26. [4]Gen. 2:17. Lam. 3:39. Rom. 6:23. Matt. 25:41. Matt. 25:46. Jude 7.

Q. 28. What are the punishments of sin in this world?
A. The punishments of sin in this world are either inward, as blindness of mind,[1] a reprobate sense,[2] strong delusions,[3] hardness of heart,[4] horror of conscience,[5] and vile affections;[6] or outward, as the curse of God upon the creatures of our sakes,[7] and all other evils that befall us in our bodies, names, estates, relations, and employments;[8] together with death itself.[9]

[1]Eph. 4:18. [2]Rom. 1:28. [3]2 Thess. 2:11. [4]Rom. 2:5. [5]Isa. 33:14. Gen. 4:13. Matt. 27:4. [6]Rom. 1:26. [7]Gen. 3:17. [8]Deut. 28:15-18. [9]Rom. 6:21, 23.

Q. 29. What are the punishments of sin in the world to come?
A. The punishments of sin in the world to come, are everlasting separation from the comfortable presence of God, and most grievous torments in soul and body, without intermission, in hell-fire forever.[1]

[1]2 Thess. 1:9. Mark 9:43-44, 46, 48. Luke 16:24.

Q. 30. Doth God leave all mankind to perish in the estate of sin and misery?
A. God doth not leave all men to perish in the estate of sin and misery,[1] into which they fell by the breach of the first covenant, commonly called the covenant of works;[2] but of His mere love and mercy delivereth His elect out of it, and bringeth them into an estate of salvation by the second covenant, commonly called the covenant of grace.[3]

[1]1 Thess. 5:9. [2]Gal. 3:10, 12. [3]Titus 3:4-7. Gal. 3:21. Rom. 3:20-22.

Q. 31. With whom was the covenant of grace made?
A. The covenant of grace was made with Christ as the second Adam, and in him with all the elect as His seed.[1]

[1]Gal. 3:16. Rom. 5:15-21. Isa. 53:10-11.

Q. 32. How is the grace of God manifested in the second covenant?
A. The grace of God is manifested in the second covenant, in that He freely provideth and offereth to sinners a Mediator,[1] and life and salvation by Him;[2] and requiring faith as the condition to interest them in Him,[3] promiseth and giveth His Holy Spirit[4] to all His elect, to work in them that faith,[5] with all other saving graces;[6] and to enable them unto all holy obedience,[7] as the evidence of the truth of their faith[8] and thankfulness to God,[9] and as the way which He hath appointed them to salvation.[10]

[1]Gen. 3:15. Isa. 42:6. John 6:27. [2]1 John 5:11-12. [3]John 3:16. John 1:12. [4]Prov. 1:23. [5]2 Cor. 4:13. [6]Gal. 5:22-23. [7]Ezek. 36:27. [8]James 2:18, 22. [9]2 Cor. 5:14-15. [10]Eph. 2:18.

Q. 33. Was the covenant of grace always administered after one and the same manner?
A. The covenant of grace was not always administered after the same manner, but the administrations of it under the Old Testament were different from those under the New.[1]

[1]2 Cor. 3:6-9.

Q. 34. How was the covenant of grace administered under the Old Testament?
A. The covenant of grace was administered under the Old Testament, by promises,[1] prophecies,[2] sacrifices,[3] circumcision,[4] the passover,[5] and other types and ordinances, which did all fore-signify Christ then to come, and were for that time sufficient to build up the elect in faith in the promised Messiah,[6] by whom they then had full remission of sin, and eternal salvation.[7]

[1]Rom. 15:8. [2]Acts 3:20, 24. [3]Heb. 10:1. [4]Rom. 4:11. [5]1 Cor. 5:7. [6]Heb. ch. 8, 9, 10. Heb. 11:13. [7]Gal. 3:7-9, 14.

Q. 35. How is the covenant of grace administered under the New Testament?
A. Under the New Testament, when Christ the substance was exhibited, the same covenant of grace was and still is to be administered in the preaching of the Word,[1] and the administration of the sacraments of Baptism[2] and the Lord's Supper;[3] in which grace and salvation are held forth in more fulness, evidence, and efficacy, to all nations.[4]

[1]Mark 16:15. [2]Matt. 28:19-20. [3]1 Cor. 11:23-25. [4]2 Cor. 3:6-9. Heb. 8:6, 10-11. Matt. 28:19.

Q. 36. Who is the Mediator of the covenant of grace?
A. The only Mediator of the covenant of grace is the Lord Jesus Christ,[1] who, being the eternal Son of God, of one substance and equal with the Father,[2] in the fulness of time became man,[3] and so was and continues to be God and man, in two entire distinct natures, and one person, forever.[4]

[1]1 Tim. 2:5. [2]John 1:1, 14. John 10:30. Phil. 2:6. [3]Gal. 4:4. [4]Luke 1:35. Rom. 9:5. Col. 2:9. Heb. 7:24-25.

Q. 37. How did Christ, being the Son of God, become man?
A. Christ the Son of God became man, by taking to Himself a true body, and a reasonable soul,[1] being conceived by the power of the Holy Ghost in the womb of the virgin Mary, of her substance, and born of her,[2] yet without sin.[3]

[1]John 1:14. Matt. 26:38. [2]Luke 1:27, 31, 35, 42. Gal. 4:4. [3]Heb. 4:15. Heb. 7:26.

Q. 38. Why was it requisite that the Mediator should be God?
A. It was requisite that the Mediator should be God, that He might sustain and keep the human nature from sinking under the infinite wrath of God, and the power of death,[1] give worth and efficacy to His sufferings, obedience, and intercession;[2] and to satisfy God's justice,[3] procure His favour,[4] purchase a peculiar people,[5] give His Spirit to them,[6] conquer all their enemies,[7] and bring them to everlasting salvation.[8]

[1]Acts 2:24-25. Rom. 1:4. Rom. 4:25. Heb. 9:14. [2]Acts 20:28. Heb. 9:14. Heb. 7:25-28. [3]Rom. 3:24-26. [4]Eph. 1:6. Matt. 3:17. [5]Titus 2:13-14. [6]Gal. 4:6. [7]Luke 1:68-69, 71, 74. [8]Heb. 5:8-9. Heb. 9:11-15.

Q. 39. Why was it requisite that the Mediator should be man?

A. It was requisite that the Mediator should be man, that He might advance our nature,[1] perform obedience to the law,[2] suffer and make intercession for us in our nature,[3] have a fellow-feeling of our infirmities;[4] that we might receive the adoption of sons,[5] and have comfort and access with boldness unto the throne of grace.[6]

[1]Heb. 2:16. [2]Gal. 4:4. [3]Heb. 2:14. Heb. 7:24-25. [14]Heb. 4:15. [5]Gal. 4:5. [6]Heb. 4:16.

Q. 40. Why was it requisite that the Mediator should be God and man in one person?
A. It was requisite that the Mediator, who was to reconcile God and man, should Himself be both God and man, and this in one person, that the proper works of each nature might be accepted of God for us,[1] and relied on by us as the works of the whole person.[2]

[1]Matt. 1:21, 23. Matt. 3:17. Heb. 9:14. [2]1 Peter 2:6.

Q. 41. Why was our Mediator called Jesus?
A. Our Mediator was called Jesus, because He saveth His people from their sins.[1]

[1]Matt. 1:21.

Q. 42. Why was our Mediator called Christ?
A. Our Mediator was called Christ, because He was anointed with the Holy Ghost above measure,[1] and so set apart, and fully furnished with all authority and ability,[2] to execute the offices of prophet,[3] priest,[4] and king of His church,[5] in the estate both of His humiliation and exaltation.

[1]John 3:34. Ps. 45:7. [2]John 6:27. Matt. 28:18-20. [3]Acts 3:21-22. Luke 4:18, 21. [4]Heb. 5:5-7. Heb. 4:14-15. [5]Ps. 2:6. Matt. 21:5. Isa. 9:6-7. Phil. 2:8-11.

Q. 43. How doth Christ execute the office of a prophet?
A. Christ executeth the office of a prophet, in His revealing to the church,[1] in all ages, by His Spirit and Word,[2] in divers ways of administration,[3] the whole will of God,[4] in all things concerning their edification and salvation.[5]

[1]John 1:18. [2]1 Peter 1:10-12. [3]Heb. 1:1-2. [4]John 15:15. [5]Acts 20:23. Eph. 4:11-13. John 20:31.

Q. 44. How doth Christ execute the office of a priest?
A. Christ executeth the office of a priest, in His once offering Himself a sacrifice without spot to God,[1] to be reconciliation for the sins of His people;[2] and in making continual intercession for them.[3]

[1]Heb. 9:14, 28. [2]Heb. 2:17. [3]Heb. 7:25.

Q. 45. How doth Christ execute the office of a king?
A. Christ executeth the office of a king, in calling out of the world a people to Himself,[1] and giving them officers,[2] laws,[3] and censures, by which He visibly governs them;[4] in bestowing saving grace upon His elect,[5] rewarding their obedience,[6] and correcting them for their sins,[7] preserving and supporting them under all their temptations and sufferings,[8] restraining and overcoming all their enemies,[9] and powerfully ordering all things for His own glory,[10] and their good;[11] and also in taking vengeance on the rest, who know not God, and obey not the gospel.[12]

[1]Acts 15:14-16. Gen. 49:10. Ps. 110:3. [2]Eph. 4:11-12. 1 Cor. 12:28. [3]Isa. 33:22. [4]Matt. 18:17-18. 1 Cor. 5:4-5. [5]Acts 5:31. [6]Rev. 22:12. Rev. 2:10. [7]Rev. 3:19. [8]Isa. 63:9. [9]1 Cor. 15:25. Ps. 110:1-2. [10]Rom. 14:10-11. [11]Rom. 8:28. [12]2 Thess. 1:8-9. Ps. 2:8-9.

Q. 46. What was the estate of Christ's humiliation?
A. The estate of Christ's humiliation was that low condition, wherein He for our sakes, emptying Himself of His glory, took upon Him the form of a servant, in His conception and birth, life, death, and after His death, until His resurrection.[1]

[1]Phil. 2:6-8. Luke 1:31. 2 Cor. 8:9. Acts 2:24.

Q. 47. How did Christ humble Himself in His conception and birth?
A. Christ humbled Himself in His conception and birth, in that, being from all eternity the Son of God, in the bosom of the Father, He was pleased in the fulness of time to become the son of man, made of a woman of low estate, and to be born of her; with divers circumstances of more than ordinary abasement.[1]

[1]John 1:14, 18. Gal. 4:4. Luke 2:7.

Q. 48. How did Christ humble Himself in His life?

A. Christ humbled Himself in His life, by subjecting Himself to the law,[1] which He perfectly fulfilled;[2] and by conflicting with the indignities of the world,[3] temptations of Satan,[4] and infirmities in His flesh, whether common to the nature of man, or particularly accompanying that His low condition.[5]

[1]Gal. 4:4. [2]Matt. 5:17. Rom. 5:19. [3]Ps. 22:6. Heb. 12:2-3. [4]Matt. 4:1-12. Luke 4:13. [5]Heb. 2:17-18. Heb. 4:15. Isa. 52:13-14.

Q. 49. How did Christ humble Himself in His death?
A. Christ humbled Himself in His death, in that having been betrayed by Judas,[1] forsaken by His disciples,[2] scorned and rejected by the world,[3] condemned by Pilate, and tormented by His persecutors;[4] having also conflicted with the terrors of death, and the powers of darkness, felt and borne the weight of God's wrath,[5] He laid down His life an offering for sin,[6] enduring the painful, shameful, and cursed death of the cross.[7]

[1]Matt. 27:4. [2]Matt. 26:56. [3]Isa. 53:2-3. [4]Matt. 27:26-50. John 19:34. [5]Luke 22:44. Matt. 27:46. [6]Isa. 53:10. [7]Phil. 2:8. Heb. 12:2. Gal. 3:13.

Q. 50. Wherein consisted Christ's humiliation after His death?
A. Christ's humiliation after His death consisted in His being buried,[1] and continuing in the state of the dead, and under the power of death till the third day;[2] which hath been otherwise expressed in these words, He descended into hell.

[1]1 Cor. 15:3-4. [2]Ps. 16:10. Acts 2:24-27, 31. Rom. 6:9. Matt. 12:40.

Q. 51. What was the estate of Christ's exaltation?
A. The estate of Christ's exaltation comprehendeth His resurrection,[1] ascension,[2] sitting at the right hand of the Father,[3] and His coming again to judge the world.[4]

[1]1 Cor. 15:4. [2]Mark 16:19. [3]Eph. 1:20. [4]Acts 1:11. Acts 17:31.

Q. 52. How was Christ exalted in His resurrection?
A. Christ was exalted in His resurrection, in that, not having seen corruption in death, (of which it was not possible for Him to be held,)[1] and having the very same body in which He suffered, with the essential properties thereof,[2] (but without mortality, and other common infirmities belonging to this life,) really united to His soul,[3] He rose again from the dead the third day by His own power;[4] whereby He declared Himself to be the Son of God,[5] to have satisfied divine justice,[6] to have vanquished death, and Him that had the power of it,[7] and to be Lord of quick and dead:[8] all which He did as a public person,[9] the head of His church,[10] for their justification,[11] quickening in grace,[12] support against enemies,[13] and to assure them of their resurrection from the dead at the last day.[14]

[1]Acts 2:24, 27. [2]Luke 24:39. [3]Rom. 6:9. Rev. 1:18. [4]John 10:18. [5]Rom. 1:4. [6]Rom. 8:34. [7]Heb. 2:14. [8]Rom. 14:9. [9]1 Cor. 15:21-22. [10]Eph. 1:20-23. Col. 1:18. [11]Rom. 4:25. [12]Eph. 2:1, 5-6. Col. 2:12. [13]1 Cor. 15:25-27. [14]1 Cor. 15:20.

Q. 53. How was Christ exalted in His ascension?
A. Christ was exalted in His ascension, in that having after His resurrection often appeared unto and conversed with His apostles, speaking to them of the things pertaining to the kingdom of God,[1] and giving them commission to preach the gospel to all nations,[2] forty days after His resurrection, he, in our nature, and as our head,[3] triumphing over enemies,[4] visibly went up into the highest heavens, there to receive gifts for men,[5] to raise up our affections thither,[6] and to prepare a place for us,[7] where He Himself is, and shall continue till His second coming at the end of the world.[8]

[1]Acts 1:2-3. [2]Matt. 28:19-20. [3]Heb. 6:20. [4]Eph. 4:8. [5]Acts 1:9-11. Eph. 4:10. Ps. 68:18. [6]Col. 3:1-2. [7]John 14:3. [8]Acts 3:21.

Q. 54. How is Christ exalted in His sitting at the right hand of God?
A. Christ is exalted in His sitting at the right hand of God, in that as God-man He is advanced to the highest favour with God the Father,[1] with all fulness of joy,[2] glory,[3] and power over all things in heaven and earth;[4] and does gather and defend His church, and subdue their enemies; furnisheth His ministers and people with

gifts and graces,[5] and maketh intercession for them.[6]

[1]Phil. 2:9. [2]Acts 2:28. Ps. 16:11. [3]John 17:5. [4]Eph. 1:22. 1 Peter 3:22. [5]Eph. 4:10-12. Ps. 110:1. [6]Rom. 8:34.

Q. 55. How doeth Christ make intercession?
A. Christ maketh intercession, by His appearing in our nature continually before the Father in heaven,[1] in the merit of His obedience and sacrifice on earth,[2] declaring His will to have it applied to all believers;[3] answering all accusations against them,[4] and procuring for them quiet of conscience, notwithstanding daily failings,[5] access with boldness to the throne of grace,[6] and acceptance of their persons[7] and services.[8]

[1]Heb. 9:12, 24. [2]Heb. 1:3. [3]John 3:16. John 17:9, 20, 24. [4]Rom. 8:33-34. [5]Rom. 5:1-2. 1 John 2:1-2. [6]Heb. 4:16. [7]Eph. 1:6. [8]1 Peter 2:5.

Q. 56. How is Christ to be exalted in His coming again to judge the world?
A. Christ is to be exalted in His coming again to judge the world, in that he, who was unjustly judged and condemned by wicked men,[1] shall come again at the last day in great power,[2] and in the full manifestation of His own glory, and of His Father's, with all His holy angels,[3] with a shout, with the voice of the archangel, and with the trumpet of God,[4] to judge the world in righteousness.[5]

[1]Acts 3:14-15. [2]Matt. 24:30. [3]Luke 9:26. Matt. 25:31. [4]1 Thess. 4:16. [5]Acts 17:31.

Q. 57. What benefits hath Christ procured by His mediation?
A. Christ, by His mediation, hath procured redemption,[1] with all other benefits of the covenant of grace.[2]

[1]Heb. 9:12. [2]2 Cor. 1:20.

Q. 58. How do we come to be made partakers of the benefits which Christ hath procured?
A. We are made partakers of the benefits which Christ hath procured, by the application of them unto us,[1] which is the work especially of God the Holy Ghost.[2]

[1]John 1:11-12. [2]Titus 3:5-6.

Q. 59. Who are made partakers of redemption through Christ?
A. Redemption is certainly applied, and effectually communicated, to all those for whom Christ hath purchased it;[1] who are in time by the Holy Ghost enabled to believe in Christ according to the gospel.[2]

[1]Eph. 1:13-14. John 6:37, 39. John 10:15-16. [2]Eph. 2:8. 2 Cor. 4:13.

Q. 60. Can they who have never heard the gospel, and so know not Jesus Christ, nor believe in Him, be saved by their living according to the light of nature?
A. They who, having never heard the gospel,[1] know not Jesus Christ,[2] and believe not in Him, cannot be saved,[3] be they never so diligent to frame their lives according to the light of nature,[4] or the laws of that religion which they profess;[5] neither is there salvation in any other, but in Christ alone,[6] who is the Savior only of His body the church.[7]

[1]Rom. 10:14. [2]2 Thess. 1:8-9. Eph. 2:12. John 1:10-12. [3]John 8:24. Mark 16:16. [4]1 Cor. 1:20-24. [5]John 4:22. Rom. 9:31-32. Phil. 3:4-9. [6]Acts 4:12. [7]Eph. 5:23.

Q. 61. Are all they saved who hear the gospel, and live in the church?
A. All that hear the gospel, and live in the visible church, are not saved; but they only who are true members of the church invisible.[1]

[1]John 12:38-40. Rom. 9:6. Matt. 22:14. Matt. 7:21. Rom. 11:7.

Q. 62. What is the visible church?
A. The visible church is a society made up of all such as in all ages and places of the world do profess the true religion,[1] and of their children.[2]

[1]1 Cor. 1:2. 1 Cor. 12:13. Rom. 15:9-12. Rev. 7:9. Ps. 2:8. Ps. 22:27-31. Ps. 45:17. Matt. 28:19-20. Isa. 59:21. [2]1 Cor. 7:14. Acts 2:39. Rom. 11:16. Gen. 17:7.

Q. 63. What are the special privileges of the visible church?
A. The visible church hath the privilege of being under God's special care and government;[1] of being protected and preserved in all ages, notwithstanding the opposition of all enemies;[2] and of enjoying the communion of saints, the ordinary means of salvation,[3] and offers of grace by Christ to all

the members of it in the ministry of the gospel, testifying, that whosoever believes in Him shall be saved,[4] and excluding none that will come unto Him.[5]

[1]Isa. 9:5-6. 1 Tim. 4:10. [2]Ps. 115:1-2, 9. Isa. 31:4-5. Zech. 12:2-4, 8-9. [3]Acts 2:39, 42. [4]Ps. 147:19-20. Rom. 9:4. Eph. 4:11-12. Mark 16:15-16. [5]John 6:37.

Q. 64. What is the invisible church?
A. The invisible church is the whole number of the elect, that have been, are, or shall be gathered into one under Christ the head.[1]

[1]Eph. 1:10. Eph. 1:22-23. John 10:16. John 11:52.

Q. 65. What special benefits do the members of the invisible church enjoy by Christ?
A. The members of the invisible church by Christ enjoy union and communion with Him in grace and glory.[1]

[1]John 17:21. Eph. 2:5-6. John 17:24.

Q. 66. What is that union which the elect have with Christ?
A. The union which the elect have with Christ is the work of God's grace,[1] whereby they are spiritually and mystically, yet really and inseparably, joined to Christ as their head and husband;[2] which is done in their effectual calling.[3]

[1]Eph. 1:22. Eph. 2:6-7. [2]1 Cor. 6:17. John 10:28. Eph. 5:23, 30. [3]1 Peter 5:10. 1 Cor. 1:9.

Q. 67. What is effectual calling?
A. Effectual calling is the work of God's almighty power and grace,[1] whereby (out of His free and special love to His elect, and from nothing in them moving Him thereunto)[2] He doth, in His accepted time, invite and draw them to Jesus Christ, by His Word and Spirit;[3] savingly enlightening their minds,[4] renewing and powerfully determining their wills,[5] so as they (although in themselves dead in sin) are hereby made willing and able freely to answer His call, and to accept and embrace the grace offered and conveyed therein.[6]

[1]John 5:25. Eph. 1:18-20. 2 Tim. 1:8-9. [2]Titus 3:4-5. Eph. 2:4-5, 7-9. Rom. 9:11. [3]2 Cor. 5:20. 2 Cor. 6:1-2. John 6:44. 2 Thess. 2:13-14. [4]Acts 26:18. 1 Cor. 2:10, 12. [5]Ezek. 11:19. Ezek. 36:26-27. John 6:45. [6]Eph. 2:5. Phil. 2:13. Deut. 30:6.

Q. 68. Are the elect only effectually called?
A. All the elect, and they only, are effectually called:[1] although others may be, and often are, outwardly called by the ministry of the Word,[2] and have some common operations of the Spirit;[3] who, for their wilful neglect and contempt of the grace offered to them, being justly left in their unbelief, do never truly come to Jesus Christ.[4]

[1]Acts 13:48. [2]Matt. 22:14. [3]Matt. 7:22. Heb. 6:4-6. [4]John 12:38-40. Acts 28:25-27. John 6:64-65. Ps. 81:11-12.

Q. 69. What is the communion in grace which the members of the invisible church have with Christ?
A. The communion in grace which the members of the invisible church have with Christ, is their partaking of the virtue of His mediation, in their justification,[1] adoption,[2] sanctification, and whatever else, in this life, manifests their union with Him.[3]

[1]Rom. 8:30. [2]Eph. 1:5. [3]1 Cor. 1:30.

Q. 70. What is justification?
A. Justification is an act of God's free grace unto sinners,[1] in which He pardoneth all their sins, accepteth and accounteth their persons righteous in His sight;[2] not for any thing wrought in them, or done by them,[3] but only for the perfect obedience and full satisfaction of Christ, by God imputed to them,[4] and received by faith alone.[5]

[1]Rom. 3:22, 24-25. Rom. 4:5. [2]2 Cor. 5:19, 21. Rom. 3:22, 24-25, 27-28. [3]Titus 3:5, 7. Eph. 1:7. [4]Rom. 5:17-19. Rom. 4:6-8. [5]Acts 10:43. Gal. 2:16. Phil. 3:9.

Q. 71. How is justification an act of God's free grace?
A. Although Christ, by His obedience and death, did make a proper, real, and full satisfaction to God's justice in the behalf of them that are justified;[1] yet in as much as God accepteth the satisfaction from a surety, which He might have demanded of them, and did provide this surety, His own only Son,[2] imputing His righteousness to them,[3] and requiring nothing of them for their justification but faith,[4] which also is His gift,[5] their justification is to them of free grace.[6]

[1]Rom. 5:8-10, 19.
[2]1 Tim. 2:5-6. Heb. 10:10. Matt. 20:28. Dan. 9:24, 26. Isa. 53:4-6, 10-12. Heb. 7:22.

Rom. 8:32. 1 Peter 1:18-19. [3]2 Cor. 5:21. [4]Rom. 3:24-25. [5]Eph. 2:8. [6]Eph. 1:17.

Q. 72. What is justifying faith?
A. Justifying faith is a saving grace,[1] wrought in the heart of a sinner by the Spirit[2] and Word of God,[3] whereby he, being convinced of his sin and misery, and of the disability in himself and all other creatures to recover him out of his lost condition,[4] not only assenteth to the truth of the promise of the gospel,[5] but receiveth and resteth upon Christ and His righteousness, therein held forth, for pardon of sin,[6] and for the accepting and accounting of his person righteous in the sight of God for salvation.[7]

[1]Heb. 10:39. [2]2 Cor. 4:13. Eph. 1:17-19. [3]Rom. 10:14-17. [4]Acts 2:37. Acts 16:30. John 16:8-9. Rom. 6:6. Eph. 2:1. Acts 4:12. [5]Eph. 1:13. [6]John 1:12. Acts 16:31. Acts 10:43. [7]Phil. 3:9. Acts 15:11.

Q. 73. How doth faith justify a sinner in the sight of God?
A. Faith justifies a sinner in the sight of God, not because of those other graces which do always accompany it, or of good works that are the fruits of it,[1] nor as if the grace of faith, or any act thereof, were imputed to him for His justification;[2] but only as it is an instrument by which He receiveth and applieth Christ and His righteousness.[3]

[1]Gal. 3:11. Rom. 3:28. [2]Rom. 4:5. Rom. 10:10. [3]John 1:12. Phil. 3:9. Gal. 1:16.

Q. 74. What is adoption?
A. Adoption is an act of the free grace of God,[1] in and for His only Son Jesus Christ,[2] whereby all those that are justified are received into the number of His children,[3] have His name put upon them,[4] the Spirit of His Son given to them,[5] are under His fatherly care and dispensations,[6] admitted to all the liberties and privileges of the sons of God, made heirs of all the promises, and fellow-heirs with Christ in glory.[7]

[1]1 John 3:1. [2]Eph. 1:5. Gal. 4:4-5. [3]John 1:12. [4]2 Cor. 6:18. Rev. 3:12. [5]Gal. 4:6. [6]Ps. 103:13. Prov. 14:26. Matt. 6:32. [7]Heb. 6:12. Rom. 8:17.

Q. 75. What is sanctification?
A. Sanctification is a work of God's grace, whereby they whom God hath, before the foundation of the world, chosen to be holy, are in time, through the powerful operation of His Spirit[1] applying the death and resurrection of Christ unto them,[2] renewed in their whole man after the image of God;[3] having the seeds of repentance unto life, and all other saving graces, put into their hearts,[4] and those graces so stirred up, increased, and strengthened,[5] as that they more and more die unto sin, and rise unto newness of life.[6]

[1]Eph. 1:4. 1 Cor. 6:11. 2 Thess. 2:13. [2]Rom. 6:4-6. [3]Eph. 4:23-24. [4]Acts 11:18. 1 John 3:9. [5]Jude 20. Heb. 6:11-12. Eph. 3:16-19. Col. 1:10-11. [6]Rom. 6:4, 6, 14. Gal. 5:24.

Q. 76. What is repentance unto life?
A. Repentance unto life is a saving grace,[1] wrought in the heart of a sinner by the Spirit[2] and Word of God,[3] whereby, out of the sight and sense, not only of the danger,[4] but also of the filthiness and odiousness of his sins,[5] and upon the apprehension of God's mercy in Christ to such as are penitent,[6] he so grieves for[7] and hates his sins,[8] as that he turns from them all to God,[9] purposing and endeavouring constantly to walk with Him in all the ways of new obedience.[10]

[1]2 Tim. 2:25. [2]Zech. 12:10. [3]Acts 11:18, 20-21. [4]Ezek. 18:28, 30, 32. Luke 15:17-18. Hosea 2:6-7. [5]Ezek. 36:31. Isa. 30:22. [6]Joel 2:12-13. [7]Jer. 31:18-19. [8]2 Cor. 7:11. [9]Acts 26:18. Exod. 14:6. 1 Kings 8:47-48. [10]Ps. 119:6, 59, 128. Luke 1:6. 2 Kings 23:25.

Q. 77. Wherein do justification and sanctification differ?
A. Although sanctification be inseparably joined with justification,[1] yet they differ, in that God in justification imputeth the righteousness of Christ;[2] in sanctification of His Spirit infuseth grace, and enableth to the exercise thereof;[3] in the former, sin is pardoned;[4] in the other, it is subdued:[5] the one doth equally free all believers from the revenging wrath of God, and that perfectly in this life, that they never fall into condemnation[6] the other is neither equal in all,[7] nor in this life perfect in any,[8] but growing up to perfection.[9]

[1]1 Cor. 6:11. 1 Cor. 1:30. [2]Rom. 4:6, 8. [3]Ezek. 36:27. [4]Rom. 3:24-25. [5]Rom. 6:6, 14. [6]Rom. 8:33-34. [7]1 John 2:12-14. Heb. 5:12-14. [8]1 John 1:8, 10. [9]2 Cor. 7:1. Phil. 3:12-14.

Q. 78. Whence ariseth the imperfection of sanctification in believers?
A. The imperfection of sanctification in believers ariseth from the remnants of sin abiding in every part of them, and the perpetual lustings of the flesh against the spirit; whereby they are often foiled with temptations, and fall into many sins,[1] are hindered in all their spiritual services,[2] and their best works are imperfect and defiled in the sight of God.[3]

[1]Rom. 7:18, 23. Mark 14:66. Gal. 2:11-12. [2]Heb. 12:1. [3]Isa. 64:6. Exod. 28:38.

Q. 79. May not true believers, by reason of their imperfections, and the many temptations and sins they are overtaken with, fall away from the state of grace?
A. True believers, by reason of the unchangeable love of God,[1] and His decree and covenant to give them perseverance,[2] their inseparable union with Christ,[3] His continual intercession for them,[4] and the Spirit and seed of God abiding in them,[5] can neither totally nor finally fall away from the state of grace,[6] but are kept by the power of God through faith unto salvation.[7]

[1]Jer. 31:3. [2]2 Tim. 2:19. Heb. 13:20-21. 2 Sam. 23:5. [3]1 Cor. 1:8-9. [4]Heb. 7:25. Luke 22:32. [5]1 John 3:9. 1 John 2:27. [6]Jer. 32:40. John 10:28. [7]1 Peter 1:5.

Q. 80. Can true believers be infallibly assured that they are in the estate of grace, and that they shall persevere therein unto salvation?
A. Such as truly believe in Christ, and endeavour to walk in all good conscience before Him,[1] may, without extraordinary revelation, by faith grounded upon the truth of God's promises, and by the Spirit enabling them to discern in themselves those graces to which the promises of life are made,[2] and bearing witness with their spirits that they are the children of God,[3] be infallibly assured that they are in the estate of grace, and shall persevere therein unto salvation.[4]

[1]1 John 2:3. [2]1 Cor. 2:12. 1 John 3:14, 18-19, 21, 24. 1 John 4:13, 16. Heb. 6:11-12. [3]Rom. 8:16. [4]1 John 5:13.

Q. 81. Are all true believers at all times assured of their present being in the estate of grace, and that they shall be saved?
A. Assurance of grace and salvation not being of the essence of faith,[1] true believers may wait long before they obtain it;[2] and, after the enjoyment thereof, may have it weakened and intermitted, through manifold distempers, sins, temptations, and desertions;[3] yet they are never left without such a presence and support of the Spirit of God as keeps them from sinking into utter despair.[4]

[1]Eph. 1:13. [2]Isa. 50:10. Ps. 88:1-3, 6-7, 9-10, 13-15. [3]Ps. 77:1-12. Song 5:2-3, 6. Ps. 51:8, 12. Ps. 31:22. Ps. 22:1. [4]1 John 3:9. Ps. 73:15, 23. Isa. 54:7-10.

Q. 82. What is the communion in glory which the members of the invisible church have with Christ?
A. The communion in glory which the members of the invisible church have with Christ, is in this life,[1] immediately after death,[2] and at last perfected at the resurrection and day of judgment.[3]

[1]2 Cor. 3:18. [2]Luke 23:43. [3]1 Thess. 4:17.

Q. 83. What is the communion in glory with Christ which the members of the invisible church enjoy in this life?
A. The members of the invisible church have communicated to them in this life the firstfruits of glory with Christ, as they are members of Him their head, and so in Him are interested in that glory which He is fully possessed of;[1] and, as an earnest thereof, enjoy the sense of God's love,[2] peace of conscience, joy in the Holy Ghost, and hope of glory;[3] as, on the contrary, sense of God's revenging wrath, horror of conscience, and a fearful expectation of judgment, are to the wicked the beginning of their torments which they shall endure after death.[4]

[1]Eph. 2:5-6. [2]Rom. 5:5. 2 Cor. 1:22. [3]Rom. 5:1-2. Rom. 14:17. [4]Gen. 4:13. Matt. 27:4. Heb. 10:27. Rom. 2:9. Mark 9:44.

Q. 84. Shall all men die?
A. Death being threatened as the wages of sin,[1] it is appointed unto all men once to die;[2] for that all have sinned.[3]

[1]Rom. 6:23. [2]Heb. 9:27. [3]Rom. 5:12.

Q. 85. Death, being the wages of sin, why are not the righteous delivered from death, seeing all their sins are forgiven in Christ?

A. The righteous shall be delivered from death itself at the last day, and even in death are delivered from the sting and curse of it;[1] so that, although they die, yet it is out of God's love,[2] to free them perfectly from sin and misery,[3] and to make them capable of further communion with Christ in glory, which they then enter upon.[4]

[1]1 Cor. 15:26, 55-57. Heb. 2:15. [2]Isa. 57:1-2. 2 Kings 22:20. [3]Rev. 14:13. Eph. 5:27. [4]Luke 23:43. Phil. 1:23.

Q. 86. What is the communion in glory with Christ, which the members of the invisible church enjoy immediately after death?
A. The communion in glory with Christ, which the members of the invisible church enjoy immediately after death is, in that their souls are then made perfect in holiness,[1] and received into the highest heavens,[2] where they behold the face of God in light and glory,[3] waiting for the full redemption of their bodies,[4] which even in death continue united to Christ,[5] and rest in their graves as in their beds,[6] till at the last day they be again united to their souls.[7] Whereas the souls of the wicked are at their death cast into hell, where they remain in torments and utter darkness, and their bodies kept in their graves, as in their prisons, till the resurrection and judgment of the great day.[8]

[1]Heb. 12:23. [2]2 Cor. 5:1, 6, 8. Phil. 1:23. Acts 3:21. Eph. 4:10. [3]1 John 3:2. 1 Cor. 13:12. [4]Rom. 8:23. Ps. 16:9. [5]1 Thess. 4:14. [6]Isa. 57:2. [7]Job 19:26-27. [8]Luke 16:23-24. Acts 1:25. Jude 6-7.

Q. 87. What are we to believe concerning the resurrection?
A. We are to believe that at the last day there shall be a general resurrection of the dead, both of the just and unjust:[1] when they that are then found alive shall in a moment be changed; and the selfsame bodies of the dead which were laid in the grave, being then again united to their souls forever, shall be raised up by the power of Christ.[2] The bodies of the just, by the Spirit of Christ, and by virtue of His resurrection as their head, shall be raised in power, spiritual, incorruptible, and made like to His glorious body;[3] and the bodies of the wicked shall be raised up in dishonour by Him, as an offended judge.[4]

[1]Acts 24:15. [2]1 Cor. 15:51-53. 1 Thess. 4:15-17. John 5:28-29. [3]1 Cor. 15:21-23, 42-44. Phil. 3:21. [4]John 5:27-29. Matt. 25:33.

Q. 88. What shall immediately follow after the resurrection?
A. Immediately after the resurrection shall follow the general and final judgment of angels and men;[1] the day and hour whereof no man knoweth, that all may watch and pray, and be ever ready for the coming of the Lord.[2]

[1]2 Peter 2:4, 6-7, 14-15. Matt. 25:46. [2]Matt. 24:36, 42, 44.

Q. 89. What shall be done to the wicked at the day of judgment?
A. At the day of judgment, the wicked shall be set on Christ's left hand,[1] and, upon clear evidence, and full conviction of their own consciences,[2] shall have the fearful but just sentence of condemnation pronounced against them;[3] and thereupon shall be cast out from the favourable presence of God, and the glorious fellowship with Christ, His saints, and all His holy angels, into hell, to be punished with unspeakable torments, both of body and soul, with the devil and his angels forever.[4]

[1]Matt. 25:33. [2]Rom. 2:15-16. [3]Matt. 25:41-43. [4]Luke 16:26. 2 Thess. 1:8-9.

Q. 90. What shall be done to the righteous at the day of judgment?
A. At the day of judgment, the righteous, being caught up to Christ in the clouds,[1] shall be set on His right hand, and there openly acknowledged and acquitted,[2] shall join with Him in the judging of reprobate angels and men,[3] and shall be received into heaven,[4] where they shall be fully and forever freed from all sin and misery;[5] filled with inconceivable joys,[6] made perfectly holy and happy both in body and soul, in the company of innumerable saints and holy angels,[7] but especially in the immediate vision and fruition of God the Father, of our Lord Jesus Christ, and of the Holy Spirit, to all eternity.[8] And this is the perfect and full communion, which the members of the invisible church shall enjoy with Christ in glory, at the resurrection and day of judgment.

[1]1 Thess. 4:17. [2]Matt. 25:33. Matt. 10:32. [3]1 Cor. 6:2-3. [4]Matt. 25:34, 46. [5]Eph. 5:27.

Rev. 14:13. [6]Ps. 16:11. [7]Heb. 12:22-23.
[8]1 John 3:2. 1 Cor. 13:12. 1 Thess. 4:17-18.

Q. 91. What is the duty which God requireth of man?
A. The duty which God requireth of man, is obedience to His revealed will.[1]

[1]Rom. 12:1-2. Micah 6:8. 1 Sam. 15:22.

Q. 92. What did God at first reveal unto man as the rule of His obedience?
A. The rule of obedience revealed to Adam in the estate of innocence, and to all mankind in him, besides a special command not to eat of the fruit of the tree of the knowledge of good and evil, was the moral law.[1]

[1]Gen. 1:26-27. Rom. 2:14-15. Rom. 10:5. Gen. 2:17.

Q. 93. What is the moral law?
A. The moral law is the declaration of the will of God to mankind, directing and binding every one to personal, perfect, and perpetual conformity and obedience thereunto, in the frame and disposition of the whole man, soul and body,[1] and in performance of all those duties of holiness and righteousness which he oweth to God and man:[2] promising life upon the fulfilling, and threatening death upon the breach of it.[3]

[1]Deut. 5:1-3, 31, 33. Luke 10:26-27. 1 Thess. 5:23. [2]Luke 1:75. Acts 24:16. [3]Rom. 10:5. Gal. 3:10. Gal. 3:12.

Q. 94. Is there any use of the moral law to man since the fall?
A. Although no man, since the fall, can attain to righteousness and life by the moral law:[1] yet there is great use thereof, as well common to all men, as peculiar either to the unregenerate, or the regenerate.[2]

[1]Rom. 8:3. Gal. 2:16. [2]1 Tim. 1:8.

Q. 95. Of what use is the moral law to all men?
A. The moral law is of use to all men, to inform them of the holy nature and the will of God,[1] and of their duty, binding them to walk accordingly;[2] to convince them of their disability to keep it, and of the sinful pollution of their nature, hearts, and lives:[3] to humble them in the sense of their sin and misery,[4] and thereby help them to a clearer sight of the need they have of Christ,[5] and of the perfection of His obedience.[6]

[1]Lev. 11:44-45. Lev. 20:7-8. Rom. 8:12. [2]Micah 6:8. James 2:10-11. [3]Ps. 19:11-12. Rom. 3:20. Rom. 7:7. [4]Rom. 3:9,23. [5]Gal. 3:21-22. [6]Rom. 10:4.

Q. 96. What particular use is there of the moral law to unregenerate men?
A. The moral law is of use to unregenerate men, to awaken their consciences to flee from wrath to come,[1] and to drive them to Christ;[2] or, upon their continuance in the estate and way of sin, to leave them inexcusable,[3] and under the curse thereof.[4]

[1]1 Tim. 1:9-10. [2]Gal. 3:24. [3]Rom. 1:20. Rom. 2:15. [4]Gal. 3:10.

Q. 97. What special use is there of the moral law to the regenerate?
A. Although they that are regenerate, and believe in Christ, be delivered from the moral law as a covenant of works,[1] so as thereby they are neither justified[2] nor condemned;[3] yet, besides the general uses thereof common to them with all men, it is of special use, to show them how much they are bound to Christ for His fulfilling it, and enduring the curse thereof in their stead, and for their good;[4] and thereby to provoke them to more thankfulness,[5] and to express the same in their greater care to conform themselves thereunto as the rule of their obedience.[6]

[1]Rom. 6:14. Rom. 7:4, 6. Gal. 4:4-5. [2]Rom. 3:20. [3]Gal. 5:23. Rom. 8:1. [4]Rom. 7:24-25. Gal. 3:13-14. Rom. 8:3-4. [5]Luke 1:68-69, 74-75. Col. 1:12-14. [6]Rom. 7:22. Rom. 12:2. Titus 2:11-14.

Q. 98. Where is the moral law summarily comprehended?
A. The moral law is summarily comprehended in the ten commandments, which were delivered by the voice of God upon Mount Sinai, and written by Him in two tables of stone;[1] and are recorded in the twentieth chapter of Exodus. The four first commandments containing our duty to God, and the other six our duty to man.[2]

[1]Deut. 10:4. Exod. 34:1-4. [2]Matt. 22:37-40.

Q. 99. What rules are to be observed for the right understanding of the ten commandments?

A. For the right understanding of the ten commandments, these rules are to be observed:

1. That the law is perfect, and bindeth everyone to full conformity in the whole man unto the righteousness thereof, and unto entire obedience forever; so as to require the utmost perfection of every duty, and to forbid the least degree of every sin.[1]
2. That it is spiritual, and so reacheth the understanding, will, affections, and all other powers of the soul; as well as words, works, and gestures.[2]
3. That one and the same thing, in divers respects, is required or forbidden in several commandments.[3]
4. That as, where a duty is commanded, the contrary sin is forbidden;[4] and, where a sin is forbidden, the contrary duty is commanded:[5] so, where a promise is annexed, the contrary threatening is included;[6] and, where a threatening is annexed, the contrary promise is included.[7]
5. That what God forbids, is at no time to be done;[8] what He commands, is always our duty;[9] and yet every particular duty is not to be done at all times.[10]
6. That under one sin or duty, all of the same kind are forbidden or commanded; together with all the causes, means, occasions, and appearances thereof, and provocations thereunto.[11]
7. That what is forbidden or commanded to ourselves, we are bound, according to our places to endeavour that it may be avoided or performed by others, according to the duty of their places.[12]
8. That in what is commanded to others, we are bound, according to our places and callings, to be helpful to them;[13] and to take heed of partaking with others in what is forbidden them.[14]

[1]Ps. 19:7. James 2:10. Matt. 5:21-22. [2]Rom. 7:14. Deut. 6:5. Matt. 22:37-39. Matt. 5:21-22, 27-28, 33-34, 37-39, 43-44. [3]Col. 3:5. Amos 8:5. Prov. 1:19. 1 Tim. 6:10. [4]Isa. 58:13. Deut. 6:13. Matt. 4:9-10. Matt. 15:4-6. [5]Matt. 5:21-25. Eph. 4:28. [6]Exod. 20:12. Prov. 30:17. [7]Jer. 18:7-8. Exod. 20:7. Ps. 15:1, 4-5. Ps. 24:4-5. [8]Job 13:7-8. Rom. 3:8. Job 36:21. Heb. 11:25. [9]Deut. 4:8-9. [10]Matt. 12:7. [11]Matt. 5:21-22, 27-28. Matt. 15:4-6. Heb. 10:24-25. 1 Thess. 5:22. Jude 23. Gal. 5:26. Col. 3:21. [12]Exod. 20:10. Lev. 19:17. Gen. 18:19. Josh. 14:15. Deut. 6:6-7. [13]2 Cor. 1:24. [14]1 Tim. 5:22. Eph. 5:11.

Q. 100. What special things are we to consider in the ten commandments?

A. We are to consider in the ten commandments, the preface, the substance of the commandments themselves, and several reasons annexed to some of them, the more to enforce them.

Q. 101. What is the preface to the ten commandments?

A. The preface to the ten commandments is contained in these words, I am the Lord thy God, which have brought thee out of the land of Egypt, out of the house of bondage.[1] Wherein God manifesteth His sovereignty, as being JEHOVAH, the eternal, immutable, and almighty God;[2] having His being in and of Himself,[3] and giving being to all His Words[4] and works:[5] and that He is a God in covenant, as with Israel of old, so with all His people;[6] who, as He brought them out of their bondage in Egypt, so He delivereth us from our spiritual thraldom;[7] and that therefore we are bound to take Him for our God alone, and to keep all His commandments.[8]

[1]Exod. 20:2. [2]Isa. 44:6. [3]Exod. 3:14. [4]Exod. 6:3. [5]Acts 17:24, 28. [6]Gen. 17:7. Rom. 3:29. [7]Luke 1:74-75. [8]1 Peter 1:15, 17-18. Lev. 18:30. Lev. 19:37.

Q. 102. What is the sum of the four commandments which contain our duty to God?

A. The sum of the four commandments containing our duty to God is, to love the Lord our God with all our heart, and with all our soul, and with all our strength, and with all our mind.[1]

[1]Luke 10:27.

Q. 103. Which is the first commandment?

A. The first commandment is, Thou shall have no other gods before me.[1]

[1]Exod. 20:3.

Q. 104. What are the duties required in the first commandment?

A. The duties required in the first commandment are, the knowing and acknowledging of God to be the only true God, and our God;[1] and to worship and glorify Him accordingly,[2] by thinking,[3] meditating,[4] remembering,[5] highly esteeming,[6] honouring,[7] adoring,[8] choosing,[9] loving,[10] desiring,[11] fearing of Him;[12] believing Him;[13] trusting[14] hoping,[15] delighting,[16] rejoicing in Him;[17] being zealous for Him;[18] calling upon Him, giving all praise and thanks,[19] and yielding all obedience and submission to Him with the whole man;[20] being careful in all things to please Him,[21] and sorrowful when in any thing He is offended;[22] and walking humbly with Him.[23]

[1] I Chron. 28:9. Deut. 26:7. Isa. 43:10. Jer. 14:22. [2] Ps. 95:6-7. Matt. 4:10. Ps. 29:2. [3] Mal. 3:16. [4] Ps. 63:6. [5] Eccles. 12:1. [6] Ps. 71:19. [7] Mal. 1:6. [8] Isa. 45:23. [9] Josh. 24:15, 22. [10] Deut. 6:5. [11] Ps. 73:25. [12] Isa. 8:13. [13] Exod. 14:31. [14] Isa. 26:4. [15] Ps. 130:7. [16] Ps. 37:4. [17] Ps. 32:11. [18] Rom. 12:11. Num. 25:11. [19] Phil. 4:6. [20] Jer. 7:23. James 4:7. [21] I John 3:22. [22] Jer. 31:18. Ps. 119:136. [23] Micah 6:8.

Q. 105. What are the sins forbidden in the first commandment?
A. The sins forbidden in the first commandment are, atheism, in denying or not having a God;[1] idolatry, in having or worshipping more gods than one, or any with or instead of the true God;[2] the not having and avouching Him for God, and our God;[3] the omission or neglect of anything due to Him, required in this commandment;[4] ignorance,[5] forgetfulness,[6] misapprehensions,[7] false opinions,[8] unworthy and wicked thoughts of Him;[9] bold and curious searching into His secrets;[10] all profaneness,[11] hatred of God;[12] self-love,[13] self-seeking,[14] and all other inordinate and immoderate setting of our mind, will, or affections upon other things, and taking them off from Him in whole or in part;[15] vain credulity,[16] unbelief,[17] heresy,[18] misbelief,[19] distrust,[20] despair,[21] incorrigibleness,[22] and insensibleness under judgments,[23] hardness of heart,[24] pride,[25] presumption,[26] carnal security,[27] tempting of God;[28] using unlawful means,[29] and trusting in lawful means;[30] carnal delights and joys;[31] corrupt, blind, and indiscreet zeal;[32] lukewarmness,[33] and deadness in the things of God;[34] estranging ourselves, and apostatizing from God;[35] praying, or giving any religious worship, to saints, angels, or any other creatures;[36] all compacts and consulting with the devil,[37] and hearkening to his suggestions;[38] making men the lords of our faith and conscience;[39] slighting and despising God and His commands;[40] resisting and grieving of His Spirit,[41] discontent and impatience at His dispensations, charging Him foolishly for the evils He inflicts on us;[42] and ascribing the praise of any good we either are, have or can do, to fortune,[43] idols,[44] ourselves,[45] or any other creature.[46]

[1] Ps. 14:1. Eph. 2:12. [2] Jer. 2:27-28. I Thess. 1:9. [3] Ps. 81:11. [4] Isa. 43:2, 23-24. [5] Jer. 4:22. Hosea 4:1, 6. [6] Jer. 2:32. [7] Acts 17:23, 29. [8] Isa. 40:18. [9] Ps. 50:21. [10] Deut. 29:29. [11] Titus 1:16. Heb. 12:16. [12] Rom. 1:30. [13] 2 Tim. 3:2. [14] Phil. 2:21. [15] I John 2:15-16. I Sam. 2:29. Col. 2:2, 5. [16] I John 4:1. [17] Heb. 3:12. [18] Gal. 5:20. Titus 3:10. [19] Acts 26:9. [20] Ps. 78:22. [21] Gen. 4:13. [22] Jer. 5:3. [23] Isa. 42:25. [24] Rom. 2:5. [25] Jer. 13:15. [26] Ps. 10:13. [27] Zeph. 1:12. [28] Matt. 4:7. [29] Rom. 3:8. [30] Jer. 17:5. [31] 2 Tim. 3:4. [32] Gal. 4:17. John 16:2. Rom. 10:2. Luke 9:54-55. [33] Rev. 3:16. [34] Rev. 2:1. [35] Ezek. 14:5. Isa. 1:4-5. [36] Rom. 10:13-14. Hosea 4:12. Acts 10:25-26. Rev. 19:10. Matt. 4:10. Col. 2:18. Rom. 1:25. [37] Lev. 20:6. I Sam. 28:7, 11. I Chron. 10:13-14. [38] Acts 5:3. [39] 2 Cor. 1:24. Matt. 23:9. [40] Deut. 32:15. 2 Sam. 12:9. Prov. 13:13. [41] Acts 7:51. Eph. 4:30. [42] Ps. 73:2-3, 13-15, 22. Job 1:22. [43] I Sam. 6:7-9. [44] Dan. 5:23. [45] Deut. 8:17. Dan. 4:30. [46] Hab. 1:16.

Q. 106. What are we specially taught by these words before me in the first commandment?
A. These words before me or before my face, in the first commandment, teach us, that God, who seeth all things, taketh special notice of, and is much displeased with, the sin of having any other God: that so it may be an argument to dissuade from it, and to aggravate it as a most impudent provocation:[1] as also to persuade us to do as in His sight, whatever we do in His service.[2]

[1] Ezek. 8:5-6. Ps. 44:20-21. [2] I Chron. 28:9.

Q. 107. Which is the second commandment?
A. The second commandment is, Thou shalt not make unto thee any graven image, or any likeness of anything that is in heaven above, or that is in the earth beneath, or

that is in the water under the earth. Thou shalt not bow down thyself to them, nor serve them: for I the Lord thy God am a jealous God, visiting the iniquity of the fathers upon the children unto the third and fourth generation of them that hate me; and showing mercy unto thousands of them that love me, and keep my commandments.[1]

[1]Exod. 20:4-6.

Q. 108. What are the duties required in the second commandment?
A. The duties required in the second commandment are, the receiving, observing, and keeping pure and entire, all such religious worship and ordinances as God hath instituted in His Word;[1] particularly prayer and thanksgiving in the name of Christ;[2] the reading, preaching, and hearing of the Word;[3] the administration and receiving of the sacraments;[4] church government and discipline;[5] the ministry and maintainance thereof;[6] religious fasting;[7] swearing by the name of God;[8] and vowing unto Him;[9] as also the disapproving, detesting, opposing all false worship;[10] and, according to each one's place and calling, removing it, and all monuments of idolatry.[11]

[1]Deut. 32:46-47. Matt. 28:20. Acts 2:42. I Tim. 6:13-14. [2]Phil. 4:6. Eph. 5:20. [3]Deut. 17:18-19. Acts 15:21. 2 Tim. 4:2. James 1:21-22. Acts 10:33. [4]Matt. 28:19. I Cor. 11:23-30. [5]Matt. 18:15-17. Matt. 16:19. I Cor. 5. I Cor. 12:28. [6]Eph. 4:11-12. I Tim. 5:17-18. I Cor. 9:7-15. [7]Joel 2:12, 18. I Cor. 7:5. [8]Deut. 6:13. [9]Ps. 76:11. [10]Acts 17:16-17. Ps. 16:4. [11]Deut. 7:5. Isa. 30:22.

Q. 109. What are the sins forbidden in the second commandment?
A. The sins forbidden in the second commandment are, all devising,[1] counseling,[2] commanding,[3] using,[4] and anywise approving, any religious worship not instituted by God Himself;[5] tolerating a false religion; the making any representation of God, of all or of any of the three persons, either inwardly in our mind, or outwardly in any kind of image or likeness of any creature whatsoever;[6] all worshipping of it,[7] or God in it or by it;[8] the making of any representation of feigned deities,[9] and all worship of them, or service belonging to them,[10] all superstitious devices,[11] corrupting the worship of God,[12] adding to it, or taking from it,[13] whether invented and taken up of ourselves,[14] or received by tradition from others,[15] though under the title of antiquity,[16] custom,[17] devotion,[18] good intent, or any other pretence whatsoever;[19] simony;[20] sacrilege;[21] all neglect,[22] contempt,[23] hindering,[24] and opposing the worship and ordinances which God hath appointed.[25]

[1]Num. 15:39. [2]Deut. 13:6-8. [3]Hosea 5:11. Micah 6:16. [4]I Kings 11:33. I Kings 12:33. [5]Deut. 12:30-32. [6]Deut. 4:15-19. Acts 17:29. Rom. 1:21-23, 25. [7]Dan. 3:18. Gal. 4:8. [8]Exod. 32:5. [9]Exod. 32:8. [10]I Kings 18:26,28. Isa. 65:11. [11]Acts 17:22. Col. 2:21-23. [12]Mal. 1:7-8, 14. [13]Deut. 4:2. [14]Ps. 106:39. [15]Matt. 15:9. [16]I Peter 1:18. [17]Jer. 44:17. [18]Isa. 65:3-5. Gal. 1:13-14. [19]I Sam. 13:11-12. I Sam. 15:21. [20]Acts 8:18. [21]Rom. 2:22. Mal. 3:8. [22]Exod. 4:24-26. [23]Matt. 22:5. Mal. 1:7, 13. [24]Matt. 23:13. [25]Acts 13:44-45. I Thess. 2:15-16.

Q. 110. What are the reasons annexed to the second commandment, the more to enforce it?
A. The reasons annexed to the second commandment, the more to enforce it, contained in these words, For I the Lord thy God am a jealous God, visiting the iniquity of the fathers upon the children unto the third and fourth generation of them that hate me; and showing mercy unto thousands of them that love me, and keep my commandments;[1] are, besides God's sovereignty over us, and propriety in us,[2] His fervent zeal for His own worship,[3] and His revengeful indignation against all false worship, as being a spiritual whoredom;[4] accounting the breakers of this commandment such as hate Him, and threatening to punish them unto divers generations;[5] and esteeming the observers of it such as love Him and keep His commandments, and promising mercy to them unto many generations.[6]

[1]Exod. 20:5-6. [2]Ps. 45:11. Rev. 15:3-4. [3]Exod. 34:13-14. [4]I Cor. 10:20-22. Deut. 32:16-20. [5]Hosea 2:2-4. [6]Deut. 5:29.

Q. 111. Which is the third commandment?
A. The third commandment is, Thou shalt not take the name of the Lord thy God in vain: for the Lord will not hold him guiltless that taketh His name in vain.[1]

[1]Exod. 20:7.

Q. 112. What is required in the third commandment?
A. The third commandment requires, That the name of God, His titles, attributes,[1] ordinances,[2] the Word,[3] sacraments,[4] prayer,[5] oaths,[6] vows,[7] lots,[8] His works,[9] and whatsoever else there is whereby He makes Himself known, be holily and reverently used in thought,[10] meditation,[11] word,[12] and writing;[13] by an holy profession,[14] and answerable conversation,[15] to the glory of God,[16] and the good of ourselves,[17] and others.[18]

[1]Matt. 11:9. Deut. 28:58. Ps. 29:2. Ps. 68:4. Rev. 15:3-4. [2]Mal. 1:14. Eccles. 5:1. [3]Ps. 138:2. [4]1 Cor. 11:24-25, 28-29. [5]1 Tim. 2:8. [6]Jer. 4:2. [7]Eccles. 5:2, 4-6. [8]Acts 1:24, 26. [9]Job 36:24. [10]Mal. 3:16. [11]Ps. 8:1, 3-4, 9. [12]Col. 3:17. Ps. 105:2, 5. [13]Ps. 102:18. [14]1 Peter 3:15. Micah 4:5. [15]Phil. 1:27. [16]1 Cor. 10:31. [17]Jer. 32:39. [18]1 Peter 2:12.

Q. 113. What are the sins forbidden in the third commandment?
A. The sins forbidden in the third commandment are, the not using of God's name as is required;[1] and the abuse of it in an ignorant,[2] vain,[3] irreverent, profane,[4] superstitious[5] or wicked mentioning or otherwise using His titles, attributes,[6] ordinances,[7] or works,[8] by blasphemy,[9] perjury;[10] all sinful cursings,[11] oaths,[12] vows,[13] and lots;[14] violating of our oaths and vows, if lawful[15] and fulfilling them, if of things unlawful;[16] murmuring and quarrelling at,[17] curious prying into,[18] and misapplying of God's decrees[19] and providences;[20] misinterpreting,[21] misapplying,[22] or any way perverting the Word, or any part of it;[23] to profane jests,[24] curious or unprofitable questions, vain janglings, or the maintaining of false doctrines;[25] abusing it, the creatures, or anything contained under the name of God, to charms,[26] or sinful lusts and practices;[27] the maligning,[28] scorning,[29] reviling,[30] or any wise opposing of God's truth, grace, and ways;[31] making profession of religion in hypocrisy, or for sinister ends;[32] being ashamed of it,[33] or a shame to it, by unconformable,[34] unwise,[35] unfruitful,[36] and offensive walking,[37] or backsliding from it.[38]

[1]Mal. 2:2. [2]Acts 17:23. [3]Prov. 30:9. [4]Mal. 1:6-7, 12. Mal. 3:14. [5]1 Sam. 4:3-5. Jer. 7:4, 9-10, 14, 31. Col. 2:20-22. [6]2 Kings 18:30, 35. Ezek. 5:2. Ps. 139:20. [7]Ps. 50:16-17. [8]Isa. 5:12. [9]2 Kings 19:22. Lev. 24:11. [10]Zech. 5:4. Zech. 8:17. [11]1 Sam. 17:43. 2 Sam. 16:5. [12]Jer. 5:7. Jer. 23:10. [13]Deut. 23:18. Acts 23:12, 14. [14]Esther 3:7. Esther 9:24. Ps. 22:18. [15]Ps. 24:4. Ezek. 17:16, 18-19. [16]Mark 6:26. 1 Sam. 25:22, 32-34. [17]Rom. 9:14, 19-20. [18]Deut. 29:29. [19]Rom. 3:5, 7. Rom. 6:1. [20]Eccles. 8:11. Eccles. 9:3. Ps. 39. etc [21]Matt. 5:21-22. etc. to the end of the chapter [22]Ezek. 13:22. [23]2 Peter 3:16. Matt. 22:24-31. Matt. 25:28-30. [24]Isa. 22:13. Jer. 23:34, 36, 38. [25]1 Tim. 1:4, 6-7. 1 Tim. 6:4-5, 20. 2 Tim. 2:14. Titus 3:9. [26]Deut. 18:10-14. etc Acts 19:13. [27]2 Tim. 4:3-4. Rom. 13:13-14. 1 Kings 21:9-10. Jude 4. [28]Acts 13:45. 1 John 3:12. [29]Ps. 1:1. 2 Peter 3:3. [30]1 Peter 4:4. [31]Acts 13:45-46, 50. Acts 4:18. Acts 19:9. 1 Thess. 2:16. Heb. 10:29. [32]2 Tim. 3:5. Matt. 23:14. Matt. 6:1-2, 5, 16. [33]Mark 8:38. [34]Ps. 73:14-15. [35]1 Cor. 6:5-6. Eph. 5:15-17. [36]Isa. 5:4. 2 Peter 1:8-9. [37]Rom. 2:23-24. [38]Gal. 3:1, 3. Heb. 6:6.

Q. 114. What reasons are annexed to the third commandment?
A. The reasons annexed to the third commandment, in these words, The Lord thy God, and, For the Lord will not hold him guiltless that taketh His name in vain,[1] are, because He is the Lord and our God, therefore His name is not to be profaned, or any way abused by us;[2] especially because He will be so far from acquitting and sparing the transgressors of this commandment, as that He will not suffer them to escape His righteous judgment;[3] albeit many such escape the censures and punishments of men.[4]

[1]Exod. 20:7. [2]Lev. 19:12. [3]Ezek. 36:21-23. Deut. 28:58-59. Zech. 5:2-4. [4]1 Sam. 2:12, 17, 22, 24. 1 Sam. 3:13.

Q. 115. Which is the fourth command-ment?
A. The fourth commandment is, Remember the sabbath day, to keep it holy. Six days shalt thou labor, and do all thy work; but the seventh day is the sabbath of the Lord thy God: in it thou shalt not do any work, thou, nor thy son, nor thy daughter, thy manservant, nor thy maid-servant, nor thy cattle, nor thy stranger that is within thy gates. For in six days the Lord made heaven and earth, the sea, and all that in them is, and rested in the seventh day: wherefore the Lord blessed the sabbath-day and hallowed it.[1]

[1]Exod. 20:8-11.

Q. 116. What is required in the fourth commandment?
A. The fourth commandment requireth of all men the sanctifying or keeping holy to God such set times as He hath appointed in His Word, expressly one whole day in seven; which was the seventh from the beginning of the world to the resurrection of Christ, and the first day of the week ever since, and so to continue to the end of the world; which is the Christian sabbath,[1] and in the New Testament called The Lord's day.[2]

[1]Deut. 5:12-14. Gen. 2:2-3. 1 Cor. 16:1-2. Matt. 5:17-18. Isa. 56:2, 4, 6-7. [2]Rev. 1:10.

Q. 117. How is the sabbath or the Lord's day to be sanctified?
A. The sabbath or Lord's day is to be sanctified by an holy resting all the day,[1] not only from such works as are at all times sinful, but even from such worldly employments and recreations as are on other days lawful;[2] and making it our delight to spend the whole time (except so much of it as is to be taken up in works of necessity and mercy[3]) in the public and private exercises of God's worship:[4] and, to that end, we are to prepare our hearts, and with such foresight, diligence, and moderation, to dispose and seasonably dispatch our worldly business, that we may be the more free and fit for the duties of that day.[5]

[1]Exod. 20:8, 10. [2]Exod. 16:25-28. Neh. 13:15-22. Jer. 17:21-22. [3]Matt. 12:1-13. etc [4]Isa. 58:13. Luke 4:16. Acts 20:7. 1 Cor. 16:1-2. Ps. 92 for the sabbath-day. Isa. 66:23. Lev. 23:3. [5]Exod. 20:8. Luke 23:54, 56. Exod. 16:22, 25-26, 29. Neh. 13:19.

Q. 118. Why is the charge of keeping the sabbath more specially directed to governors of families, and other superiors?
A. The charge of keeping the sabbath is more specially directed to governors of families, and other superiors, because they are bound not only to keep it themselves, but to see that it be observed by all those that are under their charge; and because they are prone ofttimes to hinder them by employments of their own.[1]

[1]Exod. 20:10. Josh. 24:15. Neh. 13:15, 17. Jer. 17:20-22. Exod. 23:12.

Q. 119. What are the sins forbidden in the fourth commandment?
A. The sins forbidden in the fourth commandment are, all omissions of the duties required,[1] all careless, negligent, and unprofitable performing of them, and being weary of them;[2] all profaning the day by idleness, and doing that which is in itself sinful;[3] and by all needless works, words, and thoughts, about our worldly employments and recreations.[4]

[1]Ezek. 22:26. [2]Acts 20:7, 9. Ezek. 33:30-32. Amos 8:5. Mal. 1:13. [3]Ezek. 23:38. [4]Jer. 17:24, 27. Isa. 58:13.

Q. 120. What are the reasons annexed to the fourth commandment, the more to enforce it?
A. The reasons annexed to the fourth commandment, the more to enforce it, are taken from the equity of it, God allowing us six days of seven for our own affairs, and reserving but one for Himself in these words, Six days shalt thou labor, and do all thy work:[1] from God's challenging a special propriety in that day, The seventh day is the sabbath of the Lord thy God:[2] from the example of God, who in six days made heaven and earth, the sea, and all that in them is, and rested the seventh day: and from that blessing which God put upon that day, not only in sanctifying it to be a day for His service, but in ordaining it to be a means of blessing to us in our sanctifying it; Wherefore the Lord blessed the sabbath day, and hallowed it.[3]

[1]Exod. 20:9. [2]Exod. 20:10. [3]Exod. 20:11.

Q. 121. Why is the word Remember set in the beginning of the fourth commandment?
A. The word Remember is set in the beginning of the fourth commandment,[1] partly, because of the great benefit of remembering it, we being thereby helped in our preparation to keep it,[2] and, in keeping it, better to keep all the rest of the commandments,[3] and to continue a thankful remembrance of the two great benefits of creation and redemption, which contain a short abridgment of religion;[4] and partly, because we are very ready to forget it,[5] for that there is less light of nature for it,[6] and yet it restraineth our natural liberty in things at other

times lawful;[7] that it cometh but once in seven days, and many worldly businesses come between, and too often take off our minds from thinking of it, either to prepare for it, or to sanctify it;[8] and that Satan with his instruments labors much to blot out the glory, and even the memory of it, to bring in all irreligion and impiety.[9]

[1]Exod. 20:8. [2]Exod. 16:23. Luke 23:54, 56. Mark 15:42. Neh. 13:19. [3]Ps. 92 sabbath-day. Ezek. 20:12, 19-20. [4]Gen. 2:2-3. Ps. 118:22, 24. Acts 4:10-11. Rev. 1:10. [5]Ezek. 22:26. [6]Neh. 9:14. [7]Exod. 34:21. [8]Deut. 5:14-15. Amos 8:5. [9]Lam. 1:7. Jer. 17:21-23. Neh. 13:15-22.

Q. 122. What is the sum of the six commandments which contain our duty to man?
A. The sum of the six commandments which contain our duty to man, is, to love our neighbor as ourselves,[1] and to do to others what we would have them to do to us.[2]

[1]Matt. 22:39. [2]Matt. 7:12.

Q. 123. Which is the fifth commandment?
A. The fifth commandment is, Honor thy father and thy mother: that thy days may be long upon the land which the Lord thy God giveth thee.[1]

[1]Exod. 20:12.

Q. 124. Who are meant by father and mother in the fifth commandment?
A. By father and mother, in the fifth commandment, are meant, not only natural parents,[1] but all superiors in age[2] and gifts;[3] and especially such as, by God's ordinance, are over us in place of authority, whether in family,[4] church,[5] or commonwealth.[6]

[1]Prov. 23:22, 25. Eph. 6:1-2. [2]1 Tim. 5:1-2. [3]Gen. 4:20-22. Gen. 45:8. [4]2 Kings 5:13. [5]2 Kings 2:12. 2 Kings 13:14. Gal. 4:19. [6]Isa. 49:23.

Q. 125. Why are superiors styled father and mother?
A. Superiors are styled father and mother, both to teach them in all duties toward their inferiors, like natural parents, to express love and tenderness to them, according to their several relations;[1] and to work inferiors to a greater willingness and cheerfulness in performing their duties to their superiors, as to their parents.[2]

[1]Eph. 6:4. 2 Cor. 12:14. 1 Thess. 2:7-8, 11. Num. 11:11-12. [2]1 Cor. 4:14-16. 2 Kings 5:13.

Q. 126. What is the general scope of the fifth commandment?
A. The general scope of the fifth commandment is, the performance of those duties which we mutually owe in our several relations, as inferiors, superiors, or equals.[1]

[1]Eph. 5:21. 1 Peter 2:17. Rom. 12:10.

Q. 127. What is the honour that inferiors owe to their superiors?
A. The honor which inferiors owe to their superiors is, all due reverence in heart,[1] word,[2] and behaviour;[3] prayer and thanksgiving for them;[4] imitation of their virtues and graces;[5] willing obedience to their lawful commands and counsels;[6] due submission to their corrections;[7] fidelity to,[8] defence,[9] and maintenance of their persons and authority, according to their several ranks, and the nature of their places;[10] bearing with their infirmities, and covering them in love,[11] that so they may be an honor to them and to their government.[12]

[1]Mal. 1:6. Lev. 19:3. [2]Prov. 31:28. 1 Peter 3:6. [3]Lev. 19:32. 1 Kings 2:19. [4]1 Tim. 2:1-2. [5]Heb. 13:7. Phil. 3:17. [6]Eph. 6:1-2, 6-7. 1 Peter 2:13-14. Rom. 13:1-5. Heb. 13:17. Prov. 4:3-4. Prov. 23:22. Exod. 18:19, 24. [7]Heb. 12:9. 1 Peter 2:18-20. [8]Titus 2:9-10. [9]1 Sam. 26:15-16. 2 Sam. 18:3. Esther 6:2. [10]Matt. 22:21. Rom. 13:6-7. 1 Tim. 5:17-18. Gal. 6:6. Gen. 45:11. Gen. 47:12. [11]1 Peter 2:18. Prov. 23:22. Gen. 9:23. [12]Ps. 127:3-5. Prov. 31:23.

Q. 128. What are the sins of inferiors against their superiors?
A. The sins of inferiors against their superiors are, all neglect of the duties required toward them;[1] envying at,[2] contempt of,[3] and rebellion[4] against, their persons[5] and places,[6] in their lawful counsels,[7] commands, and corrections;[8] cursing, mocking[9] and all such refractory and scandalous carriage, as proves a shame and dishonour to them and their government.[10]

[1]Matt. 15:4-6. [2]Num. 11:28-29. [3]1 Sam. 8:7. Isa. 3:5. [4]2 Sam. 15:1-12. etc [5]Exod. 24:15. [6]1 Sam. 10:27. [7]1 Sam. 2:25. [8]Deut. 21:18-21. [9]Prov. 30:11, 17. [10]Prov. 19:26.

Q. 129. What is required of superiors towards their inferiors?

A. It is required of superiors, according to that power they receive from God, and that relation wherein they stand, to love,[1] pray for,[2] and bless their inferiors;[3] to instruct,[4] counsel, and admonish them;[5] countenancing,[6] commending,[7] and rewarding such as do well;[8] and discountenancing,[9] reproving, and chastising such as do ill;[10] protecting,[11] and providing for them all things necessary for soul[12] and body:[13] and by grave, wise, holy, and exemplary carriage, to procure glory to God,[14] honor to themselves,[15] and so to preserve that authority which God hath put upon them.[16]

[1]Col. 3:19. Titus 2:4. [2]1 Sam. 12:23. Job 1:5. [3]1 Kings 8:55-56. Heb. 7:7. Gen. 49:28. [4]Deut. 6:6-7. [5]Eph. 6:4. [6]1 Peter 3:7. [7]1 Peter 2:14. Rom. 13:3. [8]Esther 6:3. [9]Rom. 13:3-4. [10]Prov. 29:15. 1 Peter 2:14. [11]Job 29:13-16. Isa. 1:10, 17. [12]Eph. 6:4. [13]1 Tim. 5:8. [14]1 Tim. 4:12. Titus 2:3-5. [15]1 Kings 3:28. [16]Titus 2:15.

Q. 130. What are the sins of superiors?
A. The sins of superiors are, besides the neglect of the duties required of them,[1] and inordinate seeking of themselves,[2] their own glory,[3] ease, profit, or pleasure;[4] commanding things unlawful,[5] or not in the power of inferiors to perform;[6] counseling,[7] encouraging,[8] or favoring them in that which is evil;[9] dissuading, discouraging, or discountenancing them in that which is good;[10] correcting them unduly;[11] careless exposing, or leaving them to wrong, temptation, and danger;[12] provoking them to wrath;[13] or any way dishonoring themselves, or lessening their authority, by an unjust, indiscreet, rigorous, or remiss behavior.[14]

[1]Ezek. 34:2-4. [2]Phil. 2:21. [3]John 5:44. John 7:18. [4]Isa. 56:10-11. Deut. 17:17. [5]Dan. 3:4-6. Acts 4:17-18. [6]Exod. 5:10-18. Matt. 23:2, 4. [7]Matt. 14:8. Mark 6:24. [8]2 Sam. 13:28. [9]1 Sam. 3:13. [10]John 7:46-49. Col. 3:21. Exod. 5:17. [11]1 Peter 2:18-20. Heb. 12:10. Deut. 25:3. [12]Gen. 38:11, 26. Acts 18:17. [13]Eph. 6:4. [14]Gen. 9:21. 1 Kings 12:13-16. 1 Kings 1:6. 1 Sam. 2:29-31.

Q. 131. What are the duties of equals?
A. The duties of equals are, to regard the dignity and worth of each other,[1] in giving honor to go one before another;[2] and to rejoice in each others' gifts and advancement, as their own.[3]

[1]1 Peter 2:17. [2]Rom. 12:10. [3]Rom. 12:15-16. Phil. 2:3-4.

Q. 132. What are the sins of equals?
A. The sins of equals are, besides the neglect of the duties required,[1] the undervaluing of the worth,[2] envying the gifts,[3] grieving at the advancement of prosperity one of another;[4] and usurping pre-eminence one over another.[5]

[1]Rom. 13:8. [2]2 Tim. 3:3. [3]Acts 7:9. Gal. 5:26. [4]Num. 12:2. Esther 6:12-13. [5]3 John 9. Luke 22:24.

Q. 133. What is the reason annexed to the fifth commandment, the more to enforce it?
A. The reason annexed to the fifth commandment, in these words, That thy days may be long upon the land which the Lord thy God giveth thee,[1] is an express promise of long life and prosperity, as far as it shall serve for God's glory and their own good, to all such as keep this commandment.[2]

[1]Exod. 20:12. [2]Deut. 5:16. 1 Kings 8:25. Eph. 6:2-3.

Q. 134. Which is the sixth commandment?
A. The sixth commandment is, Thou shalt not kill.[1]

[1]Exod. 20:13.

Q. 135. What are the duties required in the sixth commandment?
A. The duties required in the sixth commandment are all careful studies, and lawful endeavors, to preserve the life of ourselves[1] and others[2] by resisting all thoughts and purposes,[3] subduing all passions,[4] and avoiding all occasions,[5] temptations,[6] and practices, which tend to the unjust taking away the life of any;[7] by just defence thereof against violence,[8] patient bearing of the hand of God,[9] quietness of mind,[10] cheerfulness of spirit;[11] a sober use of meat,[12] drink,[13] physic,[14] sleep,[15] labor,[16] and recreations;[17] by charitable thoughts,[18] love,[19] compassion,[20] meekness, gentleness, kindness;[21] peaceable,[22] mild and courteous speeches and behavior;[23] forbearance, readiness to be reconciled, patient bearing and forgiving of injuries, and requiting good for evil;[24] comforting and succouring the distressed and protecting and defending the innocent.[25]

[1]Eph. 5:28-29. [2]1 Kings 18:4. [3]Jer. 26:15-16. Acts 23:12, 16-17, 21, 27. [4]Eph. 4:26-27. [5]2 Sam. 2:22. Deut. 22:8. [6]Matt. 4:6-7. Prov. 1:10-11, 15-16. [7]1 Sam. 24:12. 1 Sam. 26:9-11. Gen. 37:21-22. [8]Ps. 82:4. Prov. 24:11-12. 1 Sam. 14:45. [9]James 5:7-11. Heb. 12:9. [10]1 Thess. 4:11. 1 Peter 3:3-4. Ps. 37:8-11. [11]Prov. 17:22. [12]Prov. 25:16, 27. [13]1 Tim. 5:23. [14]Isa. 38:21. [15]Ps. 127:2. [16]Eccles. 5:12. 2 Thess. 3:10, 12. Prov. 16:20. [17]Eccles. 3:4, 11. [18]1 Sam. 19:4-5. 1 Sam. 22:13-14. [19]Rom. 13:10. [20]Luke 10:33-34. [21]Col. 3:12-13. [22]James 3:17. [23]1 Peter 3:8-11. Prov. 15:1. Judges 8:1-3. [24]Matt. 5:24. Eph. 5:2, 32. Rom. 12:17. [25]1 Thess. 5:14. Job 31:19-20. Matt. 25:35-36. Prov. 31:8-9.

Q. 136. What are the sins forbidden in the sixth commandment?
A. The sins forbidden in the sixth commandment are, all taking away the life of ourselves,[1] or of others,[2] except in case of public justice,[3] lawful war,[4] or necessary defence;[5] the neglecting or withdrawing the lawful and necessary means of preservation of life;[6] sinful anger,[7] hatred,[8] envy,[9] desire of revenge;[10] all excessive passions,[11] distracting cares;[12] immoderate use of meat, drink,[13] labor,[14] and recreations;[15] provoking words,[16] oppression,[17] quarreling,[18] striking, wounding,[19] and whatsoever else tends to the destruction of the life of any.[20]

[1]Acts 16:28. [2]Gen. 9:6. [3]Num. 35:31, 33. [4]Jer. 48:10. Deut. 20:1. [5]Exod. 22:2-3. [6]Matt. 25:42-43. James 2:15-16. Eccles. 6:1-2. [7]Matt. 5:22. [8]1 John 3:15. Lev. 19:17. [9]Prov. 14:30. [10]Rom. 12:19. [11]Eph. 4:31. [12]Matt. 6:31, 34. [13]Luke 21:34. Rom. 13:13. [14]Eccles. 12:12. Eccles. 2:22-23. [15]Isa. 5:12. [16]Prov. 15:1. Prov. 12:18. [17]Ezek. 18:18. Exod. 1:14. [18]Gal. 5:15. Prov. 23:29. [19]Num. 35:16-18, 21. [20]Exod. 21:18-36.

Q. 137. Which is the seventh commandment?
A. The seventh commandment is, Thou shalt not commit adultery.[1]

[1]Exod. 20:14.

Q. 138. What are the duties required in the seventh commandment?
A. The duties required in the seventh commandment are, chastity in body, mind, affections,[1] words,[2] and behavior;[3] and the preservation of it in ourselves and others;[4] watchfulness over the eyes and all the senses;[5] temperance,[6] keeping of chaste company,[7] modesty in apparel;[8] marriage by those that have not the gift of continency,[9] conjugal love,[10] and cohabitation;[11] diligent labor in our callings;[12] shunning all occasions of uncleanness, and resisting temptations thereunto.[13]

[1]1 Thess. 4:4. Job 31:1. 1 Cor. 7:34. [2]Col. 4:6. [3]1 Peter 2:3. [4]1 Cor. 7:2, 35-36. [5]Job 31:1. [6]Acts 24:24-25. [7]Prov. 2:16-20. [8]1 Tim. 2:9. [9]1 Cor. 7:2, 9. [10]Prov. 5:19-20. [11]1 Peter 3:7. [12]Prov. 31:11, 27-28. [13]Prov. 5:8. Gen. 39:8-10.

Q. 139. What are the sins forbidden in the seventh commandment?
A. The sins forbidden in the seventh commandment, besides the neglect of the duties required,[1] are, adultery, fornication,[2] rape, incest,[3] sodomy, and all unnatural lusts;[4] all unclean imaginations, thoughts, purposes, and affections;[5] all corrupt or filthy communications, or listening thereunto;[6] wanton looks,[7] impudent or light behavior, immodest apparel;[8] prohibiting of lawful,[9] and dispensing with unlawful marriages;[10] allowing, tolerating, keeping of stews, and resorting to them;[11] entangling vows of single life,[12] undue delay of marriage,[13] having more wives or husbands than one at the same time;[14] unjust divorce,[15] or desertion;[16] idleness, gluttony, drunkenness,[17] unchaste company;[18] lascivious songs, books, pictures, dancings, stage plays;[19] and all other provocations to, or acts of uncleanness, either in ourselves or others.[20]

[1]Prov. 5:7. [2]Heb. 13:4. Gal. 5:19. [3]2 Sam. 13:14. 1 Cor. 5:1. [4]Rom. 1:24, 26-27. Lev. 20:15-16. [5]Matt. 5:28. Matt. 15:19. Col. 3:5. [6]Eph. 5:3-4. Prov. 7:5, 21-22. [7]Isa. 3:16. 2 Peter 2:14. [8]Prov. 7:10, 13. [9]1 Tim. 4:3. [10]Lev. 18:1-21. Mark 6:18. Mal. 2:11-12. [11]1 Kings 15:12. 2 Kings 23:7. Deut. 23:17-18. Lev. 19:29. Jer. 5:7. Prov. 7:24-27. [12]Matt. 19:10-11. [13]1 Cor. 7:7-9. Gen. 38:26. [14]Mal. 2:14-15. Matt. 19:5. [15]Mal. 2:16. Matt. 5:32. [16]1 Cor. 7:12-13. [17]Ezek. 16:49. Prov. 23:30-33. [18]Gen. 39:19. Prov. 5:8. [19]Eph. 5:4. Ezek. 23:14-16. Isa. 23:15-17. Isa. 3:16. Mark 6:22. Rom. 13:13. 1 Peter 4:3. [20]2 Kings 9:30. Jer. 4:30. Ezek. 23:40.

Q. 140. Which is the eighth commandment?
A. The eighth commandment is, Thou shalt not steal.[1]

[1]Exod. 20:15.

Q. 141. What are the duties required in the eighth commandment?
A. The duties required in the eighth commandment are, truth, faithfulness, and justice in contracts and commerce between man and man;[1] rendering to everyone his due; restitution of goods unlawfully detained from the right owners thereof;[2] giving and lending freely, according to our abilities, and the necessities of others;[3] moderation of our judgments, wills, and affections concerning worldly goods;[4] a provident care and study to get,[5] keep, use, and dispose these things which are necessary and convenient for the sustentation of our nature, and suitable to our condition;[6] a lawful calling,[7] and diligence in it;[8] frugality;[9] avoiding unnecessary lawsuits,[10]. and suretiship, or other like engagements;[11] and an endeavor, by all just and lawful means, to procure, preserve, and further the wealth and outward estate of others, as well as our own.[12]

[1]Ps. 15:2, 4. Zech. 7:4, 10. Zech. 8:16-17. [2]Lev. 6:2-5. Luke 19:8. [3]Luke 6:30, 38. 1 John 3:17. Eph. 4:28. Gal. 6:10. [4]1 Tim. 6:6-9. Gal. 6:14. [5]1 Tim. 5:8. [6]Prov. 27:23-27. Eccles. 2:24. Eccles. 3:12-13. 1 Tim. 6:17-18. Isa. 38:1. Matt. 11:8. [7]1 Cor. 7:20. Gen. 2:15. Gen. 3:19. [8]Eph. 4:28. Prov. 10:4. [9]John 6:12. Prov. 21:20. [10]1 Cor. 6:1-9. [11]Prov. 6:1-6. Prov. 11:15. [12]Lev. 25:35. Deut. 22:1-4. Exod. 23:4-5. Gen. 47:14, 20. Phil. 2:4. Matt. 22:39.

Q. 142. What are the sins forbidden in the eighth commandment?
A. The sins forbidden in the eighth commandment, besides the neglect of the duties required,[1] are, theft,[2] robbery,[3] man-stealing,[4] and receiving any thing that is stolen;[5] fraudulent dealing,[6] false weights and measures,[7] removing landmarks,[8] injustice and unfaithfulness in contracts between man and man,[9] or in matters of trust;[10] oppression,[11] extortion,[12] usury,[13] bribery,[14] vexatious lawsuits,[15] unjust inclosures and depopulations;[16] ingrossing commodities to enhance the price;[17] unlawful callings,[18] and all other unjust or sinful ways of taking or withholding from our neighbor what belongs to him, or of enriching ourselves;[19] covetousness;[20] inordinate prizing and affecting worldly goods;[21] distrustful and distracting cares and studies in getting, keeping, and using them;[22] envying at the prosperity of others;[23] as likewise idleness,[24] prodigality, wasteful gaming; and all other ways whereby we do unduly prejudice our own outward estate,[25] and defrauding ourselves of the due use and comfort of that estate which God hath given us.[26]

[1]James 2:15-16. 1 John 3:17. [2]Eph. 4:28. [3]Ps. 62:10. [4]1 Tim. 1:10. [5]Prov. 29:24. Ps. 50:18. [6]1 Thess. 4:6. [7]Prov. 11:1. Prov. 20:10. [8]Deut. 19:14. Prov. 23:10. [9]Amos 8:5. Ps. 37:21. [10]Luke 16:10-12. [11]Ezek. 22:29. Lev. 25:17. [12]Matt. 23:25. Ezek. 22:12. [13]Ps. 15:5. [14]Job 15:34. [15]1 Cor. 6:6-8. Prov. 3:29-30. [16]Isa. 5:8. Micah 2:2. [17]Prov. 11:26. [18]Acts 19:19, 24-25. [19]Job 20:19. James 5:4. Prov. 21:6. [20]Luke 12:15. [21]1 Tim. 6:5. Col. 3:2. Prov. 23:5. Ps. 62:10. [22]Matt. 6:25, 31, 34. Eccles. 5:12. [23]Ps. 73:3. Ps. 37:1, 7. [24]2 Thess. 3:11. Prov. 18:9. [25]Prov. 21:17. Prov. 23:20-21. Prov. 28:19. [26]Eccles. 4:8. Eccles. 6:2. 1 Tim. 5:8.

Q. 143. Which is the ninth commandment?
A. The ninth commandment is, Thou shalt not bear false witness against thy neighbor.[1]

[1]Exod. 20:16.

Q. 144. What are the duties required in the ninth commandment?
A. The duties required in the ninth commandment are, the preserving and promoting of truth between man and man,[1] and the good name of our neighbor, as well as our own;[2] appearing and standing for the truth;[3] and from the heart,[4] sincerely,[5] freely,[6] clearly,[7] and fully,[8] speaking the truth, and only the truth, in matters of judgment and justice,[9] and in all other things whatsoever;[10] a charitable esteem of our neighbors;[11] loving, desiring, and rejoicing in their good name;[12] sorrowing for,[13] and covering of their infirmities;[14] freely acknowledging of their gifts and graces,[15] defending their innocency;[16] a ready receiving of a good report,[17] and unwillingness to admit of an evil report,[18] concerning them; discouraging tale-bearers,[19] flatterers,[20] and slanderers;[21] love and care of our own good name, and defending it when need requireth;[22] keeping of lawful promises;[23] studying and practicing of whatsoever things are true, honest, lovely, and of good report.[24]

[1]Zech. 8:16. [2]3 John 12. [3]Prov. 31:8-9. [4]Ps. 15:2. [5]2 Chron. 19:9. [6]1 Sam. 19:4-5. [7]Josh. 7:19. [8]2 Sam. 14:18-20. [9]Lev. 19:15. [10]2 Cor. 1:17-18.

Eph. 4:25. [11]Heb. 6:9. 1 Cor. 13:7. [12]Rom. 1:8. 2 John 4. 3 John 3-4. [13]2 Cor. 2:4. 2 Cor. 12:21. [14]Prov. 17:9. 1 Peter 4:8. [15]1 Cor. 1:4-5, 7. 2 Tim. 1:4-5. [16]1 Sam. 22:14. [17]1 Cor. 13:6-7. [18]Ps. 15:3. [19]Prov. 25:23. [20]Prov. 26:24-25. [21]Ps. 101:5. [22]Prov. 22:1. John 8:49. [23]Ps. 15:4. [24]Phil. 4:8.

Q. 145. What are the sins forbidden in the ninth commandment?
A. The sins forbidden in the ninth commandment are, all prejudicing the truth, and the good name of our neighbors, as well as our own,[1] especially in public judicature;[2] giving false evidence,[3] suborning false witnesses,[4] wittingly appearing and pleading for an evil cause, outfacing and overbearing the truth;[5] passing unjust sentence,[6] calling evil good, and good evil; rewarding the wicked according to the work of the righteous, and the righteous according to the work of the wicked;[7] forgery,[8] concealing the truth, undue silence in a just cause,[9] and holding our peace when iniquity calleth for either a reproof from ourselves,[10] or complaint to others;[11] speaking the truth unseasonably,[12] or maliciously to a wrong end,[13] or perverting it to a wrong meaning,[14] or in doubtful and equivocal expressions, to the prejudice of truth or justice;[15] speaking untruth,[16] lying,[17] slandering,[18] backbiting,[19] detracting, tale bearing,[20] whispering,[21] scoffing,[22] reviling,[23] rash,[24] harsh,[25] and partial censuring;[26] misconstructing intentions, words, and actions;[27] flattering,[28] vain-glorious boasting;[29] thinking or speaking too highly or too meanly of ourselves or others;[30] denying the gifts and graces of God;[31] aggravating smaller faults;[32] hiding, excusing, or extenuating of sins, when called to a free confession;[33] unnecessary discovering of infirmities;[34] raising false rumors,[35] receiving and countenancing evil reports,[36] and stopping our ears against just defense;[37] evil suspicion;[38] envying or grieving at the deserved credit of any,[39] endeavoring or desiring to impair it,[40] rejoicing in their disgrace and infamy;[41] scornful contempt,[42] fond admiration;[43] breach of lawful promises;[44] neglecting such things as are of good report,[45] and practicing, or not avoiding ourselves, or not hindering what we can in others, such things as procure an ill name.[46]

[1]1 Sam. 17:28. 2 Sam. 16:3. 2 Sam. 1:9-10, 15-16. [2]Lev. 19:15. Hab. 1:4. [3]Prov. 19:5. Prov. 6:16, 19. [4]Acts 6:13. [5]Jer. 9:3, 5. Acts 24:2, 5. Ps. 12:3-4. Ps. 52:1-4. [6]Prov. 17:15. 1 Kings 21:9-14. [7]Isa. 5:23. [8]Ps. 119:69. Luke 19:8. Luke 16:5-7. [9]Lev. 5:1. Deut. 13:8. Acts 5:3, 8-9. 2 Tim. 4:6. [10]1 Kings 1:6. Lev. 19:17. [11]Isa. 59:4. [12]Prov. 29:11. [13]1 Sam. 22:9-10. Ps. 52:1-5. [14]Ps. 56:5. John 2:19. Matt. 26:60-61. [15]Gen. 3:5. Gen. 26:7, 9. [16]Isa. 59:13. [17]Lev. 19:11. Col. 3:9. [18]Ps. 50:20. [19]James 4:11. Jer. 38:4. [20]Lev. 19:19. [21]Rom. 1:29-30. [22]Gen. 21:9. Gal. 4:29. [23]1 Cor. 6:10. [24]Matt. 7:1. [25]Acts 28:4. [26]Gen. 38:24. Rom. 2:1. [27]Neh. 6:6-8. Rom. 3:8. Ps. 69:10. 1 Sam. 1:13-15. 2 Sam. 10:3. [28]Ps. 12:2-3. [29]2 Tim. 3:2. [30]Luke 18:9, 11. Rom. 12:16. 1 Cor. 4:6. Acts 12:22. Exod. 4:10-14. [31]Job 27:5-6. Job 4:6. [32]Matt. 7:3-5. [33]Prov. 28:13. Prov. 30:20. Gen. 3:12-13. Jer. 2:35. 2 Kings 5:25. Gen. 4:9. [34]Gen. 9:22. Prov. 25:9-10. [35]Exod. 23:1. [36]Prov. 29:12. [37]Acts 7:56-57. Job 31:13-14. [38]1 Cor. 13:5. 1 Tim. 6:4. [39]Num. 11:29. Matt. 21:15. [40]Ezra 4:12-13. [41]Jer. 48:27. [42]Ps. 35:15-16, 21. Matt. 27:28-29. [43]Jude 16. Acts 12:22. [44]Rom. 1:31. 2 Tim. 3:3. [45]1 Sam. 2:24. [46]2 Sam. 13:12-13. Prov. 5:8-9. Prov. 6:33.

Q. 146. Which is the tenth commandment?
A. The tenth commandment is, Thou shalt not covet thy neighbor's house, thou shall not covet they neighbor's wife, nor his man-servant, nor his maid-servant, nor his ox, nor his ass, nor any thing that is thy neighbor's.[1]

[1]Exod. 20:17.

Q. 147. What are the duties required in the tenth commandment?
A. The duties required in the tenth commandment are, such a full contentment with our own condition,[1] and such a charitable frame of the whole soul toward our neighbor, as that all our inward motions and affections touching him, tend unto, and further all that good which is his.[2]

[1]Heb. 13:5. 1 Tim. 6:6. [2]Job 31:29. Rom. 12:15. Ps. 122:7-9. 1 Tim. 1:5. Esther 10:3. 1 Cor. 13:4-7.

Q. 148. What are the sins forbidden in the tenth commandment?
A. The sins forbidden in the tenth commandment are, discontentment with our own estate;[1] envying[2] and grieving at the good of our neighbor,[3] together with all inordinate motions and affections to anything that is his.[4]

[1]1 Kings 21:4. Esther 5:13. 1 Cor. 10:10. [2]Gal. 5:26. James 3:14, 16. [3]Ps. 112:9-10. Neh. 2:10. [4]Rom. 7:7-8. Rom. 13:9. Col. 3:5. Deut. 5:21.

Q. 149. Is any man able perfectly to keep the commandments of God?
A. No man is able, either of himself,[1] or by any grace received in this life, perfectly to keep the commandments of God;[2] but doth daily break them in thought,[3] word, and deed.[4]

[1]James 3:2. John 15:5. Rom. 8:3. [2]Eccles. 7:20. 1 John 1:8, 10. Gal. 5:17. Rom. 7:18-19. [3]Gen. 6:5. Gen. 8:21. [4]Rom. 3:9-19. James 3:2-13. etc.

Q. 150. Are all transgressions of the law of God equally heinous in themselves, and in the sight of God?
A. All transgressions of the law of God are not equally heinous; but some sins in themselves, and by reason of several aggravations, are more heinous in the sight of God than others.[1]

[1]John 19:11. Ezek. 8:6, 13, 15. 1 John 5:16. Ps. 78:17, 32, 56.

Q. 151. What are those aggravations that make some sins more heinous than others?
A. Sins receive their aggravations,

1. From the persons offending[1] if they be of riper age,[2] greater experience or grace,[3] eminent for profession,[4] gifts,[5] place,[6] office,[7] guides to others,[8] and whose example is likely to be followed by others.[9]
2. From the parties offended:[10] if immediately against God,[11] His attributes,[12] and worship;[13] against Christ, and His grace;[14] the Holy Spirit,[15] His witness,[16] and workings[17] against superiors, men of eminency,[18] and such as we stand especially related and engaged unto;[19] against any of the saints,[20] particularly weak brethren,[21] the souls of them, or any other,[22] and the common good of all or many.[23]
3. From the nature and quality of the offense:[24] if it be against the express letter of the law,[25] break many commandments, contain in it many sins:[26] if not only conceived in the heart, but breaks forth in words and actions,[27] scandalize others,[28] and admit of no reparation:[29] if against means,[30] mercies,[31] judgments,[32] light of nature,[33] conviction of conscience,[34] public or private admonition,[35] censures of the church,[36] civil punishments;[37] and our prayers, purposes, promises,[38] vows,[39] covenants,[40] and engagements to God or men:[41] if done deliberately,[42] wilfully,[43] presumptuously,[44] impudently,[45] boastingly,[46] maliciously,[47] frequently,[48] obstinately,[49] with delight,[50] continuance,[51] or relapsing after repentance.[52]
4. From circumstances of time[53] and place:[54] if on the Lord's day,[55] or other times of divine worship;[56] or immediately before[57] or after these,[58] or other helps to prevent or remedy such miscarriages;[59] if in public, or in the presence of others, who are thereby likely to be provoked or defiled.[60]

[1]Jer. 2:8. [2]Job 32:7, 9. Eccles. 4:13. [3]1 Kings 11:4, 9. [4]2 Sam. 12:14. 1 Cor. 5:1. [5]James 4:17. Luke 12:47-48. [6]Jer. 5:4-5. [7]2 Sam. 12:7-9. Ezek. 8:11-12. [8]Rom. 2:17-24. [9]Gal. 2:11-14. [10]Matt. 21:38-39. [11]1 Sam. 2:25. Acts 5:4. Ps. 5:4. [12]Rom. 2:4. [13]Mal. 1:8. Mal. 1:14. [14]Heb. 2:2-3. Heb. 7:25. [15]Heb. 10:29. Matt. 12:31-32. [16]Eph. 4:30. [17]Heb. 6:4-6. [18]Jude 8. Num. 12:8-9. Isa. 3:5. [19]Prov. 30:17. 2 Cor. 12:15. Ps. 55:12-15. [20]Zeph. 2:8, 10-11. Matt. 18:6. 1 Cor. 6:8. Rev. 17:6. [21]1 Cor. 8:11-12. Rom. 14:13, 15, 21. [22]Ezek. 13:19. 1 Cor. 8:12. Rev. 18:12-13. Matt. 23:15. [23]1 Thess. 2:15-16. Josh. 22:20. [24]Prov. 6:30-33. [25]Ezra 9:10-12. 1 Kings 11:9-10. [26]Col. 3:5. 1 Tim. 6:10. Prov. 5:8-12. Prov. 6:32-33. Josh. 7:21. [27]James 1:14-15. Matt. 5:22. Mic 2:1. [28]Matt. 18:7. Rom. 2:23-24. [29]Deut. 22:22, 28-29. Prov. 6:32-35. [30]Matt. 11:21-24. John 15:22. [31]Isa. 1:3. Deut. 32:6. [32]Amos 4:8-11. Jer. 5:3. [33]Rom. 1:26-27. [34]Rom. 1:32. Dan. 5:22. Titus 3:10-11. [35]Prov. 29:1. [36]Titus 3:10. Matt. 18:17. [37]Prov. 27:22. Prov. 23:35. [38]Ps. 78:34-37. Jer. 2:20. Jer. 13:5-6, 20-21. [39]Eccles. 5:4-6. Prov. 20:25. [40]Lev. 26:25. [41]Prov. 2:17. Ezek. 7:18-19. [42]Ps. 36:4. [43]Jer. 6:16. [44]Num. 15:30. Exod. 21:14. [45]Jer. 3:3. Prov. 7:13. [46]Ps. 52:1. [47]3 John 10. etc. [48]Num. 14:22. [49]Zech. 7:11-12. [50]Prov. 2:14. [51]Isa. 57:17. [52]Jer. 34:8-11. 2 Peter 2:20-22. [53]2 Kings 5:26. [54]Jer. 7:10. Isa. 26:10. [55]Ezek. 23:37-39. [56]Isa. 58:3-5. Num. 25:6-7. [57]1 Cor. 11:20-21. [58]Jer. 7:8-10. Prov. 7:14-15. John 13:27, 30. [59]Ezra 9:13-14. [60]2 Sam. 16:22. 1 Sam. 2:22-24.

Q. 152. What doth every sin deserve at the hands of God?

A. Every sin, even the least, being against the sovereignty,[1] goodness,[2] and holiness of God,[3] and against His righteous law,[4] deserveth His wrath and curse,[5] both in this life,[6] and that which is to come;[7] and cannot be expiated but by the blood of Christ.[8]

[1]James 2:10-11. [2]Exod. 20:1-2. [3]Hab. 1:13. Lev. 10:3. Lev. 11:44-45. [4]1 John 3:4. Rom. 7:12. [5]Eph. 5:6. Gal. 3:10. [6]Lam. 3:39. Deut. 28:15-18. etc. [7]Matt. 25:41. [8]Heb. 9:22. 1 Peter 1:18-19.

Q. 153. What doth God require of us, that we may escape His wrath and curse due to us by reason of the transgression of the law?
A. That we may escape the wrath and curse of God due to us by reason of the transgression of the law, He requireth of us repentance toward God, and faith toward our Lord Jesus Christ,[1] and the diligent use of the outward means whereby Christ communicates to us the benefits of His mediation.[2]

[1]Acts 20:21. Matt. 3:7-8. Luke 13:3, 5. Acts 16:30-31. John 3:16, 18. [2]Prov. 2:1-5. Prov. 8:33-36.

Q. 154. What are the outward means whereby Christ communicates to us the benefits of His mediation?
A. The outward and ordinary means whereby Christ communicates to His church the benefits of His mediation, are all His ordinances; especially the Word, sacraments, and prayer; all which are made effectual to the elect for their salvation.[1]

[1]Matt. 28:19-20. Acts 2:42, 46-47.

Q. 155. How is the Word made effectual to salvation?
A. The Spirit of God maketh the reading, but especially the preaching of the Word, an effectual means of enlightening,[1] convincing, and humbling sinners;[2] of driving them out of themselves, and drawing them unto Christ;[3] of conforming them to His image,[4] and subduing them to His will;[5] of strengthening them against temptations and corruptions;[6] of building them up in grace,[7] and establishing their hearts in holiness and comfort through faith unto salvation.[8]

[1]Neh. 8:8. Acts 26:18. Ps. 19:8. [2]1 Cor. 14:24-25. 2 Chron. 34:18-19, 26-28, etc. [3]Acts 2:37, 41. Acts 8:27-30, 35-38. [4]2 Cor. 3:18. [5]2 Cor. 10:4-6. Rom. 6:17. [6]Matt. 4:4, 7, 10. Eph. 6:16-17. Ps. 19:11. 1 Cor. 10:11. [7]Acts 20:32. 2 Tim. 3:15-17. [8]Rom. 16:25. 1 Thess. 3:2, 10-11, 13. Rom. 15:4. Rom. 10:13-17. Rom. 1:16.

Q. 156. Is the Word of God to be read by all?
A. Although all are not to be permitted to read the Word publicly to the congregation,[1] yet all sorts of people are bound to read it apart by themselves,[2] and with their families:[3] to which end, the holy scriptures are to be translated out of the original into vulgar languages.[4]

[1]Deut. 31:9, 11-13. Neh. 8:2-3. Neh. 9:3-5. etc. [2]Deut. 17:19. Rev. 1:3. John 5:39. Isa. 34:16. etc. [3]Deut. 6:6-9. Gen. 18:17. Ps. 78:5-7. [4]1 Cor. 14:6, 9, 11-12, 15-16, 24, 27-28.

Q. 157. How is the Word of God to be read?
A. The holy Scriptures are to be read with an high and reverent esteem of them;[1] with a firm persuasion that they are the very Word of God,[2] and that He only can enable us to understand them;[3] with desire to know, believe, and obey the will of God revealed in them;[4] with diligence,[5] and attention to the matter and scope of them;[6] with meditation,[7] application,[8] self-denial,[9] and prayer.[10]

[1]Ps. 19:10. Neh. 8:3-6, 10. etc. Exod. 24:7. 2 Chron. 34:27. Isa. 66:2. [2]2 Peter 1:19-21. [3]Luke 24:45. 2 Cor. 3:13-16. [4]Deut. 17:10, 20. [5]Acts 17:11. [6]Acts 8:30, 34. Luke 10:26-28. [7]Ps. 1:2. Ps. 119:97. [8]2 Chron. 34:21. [9]Prov. 3:5. Deut. 33:3. [10]Prov. 2:1-6. Ps. 119:18. Neh. 7:6, 8.

Q. 158. By whom is the Word of God to be preached?
A. The Word of God is to be preached only by such as are sufficiently gifted,[1] and also duly approved and called to that office.[2]

[1]1 Tim. 3:2, 6. Eph. 4:8-11. Hosea 4:6. Mal. 2:7. 2 Cor. 3:6. [2]Jer. 14:15. Rom. 10:15. Heb. 5:4. 1 Cor. 12:28-29. 1 Tim. 3:10. 1 Tim. 4:14. 1 Tim. 5:22.

Q. 159. How is the Word of God to be preached by those that are called thereunto?
A. They that are called to labor in the ministry of the Word, are to preach sound doctrine,[1] diligently,[2] in season and out of season;[3] plainly,[4] not in the enticing words

of man's wisdom, but in demonstration of the Spirit, and of power;[5] faithfully,[6] making known the whole counsel of God;[7] wisely,[8] applying themselves to the necessities and capacities of the hearers;[9] zealously,[10] with fervent love to God[11] and the souls of His people;[12] sincerely,[13] aiming at His glory,[14] and their conversion,[15] edification,[16] and salvation.[17]

[1]Titus 2:1, 8. [2]Acts 18:25. [3]2 Tim. 4:2. [4]1 Cor. 14:19. [5]1 Cor. 2:4. [6]Jer. 23:28. 1 Cor. 4:1-2. [7]Acts 20:27. [8]Col. 1:28. 2 Tim. 2:15. [9]1 Cor. 3:2. Heb. 5:12-14. Luke 12:42. [10]Acts 18:25. [11]2 Cor. 5:13-14. Phil. 1:15-17. [12]Col. 4:12. 2 Cor. 12:15. [13]2 Cor. 2:17. 2 Cor. 4:2. [14]1 Thess. 2:4-6. John 7:18. [15]1 Cor. 9:19-22. [16]2 Cor. 12:19. Eph. 4:12. [17]1 Tim. 4:16. Acts 26:16-18.

Q. 160. What is required of those that hear the Word preached?
A. It is required of those that hear the Word preached, that they attend upon it with diligence,[1] preparation,[2] and prayer;[3] examine what they hear by the Scriptures;[4] receive the truth with faith,[5] love,[6] meekness,[7] and readiness of mind,[8] as the Word of God;[9] meditate,[10] and confer of it;[11] hide it in their hearts,[12] and bring forth the fruit of it in their lives.[13]

[1]Prov. 8:34. [2]1 Peter 2:1-2. Luke 8:18. [3]Ps. 119:18. Eph. 6:18-19. [4]Acts 17:11. [5]Heb. 4:2. [6]2 Thess. 2:10. [7]James 1:21. [8]Acts 17:11. [9]1 Thess. 2:13. [10]Luke 9:44. Heb. 2:1. [11]Luke 24:14. Deut. 6:6-7. [12]Prov. 2:1. Ps. 119:11. [13]Luke 8:15. James 1:25.

Q. 161. How do the sacraments become effectual means of salvation?
A. The sacraments become effectual means of salvation, not by any power in themselves, or any virtue derived from the piety or intention of him by whom they are administered, but only by the working of the Holy Ghost, and the blessing of Christ, by whom they are instituted.[1]

[1]1 Peter 3:21. Acts 8:13, 23. 1 Cor. 3:6-7. 1 Cor. 12:13.

Q. 162. What is a sacrament?
A. A sacrament is an holy ordinance instituted by Christ in His church,[1] to signify, seal, and exhibit[2] unto those that are within the covenant of grace,[3] the benefits of His mediation;[4] to strengthen and increase their faith, and all other graces;[5] to oblige them to obedience;[6] to testify and cherish their love and communion one with another;[7] and to distinguish them from those that are without.[8]

[1]Gen. 17:7, 10. Exod. 12. Matt. 28:19. Matt. 26:26-28. [2]Rom. 4:11. 1 Cor. 11:24-25. [3]Rom. 15:8. Exod. 12:48. [4]Acts 2:38. 1 Cor. 10:16. [5]Rom. 4:11. Gal. 3:27. [6]Rom. 6:3-4. 1 Cor. 10:21. [7]Eph. 4:2-5. 1 Cor. 12:13. [8]Eph. 2:11-12. Gen. 34:14.

Q. 163. What are the parts of a sacrament?
A. The parts of the sacrament are two; the one an outward and sensible sign, used according to Christ's own appointment; the other an inward and spiritual grace thereby signified.[1]

[1]Matt. 3:11. 1 Peter 3:21. Rom. 2:28-29.

Q. 164. How many sacraments hath Christ instituted in His church under the New Testament?
A. Under the New Testament Christ hath instituted in His church only two sacraments, baptism and the Lord's supper.[1]

[1]Matt. 28:19. 1 Cor. 11:20, 23. Matt. 26:26-28.

Q. 165. What is baptism?
A. Baptism is a sacrament of the New Testament, wherein Christ hath ordained the washing with water in the name of the Father, and of the Son, and of the Holy Ghost,[1] to be a sign and seal of ingrafting into Himself,[2] of remission of sins by His blood,[3] and regeneration by His Spirit;[4] of adoption,[5] and resurrection unto everlasting life;[6] and whereby the parties baptized are solemnly admitted into the visible church,[7] and enter into an open and professed engagement to be wholly and only the Lord's.[8]

[1]Matt. 28:19. [2]Gal. 3:27. [3]Mark 1:4. Rev. 1:5. [4]Titus 3:5. Eph. 5:26. [5]Gal. 3:26-27. [6]1 Cor. 15:29. Rom. 6:5. [7]1 Cor. 12:13. [8]Rom. 6:4.

Q. 166. Unto whom is baptism to be administered?
A. Baptism is not to be administered to any that are out of the visible church, and so strangers from the covenant of promise, till they profess their faith in Christ, and obedi-

ence to Him,[1] but infants descending from parents, either both, or but one of them, professing faith in Christ, and obedience to Him, are in that respect within the covenant, and to be baptized.[2]

[1]Acts 8:36-37. Acts 2:38. [2]Gen. 17:7, 9. Gal. 3:9, 14. Col. 2:11-12. Acts 2:38-39. Rom. 4:11-12. 1 Cor. 7:14. Matt. 28:19. Luke 18:15-16. Rom. 11:16.

Q. 167. How is our baptism to be improved by us?
A. The needful but much neglected duty of improving our baptism, is to be performed by us all our life long, especially in the time of temptation, and when we are present at the administration of it to others;[1] by serious and thankful consideration of the nature of it, and of the ends for which Christ instituted it, the privileges and benefits conferred and sealed thereby, and our solemn vow made therein;[2] by being humbled for our sinful defilement, our falling short of, and walking contrary to, the grace of baptism, and our engagements;[3] by growing up to assurance of pardon of sin, and of all other blessings sealed to us in that sacrament;[4] by drawing strength from the death and resurrection of Christ, into whom we are baptized, for the mortifying of sin, and quickening of grace;[5] and by endeavoring to live by faith,[6] to have our conversation in holiness and righteousness,[7] as those that have therein given up their names to Christ;[8] and to walk in brotherly love, as being baptized by the same Spirit into one body.[9]

[1]Col. 2:11-12. Rom. 6:4, 6, 11. [2]Rom. 6:3-5. [3]1 Cor. 1:11-13. Rom. 6:2-3. [4]Rom. 4:11-12. 1 Peter 3:21. [5]Rom. 6:3-5. [6]Gal. 3:26-27. [7]Rom. 6:22. [8]Acts 2:38. [9]1 Cor. 12:13, 25.

Q. 168. What is the Lord's supper?
A. The Lord's supper is a sacrament of the New Testament,[1] wherein, by giving and receiving bread and wine according to the appointment of Jesus Christ, His death is showed forth; and they that worthily communicate feed upon His body and blood, to their spiritual nourishment and growth in grace;[2] have their union and communion with Him confirmed;[3] testify and renew their thankfulness,[4] and engagement to God,[5] and their mutual love and fellowship each with the other, as members of the same mystical body.[6]

[1]Luke 22:20. [2]Matt. 26:26-28. 1 Cor. 11:23-26. [3]1 Cor. 10:16. [4]1 Cor. 11:24. [5]1 Cor. 10:14-16, 21. [6]1 Cor. 10:17.

Q. 169. How hath Christ appointed bread and wine to be given and received in the sacrament of the Lord's supper?
A. Christ hath appointed the ministers of His Word, in the administration of this sacrament of the Lord's supper, to set apart the bread and wine from common use, by the word of institution, thanksgiving, and prayer; to take and break the bread, and to give both the bread and the wine to the communicants: who are, by the same appointment, to take and eat the bread, and to drink the wine, in thankful remembrance that the body of Christ was broken and given, and His blood shed, for them.[1]

[1]1 Cor. 11:23-24. Matt. 26:26-28. Mark 14:22-24. Luke 22:19-20.

Q. 170. How do they that worthily communicate in the Lord's supper feed upon the body and blood of Christ therein?
A. As the body and blood of Christ are not corporally or carnally present in, with, or under the bread and wine in the Lord's supper,[1] and yet are spiritually present to the faith of the receiver, no less truly and really than the elements themselves are to their outward senses;[2] so they that worthily communicate in the sacrament of the Lord's supper, do therein feed upon the body and blood of Christ, not after a corporal and carnal, but in a spiritual manner; yet truly and really,[3] while by faith they receive and apply unto themselves Christ crucified, and all the benefits of His death.[4]

[1]Acts 3:21. [2]Matt. 26:26, 28. [3]1 Cor. 11:24-29. [4]1 Cor. 10:16.

Q. 171. How are they that receive the sacrament of the Lord's supper to prepare themselves before they come unto it?
A. They that receive the sacrament of the Lord's supper are, before they come, to prepare themselves thereunto, by examining themselves[1] of their being in Christ,[2] of their sins and wants;[3] of the truth and measure of their knowledge,[4] faith,[5] repentance;[6] love to God and the

brethren,[7] charity to all men,[8] forgiving those that have done them wrong;[9] of their desires after Christ,[10] and of their new obedience;[11] and by renewing the exercise of these graces,[12] by serious meditation,[13] and fervent prayer.[14]

[1]1 Cor. 11:28. [2]2 Cor. 13:5. 1 Cor. 5:7. Exod. 12:15. [4]1 Cor. 11:29. [5]1 Cor. 13:5. Matt. 26:28. [6]Zech. 12:10. 1 Cor. 11:31. [7]1 Cor. 10:16-17. Acts 2:46-47. [8]1 Cor. 5:8. 1 Cor. 11:18, 20. [9]Matt. 5:23-24. [10]Isa. 55:1 John 7:37. [11]1 Cor. 5:7-8. [12]1 Cor. 11:25-26, 28. Heb. 10:21-22 Heb. 10:24. Ps. 26:6. [13]1 Cor. 11:24-25. [14]2 Chron. 30:18-19. Matt. 26:26.

Q. 172. May one who doubteth of His being in Christ, or of His due preparation, come to the Lord's supper?

A. One who doubteth of His being in Christ, or of His due preparation to the sacrament of the Lord's supper, may have true interest in Christ, though he be not yet assured thereof;[1] and in God's account hath it, if he be duly affected with the apprehension of the want of it,[2] and unfeignedly desires to be found in Christ,[3] and to depart from iniquity:[4] in which case (because promises are made, and this sacrament is appointed, for the relief even of weak and doubting Christians[5]) he is to bewail His unbelief,[6] and labor to have His doubts resolved;[7] and, so doing, he may and ought to come to the Lord's supper, that he may be further strengthened.[8]

[1]Isa. 50:10. 1 John 5:13. Ps. 88. Ps. 77:1-4, 7-10. Jonah 2:4. [2]Isa. 54:7-10. Matt. 5:3-4. Ps. 31:22. Ps. 73:13, 22-23. [3]Phil. 3:8-9. Ps. 10:17. Ps. 42:1-2, 5, 11. [4]2 Tim. 2:19. Isa. 50:10. Ps. 66:18-20. [5]Isa. 40:11, 29, 31. Matt. 11:28. Matt. 12:20. Matt. 26:28. [6]Mark 9:24. [7]Acts 2:37. Acts 16:30. [8]Rom. 4:11. 1 Cor. 11:28.

Q. 173. May any who profess the faith, and desire to come to the Lord's supper, be kept from it?

A. Such as are found to be ignorant or scandalous, notwithstanding their profession of the faith, and desire to come to the Lord's supper, may and ought to be kept from that sacrament, by the power which Christ hath left in His church,[1] until they receive instruction, and manifest their reformation.[2]

[1]1 Cor. 11:27-34. Matt. 7:6. 1 Cor. 5. Jude 23. 1 Tim. 5:22. [2]2 Cor. 2:7.

Q. 174. What is required of them that receive the sacrament of the Lord's supper in the time of the administration of it?

A. It is required of them that receive the sacrament of the Lord's supper, that, during the time of the administration of it, with all holy reverence and attention they wait upon God in that ordinance,[1] diligently observe the sacramental elements and actions,[2] heedfully discern the Lord's body,[3] and affectionately meditate on His death and sufferings,[4] and thereby stir up themselves to a vigorous exercise of their graces;[5] in judging themselves,[6] and sorrowing for sin;[7] in earnest hungering and thirsting after Christ,[8] feeding on Him by faith,[9] receiving of His fullness,[10] trusting in His merits,[11] rejoicing in His love,[12] giving thanks for His grace;[13] in renewing of their covenant with God,[14] and love to all the saints.[15]

[1]Lev. 10:3. Heb. 12:28. Ps. 5:7. 1 Cor. 11:17, 26-27. [2]Exod. 24:8. Matt. 26:28. [3]1 Cor. 11:29. [4]Luke 22:19. [5]1 Cor. 11:26. 1 Cor. 10:3-5, 11, 14. [6]1 Cor. 11:31. [7]Zech. 12:10. [8]Rev. 22:17. [9]John 6:35. [10]John 1:16. [11]Phil. 1:16. [12]Ps. 58:4-5. 2 Chron. 30:21. [13]Ps. 22:26. [14]Jer. 50:5. Ps. 50:5. [15]Acts 2:42.

Q. 175. What is the duty of Christians, after they have received the sacrament of the Lord's supper?

A. The duty of Christians, after they have received the sacrament of the Lord's supper, is seriously to consider how they have behaved themselves therein, and with what success;[1] if they find quickening and comfort, to bless God for it,[2] beg the continuance of it,[3] watch against relapses,[4] fulfill their vows,[5] and encourage themselves to a frequent attendance on that ordinance:[6] but if they find no present benefit, more exactly to review their preparation to, and carriage at, the sacrament;[7] in both which, if they can approve themselves to God and their own consciences, they are to wait for the fruit of it in due time:[8] but, if they see they have failed in either, they are to be humbled,[9] and to attend upon it afterwards with more care and diligence.[10]

[1]Ps. 28:7. Ps. 85:8. 1 Cor. 11:7, 30-31. [2]2 Chron. 30:21-23, 25-26. Acts 2:42, 46-47. [3]Ps. 36:10. Song 3:4. 1 Chron. 29:18. [4]1 Cor. 10:3-5, 12. [5]Ps. 50:14. [6]1 Cor. 11:25-26. Acts 2:42, 46. [7]Song 5:1-6. Eccles. 5:1-6.

[8]Ps. 123:1-2. Ps. 42:5, 8. Ps. 43:3-5. [9]2 Chron. 30:18-19. [10]2 Cor. 7:11. 1 Chron. 15:12-14.

Q. 176. Wherein do the sacraments of baptism and the Lord's supper agree?
A. The sacraments of baptism and the Lord's supper agree, in that the author of both is God;[1] the spiritual part of both is Christ and His benefits;[2] both are seals of the same covenant,[3] are to be dispensed by ministers of the gospel, and by none other;[4] and to be continued in the church of Christ until His second coming.[5]

[1]Matt. 28:19. 1 Cor. 11:23. [2]Rom. 6:3-4. 1 Cor. 10:16. [3]Rom. 4:11. Col. 2:12. Matt. 26:27-28. [4]John 1:33. Matt. 28:19. 1 Cor. 11:23. 1 Cor. 4:1. Heb. 5:4. [5]Matt. 28:19-20. 1 Cor. 11:26.

Q. 177. Wherein do the sacraments of baptism and the Lord's supper differ?
A. The sacraments of baptism and the Lord's supper differ, in that baptism is to be administered but once, with water, to be a sign and seal of our regeneration and ingrafting into Christ,[1] and that even to infants;[2] whereas the Lord's supper is to be administered often, in the elements of bread and wine, to represent and exhibit Christ as spiritual nourishment to the soul,[3] and to confirm our continuance and growth in Him,[4] and that only to such as are of years and ability to examine themselves.[5]

[1]Matt. 3:11. Titus 3:5. Gal. 3:27. [2]Gen. 17:7, 9. Acts 2:38-39. 1 Cor. 7:14. [3]1 Cor. 11:23-26. [4]1 Cor. 10:16. [5]1 Cor. 11:28-29.

Q. 178. What is prayer?
A. Prayer is an offering up of our desires unto God,[1] in the name of Christ,[2] by the help of His Spirit;[3] with confession of our sins,[4] and thankful acknowledgment of His mercies.[5]

[1]Ps. 62:8. [2]John 16:23. [3]Rom. 8:26. [4]Ps. 32:5-6. Dan. 9:4. [5]Phil. 4:6.

Q. 179. Are we to pray unto God only?
A. God only being able to search the hearts,[1] hear the requests,[2] pardon the sins,[3] and fulfill the desires of all;[4] and only to be believed in,[5] and worshipped with religious worship;[6] prayer, which is a special part thereof,[7] is to be made by all to Him alone,[8] and to none other.[9]

[1]1 Kings 8:39. Acts 1:24. Rom. 8:27. [2]Ps. 65:2. [3]Micah 7:18. [4]Ps. 145:18. [5]Rom. 10:14. [6]Matt. 4:10. [7]1 Cor. 1:2. [8]Ps. 50:15. [9]Rom. 10:14.

Q. 180. What is it to pray in the name of Christ?
A. To pray in the name of Christ is, in obedience to His command, and in confidence on His promises, to ask mercy for His sake;[1] not by bare mentioning of His name,[2] but by drawing our encouragement to pray, and our boldness, strength, and hope of acceptance in prayer, from Christ and His mediation.[3]

[1]John 14:13-14. John 16:24. Dan. 9:17. [2]Matt. 7:21. [3]Heb. 4:14-16. 1 John 5:13-15.

Q. 181. Why are we to pray in the name of Christ?
A. The sinfulness of man, and His distance from God by reason thereof, being so great, as that we can have no access into His presence without a mediator;[1] and there being none in heaven or earth appointed to, or fit for, that glorious work but Christ alone,[2] we are to pray in no other name but His only.[3]

[1]John 14:6. Isa. 59:2. Eph. 3:12. [2]John 6:27. Heb. 7:25-27. 1 Tim. 2:5. [3]Col. 3:17. Heb. 13:15.

Q. 182. How doth the Spirit help us to pray?
A. We not knowing what to pray for as we ought, the Spirit helpeth our infirmities, by enabling us to understand both for whom, and what, and how prayer is to be made; and by working and quickening in our hearts (although not in all persons, nor at all times, in the same measure) those apprehensions, affections, and graces which are requisite for the right performance of that duty.[1]

[1]Rom. 8:26-27. Ps. 10:17. Zech. 12:10.

Q. 183. For whom are we to pray?
A. We are to pray for the whole church of Christ upon earth;[1] for magistrates,[2] and ministers;[3] for ourselves,[4] our brethren,[5] yea, our enemies;[6] and for all sorts of men living,[7] or that shall live hereafter;[8] but not for the dead,[9] nor for those that are known to have sinned the sin unto death.[10]

[1]Eph. 6:18. Ps. 28:9. [2]1 Tim. 2:1-2. [3]Col. 4:3. [4]Gen. 32:11. [5]James 5:16. [6]Matt. 5:44. [7]1 Tim. 2:1-2. [8]John 17:20. 2 Sam. 7:29. [9]2 Sam. 12:21-23. [10]1 John 5:16.

Q. 184. For what things are we to pray?
A. We are to pray for all things tending to the glory of God,[1] the welfare of the church,[2] our own[3] or others' good;[4] but not for anything that is unlawful.[5]

[1]Matt. 6:9. [2]Ps. 51:18. Ps. 122:6. [3]Matt. 7:11. [4]Ps. 125:4. [5]1 John 5:14.

Q. 185. How are we to pray?
A. We are to pray with an awful apprehension of the majesty of God,[1] and deep sense of our own unworthiness,[2] necessities,[3] and sins;[4] with penitent,[5] thankful,[6] and enlarged hearts;[7] with understanding,[8] faith,[9] sincerity,[10] fervency,[11] love,[12] and perseverance,[13] waiting upon Him,[14] with humble submission to His will.[15]

[1]Eccles. 5:1. [2]Gen. 18:27. Gen. 32:10. [3]Luke 15:17-19. [4]Luke 18:13-14. [5]Ps. 51:17. [6]Phil. 4:6. [7]1 Sam. 1:15. 1 Sam. 2:1. [8]1 Cor. 14:15. [9]Mark 11:24. James 1:6. [10]Ps. 145:18. Ps. 17:1. [11]James 5:16. [12]1 Tim. 2:8. [13]Eph. 6:18. [14]Micah 7:7. [15]Matt. 26:39.

Q. 186. What rule hath God given for our direction in the duty of prayer?
A. The whole Word of God is of use to direct us in the duty of prayer;[1] but the special rule of direction is that form of prayer which our Savior Christ taught His disciples, commonly called The Lord's Prayer.[2]

[1]1 John 5:14. [2]Matt. 6:9-13. Luke 11:2-4.

Q. 187. How is the Lord's Prayer to be used?
A. The Lord's Prayer is not only for direction, as a pattern, according to which we are to make other prayers; but may also be used as a prayer, so that it be done with understanding, faith, reverence, and other graces necessary to the right performance of the duty of prayer.[1]

[1]Matt. 6:9. Luke 11:2.

Q. 188. Of how many parts doth the Lord's Prayer consist?
A. The Lord's Prayer consists of three parts; a preface, petitions, and a conclusion.

Q. 189. What doth the preface of the Lord's Prayer teach us?
A. The preface of the Lord's Prayer (contained in these words, Our Father which art in heaven,[1]) teacheth us, when we pray, to draw near to God with confidence of His fatherly goodness, and our interest therein;[2] with reverence, and all other childlike dispositions,[3] heavenly affections,[4] and due apprehensions of His sovereign power, majesty, and gracious condescension:[5] as also, to pray with and for others.[6]

[1]Matt. 6:9. [2]Luke 11:13. Rom. 8:15. [3]Isa. 64:9. [4]Ps. 123:1. Lam. 3:41. [5]Isa. 63:15-16. Neh. 1:4-6. [6]Acts 12:5.

Q. 190. What do we pray for in the first petition?
A. In the first petition, (which is, Hallowed by thy name,[1]) acknowledging the utter inability and indisposition that is in ourselves and all men to honor God aright,[2] we pray, that God would by His grace enable and incline us and others to know, to acknowledge, and highly to esteem Him,[3] His titles,[4] attributes,[5] ordinances, Word,[6] works, and whatsoever He is pleased to make Himself known by;[7] and to glorify Him in thought, word,[8] and deed:[9] that He would prevent and remove atheism,[10] ignorance,[11] idolatry,[12] profaneness,[13] and whatsoever is dishonorable to Him;[14] and, by His over-ruling providence, direct and dispose of all things to His own glory.[15]

[1]Matt. 6:9. [2]2 Cor. 3:5. Ps. 51:15. [3]Ps. 67:2-3. [4]Ps. 83:18. [5]Ps. 86:10-13, 15. [6]2 Thess. 3:1. Ps. 147:19-20. Ps. 138:1-3. 2 Cor. 2:14-15. [7]Ps. 145. etc Ps. 8. etc [8]Ps. 103:1. Ps. 19:14. [9]Phil. 1:9, 11. [10]Ps. 67:1-4. [11]Eph. 1:17-18. [12]Ps. 97:7. [13]Ps. 74:18, 22-23. [14]2 Kings 19:15-16. [15]2 Chron. 20:6, 10-12. Ps. 83. etc Ps. 140:4, 8.

Q. 191. What do we pray for in the second petition?
A. In the second petition, (which is, Thy kingdom come,[1]) acknowledging ourselves and all mankind to be by nature under the dominion of sin and Satan,[2] we pray, that the kingdom of sin and Satan may be destroyed,[3] the gospel propagated throughout the world,[4] the Jews called,[5] the fullness of the Gentiles brought in;[6] the church furnished with all gospel-officers and ordinances,[7] purged from corruption,[8] countenanced and maintained by the civil magistrate:[9] that the ordinances of Christ may be purely dispensed, and made effectual to the converting of those that are yet in their sins, and the confirming, comforting, and building up of those that are already converted:[10]

that Christ would rule in our hearts here,[11] and hasten the time of His second coming, and our reigning with Him forever:[12] and that He would be pleased so to exercise the kingdom of His power in all the world, as may best conduce to these ends.[13]

[1]Matt. 6:10. [2]Eph. 2:2-3. [3]Ps. 68:1. Rev. 12:10-11. [4]2 Thess. 3:1. [5]Rom. 10:1. [6]John 17:9, 20. Rom. 11:25-26. Ps. 67. [7]Matt. 9:38. 2 Thess. 3:1. [8]Mal. 1:11. Zeph. 3:9. [9]1 Tim. 2:1-2. [10]Acts 4:29-30. Eph. 6:18-20. Rom. 15:29-30, 32. 2 Thess. 1:11. 2 Thess. 2:16-17. [11]Eph. 3:14-20. [12]Rev. 22:20. [13]Isa. 64:1-2. Rev. 4:8-11.

Q. 192. What do we pray for in the third petition?
A. In the third petition, (which is, Thy will be done in earth as it is in heaven,[1]) acknowledging, that by nature we and all men are not only utterly unable and unwilling to know and do the will of God,[2] but prone to rebel against His Word,[3] to repine and murmur against His providence,[4] and wholly inclined to do the will of the flesh, and of the devil:[5] we pray, that God would by His Spirit take away from ourselves and others all blindness,[6] weakness,[7] indisposedness,[8] and perverseness of heart;[9] and by His grace make us able and willing to know, do, and submit to His will in all things,[10] with the like humility,[11] cheerfulness,[12] faithfulness,[13] diligence,[14] zeal,[15] sincerity,[16] and constancy,[17] as the angels do in heaven.[18]

[1]Matt. 6:10. [2]Rom. 7:18. Job 21:14. 1 Cor. 2:14. [3]Rom. 8:7. [4]Exod. 17:7. Num. 14:2. [5]Eph. 2:2. [6]Eph. 1:17-18. [7]Eph. 3:16. [8]Matt. 26:40-41. [9]Jer. 31:18-19. [10]Ps. 119:1, 8, 35-36. Acts 21:14. [11]Micah 6:8. [12]Ps. 100:2. Job 1:21. 2 Sam. 15:25-26. [13]Isa. 38:3. [14]Ps. 119:4-5. [15]Rom. 12:11. [16]Ps. 119:80. [17]Ps. 119:112. [18]Isa. 6:2-3. Ps. 103:20-21. Matt. 18:10.

Q. 193. What do we pray for in the fourth petition?
A. In the fourth petition, (which is, Give us this day our daily bread,[1]) acknowledging, that in Adam, and by our own sin, we have forfeited our right to all the outward blessings of this life, and deserve to be wholly deprived of them by God, and to have them cursed to us in the use of them;[2] and that neither they of themselves are able to sustain us,[3] nor we to merit,[4] or by our own industry to procure them;[5] but prone to desire,[6] get,[7] and use them unlawfully:[8] we pray for ourselves and others, that both they and we, waiting upon the providence of God from day to day in the use of lawful means, may, of His free gift, and as to His fatherly wisdom shall seem best, enjoy a competent portion of them;[9] and have the same continued and blessed unto us in our holy and comfortable use of them,[10] and contentment in them;[11] and be kept from all things that are contrary to our temporal support and comfort.[12]

[1]Matt. 6:11. [2]Gen. 2:17. Gen. 3:17. Rom. 8:20-22. Jer. 5:25. Deut. 28:15-17. etc [3]Deut. 8:3. [4]Gen. 32:10. [5]Deut. 8:17-18. [6]Jer. 6:13. Mark 7:21-22. [7]Hosea 12:7. [8]James 4:3. [9]Gen. 43:12-14. Gen. 28:20. Eph. 4:28. 2 Thess. 3:11-12. Phil. 4:6. [10]1 Tim. 4:3-5. [11]1 Tim. 6:6-8. [12]Prov. 30:8-9.

Q. 194. What do we pray for in the fifth petition?
A. In the fifth petition, (which is, Forgive us our debts, as we forgive our debtors,[1]) acknowledging, that we and all others are guilty both of original and actual sin, and thereby become debtors to the justice of God; and that neither we, nor any other creature, can make the least satisfaction for that debt:[2] we pray for ourselves and others, that God of His free grace would, through the obedience and satisfaction of Christ, apprehended and applied by faith, acquit us both from the guilt and punishment of sin,[3] accept us in His Beloved;[4] continue His favor and grace to us,[5] pardon our daily failings,[6] and fill us with peace and joy, in giving us daily more and more assurance of forgiveness;[7] which we are the rather emboldened to ask, and encouraged to expect, when we have this testimony in ourselves, that we from the heart forgive others their offenses.[8]

[1]Matt. 6:12. [2]Rom. 3:9-22. etc Matt. 18:24-25. Ps. 130:3-4. [3]Rom. 3:24-26. Heb. 9:22. [4]Eph. 1:6-7. [5]2 Peter 1:2. [6]Hosea 14:2. Jer. 14:7. [7]Rom. 15:13. Ps. 51:7-10, 12. [8]Luke 11:4. Matt. 6:14-15. Matt. 18:35.

Q. 195. What do we pray for in the sixth petition?
A. In the sixth petition, (which is, And lead us not into temptation, but deliver us from

evil,[1]) acknowledging, that the most wise, righteous, and gracious God, for divers holy and just ends, may so order things, that we may be assaulted, foiled, and for a time led captive by temptations;[2] that Satan,[3] the world,[4] and the flesh, are ready powerfully to draw us aside, and ensnare us;[5] and that we, even after the pardon of our sins, by reason of our corruption,[6] weakness, and want of watchfulness,[7] are not only subject to be tempted, and forward to expose ourselves unto temptations,[8] but also of ourselves unable and unwilling to resist them, to recover out of them, and to improve them;[9] and worthy to be left under the power of them:[10] we pray, that God would so overrule the world and all in it,[11] subdue the flesh,[12] and restrain Satan,[13] order all things,[14] bestow and bless all means of grace,[15] and quicken us to watchfulness in the use of them, that we and all His people may by His providence be kept from being tempted to sin;[16] or, if tempted, that by His Spirit we may be powerfully supported and enabled to stand in the hour of temptation;[17] or when fallen, raised again and recovered out of it,[18] and have a sanctified use and improvement thereof:[19] that our sanctification and salvation may be perfected,[20] Satan trodden under our feet,[21] and we fully freed from sin, temptation, and all evil, forever.[22]

[1]Matt. 6:13. [2]2 Chron. 32:31. [3]1 Chron. 21:1. [4]Luke 21:34. Mark 4:19. [5]James 1:14. [6]Gal. 5:17. [7]Matt. 26:41. [8]Matt. 26:69-72. Gal. 2:11-14. 2 Chron. 18:3. 2 Chron. 19:2. [9]Rom. 7:23-24. 1 Chron. 21:1-4. 2 Chron. 16:7-10. [10]Ps. 81:11-12. [11]John 17:15. [12]Ps. 51:10. Ps. 119:133. [13]2 Cor. 12:7-8. [14]1 Cor. 10:12-13.[15]Heb. 13:20-21.[16]Matt. 26:41. Ps. 19:13. [17]Eph. 3:14-17. 1 Thess. 3:13. Jude 24. [18]Ps. 51:12. [19]1 Peter 5:8-10. [20]2 Cor. 13:7, 9. [21]Rom. 16:20. Luke 22:31-32. [22]John 17:15. 1 Thess. 5:23.

Q. 196. What doth the conclusion of the Lord's Prayer teach us?

A. The conclusion of the Lord's Prayer, (which is, For thine is the kingdom, and the power, and the glory, for ever. Amen.[1]) teacheth us to enforce our petitions with arguments,[2] which are to be taken, not from any worthiness in ourselves, or in any other creature, but from God;[3] and with our prayers to join praises,[4] ascribing to God alone eternal sovereignty, omnipotency, and glorious excellency;[5] in regard whereof, as He is able and willing to help us,[6] so we by faith are emboldened to plead with Him that He would,[7] and quietly to rely upon Him, that He will fulfill our requests.[8] And, to testify this our desire and assurance, we say, Amen.[9]

[1]Matt. 6:13. [2]Rom. 15:30. [3]Dan. 9:4, 7-9, 16-19. [4]Phil. 4:6. [5]1 Chron. 29:10-13. [6]Eph. 3:20-21. Luke 11:13. [7]2 Chron. 20:6, 11. [8]2 Chron. 14:11. [9]1 Cor. 14:16. Rev. 22:20-21.

APPENDIX 3

THE SHORTER CATECHISM

Q. 1. What is the chief end of man?
A. Man's chief end is to glorify God,[1] and to enjoy Him forever.[2]

[1]Ps. 86. Isa. 60:21. Rom. 11:36. 1 Cor. 6:20, 31. Rev. 4:11. [2]Ps. 16:5-11. Ps. 144:15. Isa. 12:2. Luke 2:10. Phil. 4:4. Rev. 21:3-4.

Q. 2. What rule hath God given to direct us how we may glorify and enjoy Him?
A. The Word of God, which is contained in the Scriptures of the Old and New Testaments,[1] is the only rule to direct us how we may glorify and enjoy Him.[2]

[1]Matt. 19:4-5. With Gen. 2:24. Luke 24:27, 44. 1 Cor. 2:13. 1 Cor. 14:37. 2 Peter 1:20-21. 2 Peter 3:2, 15-16. [2]Deut. 4:2. Ps. 19:7-11. Isa. 8:20. John 15:11. John 20:30-31. Acts 17:11. 2 Tim. 3:15-17. 1 John 1:4.

Q. 3. What do the Scriptures principally teach?
A. The Scriptures principally teach, what man is to believe concerning God,[1] and what duty God requires of man.[2]

[1]Gen. 1:1. John 5:39. John 20:31. Rom. 10:17 2 Tim. 3:15. [2]Deut. 10:12-13. Josh. 1:8. Ps. 119:105. Micah 6:8. 2 Tim. 3:16-17.

Q. 4. What is God?
A. God is a Spirit,[1] infinite,[2] eternal,[3] and unchangeable,[4] in His being,[5] wisdom,[6] power,[7] holiness,[8] justice,[9] goodness,[10] and truth.[11]

[1]Deut. 4:15-19. Luke 24:39. John 1:18. John 4:24. Acts 17:29. [2]1 Kings 8:27. Ps. 139:7-10. Ps. 145:3. Ps. 147:5. Jer. 23:24. Rom. 11:33-36. [3]Deut. 33:27. Ps. 90:2. Ps. 102:12, 24-27. Rev. 1:4, 8. [4]Ps. 33:11. Mal. 3:6. Heb. 1:12. Heb. 6:17-18. Heb. 13:8. James 1:17. [5]Exod. 3:14. Ps. 115:2-3. 1 Tim. 1:17. 1 Tim. 6:15-16. [6]Ps. 104:24. Rom. 11:33-34. Heb. 4:13. 1 John 3:20. [7]Gen. 17:1. Ps. 62:11. Jer. 32:17. Matt. 19:26. Rev. 1:8. [8]Heb. 1:13. 1 Peter 1:15-16. 1 John 3:3, 5. Rev. 15:4. [9]Gen. 18:25. Exod. 34:6-7. Deut. 32:4. Ps. 96:13. Rom. 3:5, 26. [10]Ps. 103:5. Ps. 107:8. Matt. 19:7. Rom. 2:4. [11]Exod. 34:6. Deut. 32:4. Ps. 86:15. Ps. 117:2. Heb. 6:18.

Q. 5. Are there more Gods than one?
A. There is but one only,[1] the living and true God.[2]

[1]Deut. 6:4. Isa. 44:6. Isa. 45:21-22. 1 Cor. 8:4-6. [2]Jer. 10:10. John 17:3. 1 Thess. 1:9. 1 John 5:20.

Q. 6. How many persons are there in the Godhead?
A. There are three persons in the Godhead: the Father, the Son, and the Holy Ghost;[1] and these three are one God, the same in substance, equal in power and glory.[2]

[1]Matt. 3:16-17. Matt. 28:19. 2 Cor. 13:14. 1 Peter 1:2. [2]Ps. 45:6. John 1:1. John 17:5. Acts 5:3-4. Rom. 9:5. Col. 2:9. Jude 1:24-25.

Q. 7. What are the decrees of God?
A. The decrees of God are, His eternal purpose, according to the counsel of His will, whereby, for His own glory, He hath foreordained whatsoever comes to pass.[1]

[1]Ps. 33:11. Isa. 14:24. Acts 2:23. Eph. 1:11-12.

Q. 8. How doth God execute His decrees?
A. God executeth His decrees in the works of creation and providence.[1]

[1]Ps. 148:8. Isa. 40:26. Dan. 4:35. Acts 4:24-28. Rev. 4:11.

Q. 9. What is the work of creation?
A. The work of creation is, God's making all things of nothing, by the word of His power,[1] in the space of six days, and all very good.[2]

[1]Gen. 1:1. Ps. 33:6, 9. Heb. 11:3. [2]Gen. 1:31.

Q. 10. How did God create man?
A. God created man male and female, after His own image,[1] in knowledge,[2] righteousness, and holiness,[3] with dominion over the creatures.[4]

[1]Gen. 1:27. [2]Col. 3:10. [3]Eph. 4:24. [4]Gen. 1:28. Ps. 8.

Q. 11. What are God's works of providence?
A. God's works of providence are, His most holy,[1] wise,[2] and powerful[3] preserving[4] and governing[5] all His creatures, and all their actions.[6]

[1]Ps. 145:17. [2]Ps. 104:24. [3]Heb. 1:3. [4]Neh. 9:6. [5]Eph. 1:19-22. [6]Ps. 36:6. Prov. 16:33. Matt. 10:30.

Q. 12. What special act of providence did God exercise towards man in the estate wherein he was created?
A. When God had created man, he entered into a covenant of life with him, upon condition of perfect obedience; forbidding him to eat of the tree of the knowledge of good and evil, upon pain of death.[1]

[1]Gen. 2:16-17. James 2:10.

Q. 13. Did our first parents continue in the estate wherein they were created?
A. Our first parents, being left to the freedom of their own will, fell from the estate wherein they were created, by sinning against God.[1]

[1]Gen. 3:6-8, 13. 2 Cor. 11:3.

Q. 14. What is sin?
A. Sin is any want of conformity unto, or transgression of, the law of God.[1]

[1]Lev. 5:17. James 4:17. 1 John 3:4.

Q. 15. What was the sin whereby our first parents fell from the estate wherein they were created?
A. The sin whereby our first parents fell from the estate wherein they were created, was their eating the forbidden fruit.[1]

[1]Gen. 3:6.

Q. 16. Did all mankind fall in Adam's first transgression?
A. The covenant being made with Adam,[1] not only for himself, but for his posterity; all mankind, descending from him by ordinary generation, sinned in him, and fell with him, in his first transgression.[2]

[1]Gen. 2:16-17. James 2:10. [2]Rom. 5:12-21. 1 Cor. 15:22.

Q. 17. Into what estate did the fall bring mankind?
A. The fall brought mankind into an estate of sin and misery.[1]

[1]Gen. 3:16-19, 23. Rom. 3:16. Rom. 5:12. Eph. 2:1.

Q. 18. Wherein consists the sinfulness of that estate whereinto man fell?
A. The sinfulness of that estate whereinto man fell, consists in the guilt of Adam's first sin,[1] the want of original righteousness,[2] and the corruption of his whole nature,[3] which is commonly called original sin; together with all actual transgressions which proceed from it.[4]

[1]Rom. 5:12, 19. [2]Rom. 3:10. Col. 3:10. Eph. 4:24. [3]Ps. 51:5. John 3:6. Rom. 3:18. Rom. 8:7-8. Eph. 2:3. [4]Gen. 6:5. Ps. 53:1-3. Matt. 15:19. Rom. 3:10-18, 23. Gal. 5:19-21. James 1:14-15.

Q. 19. What is the misery of that estate whereinto man fell?
A. All mankind by their fall lost communion with God,[1] are under His wrath[2] and curse,[3] and so made liable to all the miseries of this life,[4] to death[5] itself, and to the pains of hell forever.[6]

[1]Gen. 3:8, 24. John 8:34, 42, 44. Eph. 2:12. Eph. 4:18. [2]John 3:36. Rom. 1:18. Eph. 2:3. Eph. 5:6. [3]Gal. 3:10. Rev. 22:3. [4]Gen. 3:16-19. Job 5:7. Eccles. 2:22-23. Rom. 8:18-23. [5]Ezek 18:4. Rom. 5:12. Rom. 6:23. [6]Matt. 25:41, 46. 2 Thess. 1:9. Rev. 14:9-11.

Q. 20. Did God leave all mankind to perish in the estate of sin and misery?
A. God, having out of His mere good pleasure, from all eternity, elected some to everlasting life,[1] did enter into a covenant of grace to deliver them out of the estate of sin and misery, and to bring them into an estate of salvation by a Redeemer.[2]

[1]Acts 13:48. Eph. 1:4-5. 2 Thess. 2:13-14. [2]Gen. 3:15. Gen. 17:7. Exod. 19:5-6. Jer. 31:31-34. Matt. 20:28. 1 Cor. 11:25. Heb. 9:15.

Q. 21. Who is the Redeemer of God's elect?
A. The only Redeemer of God's elect is the Lord Jesus Christ,[1] who, being the eternal Son of God,[2] became man,[3] and so was, and continueth to be, God and man in two distinct natures, and one person, forever.[4]

[1]John 14:6. Acts 4:12. 1 Tim. 2:5-6. [2]Ps. 2:7. Matt. 3:17. Matt. 17:5. John 1:18. [3]Isa. 9:6. Matt. 1:23. John 1:14. Gal. 4:4. [4]Acts 1:11. Heb. 7:24-25.

Q. 22. How did Christ, being the Son of God, become man?
A. Christ, the Son of God, became man, by taking to Himself a true body, and a reasonable soul,[1] being conceived by the power of the Holy Ghost, in the womb of the virgin Mary, and born of her,[2] yet without sin.[3]

[1]Phil. 2:7. Heb. 2:14, 17. [2]Luke 1:27, 31, 35. [3]2 Cor. 5:21. Heb. 4:15. Heb. 7:26. 1 John 3:5.

Q. 23. What offices doth Christ execute as our Redeemer?
A. Christ, as our Redeemer, executeth the offices of a prophet,[1] of a priest,[2] and of a king,[3] both in His estate of humiliation and exaltation.

[1]Deut. 18:18. Acts 2:33. Acts 3:22-23. Heb. 1:1-2. [2]Heb. 4:14-15. Heb. 5:5-6. [3]Isa. 9:6-7. Luke 1:32-33. John 18:37. 1 Cor. 15:25.

Q. 24. How doth Christ execute the office of a prophet?
A. Christ executeth the office of a prophet, in revealing to us, by His Word[1] and Spirit,[2] the will of God for our salvation.[3]

[1]Luke 4:18-19, 21. Acts 1:1-2. Heb. 2:3. [2]John 15:26-27. Acts 1:8. 1 Peter 1:11. [3]John 4:41-42. John 20:30-31.

Q. 25. How doth Christ execute the office of a priest?
A. Christ executeth the office of a priest, in His once offering up of Himself a sacrifice to satisfy divine justice,[1] and reconcile us to God,[2] and in making continual intercession for us.[3]

[1]Isa. 53. Acts 8:32-35. Heb. 9:26-28. Heb. 10:12. [2]Rom. 5:10-11. 2 Cor. 5:18. Col. 1:21-22. [3]Rom. 8:34. Heb. 7:25. Heb. 9:24.

Q. 26. How doth Christ execute the office of a king?
A. Christ executeth the office of a king, in subduing us to Himself, in ruling and defending us,[1] and in restraining and conquering all His and our enemies.[2]

[1]Ps. 110:3. Matt. 28:18-20. John 17:2. Col. 1:13. [2]Ps. 2:6-9. Ps. 110:1-2. Matt. 12:28. 1 Cor. 15:24-26. Col. 2:15.

Q. 27. Wherein did Christ's humiliation consist?
A. Christ's humiliation consisted in His being born, and that in a low condition,[1] made under the law,[2] undergoing the miseries of this life,[3] the wrath of God,[4] and the cursed death of the cross;[5] in being buried, and continuing under the power of death for a time.[6]

[1]Luke 2:7. 2 Cor. 8:9. Gal. 4:4. [2]Gal. 4:4. [3]Isa. 53:3. Luke 9:58. John 4:6. John 11:35. Heb. 2:18. [4]Ps. 22:1. Matt. 27:46. Isa. 53:10. 1 John 2:2. [5]Gal. 3:13. Phil. 2:8. [6]Matt. 12:40. 1 Cor. 15:3-4.

Q. 28. Wherein consisteth Christ's exaltation?
A. Christ's exaltation consisteth in His rising again from the dead on the third day,[1] in ascending up into heaven,[2] in sitting at the right hand[3] of God the Father, and in coming to judge the world at the last day.[4]

[1]1 Cor. 15:4. [2]Ps. 68:18. Acts 1:11. Eph. 4:8. [3]Ps. 110:1. Acts 2:33-34. Heb. 1:3. [4]Matt. 16:27. Acts 17:31.

Q. 29. How are we made partakers of the redemption purchased by Christ?
A. We are made partakers of the redemption purchased by Christ, by the effectual application of it to us by His Holy Spirit.[1]

[1]Titus 3:4-7.

Q. 30. How doth the Spirit apply to us the redemption purchased by Christ?
A. The Spirit applieth to us the redemption purchased by Christ, by working faith in us,[1] and thereby uniting us to Christ in our effectual calling.[2]

[1]Rom. 10:17. 1 Cor. 2:12-16. Eph. 2:8. Phil. 1:29. [2]John 15:5. 1 Cor. 1:9. Eph. 3:17.

Q. 31. What is effectual calling?
A. Effectual calling is the work of God's Spirit, whereby, convincing us of our sin

and misery, enlightening our minds in the knowledge of Christ,[1] and renewing our wills,[2] He doth persuade and enable us to embrace Jesus Christ,[3] freely offered to us in the gospel.[4]

[1]Acts 26:18. I Cor. 2:10, 12. 2 Cor. 4:6. Eph. 1:17-18. [2]Deut. 30:6. Ezek 36:26-27. John 3:5. Titus 3:5. [3]John 6:44-45. Acts 16:14. [4]Isa. 45:22. Matt. 11:28-30. Rev. 22:17.

Q. 32. What benefits do they that are effectually called partake of in this life?
A. They that are effectually called do in this life partake of justification, adoption, and sanctification, and the several benefits which in this life do either accompany or flow from them.[1]

[1]Rom. 8:30. I Cor. 1:30. I Cor. 6:11. Eph. 1:5.

Q. 33. What is justification?
A. Justification is an act of God's free grace,[1] wherein He pardoneth all our sins,[2] and accepteth us as righteous in His sight,[3] only for the righteousness of Christ imputed to us,[4] and received by faith alone.[5]

[1]Rom. 3:24. [2]Rom. 4:6-8. 2 Cor. 5:19. [3]2 Cor. 5:21. [4]Rom. 4:6, 11. Rom. 5:19. [5]Gal. 2:16. Phil. 3:9.

Q. 34. What is adoption?
A. Adoption is an act of God's free grace, whereby we are received into the number, and have a right to all the privileges, of the sons of God.[1]

[1]I John 3:1.

Q. 35. What is sanctification?
A. Sanctification is the work of God's free grace,[1] whereby we are renewed in the whole man after the image of God,[2] and are enabled more and more to die unto sin, and live unto righteousness.[3]

[1]Ezek 36:27. Phil. 2:13. 2 Thess. 2:13. [2]2 Cor. 5:17. Eph. 4:23-24. I Thess. 5:23. [3]Ezek 36:25-27. Rom. 6:4, 6, 12-14. 2 Cor. 7:1. I Peter 2:24.

Q. 36. What are the benefits which in this life do accompany or flow from justification, adoption, and sanctification?
A. The benefits which in this life do accompany or flow from justification, adoption, and sanctification, are, assurance of God's love,[1] peace of conscience,[2] joy in the Holy Ghost,[3] increase of grace,[4] and perseverance therein to the end.[5]

[1]Rom. 5:5. [2]Rom. 5:1. [3]Rom. 14:17. [4]2 Peter 3:18. [5]Phil. 1:6. I Peter 1:5.

Q. 37. What benefits do believers receive from Christ at death?
A. The souls of believers are at their death made perfect in holiness,[1] and do immediately pass into glory;[2] and their bodies, being still united in Christ,[3] do rest in their graves, till the resurrection.[4]

[1]Heb. 12:23. [2]Luke 23:43. 2 Cor. 5:6, 8. Phil. 1:23. [3]I Thess. 4:14. [4]Dan. 12:2. John 5:28-29. Acts 24:15.

Q. 38. What benefits do believers receive from Christ at the resurrection?
A. At the resurrection, believers, being raised up in glory,[1] shall be openly acknowledged and acquitted in the day of judgment,[2] and made perfectly blessed in the full enjoying of God[3] to all eternity.[4]

[1]I Cor. 15:42-43. [2]Matt. 25:33-34, 46. [3]Rom. 8:29. I John 3:2. [4]Ps. 16:11. I Thess. 4:17.

Q. 39. What is the duty which God requireth of man?
A. The duty which God requireth of man, is obedience to His revealed will.[1]

[1]Deut. 29:29. Micah 6:8. I John 5:2-3.

Q. 40. What did God at first reveal to man for the rule of His obedience?
A. The rule which God at first revealed to man for His obedience, was the moral law.[1]

[1]Rom. 2:14-15. Rom. 10:5.

Q. 41. Wherein is the moral law summarily comprehended?
A. The moral law is summarily comprehended in the ten commandments.[1]

[1]Deut. 4:13. Matt. 19:17-19.

Q. 42. What is the sum of the ten commandments?
A. The sum of the ten commandments is, to love the Lord our God with all our heart, with all our soul, with all our strength, and with all our mind; and our neighbor as ourselves.[1]

[1]Matt. 22:37-40.

Q. 43. What is the preface to the ten commandments?
A. The preface to the ten commandments is in these words, I am the Lord thy God,

which have brought thee out of the land of Egypt, out of the house of bondage.[1]

[1]Exod. 20:2. Deut. 5:6.

Q. 44. What doth the preface to the ten commandments teach us?
A. The preface to the ten commandments teacheth us, that because God is the Lord, and our God, and Redeemer, therefore we are bound to keep all His commandments.[1]

[1]Luke 1:74-75. 1 Peter 1:14-19.

Q. 45. Which is the first commandment?
A. The first commandment is, Thou shalt have no other gods before me.[1]

[1]Exod. 20:3. Deut. 5:7.

Q. 46. What is required in the first commandment?
A. The first commandment requireth us to know and acknowledge God to be the only true God, and our God; and to worship and glorify Him accordingly.[1]

[1]1 Chron. 28:9. Isa. 45:20-25. Matt. 4:10.

Q. 47. What is forbidden in the first commandment?
A. The first commandment forbiddeth the denying,[1] or not worshiping and glorifying, the true God as God,[2] and our God;[3] and the giving of that worship and glory to any other, which is due to Him alone.[4]

[1]Ps. 14:1. [2]Rom. 1:20-21. [3]Ps. 81:10-11. [4]Ezek 8:16-18. Rom. 1:25.

Q. 48. What are we specially taught by these words before me in the first commandment?
A. These words before me in the first commandment teach us, that God, who seeth all things, taketh notice of, and is much displeased with, the sin of having any other God.[1]

[1]Deut. 30:17-18. Ps. 44:20-21. Ezek 8:12.

Q. 49. Which is the second commandment?
A. Thou shalt not make unto thee any graven image, or any likeness of any thing that is in heaven above, or that is in the earth beneath, or that is in the water under the earth: Thou shalt not bow down thyself to them, nor serve them: for I the LORD thy God am a jealous God, visiting the iniquity of the fathers upon the children unto the third and fourth generation of them that hate me; And shewing mercy unto thousands of them that love me, and keep my commandments.[1]

[1]Exod. 20:4-6. Deut. 5:8-10.

Q. 50. What is required in the second commandment?
A. The second commandment requireth the receiving, observing, and keeping pure and entire, all such religious worship and ordinances as God hath appointed in His Word.[1]

[1]Deut. 12:32. Matt. 28:20.

Q. 51. What is forbidden in the second commandment?
A. The second commandment forbiddeth the worshiping of God by images,[1] or any other way not appointed in His Word.[2]

[1]Deut. 4:15-19. Rom. 1:22-23. [2]Lev. 10:1-2. Jer. 19:4-5. Col. 2:18-23.

Q. 52. What are the reasons annexed to the second commandment?
A. The reasons annexed to the second commandment are, God's sovereignty over us,[1] His propriety in us,[2] and the zeal He hath to His own worship.[3]

[1]Ps. 95:2-3, 6-7. Ps. 96:9-10. [2]Exod. 19:5. Ps. 45:11. Isa. 54:5. [3]Exod. 34:14. 1 Cor. 10:22.

Q. 53. Which is the third commandment?
A. The third commandment is, Thou shalt not take the name of the Lord thy God in vain: for the Lord will not hold him guiltless that taketh His name in vain.[1]

[1]Exod. 20:7. Deut. 5:11.

Q. 54. What is required in the third commandment?
A. The third commandment requireth the holy and reverent use of God's names, titles,[1] attributes,[2] ordinances,[3] Word,[4] and works.[5]

[1]Deut. 10:20. Ps. 29:2. Matt. 6:9. [2]1 Chron. 29:10-13. Rev. 15:3-4. [3]Acts 2:42. 1 Cor. 11:27-28. [4]Ps. 138:2. Rev. 22:18-19. [5]Ps. 107:21-22. Rev. 4:11.

Q. 55. What is forbidden in the third commandment?

A. The third commandment forbiddeth all profaning or abusing of anything whereby God maketh Himself known.[1]

[1]Lev. 19:12. Matt. 5:33-37. James 5:12.

Q. 56. What is the reason annexed to the third commandment?
A. The reason annexed to the third commandment is, that however the breakers of this commandment may escape punishment from men, yet the Lord our God will not suffer them to escape His righteous judgment.[1]

[1]Deut. 28:58-59. I Sam. 3:13. I Sam. 4:11.

Q. 57. Which is the fourth commandment?
A. The fourth commandment is, Remember the sabbath day to keep it holy. Six days shalt thou labor, and do all thy work: but the seventh day is the sabbath of the Lord thy God: in it thou shalt not do any work, thou, nor thy son, nor thy daughter, thy manservant, nor thy maidservent, nor thy cattle, nor thy stranger that is within thy gates: For in six days the Lord made heaven and earth, the sea, and all that in them is, and rested the seventh day: wherefore the Lord blessed the sabbath day, and hallowed it.[1]

[1]Exod. 20:8-11. Deut. 5:12-15.

Q. 58. What is required in the fourth commandment?
A. The fourth commandment requireth the keeping holy to God such set times as He hath appointed in His Word; expressly one whole day in seven, to be a holy sabbath to Himself.[1]

[1]Exod. 31:13, 16-17.

Q. 59. Which day of the seven hath God appointed to be the weekly sabbath?
A. From the beginning of the world to the resurrection of Christ, God appointed the seventh day of the week to be the weekly sabbath;[1] and the first day of the week ever since, to continue to the end of the world, which is the Christian sabbath.[2]

[1]Gen. 2:2-3. Exod. 20:11. [2]Mark 2:27-28. Acts 20:7. I Cor. 16:2. Rev. 1:10.

Q. 60. How is the sabbath to be sanctified?
A. The sabbath is to be sanctified by a holy resting all that day, even from such worldly employments and recreations as are lawful on other days;[1] and spending the whole time in the public and private exercises of God's worship,[2] except so much as is to be taken up in the works of necessity and mercy.[3]

[1]Exod. 20:10. Neh. 13:15-22. Isa. 58:13-14.
[2]Exod. 20:8. Lev. 23:3. Luke 4:16. Acts 20:7.
[3]Matt. 12:1-13.

Q. 61. What is forbidden in the fourth commandment?
A. The fourth commandment forbiddeth the omission, or careless performance, of the duties required, and the profaning the day by idleness, or doing that which is in itself sinful, or by unnecessary thoughts, words, or works, about our worldly employments or recreations.[1]

[1]Neh. 13:15-22. Isa. 58:13-14. Amos 8:4-6.

Q. 62. What are the reasons annexed to the fourth commandment?
A. The reasons annexed to the fourth commandment are, God's allowing us six days of the week for our own employments,[1] His challenging a special propriety in the seventh, His own example, and His blessing the sabbath day.[2]

[1]Exod. 20:9. Exod. 31:15. Lev. 23:3. [2]Gen. 2:2-3. Exod. 20:11. Exod. 31:17.

Q. 63. Which is the fifth commandment?
A. The fifth commandment is, Honor thy father and thy mother: that thy days may be long upon the land which the Lord thy God giveth thee.[1]

[1]Exod. 20:12. Deut. 5:16.

Q. 64. What is required in the fifth commandment?
A. The fifth commandment requireth the preserving the honor, and performing the duties, belonging to everyone in their several places and relations, as superiors, inferiors, or equals.[1]

[1]Rom. 13:1, 7. Eph. 5:21-22, 24. Eph. 6:1, 4-5, 9. I Peter 2:17.

Q. 65. What is forbidden in the fifth commandment?
A. The fifth commandment forbiddeth the neglecting of, or doing anything against, the honor and duty which belongeth to everyone in their several places and relations.[1]

[1]Matt. 15:4-6. Rom. 13:8.

Q. 66. What is the reason annexed to the fifth commandment?
A. The reason annexed to the fifth commandment is, a promise of long life and prosperity (as far as it shall serve for God's glory and their own good) to all such as keep this commandment.[1]

[1]Exod. 20:12. Deut. 5:16. Eph. 6:2-3.

Q. 67. Which is the sixth commandment?
A. The sixth commandment is, Thou shalt not kill.[1]

[1]Exod. 20:13. Deut. 5:17.

Q. 68. What is required in the sixth commandment?
A. The sixth commandment requireth all lawful endeavors to preserve our own life, and the life of others.[1]

[1]Eph. 5:28-29.

Q. 69. What is forbidden in the sixth commandment?
A. The sixth commandment forbiddeth the taking away of our own life, or the life of our neighbor, unjustly, or whatsoever tendeth thereunto.[1]

[1]Gen. 9:6. Matt. 5:22. 1 John 3:15.

Q. 70. Which is the seventh commandment?
A. The seventh commandment is, Thou shalt not commit adultery.[1]

[1]Exod. 20:14. Deut. 5:18.

Q. 71. What is required in the seventh commandment?
A. The seventh commandment requireth the preservation of our own and our neighbor's chastity, in heart, speech, and behavior.[1]

[1]1 Cor. 7:2-3, 5. 1 Thess. 4:3-5.

Q. 72. What is forbidden in the seventh commandment?
A. The seventh commandment forbiddeth all unchaste thoughts, words, and actions.[1]

[1]Matt. 5:28. Eph. 5:3-4.

Q. 73. Which is the eighth commandment?
A. The eighth commandment is, Thou shalt not steal.[1]

[1]Exod. 20:15. Deut. 5:19.

Q. 74. What is required in the eighth commandment?
A. The eighth commandment requireth the lawful procuring and furthering the wealth and outward estate of ourselves and others.[1]

[1]Lev. 25:35. Eph. 4:28b. Phil. 2:4.

Q. 75. What is forbidden in the eighth commandment?
A. The eighth commandment forbiddeth whatsoever doth, or may, unjustly hinder our own, or our neighbor's wealth or outward estate.[1]

[1]Prov. 28:19 ff. Eph. 4:28a. 2 Thess. 3:10. 1 Tim. 5:8.

Q. 76. Which is the ninth commandment?
A. The ninth commandment is, Thou shalt not bear false witness against thy neighbor.[1]

[1]Exod. 20:16. Deut. 5:20.

Q. 77. What is required in the ninth commandment?
A. The ninth commandment requireth the maintaining and promoting of truth between man and man, and of our own and our neighbor's good name,[1] especially in witness-bearing.[2]

[1]Zech. 8:16. Acts 25:10. 3 John 12.
[2]Prov. 14:5, 25.

Q. 78. What is forbidden in the ninth commandment?
A. The ninth commandment forbiddeth whatsoever is prejudicial to truth, or injurious to our own, or our neighbor's, good name.[1]

[1]Lev. 19:16. Ps. 15:3. Prov. 6:16-19. Luke 3:14.

Q. 79. Which is the tenth commandment?
A. The tenth commandment is, Thou shalt not covet thy neighbor's house, thou shalt not covet thy neighbor's wife, nor his manservant, nor his maidservant, nor his ox, nor his ass, nor anything that is thy neighbor's.[1]

[1]Exod. 20:17. Deut. 5:21.

Q. 80. What is required in the tenth commandment?
A. The tenth commandment requireth full contentment with our own condition,[1] with a right and charitable frame of spirit toward our neighbor, and all that is his.[2]

[1]Ps. 34:1. Phil. 4:11. 1 Tim. 6:6. Heb. 13:5. [2]Luke 15:6, 9, 11-32. Rom. 12:15. Phil. 2:4.

Q. 81. What is forbidden in the tenth commandment?
A. The tenth commandment forbiddeth all discontentment with our own estate,[1] envying or grieving at the good of our neighbor, and all inordinate motions and affections to anything that is his.[2]

[1]1 Cor. 10:10. James 3:14-16. [2]Gal. 5:26. Col. 3:5.

Q. 82. Is any man able perfectly to keep the commandments of God?
A. No mere man, since the fall, is able in this life perfectly to keep the commandments of God, but doth daily break them in thought, word, and deed.[1]

[1]Gen. 8:21. Rom. 3:9 ff., 23.

Q. 83. Are all transgressions of the law equally heinous?
A. Some sins in themselves, and by reason of several aggravations, are more heinous in the sight of God than others.[1]

[1]Ezek 8:6, 13, 15. Matt. 11:20-24. John 19:11.

Q. 84. What doth every sin deserve?
A. Every sin deserveth God's wrath and curse, both in this life, and that which is to come.[1]

[1]Matt. 25:41. Gal. 3:10. Eph. 5:6. James 2:10.

Q. 85. What doth God require of us, that we may escape His wrath and curse, due to us for sin?
A. To escape the wrath and curse of God, due to us for sin, God requireth of us faith in Jesus Christ, repentance unto life,[1] with the diligent use of all the outward means whereby Christ communicateth to us the benefits of redemption.[2]

[1]Mark 1:15. Acts 20:21. [2]Acts 2:38. 1 Cor. 11:24-25. Col. 3:16.

Q. 86. What is faith in Jesus Christ?
A. Faith in Jesus Christ is a saving grace,[1] whereby we receive and rest upon Him alone for salvation, as He is offered to us in the gospel.[2]

[1]Eph. 2:8-9. Cf. Rom. 4:16. [2]John 20:30-31. Gal. 2:15-16. Phil. 3:3-11.

Q. 87. What is repentance unto life?
A. Repentance unto life is a saving grace,[1] whereby a sinner, out of a true sense of his sin, and apprehension of the mercy of God in Christ,[2] doth, with grief and hatred of his sin, turn from it unto God,[3] with full purpose of, and endeavor after, new obedience.[4]

[1]Acts 11:18. 2 Tim. 2:25. [2]Ps. 51:1-4. Joel 2:13. Luke 15:7, 10. Acts 2:37. [3]Jer. 31:18-19. Luke 1:16-17. 1 Thess. 1:9. [4]2 Chron. 7:14. Ps. 119:57-64. Matt. 3:8. 2 Cor. 7:10.

Q. 88. What are the outward and ordinary means whereby Christ communicateth to us the benefits of redemption?
A. The outward and ordinary means whereby Christ communicateth to us the benefits of redemption are, His ordinances, especially the Word, sacraments, and prayer; all which are made effectual to the elect for salvation.[1]

[1]Matt. 28:18-20. Acts 2:41-42.

Q. 89. How is the Word made effectual to salvation?
A. The Spirit of God maketh the reading, but especially the preaching, of the Word, an effectual means of convincing and converting sinners, and of building them up in holiness and comfort, through faith, unto salvation.[1]

[1]Neh. 8:8-9. Acts 20:32. Rom. 10:14-17. 2 Tim. 3:15-17.

Q. 90. How is the Word to be read and heard, that it may become effectual to salvation?
A. That the Word may become effectual to salvation, we must attend thereunto with diligence, preparation, and prayer;[1] receive it with faith and love, lay it up in our hearts, and practice it in our lives.[2]

[1]Deut. 6:16ff. Ps. 119:18. 1 Peter 2:1-2. [2]Ps. 119:11. 2 Thess. 2:10. Heb. 4:2. James 1:22-25.

Q. 91. How do the sacraments become effectual means of salvation?
A. The sacraments become effectual means of salvation, not from any virtue in them, or in him that doth administer them; but only by the blessing of Christ, and the working of His Spirit in them that by faith receive them.[1]

[1]1 Cor. 3:7. Cf. 1 Cor. 1:12-17.

Q. 92. What is a sacrament?
A. A sacrament is a holy ordinance instituted by Christ;[1] wherein, by sensible signs, Christ, and the benefits of the new covenant, are represented, sealed, and applied to believers.[2]

[1]Matt. 28:19. Matt. 26:26-28. Mark 14:22-25. Luke 22:19-20. I Cor. 1:22-26. [2]Gal. 3:27. I Cor. 10:16-17.

Q. 93. Which are the sacraments of the New Testament?
A. The sacraments of the New Testament are, baptism,[1] and the Lord's Supper.[2]

[1]Matt. 28:19. [2]I Cor. 11:23-26.

Q. 94. What is baptism?
A. Baptism is a sacrament, wherein the washing with water in the name of the Father, and of the Son, and of the Holy Ghost,[1] doth signify and seal our ingrafting into Christ, and partaking of the benefits of the covenant of grace, and our engagement to be the Lord's.[2]

[1]Matt. 28:19. [2]Acts 2:38-42. Acts 22:16. Rom. 6:3-4. Gal. 3:26-27. I Peter 3:21.

Q. 95. To whom is Baptism to be administered?
A. Baptism is not to be administered to any that are out of the visible church, till they profess their faith in Christ, and obedience to Him;[1] but the infants of such as are members of the visible church are to be baptized.[2]

[1]Acts 2:41. Acts 8:12, 36, 38. Acts 18:8. [2]Gen. 17:7. Gen. 17:9-11. Acts 2:38-39. Acts 16:32-33. Col. 2:11-12.

Q. 96. What is the Lord's Supper?
A. The Lord's Supper is a sacrament, wherein, by giving and receiving bread and wine, according to Christ's appointment, His death is showed forth;[1] and the worthy receivers are, not after a corporal and carnal manner, but by faith, made partakers of His body and blood, with all His benefits, to their spiritual nourishment, and growth in grace.[2]

[1]Luke 22:19-20. I Cor. 11:23-26. [2]I Cor. 10:16-17.

Q. 97. What is required for the worthy receiving of the Lord's Supper?
A. It is required of them that would worthily partake of the Lord's Supper, that they examine themselves of their knowledge to discern the Lord's body, of their faith to feed upon Him, of their repentance, love, and new obedience; lest, coming unworthily, they eat and drink judgment to themselves.[1]

[1]I Cor. 11:27-32.

Q. 98. What is prayer?
A. Prayer is an offering up of our desires unto God,[1] for things agreeable to His will,[2] in the name of Christ,[3] with confession of our sins,[4] and thankful acknowledgment of His mercies.[5]

[1]Ps. 10:17. Ps. 62:8. Matt. 7:7-8. [2]I John 5:14. [3]John 16:23-24. [4]Ps. 32:5-6. Dan. 9:4-19. I John 1:9. [5]Ps. 103:1-5. Ps. 136. Phil. 4:6.

Q. 99. What rule hath God given for our direction in prayer?
A. The whole Word of God is of use to direct us in prayer;[1] but the special rule of direction is that form of prayer which Christ taught His disciples, commonly called the Lord's Prayer.[2]

[1]I John 5:14. [2]Matt. 6:9-13.

Q. 100. What doth the preface of the Lord's Prayer teach us?
A. The preface of the Lord's Prayer, which is, Our Father which art in heaven, teacheth us to draw near to God with all holy reverence[1] and confidence,[2] as children to a father,[3] able and ready to help us;[4] and that we should pray with and for others.[5]

[1]Ps. 95:6. [2]Eph. 3:12. [3]Matt. 7:9-11. Cf. Luke 11:11-13. Rom. 8:15. [4]Eph. 3:20. [5]Eph. 6:18. I Tim. 2:1-2.

Q. 101. What do we pray for in the first petition?
A. In the first petition, which is, Hallowed be thy name, we pray that God would enable us, and others, to glorify Him in all that whereby He maketh Himself known;[1] and that He would dispose all things to His own glory.[2]

[1]Ps. 67:1-3. Ps. 99:3. Ps. 100:3-4. [2]Rom. 11:33-36. Rev. 4:11.

Q. 102. What do we pray for in the second petition?
A. In the second petition, which is, Thy kingdom come, we pray that Satan's kingdom

may be destroyed;[1] and that the kingdom of grace may be advanced,[2] ourselves and others brought into it, and kept in it;[3] and that the kingdom of glory may be hastened.[4]

[1]Matt. 12:25-28. Rom. 16:20. 1 John 3:8. [2]Ps. 72:8-11. Matt. 24:14. 1 Cor. 15:24-25. [3]Ps. 119:5. Luke 22:32. 2 Thess. 3:1-5. [4]Rev. 22:20.

Q. 103. What do we pray for in the third petition?
A. In the third petition, which is, Thy will be done in earth, as it is in heaven, we pray that God, by His grace, would make us able and willing to know, obey, and submit to His will in all things,[1] as the angels do in heaven.[2]

[1]Ps. 19:14. Ps. 119. etc. 1 Thess. 5:23. Heb. 13:20-21. [2]Ps. 103:20-21. Heb. 1:14.

Q. 104. What do we pray for in the fourth petition?
A. In the fourth petition, which is, Give us this day our daily bread, we pray that of God's free gift we may receive a competent portion of the good things of this life, and enjoy His blessing with them.[1]

[1]Prov. 30:8-9. Matt. 6:31-34. Phil. 4:11, 19. 1 Tim. 6:6-8.

Q. 105. What do we pray for in the fifth petition?
A. In the fifth petition, which is, And forgive us our debts, as we forgive our debtors, we pray that God, for Christ's sake, would freely pardon all our sins;[1] which we are the rather encouraged to ask, because by His grace we are enabled from the heart to forgive others.[2]

[1]Ps. 51:1-2, 7, 9. Dan. 9:17-19. 1 John 1:7. [2]Matt. 18:21-35. Eph. 4:32. Col. 3:13.

Q. 106. What do we pray for in the sixth petition?
A. In the sixth petition, which is, And lead us not into temptation, but deliver us from evil, we pray that God would either keep us from being tempted to sin,[1] or support and deliver us when we are tempted.[2]

[1]Ps. 19:13. Matt. 26:41. John 17:15. [2]Luke 22:31-32. 1 Cor. 10:13. 2 Cor. 12:7-9. Heb. 2:18.

Q. 107. What doth the conclusion of the Lord's Prayer teach us?
A. The conclusion of the Lord's Prayer, which is, For thine is the kingdom, and the power, and the glory, forever. Amen, teacheth us to take our encouragement in prayer from God only,[1] and in our prayers to praise Him, ascribing kingdom, power, and glory to Him;[2] and, in testimony of our desire, and assurance to be heard, we say, Amen.[3]

[1]Dan. 9:4, 7-9, 16-19. Luke 18:1, 7-8. [2]1 Chron. 29:10-13. 1 Tim. 1:17. Rev. 5:11-13. [3]1 Cor. 14:16. Rev. 22:20.

APPENDIX 4

THE BELGIC CONFESSION

Article 1: The Only God

We all believe in our hearts and confess with our mouths that there is a single and simple spiritual being, whom we call God – eternal, incomprehensible, invisible, unchangeable, infinite, almighty; completely wise, just, and good, and the overflowing source of all good.

Article 2: The Means by Which We Know God

We know Him by two means:

First, by the creation, preservation, and government of the universe, since that universe is before our eyes like a beautiful book in which all creatures, great and small, are as letters to make us ponder the invisible things of God: His eternal power and His divinity, as the apostle Paul says in Rom. 1:20.

All these things are enough to convict men and to leave them without excuse.

Second, He makes Himself known to us more openly by His holy and divine Word, as much as we need in this life, for His glory and for the salvation of His own.

Article 3: The Written Word of God

We confess that this Word of God was not sent nor delivered by the will of men, but that holy men of God spoke, being moved by the Holy Spirit, as Peter says.[1]

Afterwards our God – because of the special care He has for us and our salvation – commanded His servants, the prophets and apostles, to commit this revealed Word to writing. He Himself wrote with His own finger the two tables of the law.

Therefore we call such writings holy and divine Scriptures.

[1] 2 Peter 1:21

Article 4: The Canonical Books

We include in the Holy Scripture the two volumes of the Old and New Testaments. They are canonical books with which there can be no quarrel at all.

In the church of God the list is as follows: In the Old Testament, the five books of Moses – Genesis, Exodus, Leviticus, Numbers, Deuteronomy; the books of Joshua, Judges, and Ruth; the two books of Samuel, and two of Kings; the two books of Chron., called Paralipomenon; the first book of Ezra; Nehemiah, Esther, Job; the Psalms of David; the three books of Solomon – Proverbs, Ecclesiastes, and the Song; the four major prophets – Isaiah, Jeremiah, Ezekiel, Daniel; and then the other twelve minor prophets – Hosea, Joel, Amos, Obadiah, Jonah, Micah, Nahum, Habakkuk, Zephaniah, Haggai, Zechariah, Malachi.

In the New Testament, the four gospels – Matt., Mark, Luke, and John; the Acts of the Apostles; the fourteen letters of Paul – to the Romans; the two letters to the Corinthians; to the Galatians, Ephesians, Philippians, and Colossians; the two letters to the Thessalonians; the two letters to Timothy; to Titus, Philemon, and to the Hebrews; the seven letters of the other apostles – one of James; two of Peter; three of John; one of Jude; and the Revelation of the apostle John.

Article 5: The Authority of Scripture

We receive all these books and these only as holy and canonical, for the regulating, founding, and establishing of our faith.

And we believe without a doubt all things contained in them – not so much because the church receives and approves them as such but above all because the Holy Spirit testifies in our hearts that they are from God, and also because they prove themselves to be from God.

For even the blind themselves are able to see that the things predicted in them do happen.

Article 6: The Difference Between Canonical and Apocryphal Books

We distinguish between these holy books and the apocryphal ones, which are the third and fourth books of Esdras; the books of Tobit, Judith, Wisdom, Jesus Sirach, Baruch; what was added to the Story of Esther; the Song of the Three Children in the Furnace; the Story of Susannah; the Story of Bell and the Dragon; the Prayer of Manasseh; and the two books of Maccabees.

The church may certainly read these books and learn from them as far as they agree with the canonical books. But they do not have such power and virtue that one could confirm from their testimony any point of faith or of the Christian religion. Much less can they detract from the authority of the other holy books.

Article 7: The Sufficiency of Scripture

We believe that this Holy Scripture contains the will of God completely and that everything one must believe to be saved is sufficiently taught in it. For since the entire manner of service which God requires of us is described in it at great length, no one, even an apostle or an angel from heaven, as Paul says,[1] ought to teach other than what the Holy Scriptures have already taught us. For since it is forbidden to add to or subtract from the Word of God,[2] this plainly demonstrates that the teaching is perfect and complete in all respects.

Therefore we must not consider human writings, no matter how holy their authors may have been, equal to the divine writings; nor may we put custom, nor the majority, nor age, nor the passage of time or persons, nor councils, decrees, or official decisions above the truth of God, for truth is above everything else.

For all human beings are liars by nature and more vain than vanity itself.

Therefore we reject with all our hearts everything that does not agree with this infallible rule, as we are taught to do by the apostles when they say, "Test the spirits to see if they are of God,"[3] and also, "If anyone comes to you and does not bring this teaching, do not receive him into your house."[4]

[1]Gal. 1:8 [2]Deut. 12:32; Rev. 22:18-19
[3]1 John 4:1 [4]2 John 10

Article 8: The Trinity

In keeping with this truth and Word of God we believe in one God, who is one single essence, in whom there are three persons, really, truly, and eternally distinct according to their incommunicable properties – namely, Father, Son, and Holy Spirit. The Father is the cause, origin, and source of all things, visible as well as invisible.

The Son is the Word, the Wisdom, and the image of the Father.

The Holy Spirit is the eternal power and might, proceeding from the Father and the Son.

Nevertheless, this distinction does not divide God into three, since Scripture teaches us that the Father, the Son, and the Holy Spirit each has His own subsistence distinguished by characteristics – yet in such a way that these three persons are only one God.

It is evident then that the Father is not the Son and that the Son is not the Father, and that likewise the Holy Spirit is neither the Father nor the Son.

Nevertheless, these persons, thus distinct, are neither divided nor fused or mixed together.

For the Father did not take on flesh, nor did the Spirit, but only the Son.

The Father was never without His Son, nor without His Holy Spirit, since all these are equal from eternity, in one and the same essence.

There is neither a first nor a last, for all three are one in truth and power, in goodness and mercy.

Article 9: The Scriptural Witness on the Trinity

All these things we know from the testimonies of Holy Scripture as well as from the effects of the persons, especially from those we feel within ourselves.

The testimonies of the Holy Scriptures, which teach us to believe in this Holy Trinity, are written in many places of the Old Testament, which need not be enumerated but only chosen with discretion.

In the book of Genesis God says, "Let us make man in our image, according to our likeness." So "God created man in His own image" – indeed, "male and female He created them."[1] "Behold, man has become like one of us."[2]

It appears from this that there is a plurality of persons within the Deity, when He says, "Let us make man in our image" – and afterwards He indicates the unity when He says, "God created."

It is true that He does not say here how many persons there are – but what is somewhat obscure to us in the Old Testament is very clear in the New.

For when our Lord was baptized in the Jordan, the voice of the Father was heard saying, "This is my dear Son";[3] the Son was seen in the water; and the Holy Spirit appeared in the form of a dove.

So, in the baptism of all believers this form was prescribed by Christ: "Baptize all people in the name of the Father, and of the Son, and of the Holy Spirit."[4]

In the Gospel according to Luke the angel Gabriel says to Mary, the mother of our Lord: "The Holy Spirit will come upon you, and the power of the Most High will overshadow you; and therefore that holy one to be born of you shall be called the Son of God."[5]

And in another place it says: "The grace of our Lord Jesus Christ, and the love of God, and the fellowship of the Holy Spirit be with you."[6]

"There are three who bear witness in heaven – the Father, the Word, and the Holy Spirit – and these three are one."[7]

In all these passages we are fully taught that there are three persons in the one and only divine essence. And although this doctrine surpasses human understanding, we nevertheless believe it now, through the Word, waiting to know and enjoy it fully in heaven.

Furthermore, we must note the particular works and activities of these three persons in relation to us. The Father is called our Creator, by reason of His power. The Son is our Savior and Redeemer, by His blood. The Holy Spirit is our Sanctifier, by His living in our hearts.

This doctrine of the holy Trinity has always been maintained in the true church, from the time of the apostles until the present, against Jews, Muslims, and certain false Christians and heretics, such as Marcion, Mani, Praxeas, Sabellius, Paul of Samosata, Arius, and others like them, who were rightly condemned by the holy fathers.

And so, in this matter we willingly accept the three ecumenical creeds – the Apostles', Nicene, and Athanasian – as well as what the ancient fathers decided in agreement with them.

[1]Gen. 1:26-27 [2]Gen. 3:22 [3]Matt. 3:17
[4]Matt. 28:19 [5]Luke 1:35 [6]2 Cor. 13:14
[7]1 John 5:7 (KJV)

Article 10: The Deity of Christ

We believe that Jesus Christ, according to His divine nature, is the only Son of God – eternally begotten, not made nor created, for then He would be a creature.

He is one in essence with the Father; coeternal; the exact image of the person of the Father and the "reflection of His glory,"[1] being in all things like Him.

He is the Son of God not only from the time He assumed our nature but from all eternity, as the following testimonies teach us when they are taken together.

Moses says that God "created the world";[2] and John says that "all things were created by the Word,"[3] which he calls God. The apostle says that "God made the world by His Son."[4] He also says that "God created all things by Jesus Christ."[5]

And so it must follow that He who is called God, the Word, the Son, and Jesus Christ already existed when all things were created by Him.

Therefore the prophet Micah says that His origin is "from ancient times, from eternity."[6] And the apostle says that He has "neither beginning of days nor end of life."[7]

So then, He is the true eternal God, the Almighty, whom we invoke, worship, and serve.

[1]Col. 1:15; Heb. 1:3 [2]Gen. 1:1 [3]John 1:3 [4]Heb. 1:2 [5]Col. 1:16 [6]Micah 5:2 [7]Heb. 7:3

Article 11: The Deity of the Holy Spirit
We believe and confess also that the Holy Spirit proceeds eternally from the Father and the Son – neither made, nor created, nor begotten, but only proceeding from the two of them. In regard to order, He is the third person of the Trinity – of one and the same essence, and majesty, and glory, with the Father and the Son.

He is true and eternal God, as the Holy Scriptures teach us.

Article 12: The Creation of All Things
We believe that the Father created heaven and earth and all other creatures from nothing, when it seemed good to Him, by His Word – that is to say, by His Son.

He has given all creatures their being, form, and appearance, and their various functions for serving their Creator.

Even now He also sustains and governs them all, according to His eternal providence, and by His infinite power, that they may serve man, in order that man may serve God.

He has also created the angels good, that they might be His messengers and serve His elect.

Some of them have fallen from the excellence in which God created them into eternal perdition; and the others have persisted and remained in their original state, by the grace of God.

The devils and evil spirits are so corrupt that they are enemies of God and of everything good. They lie in wait for the church and every member of it like thieves, with all their power, to destroy and spoil everything by their deceptions.

So then, by their own wickedness they are condemned to everlasting damnation, daily awaiting their torments.

For that reason we detest the error of the Sadducees, who deny that there are spirits and angels, and also the error of the Manicheans, who say that the devils originated by themselves, being evil by nature, without having been corrupted.

Article 13: The Doctrine of God's Providence
We believe that this good God, after He created all things, did not abandon them to chance or fortune but leads and governs them according to His holy will, in such a way that nothing happens in this world without His orderly arrangement.

Yet God is not the author of, nor can He be charged with, the sin that occurs. For His power and goodness are so great and incomprehensible that He arranges and does His work very well and justly even when the devils and wicked men act unjustly.

We do not wish to inquire with undue curiosity into what He does that surpasses human understanding and is beyond our ability to comprehend. But in all humility and reverence we adore the just judgments of God, which are hidden from us, being content to be Christ's disciples, so as to learn only what He shows us in His Word, without going beyond those limits.

This doctrine gives us unspeakable comfort since it teaches us that nothing can happen to us by chance but only by the arrangement of our gracious heavenly Father. He watches over us with fatherly care, keeping all creatures under His control, so that not one of the hairs on our heads (for they are all numbered) nor even a little bird can fall to the ground[1] without the will of our Father.

In this thought we rest, knowing that He holds in check the devils and all our enemies, who cannot hurt us without His permission and will.

For that reason we reject the damnable error of the Epicureans, who say that God involves Himself in nothing and leaves everything to chance.

[1]Matt. 10:29-30

Article 14: The Creation and Fall of Man
We believe that God created man from the dust of the earth and made and formed him in His image and likeness – good, just, and holy; able by His own will to conform in all things to the will of God.

But when he was in honor he did not understand it[1] and did not recognize His excellence. But he subjected himself willingly to sin and consequently to death and the curse, lending His ear to the word of the devil.

For He transgressed the commandment of life, which he had received, and by his sin he separated himself from God, who was his true life, having corrupted his entire nature.

So he made himself guilty and subject to physical and spiritual death, having become wicked, perverse, and corrupt in all his ways. He lost all his excellent gifts which he had received from God, and he retained none of them except for small traces which are enough to make him inexcusable.

Moreover, all the light in us is turned to darkness, as the Scripture teaches us: "The light shone in the darkness, and the darkness did not receive it."[2] Here John calls men "darkness."

Therefore we reject everything taught to the contrary concerning man's free will, since man is nothing but the slave of sin and cannot do a thing unless it is "given him from heaven."[3]

For who can boast of being able to do anything good by himself, since Christ says, "No one can come to me unless my Father who sent me draws him"?[4]

Who can glory in his own will when he understands that "the mind of the flesh is enmity against God"?[5] Who can speak of his own knowledge in view of the fact that "the natural man does not understand the things of the Spirit of God"?[6]

In short, who can produce a single thought, since he knows that we are "not able to think a thing" about ourselves, by ourselves, but that "our ability is from God"?[7]

And therefore, what the apostle says ought rightly to stand fixed and firm: "God works within us both to will and to do according to His good pleasure."[8]

For there is no understanding nor will conforming to God's understanding and will apart from Christ's involvement, as He teaches us when He says, "Without me you can do nothing."[9]

[1]Ps. 49:20 [2]John 1:5 [3]John 3:27 [4]John 6:44 [5]Rom. 8:7 [6]1 Cor. 2:14 [7]2 Cor. 3:5 [8]Phil. 2:13 [9]John 15:5

Article 15: The Doctrine of Original Sin

We believe that by the disobedience of Adam original sin has been spread through the whole human race.

It is a corruption of all nature – an inherited depravity which even infects small infants in their mother's womb, and the root which produces in man every sort of sin. It is therefore so vile and enormous in God's sight that it is enough to condemn the human race, and it is not abolished or wholly uprooted even by baptism, seeing that sin constantly boils forth as though from a contaminated spring.

Nevertheless, it is not imputed to God's children for their condemnation but is forgiven by His grace and mercy – not to put them to sleep but so that the awareness of this corruption might often make believers groan as they long to be set free from the "body of this death."[1]

Therefore we reject the error of the Pelagians who say that this sin is nothing else than a matter of imitation.

[1]Rom. 7:24

Article 16: The Doctrine of Election

We believe that – all Adam's descendants having thus fallen into perdition and ruin by the sin of the first man – God showed Himself to be as He is: merciful and just.

He is merciful in withdrawing and saving from this perdition those whom he, in His eternal and unchangeable counsel, has elected and chosen in Jesus Christ our Lord by His pure goodness, without any consideration of their works.

He is just in leaving the others in their ruin and fall into which they plunged themselves.

Article 17: The Recovery of Fallen Man

We believe that our good God, by His marvelous wisdom and goodness, seeing that man had plunged himself in this manner into both physical and spiritual death and made himself completely miserable, set out to find him, though man, trembling all over, was fleeing from Him.

And He comforted him, promising to give him His Son, "born of a woman,"[1] to crush the head of the serpent,[2] and to make him blessed.

[1]Gal. 4:4 [2]Gen. 3:15

Article 18: The Incarnation

So then we confess that God fulfilled the promise which He had made to the early fathers by the mouth of His holy prophets when He sent His only and eternal Son into the world at the time set by Him.

The Son took the "form of a servant" and was made in the "likeness of man,"[1] truly assuming a real human nature, with all its weaknesses, except for sin; being conceived in the womb of the blessed virgin Mary by the power of the Holy Spirit, without male participation.

And He not only assumed human nature as far as the body is concerned but also a real human soul, in order that He might be a real human being. For since the soul had been lost as well as the body He had to assume them both to save them both together.

Therefore we confess, against the heresy of the Anabaptists who deny that Christ assumed human flesh from His mother, that He "shared the very flesh and blood of children";[2] that He is "fruit of the loins of David" according to the flesh;[3] "born of the seed of David" according to the flesh;[4] "fruit of the womb of the virgin Mary";[5] "born of a woman";[6] "the seed of David";[7] "a shoot from the root of Jesse";[8] "the offspring of Judah,"[9] having descended from the Jews according to the flesh; "from the seed of Abraham" – for He "assumed Abraham's seed" and was "made like his brothers except for sin."[10]

In this way He is truly our Immanuel – that is: "God with us."[11]

[1]Phil. 2:7 [2]Heb. 2:14 [3]Acts 2:30 [4]Rom. 1:3 [5]Luke 1:42 [6]Gal. 4:4 [7]2 Tim. 2:8 [8]Rom. 15:12 [9]Heb. 7:14 [10]Heb. 2:17; 4:15 [11]Matt. 1:23

Article 19: The Two Natures of Christ

We believe that by being thus conceived the person of the Son has been inseparably united and joined together with human nature, in such a way that there are not two Sons of God, nor two persons, but two natures united in a single person, with each nature retaining its own distinct properties.

Thus His divine nature has always remained uncreated, without beginning of days or end of life,[1] filling heaven and earth.

His human nature has not lost its properties but continues to have those of a creature – it has a beginning of days; it is of a finite nature and retains all that belongs to a real body. And even though he, by His resurrection, gave it immortality, that nonetheless did not change the reality of His human nature; for our salvation and resurrection depend also on the reality of His body.

But these two natures are so united together in one person that they are not even separated by His death.

So then, what He committed to His Father when He died was a real human spirit which left His body. But meanwhile His divine nature remained united with His human nature even when He was lying in the grave; and His deity never ceased to be in Him, just as it was in Him when He was a little child, though for a while it did not show itself as such.

These are the reasons why we confess Him to be true God and true man – true God in order to conquer death by His power, and true man that He might die for us in the weakness of His flesh.

[1]Heb. 7:3

Article 20: The Justice and Mercy of God in Christ

We believe that God – who is perfectly merciful and also very just – sent His Son to assume the nature in which the disobedience had been committed, in order to bear in it the punishment of sin by His most bitter passion and death.

So God made known His justice toward His Son, who was charged with our sin, and He poured out His goodness and mercy on us, who are guilty and worthy of damnation, giving to us His Son to die, by a most perfect love, and raising Him to life for our justification, in order that by Him we might have immortality and eternal life.

Article 21: The Atonement

We believe that Jesus Christ is a high priest forever according to the order of Melchizedek – made such by an oath – and that He presented Himself in our name before His Father, to appease His wrath with full satisfaction by offering Himself on the tree of the cross and pouring out His precious blood for the cleansing of our sins, as the prophets had predicted.

For it is written that "the chastisement of our peace" was placed on the Son of God and that "we are healed by His wounds." He was "led to death as a lamb"; He was "numbered among sinners"[1] and condemned as a criminal by Pontius Pilate, though Pilate had declared that He was innocent.

So He paid back what He had not stolen,[2] and He suffered – the "just for the unjust,"[3] in both His body and His soul – in such a way that when He sensed the horrible punishment required by our sins His sweat became like "big drops of blood falling on the ground."[4] He cried, "My God, my God, why have you abandoned me?"[5]

And He endured all this for the forgiveness of our sins.

Therefore we rightly say with Paul that we "know nothing but Jesus and Him crucified";[6] we consider all things as "dung for the excellence of the knowledge of our Lord Jesus Christ."[7] We find all comforts in His wounds and have no need to seek or invent any other means to reconcile ourselves with God than this one and only sacrifice, once made, which renders believers perfect forever.

This is also why the angel of God called Him Jesus – that is, "Savior" – because He would save His people from their sins.[8]

[1]Isa. 53:4-12 [2]Ps. 69:4 [3]1 Peter 3:18
[4]Luke 22:44 [5]Matt. 27:46 [6]1 Cor. 2:2 [7]Phil. 3:8
[8]Matt. 1:21

Article 22: The Righteousness of Faith

We believe that for us to acquire the true knowledge of this great mystery the Holy Spirit kindles in our hearts a true faith that embraces Jesus Christ, with all His merits, and makes Him its own, and no longer looks for anything apart from Him.

For it must necessarily follow that either all that is required for our salvation is not in Christ or, if all is in Him, then He who has Christ by faith has His salvation entirely.

Therefore, to say that Christ is not enough but that something else is needed as well is a most enormous blasphemy against God – for it then would follow that Jesus Christ is only half a Savior. And therefore we justly say with Paul that we are justified "by faith alone" or by faith "apart from works."[1]

However, we do not mean, properly speaking, that it is faith itself that justifies us – for faith is only the instrument by which we embrace Christ, our righteousness.

But Jesus Christ is our righteousness in making available to us all His merits and all the holy works He has done for us and in our place. And faith is the instrument that keeps us in communion with Him and with all His benefits.

When those benefits are made ours they are more than enough to absolve us of our sins.

[1]Rom. 3:28

Article 23: The Justification of Sinners

We believe that our blessedness lies in the forgiveness of our sins because of Jesus Christ, and that in it our righteousness before God is contained, as David and Paul teach us when they declare that man blessed to whom God grants righteousness apart from works.[1]

And the same apostle says that we are justified "freely" or "by grace" through redemption in Jesus Christ.[2] And therefore we cling to this foundation, which is firm forever, giving all glory to God, humbling ourselves, and recognizing ourselves as we are; not claiming a thing for ourselves or our merits and leaning and resting on the sole obedience of Christ crucified, which is ours when we believe in Him.

That is enough to cover all our sins and to make us confident, freeing the conscience from the fear, dread, and terror of God's approach, without doing what our first father, Adam, did, who trembled as He tried to cover himself with fig leaves.

In fact, if we had to appear before God relying – no matter how little – on ourselves or some other creature, then, alas, we would be swallowed up.

Therefore everyone must say with David: "Lord, do not enter into judgment with your servants, for before you no living person shall be justified."[3]

[1]Ps. 32:1; Rom. 4:6 [2]Rom. 3:24 [3]Ps. 143:2

Article 24: The Sanctification of Sinners

We believe that this true faith, produced in man by the hearing of God's Word and by the work of the Holy Spirit, regenerates him and makes him a "new man,"[1] causing him to live the "new life"[2] and freeing him from the slavery of sin.

Therefore, far from making people cold toward living in a pious and holy way, this justifying faith, quite to the contrary, so works within them that apart from it they will never do a thing out of love for God but only out of love for themselves and fear of being condemned.

So then, it is impossible for this holy faith to be unfruitful in a human being, seeing that we do not speak of an empty faith but of what Scripture calls "faith working through love,"[3] which leads a man to do by himself the works that God has commanded in His Word.

These works, proceeding from the good root of faith, are good and acceptable to God, since they are all sanctified by His grace. Yet they do not count toward our justification – for by faith in Christ we are justified, even before we do good works. Otherwise they could not be good, any more than the fruit of a tree could be good if the tree is not good in the first place.

So then, we do good works, but not for merit – for what would we merit? Rather, we are indebted to God for the good works we do, and not He to us, since it is He who "works in us both to will and do according to His good pleasure", [4] thus keeping in mind what is written: "When you have done all that is commanded you, then you shall say, 'We are unworthy servants; we have done what it was our duty to do.' "[5]

Yet we do not wish to deny that God rewards good works – but it is by His grace that He crowns His gifts.

Moreover, although we do good works we do not base our salvation on them; for we cannot do any work that is not defiled by our flesh and also worthy of punishment.And even if we could point to one, memory of a single sin is enough for God to reject that work.

So we would always be in doubt, tossed back and forth without any certainty, and our poor consciences would be tormented constantly if they did not rest on the merit of the suffering and death of our Savior.

[1]2 Cor. 5:17 [2]Rom. 6:4 [3]Gal. 5:6 [4]Phil. 2:13 [5]Luke 17:10

Article 25: The Fulfillment of the Law

We believe that the ceremonies and symbols of the law have ended with the coming of Christ, and that all foreshadowings have come to an end, so that the use of them ought to be abolished among Christians. Yet the truth and substance of these things remain for us in Jesus Christ, in whom they have been fulfilled.

Nevertheless, we continue to use the witnesses drawn from the law and prophets to confirm us in the gospel and to regulate our lives with full integrity for the glory of God, according to His will.

Article 26: The Intercession of Christ

We believe that we have no access to God except through the one and only Mediator and Intercessor: Jesus Christ the Righteous.[1]

He therefore was made man, uniting together the divine and human natures, so that we human beings might have access to the divine Majesty. Otherwise we would have no access.

But this Mediator, whom the Father has appointed between Himself and us, ought not terrify us by His greatness, so that we have to look for another one, according to our fancy. For neither in heaven nor among the creatures on earth is there anyone who loves us more than Jesus Christ does. Although He was "in the form of God," He nevertheless "emptied Himself," taking the form of "a man" and "a servant" for us;[2] and He made Himself "completely like His brothers."[3]

Suppose we had to find another intercessor. Who would love us more than He who gave His life for us, even though "we were His enemies"?[4] And suppose we had to find one who has prestige and power. Who has as much of these as He who is seated "at the right hand of the Father,"[5]and who has all power "in heaven and on earth"?[6]And who will be heard more readily than God's own dearly beloved Son?

So then, sheer unbelief has led to the practice of dishonoring the saints, instead of honoring them. That was something the saints never did nor asked for, but which in keeping with their duty, as appears from their writings, they consistently refused.

We should not plead here that we are unworthy – for it is not a question of offering our prayers on the basis of our own dignity but only on the basis of the excellence and dignity of Jesus Christ, whose righteousness is ours by faith.

Since the apostle for good reason wants us to get rid of this foolish fear – or rather, this unbelief – he says to us that Jesus

Christ was "made like His brothers in all things," that He might be a high priest who is merciful and faithful to purify the sins of the people.[7] For since He suffered, being tempted, He is also able to help those who are tempted.[8]

And further, to encourage us more to approach Him he says, "Since we have a high priest, Jesus the Son of God, who has entered into heaven, we maintain our confession. For we do not have a high priest who is unable to have compassion for our weaknesses, but one who was tempted in all things, just as we are, except for sin. Let us go then with confidence to the throne of grace that we may obtain mercy and find grace, in order to be helped."[9]

The same apostle says that we "have liberty to enter into the holy place by the blood of Jesus. Let us go, then, in the assurance of faith...."[10]

Likewise, "Christ's priesthood is forever. By this He is able to save completely those who draw near to God through Him who always lives to intercede for them."[11]

What more do we need? For Christ Himself declares: "I am the way, the truth, and the life; no one comes to my Father but by me."[12] Why should we seek another intercessor?

Since it has pleased God to give us His Son as our Intercessor, let us not leave Him for another – or rather seek, without ever finding. For when God gave Him to us He knew well that we were sinners.

Therefore, in following the command of Christ we call on the heavenly Father through Christ, our only Mediator, as we are taught by the Lord's Prayer, being assured that we shall obtain all we ask of the Father in His name.

[1] I John 2:1 [2]Phil. 2:6-8 [3]Heb. 2:17 [4]Rom. 5:10 [5]Rom. 8:34; Heb. 1:3 [6]Matt. 28:18 [7]Heb. 2:17 [8]Heb. 2:18 [9]Heb. 4:14-16 [10]Heb. 10:19, 22 [11]Heb. 7:24-25 [12]John 14:6

Article 27: The Holy Catholic Church

We believe and confess one single catholic or universal church – a holy congregation and gathering of true Christian believers, awaiting their entire salvation in Jesus Christ being washed by His blood, and sanctified and sealed by the Holy Spirit.

This church has existed from the beginning of the world and will last until the end, as appears from the fact that Christ is eternal King who cannot be without subjects.

And this holy church is preserved by God against the rage of the whole world, even though for a time it may appear very small in the eyes of men – as though it were snuffed out.

For example, during the very dangerous time of Ahab the Lord preserved for Himself seven thousand men who did not bend their knees to Baal.[1]

And so this holy church is not confined, bound, or limited to a certain place or certain persons. But it is spread and dispersed throughout the entire world, though still joined and united in heart and will, in one and the same Spirit, by the power of faith.

[1] I Kings 19:18

Article 28: The Obligations of Church Members

We believe that since this holy assembly and congregation is the gathering of those who are saved and there is no salvation apart from it, no one ought to withdraw from it, content to be by himself, regardless of His status or condition.

But all people are obliged to join and unite with it, keeping the unity of the church by submitting to its instruction and discipline, by bending their necks under the yoke of Jesus Christ, and by serving to build up one another, according to the gifts God has given them as members of each other in the same body.

And to preserve this unity more effectively, it is the duty of all believers, according to God's Word, to separate themselves from those who do not belong to the church, in order to join this assembly wherever God has established it, even if civil authorities and royal decrees forbid and death and physical punishment result.

And so, all who withdraw from the church or do not join it act contrary to God's ordinance.

Article 29: The Marks of the True Church

We believe that we ought to discern diligently and very carefully, by the Word of God, what is the true church – for all sects in the world today claim for themselves the name of "the church."

We are not speaking here of the company of hypocrites who are mixed among the good in the church and who nonetheless are not part of it, even though they are physically there. But we are speaking of distinguishing the body and fellowship of the true church from all sects that call themselves "the church."

The true church can be recognized if it has the following marks: The church engages in the pure preaching of the gospel; it makes use of the pure administration of the sacraments as Christ instituted them; it practices church discipline for correcting faults. In short, it governs itself according to the pure Word of God, rejecting all things contrary to it and holding Jesus Christ as the only Head. By these marks one can be assured of recognizing the true church – and no one ought to be separated from it.

As for those who can belong to the church, we can recognize them by the distinguishing marks of Christians: namely by faith, and by their fleeing from sin and pursuing righteousness, once they have received the one and only Savior, Jesus Christ. They love the true God and their neighbors, without turning to the right or left, and they crucify the flesh and its works.

Though great weakness remains in them, they fight against it by the Spirit all the days of their lives, appealing constantly to the blood, suffering, death, and obedience of the Lord Jesus, in whom they have forgiveness of their sins, through faith in Him.

As for the false church, it assigns more authority to itself and its ordinances than to the Word of God; it does not want to subject itself to the yoke of Christ; it does not administer the sacraments as Christ commanded in His Word; it rather adds to them or subtracts from them as it pleases; it bases itself on men, more than on Jesus Christ; it persecutes those who live holy lives according to the Word of God and who rebuke it for its faults, greed, and idolatry.

These two churches are easy to recognize and thus to distinguish from each other.

Article 30: The Government of the Church

We believe that this true church ought to be governed according to the spiritual order that our Lord has taught us in His Word. There should be ministers or pastors to preach the Word of God and administer the sacraments. There should also be elders and deacons, along with the pastors, to make up the council of the church.

By this means true religion is preserved; true doctrine is able to take its course; and evil men are corrected spiritually and held in check, so that also the poor and all the afflicted may be helped and comforted according to their need.

By this means everything will be done well and in good order in the church, when such persons are elected who are faithful and are chosen according to the rule that Paul gave to Timothy.[1]

[1] I Tim. 3

Article 31: The Officers of the Church

We believe that ministers of the Word of God, elders, and deacons ought to be chosen to their offices by a legitimate election of the church, with prayer in the name of the Lord, and in good order, as the Word of God teaches.

So everyone must be careful not to push himself forward improperly, but he must wait for God's call, so that he may be assured of His calling and be certain that he is chosen by the Lord.

As for the ministers of the Word, they all have the same power and authority, no matter where they may be, since they are all servants of Jesus Christ, the only universal bishop, and the only head of the church.

Moreover, to keep God's holy order from being violated or despised, we say that everyone ought, as much as possible, to hold the ministers of the Word and elders of the church in special esteem, because of the work they do, and be at peace with them, without grumbling, quarreling, or fighting.

Article 32: The Order and Discipline of the Church

We also believe that although it is useful and good for those who govern the churches to establish and set up a certain order among themselves for maintaining the body of the church, they ought always to guard against deviating from what Christ, our only Master, has ordained for us.

Therefore we reject all human innovations and all laws imposed on us, in our worship of God, which bind and force our consciences in any way.

So we accept only what is proper to maintain harmony and unity and to keep all in obedience to God.

To that end excommunication, with all it involves, according to the Word of God, is required.

Article 33: The Sacraments

We believe that our good God, mindful of our crudeness and weakness, has ordained sacraments for us to seal His promises in us, to pledge His good will and grace toward us, and also to nourish and sustain our faith.

He has added these to the Word of the gospel to represent better to our external senses both what He enables us to understand by His Word and what He does inwardly in our hearts, confirming in us the salvation He imparts to us.

For they are visible signs and seals of something internal and invisible, by means of which God works in us through the power of the Holy Spirit. So they are not empty and hollow signs to fool and deceive us, for their truth is Jesus Christ, without whom they would be nothing.

Moreover, we are satisfied with the number of sacraments that Christ our Master has ordained for us. There are only two: the sacrament of baptism and the Holy Supper of Jesus Christ.

Article 34: The Sacrament of Baptism

We believe and confess that Jesus Christ, in whom the law is fulfilled, has by His shed blood put an end to every other shedding of blood, which anyone might do or wish to do in order to atone or satisfy for sins.

Having abolished circumcision, which was done with blood, He established in its place the sacrament of baptism. By it we are received into God's church and set apart from all other people and alien religions, that we may be dedicated entirely to Him, bearing His mark and sign. It also witnesses to us that He will be our God forever, since He is our gracious Father.

Therefore He has commanded that all those who belong to Him be baptized with pure water in the name of the Father, and the Son, and the Holy Spirit.[1]

In this way He signifies to us that just as water washes away the dirt of the body when it is poured on us and also is seen on the body of the baptized when it is sprinkled on him, so too the blood of Christ does the same thing internally, in the soul, by the Holy Spirit. It washes and cleanses it from its sins and transforms us from being the children of wrath into the children of God.

This does not happen by the physical water but by the sprinkling of the precious blood of the Son of God, who is our Red Sea, through which we must pass to escape the tyranny of Pharoah, who is the devil, and to enter the spiritual land of Canaan.

So ministers, as far as their work is concerned, give us the sacrament and what is visible, but our Lord gives what the sacrament signifies – namely the invisible gifts and graces; washing, purifying, and cleansing our souls of all filth and unrighteousness; renewing our hearts and filling them with all comfort; giving us true assurance of His fatherly goodness; clothing us with the "new man" and stripping off the "old," with all its works.

For this reason we believe that anyone who aspires to reach eternal life ought to be baptized only once without ever repeating it – for we cannot be born twice. Yet this baptism is profitable not only when the water is on us and when we receive it but throughout our entire lives.

For that reason we detest the error of the Anabaptists who are not content with a single baptism once received and also condemn the baptism of the children of believers. We believe our children ought to be baptized and sealed with the sign of the covenant, as little children were circumcised in Israel on the basis of the same promises made to our children.

And truly, Christ has shed His blood no less for washing the little children of believers than He did for adults.

Therefore they ought to receive the sign and sacrament of what Christ has done for them, just as the Lord commanded in the law that by offering a lamb for them the sacrament of the suffering and death of Christ would be granted them shortly after their birth. This was the sacrament of Jesus Christ.

Furthermore, baptism does for our children what circumcision did for the Jewish people. That is why Paul calls baptism the "circumcision of Christ."[2]

[1]Matt. 28:19 [2]Col. 2:11

Article 35: The Sacrament of the Lord's Supper

We believe and confess that our Savior Jesus Christ has ordained and instituted the sacrament of the Holy Supper to nourish and sustain those who are already born again and ingrafted into His family: His church.

Now those who are born again have two lives in them. The one is physical and temporal – they have it from the moment of their first birth, and it is common to all. The other is spiritual and heavenly, and is given them in their second birth; it comes through the Word of the gospel in the communion of the body of Christ; and this life is common to God's elect only.

Thus, to support the physical and earthly life God has prescribed for us an appropriate earthly and material bread, which is as common to all as life itself also is. But to maintain the spiritual and heavenly life that belongs to believers He has sent a living bread that came down from heaven: namely Jesus Christ, who nourishes and maintains the spiritual life of believers when eaten – that is, when appropriated and received spiritually by faith.

To represent to us this spiritual and heavenly bread Christ has instituted an earthly and visible bread as the sacrament of His body and wine as the sacrament of His blood. He did this to testify to us that just as truly as we take and hold the sacraments in our hands and eat and drink it in our mouths, by which our life is then sustained, so truly we receive into our souls, for our spiritual life, the true body and true blood of Christ, our only Savior. We receive these by faith, which is the hand and mouth of our souls.

Now it is certain that Jesus Christ did not prescribe His sacraments for us in vain, since He works in us all He represents by these holy signs, although the manner in which He does it goes beyond our understanding and is incomprehensible to us, just as the operation of God's Spirit is hidden and incomprehensible.

Yet we do not go wrong when we say that what is eaten is Christ's own natural body and what is drunk is His own blood – but the manner in which we eat it is not by the mouth but by the Spirit, through faith.

In that way Jesus Christ remains always seated at the right hand of God the Father in heaven – but He never refrains on that account to communicate Himself to us through faith.

This banquet is a spiritual table at which Christ communicates Himself to us with all His benefits. At that table He makes us enjoy Himself as much as the merits of His suffering and death, as He nourishes, strengthens, and comforts our poor, desolate souls by the eating of His flesh, and relieves and renews them by the drinking of His blood.

Moreover, though the sacraments and thing signified are joined together, not all receive both of them. The wicked person certainly takes the sacrament, to His condemnation, but does not receive the truth of the sacrament, just as Judas and Simon the Sorcerer both indeed received the sacrament, but not Christ, who was signified by it. He is communicated only to believers.

Finally, with humility and reverence we receive the holy sacrament in the gathering of God's people, as we engage together, with thanksgiving, in a holy remembrance of the death of Christ our Savior, and as we thus confess our faith and Christian religion. Therefore no one should come to this table without examining himself carefully, lest "by eating this bread and drinking this cup he eat and drink to His own judgment."[1]

In short, by the use of this holy sacrament we are moved to a fervent love of God and our neighbors.

Therefore we reject as desecrations of the sacraments all the muddled ideas and damnable inventions that men have added and mixed in with them. And we say that we should be content with the procedure that Christ and the apostles have taught us and speak of these things as they have spoken of them.

[1]1 Cor. 11:27

Article 36: The Civil Government

We believe that because of the depravity of the human race our good God has ordained kings, princes, and civil officers. He wants the world to be governed by laws and policies so that human lawlessness may be restrained and that everything may be conducted in good order among human beings.

For that purpose He has placed the sword in the hands of the government, to punish evil people and protect the good.

And being called in this manner to contribute to the advancement of a society that is pleasing to God, the civil rulers have the task, subject to God's law, of removing every obstacle to the preaching of the gospel and to every aspect of divine worship.

They should do this while completely refraining from every tendency toward exercising absolute authority, and while functioning in the sphere entrusted to them, with the means belonging to them.

And the government's task is not limited to caring for and watching over the public domain but extends also to upholding the sacred ministry, with a view to removing and destroying all idolatry and false worship of the Antichrist; to promoting the kingdom of Jesus Christ; and to furthering the preaching of the gospel everywhere; to the end that God may be honored and served by everyone, as He requires in His Word.

Moreover everyone, regardless of status, condition, or rank, must be subject to the government, and pay taxes, and hold its representatives in honor and respect, and obey them in all things that are not in conflict with God's Word, praying for them that the Lord may be willing to lead them in all their ways and that we may live a peaceful and quiet life in all piety and decency.

And on this matter we denounce the Anabaptists, other anarchists, and in general all those who want to reject the authorities and civil officers and to subvert justice by introducing common ownership of goods and corrupting the moral order that God has established among human beings.

Article 37: The Last Judgment

Finally we believe, according to God's Word, that when the time appointed by the Lord is come (which is unknown to all creatures) and the number of the elect is complete, our Lord Jesus Christ will come from heaven, bodily and visibly, as He ascended, with great glory and majesty, to declare Himself the judge of the living and the dead. He will burn this old world, in fire and flame, in order to cleanse it.

Then all human creatures will appear in person before the great judge – men, women, and children, who have lived from the beginning until the end of the world.

They will be summoned there by the voice of the archangel and by the sound of the divine trumpet.[1]

For all those who died before that time will be raised from the earth, their spirits being joined and united with their own bodies in which they lived. And as for those who are still alive, they will not die like the others but will be changed "in the twinkling of an eye" from "corruptible to incorruptible."[2]

Then "the books" (that is, the consciences) will be opened, and the dead will be judged according to the things they did in the world,[3] whether good or evil. Indeed, all people will give account of all the idle words they have spoken,[4] which the world regards as only playing games. And then the secrets and hypocrisies of men will be publicly uncovered in the sight of all.

Therefore, with good reason the thought of this judgment is horrible and dreadful to wicked and evil people. But it is very pleasant and a great comfort to the righteous and elect, since their total redemption will then be accomplished. They will then receive the fruits of their labor and of the trouble they have suffered; their innocence will be openly recognized by all; and they will see the terrible vengeance that God will bring on the evil ones who tyrannized, oppressed, and tormented them in this world.

The evil ones will be convicted by the witness of their own consciences, and shall be made immortal – but only to be tormented in the everlasting fire prepared for the devil and His angels.[5]

In contrast, the faithful and elect will be crowned with glory and honor. The Son of God will "confess their names"[6] before God His Father and the holy and elect angels; all tears will be "wiped from their eyes";[7] and their cause – at present condemned as heretical and evil by many judges and civil officers – will be acknowledged as the "cause of the Son of God."

And as a gracious reward the Lord will make them possess a glory such as the heart of man could never imagine.

So we look forward to that great day with longing in order to enjoy fully the promises of God in Christ Jesus, our Lord.

[1] I Thess. 4:16 [2] I Cor. 15:51-53 [3] Rev. 20:12
[4] Matt. 12:36 [5] Matt. 25:14 [6] Matt. 10:32
[7] Rev. 7:17

APPENDIX 5

THE HEIDELBERG CATECHISM

LORD'S DAY 1

1. Q. What is your only comfort in life and death?
A. That I am not my own,[1] but belong with body and soul, both in life and in death,[2] to my faithful Savior Jesus Christ.[3] He has fully paid for all my sins with His precious blood,[4] and has set me free from all the power of the devil.[5] He also preserves me in such a way[6] that without the will of my heavenly Father not a hair can fall from my head;[7] indeed, all things must work together for my salvation.[8] Therefore, by His Holy Spirit He also assures me of eternal life[9] and makes me heartily willing and ready from now on to live for Him.[10]

[1]1 Cor. 6:19, 20. [2]Rom. 14:7-9. [3]1 Cor. 3:23; Titus 2:14. [4]1 Peter 1:18, 19; 1 John 1:7; 2:2. [5]John 8:34-36; Heb. 2:14, 15; 1 John 3:8. [6]John 6:39, 40; 10:27-30; 2 Thess. 3:3; 1 Peter 1:5. [7]Matt. 10:29-31; Luke 21:16-18. [8]Rom. 8:28. [9]Rom. 8:15, 16; 2 Cor. 1:21, 22; 5:5; Eph. 1:13, 14. [10]Rom. 8:14.

2. Q. What do you need to know in order to live and die in the joy of this comfort?
A. First, how great my sins and misery are;[1] second, how I am delivered from all my sins and misery;[2] third, how I am to be thankful to God for such deliverance.[3]

[1]Rom. 3:9, 10; 1 John 1:10. [2]John 17:3; Acts 4:12; 10:43. [3]Matt. 5:16; Rom. 6:13; Eph. 5:8-10; 1 Peter 2:9, 10.

The First Part
OUR SIN AND MISERY
LORD'S DAY 2

3. Q. From where do you know your sins and misery?
A. From the law of God.[1]

[1]Rom. 3:20; 7:7-25.

4. Q. What does God's law require of us?
A. Christ teaches us this in a summary in Matt. 22: You shall love the Lord your God with all your heart, and with all your soul, and with all your mind.[1] This is the great and first commandment. And a second is like it, You shall love your neighbor as yourself. On these two commandments depend all the law and the prophets.[2]

[1]Deut. 6:5. [2]Lev. 19:18.

5. Q. Can you keep all this perfectly?
A. No,[1] I am inclined by nature to hate God and my neighbor.[2]

[1]Rom. 3:10, 23; 1 John 1:8, 10. [2]Gen. 6:5; 8:21; Jer. 17:9; Rom. 7:23; 8:7; Eph. 2:3; Titus 3:3.

LORD'S DAY 3

6. Q. Did God, then, create man so wicked and perverse?
A. No, on the contrary, God created man good[1] and in His image,[2] that is, in true righteousness and holiness,[3] so that he might rightly know God His Creator,[4] heartily love Him, and live with Him in eternal blessedness to praise and glorify Him.[5]

[1]Gen. 1:31. [2]Gen. 1:26, 27. [3]Eph. 4:24. [4]Col. 3:10. [5]Ps. 8.

7. Q. From where, then, did man's depraved nature come?
A. From the fall and disobedience of our first parents, Adam and Eve, in Paradise,[1] for there our nature became so corrupt[2] that we are all conceived and born in sin.[3]

[1]Gen. 3. [2]Rom. 5:12, 18, 19. [3]Ps. 51:5.

8. Q. But are we so corrupt that we are totally unable to do any good and inclined to all evil?
A. Yes,[1] unless we are regenerated by the Spirit of God.[2]

[1]Gen. 6:5; 8:21; Job 14:4; Isa. 53:6. [2]John 3:3-5.

LORD'S DAY 4

9. Q. But does not God do man an injustice by requiring in His law what man cannot do?
A. No, for God so created man that he was able to do it.[1] But man, at the instigation of the devil,[2] in deliberate disobedience[3] robbed himself and all his descendants of these gifts.[4]

[1]Gen. 1:31. [2]Gen. 3:13; John 8:44; I Tim. 2:13, 14. [3]Gen. 3:6. [4]Rom. 5:12, 18, 19.

10. Q. Will God allow such disobedience and apostasy to go unpunished?
A. Certainly not. He is terribly displeased with our original sin as well as our actual sins. Therefore He will punish them by a just judgment both now and eternally,[1] as He has declared:[2] Cursed be every one who does not abide by all things written in the book of the law, and do them (Gal. 3:10).

[1]Gen. 2:17; Ex 34:7; Ps. 5:4-6; 7:11; Nahum 1:2; Rom. 1:18; 5:12; [2]Deut. 27:26.

11. Q. But is God not also merciful?
A. God is indeed merciful,[1] but He is also just.[2] His justice requires that sin committed against the most high majesty of God also be punished with the most severe, that is, with everlasting, punishment of body and soul.[3]

[1]Ex 20:6; 34:6, 7; Ps. 103:8, 9. [2]Ex 20:5; 34:7; Deut. 7:9-11; Ps. 5:4-6; Heb. 10:30, 31. [3]Matt. 25:45, 46.

The Second Part
OUR DELIVERANCE

LORD'S DAY 5

12. Q. Since, according to God's righteous judgment we deserve temporal and eternal punishment, how can we escape this punishment and be again received into favour?
A. God demands that His justice be satisfied.[1] Therefore we must make full payment, either by ourselves or through another.[2]

[1]Ex 20:5; 23:7; Rom. 2:1-11. [2]Isa. 53:11; Rom. 8:3, 4.

13. Q. Can we by ourselves make this payment?

A. Certainly not. On the contrary, we daily increase our debt.[1]

[1]Ps. 130:3; Matt. 6:12; Rom. 2:4, 5.

14. Q. Can any mere creature pay for us?

A. No. In the first place, God will not punish another creature for the sin which man has committed.[1] Furthermore, no mere creature can sustain the burden of God's eternal wrath against sin and deliver others from it.[2]

[1]Ezek 18:4, 20; Heb. 2:14-18. [2]Ps. 130:3; Nahum 1:6.

15. Q. What kind of mediator and deliverer must we seek?

A. One who is a true[1] and righteous[2] man, and yet more powerful than all creatures; that is, one who is at the same time true God.[3]

[1]I Cor. 15:21; Heb. 2:17. [2]Isa. 53:9; 2 Cor. 5:21; Heb. 7:26. [3]Isa. 7:14; 9:6; Jer. 23:6; John 1:1; Rom. 8:3, 4.

LORD'S DAY 6

16. Q. Why must He be a true and righteous man?

A. He must be a true man because the justice of God requires that the same human nature which has sinned should pay for sin.[1] He must be a righteous man because one who himself is a sinner cannot pay for others.[2]

[1]Rom. 5:12, 15; I Cor. 15:21; Heb. 2:14-16. [2]Heb. 7:26, 27; I Peter 3:18.

17. Q. Why must He at the same time be true God?
A. He must be true God so that by the power of His divine nature[1] He might bear in His human nature the burden of God's wrath,[2] and might obtain for us and restore to us righteousness and life.[3]

[1]Isa. 9:6. [2]Deut. 4:24; Nahum 1:6; Ps. 130:3. [3]Isa. 53:5, 11; John 3:16; 2 Cor. 5:21.

18. Q. But who is that Mediator who at the same time is true God and a true and righteous man?

A. Our Lord Jesus Christ,[1] whom God made our wisdom, our righteousness and sanctification and redemption (1 Cor. 1:30).

[1]Matt. 1:21-23; Luke 2:11; 1 Tim. 2:5; 3:16.

19. Q. From where do you know this?
A. From the holy gospel, which God Himself first revealed in Paradise.[1] Later, He had it proclaimed by the patriarchs[2] and prophets,[3] and foreshadowed by the sacrifices and other ceremonies of the law.[4] Finally, He had it fulfilled through His only Son.[5]

[1]Gen. 3:15. [2]Gen. 12:3; 22:18; 49:10. [3]Isa. 53; Jer. 23:5, 6; Micah 7:18-20; Acts 10:43; Heb. 1:1. [4]Lev. 1–7; John 5:46; Heb. 10:1-10. [5]Rom. 10:4; Gal. 4:4, 5; Col. 2:17.

LORD'S DAY 7

20. Q. Are all men, then, saved by Christ just as they perished through Adam?
A. No. Only those are saved who by a true faith are grafted into Christ and accept all His benefits.[1]

[1]Matt. 7:14; John 1:12; 3:16, 18, 36; Rom. 11:16-21.

21. Q. What is true faith?
A. True faith is a sure knowledge whereby I accept as true all that God has revealed to us in His Word.[1] At the same time it is a firm confidence[2] that not only to others, but also to me,[3] God has granted forgiveness of sins, everlasting righteousness, and salvation,[4] out of mere grace, only for the sake of Christ's merits.[5] This faith the Holy Spirit works in my heart by the gospel.[6]

[1]John 17:3, 17; Heb. 11:1-3; James 2:19. [2]Rom. 4:18-21; 5:1; 10:10; Heb. 4:16. [3]Gal 2:20. [4]Rom. 1:17; Heb. 10:10. [5]Rom. 3:20-26; Gal 2:16; Eph. 2:8-10. [6]Acts 16:14; Rom. 1:16; 10:17; 1 Cor. 1:21.

22. Q. What, then, must a Christian believe?
A. All that is promised us in the gospel,[1] which the articles of our catholic and undoubted Christian faith teach us in a summary.

[1]Matt. 28:19; John 20:30, 31.

23. Q. What are these articles?
A.

1. I believe in God the Father almighty, Creator of heaven and earth.
2. I believe in Jesus Christ, His only-begotten Son, our Lord;
3. He was conceived by the Holy Spirit, born of the virgin Mary;
4. suffered under Pontius Pilate, was crucified, dead, and buried; He descended into hell.
5. On the third day He arose from the dead;
6. He ascended into heaven, and sits at the right hand of God the Father almighty;
7. From there He will come to judge
8. the living and the dead.
9. I believe in the Holy Spirit;
10. i believe a holy catholic Christian church, the communion of saints;
11. the forgiveness of sins;
12. the resurrection of the body;
13. and the life everlasting. Amen.

LORD'S DAY 8

24. Q. How are these articles divided?
A. Into three parts: the first is about God the Father and our creation; the second about God the Son and our redemption; the third about God the Holy Spirit and our sanctification.

25. Q. Since there is only one God,[1] why do you speak of three persons, Father, Son, and Holy Spirit?
A. Because God has so revealed Himself in His Word[2] that these three distinct persons are the one, true, eternal God.

[1]Deut. 6:4; Isa. 44:6; 45:5; 1 Cor. 8:4, 6. [2]Gen. 1:2, 3; Isa. 61:1; 63:8-10; Matt. 3:16, 17; 28:18, 19; Luke 4:18; John 14:26; 15:26; 2 Cor. 13:14; Gal 4:6; Titus 3:5, 6.

LORD'S DAY 9

26. Q. What do you believe when you say: I believe in God the Father almighty, Creator of heaven and earth?
A. That the eternal Father of our Lord Jesus Christ, who out of nothing created heaven and earth and all that is in them,[1] and who still upholds and governs them by His eternal counsel and providence,[2] is, for the sake of Christ His Son, my God and my Father.[3] In Him I trust so completely as to have no doubt that He will provide me with all things necessary for body and soul,[4] and will also turn to

my good whatever adversity He sends me in this life of sorrow.[5] He is able to do so as almighty God,[6] and willing also as a faithful Father.[7]

[1]Gen. 1 and 2; Ex 20:11; Job 38 and 39; Ps. 33:6; Isa. 44:24; Acts 4:24; 14:15. [2]Ps. 104:27-30; Matt. 6:30; 10:29; Eph. 1:11. [3]John 1:12, 13; Rom. 8:15, 16; Gal 4:4-7; Eph. 1:5. [4]Ps. 55:22; Matt. 6:25, 26; Luke 12:22-31. [5]Rom. 8:28. [6]Gen. 18:14; Rom. 8:31-39. [7]Matt. 6:32, 33; 7:9-11.

LORD'S DAY 10

27. Q. What do you understand by the providence of God?
A. God's providence is His almighty and ever present power,[1] whereby, as with His hand, He still upholds heaven and earth and all creatures,[2] and so governs them that leaf and blade, rain and drought, fruitful and barren years, food and drink, health and sickness, riches and poverty,[3] indeed, all things, come to us not by chance[4] but by His fatherly hand.[5]

[1]Jer. 23:23, 24; Acts 17:24-28. [2]Heb. 1:3. [3]Jer. 5:24; Acts 14:15-17; John 9:3; Prov. 22:2. [4]Prov. 16:33. [5]Matt. 10:29.

28. Q. What does it benefit us to know that God has created all things and still upholds them by His providence?
A. We can be patient in adversity,[1] thankful in prosperity,[2] and with a view to the future we can have a firm confidence in our faithful God and Father that no creature shall separate us from His love;[3] for all creatures are so completely in His hand that without His will they cannot so much as move.[4]

[1]Job 1:21, 22; Ps. 39:10; James 1:3. [2]Deut. 8:10; 1 Thess. 5:18. [3]Ps. 55:22; Rom. 5:3-5; 8:38, 39. [4]Job 1:12; 2:6; Prov 21:1; Acts 17:24-28.

LORD'S DAY 11

29. Q. Why is the Son of God called Jesus, that is, Savior?
A. Because He saves us from all our sins,[1] and because salvation is not to be sought or found in anyone else.[2]

[1]Matt. 1:21; Heb. 7:25. [2]Isa. 43:11; John 15:4, 5; Acts 4:11, 12; 1 Tim. 2:5.

30. Q. Do those who seek their salvation or well-being in saints, in themselves, or anywhere else, also believe in the only Savior Jesus?
A. No. Though they boast of Him in words, they in fact deny the only Savior Jesus.[1] For one of two things must be true: either Jesus is not a complete Savior, or those who by true faith accept this Savior must find in Him all that is necessary for their salvation.[2]

[1]1 Cor. 1:12, 13; Gal 5:4. [2]Col. 1:19, 20; 2:10; 1 John 1:7.

LORD'S DAY 12

31. Q. Why is He called Christ, that is, Anointed?
A. Because He has been ordained by God the Father, and anointed with the Holy Spirit,[1] to be our chief Prophet and Teacher,[2] who has fully revealed to us the secret counsel and will of God concerning our redemption;[3] our only High Priest,[4] who by the one sacrifice of His body has redeemed us,[5] and who continually intercedes for us before the Father;[6] and our eternal King,[7] who governs us by His Word and Spirit, and who defends and preserves us in the redemption obtained for us.[8]

[1]Ps. 45:7 (Heb. 1:9); Isa. 61:1 (Luke 4:18); Luke 3:21, 22. [2]Deut. 18:15 (Acts 3:22). [3]John 1:18; 15:15. [4]Ps. 110:4 (Heb. 7:17). [5]Heb. 9:12; 10:11-14. [6]Rom. 8:34; Heb. 9:24; 1 John 2:1. [7]Zech. 9:9 (Matt. 21:5); Luke 1:33. [8]Matt. 28:18-20; John 10:28; Rev. 12:10, 11.

32. Q. Why are you called a Christian?
A. Because I am a member of Christ by faith[1] and thus share in His anointing,[2] so that I may as prophet confess His Name,[3] as priest present myself a living sacrifice of thankfulness to Him,[4] and as king fight with a free and good conscience against sin and the devil in this life,[5] and hereafter reign with Him eternally over all creatures.[6]

[1]1 Cor. 12:12-27. [2]Joel 2:28 (Acts 2:17); 1 John 2:27. [3]Matt. 10:32; Rom. 10:9, 10; Heb. 13:15. [4]Rom. 12:1; 1 Peter 2:5, 9. [5]Gal. 5:16, 17; Eph. 6:11; 1 Tim. 1:18, 19. [6]Matt. 25:34; 2 Tim. 2:12.

LORD'S DAY 13

33. Q. Why is He called God's only-begotten Son, since we also are children of God?
A. Because Christ alone is the eternal, natural Son of God.[1] We, however, are

children of God by adoption, through grace, for Christ's sake.[2]

[1]John 1:1-3, 14, 18; 3:16; Rom. 8:32; Heb. 1; 1 John 4:9. [2]John 1:12; Rom. 8:14-17; Gal 4:6; Eph. 1:5, 6.

34. Q. Why do you call Him our Lord?
A. Because He has ransomed us, body and soul,[1] from all our sins, not with silver or gold but with His precious blood,[2] and has freed us from all the power of the devil to make us His own possession.[3]

[1]1 Cor. 6:20; 1 Tim. 2:5, 6. [2]1 Peter 1:18, 19. [3]Col. 1:13, 14; Heb. 2:14, 15.

LORD'S DAY 14

35. Q. What do you confess when you say: He was conceived by the Holy Spirit, born of the virgin Mary?
A. The eternal Son of God, who is and remains true and eternal God,[1] took upon Himself true human nature from the flesh and blood of the virgin Mary,[2] through the working of the Holy Spirit.[3] Thus He is also the true seed of David,[4] and like His brothers in every respect,[5] yet without sin.[6]

[1]John 1:1; 10:30-36; Rom. 1:3; 9:5; Col. 1:15-17; 1 John 5:20. [2]Matt. 1:18-23; John 1:14; Gal 4:4; Heb. 2:14. [3]Luke 1:35. [4]2 Sam. 7:12-16; Ps. 132:11; Matt. 1:1; Luke 1:32; Rom. 1:3. [5]Phil. 2:7; Heb. 2:17. [6]Heb. 4:15; 7:26, 27.

36. Q. What benefit do you receive from the holy conception and birth of Christ?
A. He is our Mediator,[1] and with His innocence and perfect holiness covers, in the sight of God, my sin, in which I was conceived and born.[2]

[1]1 Tim. 2:5, 6; Heb. 9:13-15. [2]Rom. 8:3, 4; 2 Cor. 5:21; Gal 4:4, 5; 1 Peter 1:18, 19.

LORD'S DAY 15

37. Q. What do you confess when you say that He suffered?
A. During all the time He lived on earth, but especially at the end, Christ bore in body and soul the wrath of God against the sin of the whole human race.[1] Thus, by His suffering, as the only atoning sacrifice,[2] He has redeemed our body and soul from everlasting damnation,[3] and obtained for us the grace of God, righteousness, and eternal life.[4]

[1]Isa. 53; 1 Tim. 2:6; 1 Peter 2:24; 3:18. [2]Rom. 3:25; 1 Cor. 5:7; Eph. 5:2; Heb. 10:14; 1 John 2:2; 4:10. [3]Rom. 8:1-4; Gal 3:13; Col. 1:13; Heb. 9:12; 1 Peter 1:18, 19. [4]John 3:16; Rom. 3:24-26; 2 Cor. 5:21; Heb. 9:15.

38. Q. Why did He suffer under Pontius Pilate as judge?
A. Though innocent, Christ was condemned by an earthly judge,[1] and so He freed us from the severe judgment of God that was to fall on us.[2]

[1]Luke 23:13-24; John 19:4, 12-16. [2]Isa. 53:4, 5; 2 Cor. 5:21; Gal 3:13.

39. Q. Does it have a special meaning that Christ was crucified and did not die in a different way?
A. Yes. Thereby I am assured that He took upon Himself the curse which lay on me, for a crucified one was cursed by God.[1]

[1]Deut. 21:23; Gal 3:13.

LORD'S DAY 16

40. Q. Why was it necessary for Christ to humble Himself even unto death?
A. Because of the justice and truth of God[1] satisfaction for our sins could be made in no other way than by the death of the Son of God.[2]

[1]Gen. 2:17. [2]Rom. 8:3; Phil 2:8; Heb. 2:9, 14, 15.

41. Q. Why was He buried?
A. His burial testified that He had really died.[1]

[1]Isa. 53:9; John 19:38-42; Acts 13:29; 1 Cor. 15:3, 4.

42. Q. Since Christ has died for us, why do we still have to die?
A. Our death is not a payment for our sins, but it puts an end to sin and is an entrance into eternal life.[1]

[1]John 5:24; Phil 1:21-23; 1 Thess. 5:9, 10.

43. Q. What further benefit do we receive from Christ's sacrifice and death on the cross?
A. Through Christ's death our old nature is crucified, put to death, and buried with Him,[1] so that the evil desires of the flesh may no longer reign in us,[2] but that we may offer ourselves to Him as a sacrifice of thankfulness.[3]

[1]Rom. 6:5-11; Col. 2:11, 12. [2]Rom. 6:12-14. [3]Rom. 12:1; Eph. 5:1, 2.

44. Q. Why is there added: He descended into hell?
A. In my greatest sorrows and temptations I may be assured and comforted that my Lord Jesus Christ, by His unspeakable anguish, pain, terror, and agony, which He endured throughout all His sufferings[1] but especially on the cross, has delivered me from the anguish and torment of hell.[2]

[1]Ps. 18:5, 6; 116:3; Matt. 26:36-46; 27:45, 46; Heb. 5:7-10. [2]Isa. 53.

LORD'S DAY 17

45. Q. How does Christ's resurrection benefit us?
A. First, by His resurrection He has overcome death, so that He could make us share in the righteousness which He had obtained for us by His death.[1] Second, by His power we too are raised up to a new life.[2] Third, Christ's resurrection is to us a sure pledge of our glorious resurrection.[3]

[1]Rom. 4:25; 1 Cor. 15:16-20; 1 Peter 1:3-5. [2]Rom. 6:5-11; Eph. 2:4-6; Col. 3:1-4. [3]Rom. 8:11; 1 Cor. 15:12-23; Phil 3:20, 21.

LORD'S DAY 18

46. Q. What do you confess when you say, He ascended into heaven?
A. That Christ, before the eyes of His disciples, was taken up from the earth into heaven,[1] and that He is there for our benefit[2] until He comes again to judge the living and the dead.[3]

[1]Mark 16:19; Luke 24:50, 51; Acts 1:9-11. [2]Rom. 8:34; Heb. 4:14; 7:23-25; 9:24. [3]Matt. 24:30; Acts 1:11.

47. Q. Is Christ, then, not with us until the end of the world, as He has promised us?[1]
A. Christ is true man and true God. With respect to His human nature He is no longer on earth,[2] but with respect to His divinity, majesty, grace, and Spirit He is never absent from us.[3]

[1]Matt. 28:20. [2]Matt. 26:11; John 16:28; 17:11; Acts 3:19-21; Heb. 8:4. [3]Matt. 28:18-20; John 14:16-19; 16:13.

48. Q. But are the two natures in Christ not separated from each other if His human nature is not present wherever His divinity is?
A. Not at all, for His divinity has no limits and is present everywhere.[1] So it must follow that His divinity is indeed beyond the human nature which He has taken on and nevertheless is within this human nature and remains personally united with it.[2]

[1]Jer. 23:23, 24; Acts 7:48, 49. [2]John 1:14; 3:13; Col. 2:9.

49. Q. How does Christ's ascension into heaven benefit us?
A. First, He is our Advocate in heaven before His Father.[1] Second, we have our flesh in heaven as a sure pledge that He, our Head, will also take us, His members, up to Himself.[2] Third, He sends us His Spirit as a counter-pledge,[3] by whose power we seek the things that are above, where Christ is, seated at the right hand of God, and not the things that are on earth.[4]

[1]Rom. 8:34; 1 John 2:1. [2]John 14:2; 17:24; Eph. 2:4-6. [3]John 14:16; Acts 2:33; 2 Cor. 1:21, 22; 5:5. [4]Col. 3:1-4.

LORD'S DAY 19

50. Q. Why is it added, And sits at the right hand of God?
A. Christ ascended into heaven to manifest Himself there as Head of His church,[1] through whom the Father governs all things.[2]

[1]Eph. 1:20-23; Col. 1:18. [2]Matt. 28:18; John 5:22, 23.

51. Q. How does the glory of Christ, our Head, benefit us?
A. First, by His Holy Spirit He pours out heavenly gifts upon us, His members.[1] Second, by His power He defends and preserves us against all enemies.[2]

[1]Acts 2:33; Eph. 4:7-12. [2]Ps. 2:9; 110:1, 2; John 10:27-30; Rev. 19:11-16.

52. Q. What comfort is it to you that Christ will come to judge the living and the dead?
A. In all my sorrow and persecution I lift up my head and eagerly await as judge from heaven the very same person who before has submitted Himself to the judgment of God for my sake, and has removed all the curse from me.[1] He will cast all His and my

enemies into everlasting condemnation, but He will take me and all His chosen ones to Himself into heavenly joy and glory.[2]

[1]Luke 21:28; Rom. 8:22-25; Phil 3:20,21; Titus 2:13, 14. [2]Matt. 25:31-46; 1 Thess. 4:16, 17; 2 Thess. 1:6-10.

God the Holy Spirit and our Sanctification

LORD'S DAY 20

53. Q. What do you believe concerning the Holy Spirit?
A. First, He is, together with the Father and the Son, true and eternal God.[1] Second, He is also given to me,[2] to make me by true faith share in Christ and all His benefits,[3] to comfort me,[4] and to remain with me forever.[5]

[1]Gen. 1:1, 2; Matt. 28:19; Acts 5:3, 4; 1 Cor. 3:16. [2]1 Cor. 6:19; 2 Cor. 1:21, 22; Gal 4:6; Eph. 1:13. [3]Gal 3:14; 1 Peter 1:2. [4]John 15:26; Acts 9:31. [5]John 14:16, 17; 1 Peter 4:14.

LORD'S DAY 21

54. Q. What do you believe concerning the holy catholic Christian church?
A. I believe that the Son of God,[1] out of the whole human race,[2] from the beginning of the world to its end,[3] gathers, defends, and preserves for Himself,[4] by His Spirit and Word,[5] in the unity of the true faith,[6] a church chosen to everlasting life.[7] And I believe that I am[8] and forever shall remain a living member of it.[9]

[1]John 10:11; Acts 20:28; Eph. 4:11-13; Col. 1:18. [2]Gen. 26:4; Rev. 5:9. [3]Isa. 59:21; 1 Cor. 11:26. [4]Ps. 129:1-5; Matt. 16:18; John 10:28-30. [5]Rom. 1:16; 10:14-17; Eph. 5:26. [6]Acts 2:42-47; Eph. 4:1-6. [7]Rom. 8:29; Eph. 1:3-14. [8]1 John 3:14, 19-21. [9]Ps. 23:6; John 10:27, 28; 1 Cor. 1:4-9; 1 Peter 1:3-5.

55. Q. What do you understand by the communion of saints?
A. First, that believers, all and everyone, as members of Christ have communion with Him and share in all His treasures and gifts.[1] Second, that everyone is duty-bound to use his gifts readily and cheerfully for the benefit and well-being of the other members.[2]

[1]Rom. 8:32; 1 Cor. 6:17; 12:4-7, 12, 13; 1 John 1:3. [2]Rom. 12:4-8; 1 Cor. 12:20-27; 13:1-7; Phil 2:4-8.

56. Q. What do you believe concerning the forgiveness of sins?
A. I believe that God, because of Christ's satisfaction, will no more remember my sins,[1] nor my sinful nature, against which I have to struggle all my life,[2] but will graciously grant me the righteousness of Christ, that I may never come into condemnation.[3]

[1]Ps. 103:3, 4, 10, 12; Mic 7:18, 19; 2 Cor. 5:18-21; 1 John 1:7; 2:2. [2]Rom. 7:21-25. [3]John 3:17, 18; 5:24; Rom. 8:1, 2.

LORD'S DAY 22

57. Q. What comfort does the resurrection of the body offer you?
A. Not only shall my soul after this life immediately be taken up to Christ, my Head,[1] but also this my flesh, raised by the power of Christ, shall be reunited with my soul and made like Christ's glorious body.[2]

[1]Luke 16:22; 23:43; Phil 1:21-23. [2]Job 19:25, 26; 1 Cor. 15:20, 42-46, 54; Phil 3:21; 1 John 3:2.

58. Q. What comfort do you receive from the article about the life everlasting?
A. Since I now already feel in my heart the beginning of eternal joy,[1] I shall after this life possess perfect blessedness, such as no eye has seen, nor ear heard, nor the heart of man conceived – a blessedness in which to praise God forever.[2]

[1]John 17:3; Rom. 14:17; 2 Cor. 5:2, 3. [2]John 17:24; 1 Cor. 2:9.

LORD'S DAY 23

59. Q. But what does it help you now that you believe all this?
A. In Christ I am righteous before God and heir to life everlasting.[1]

[1]Hab. 2:4; John 3:36; Rom. 1:17; 5:1, 2.

60. Q. How are you righteous before God?
A. Only by true faith in Jesus Christ.[1] Although my conscience accuses me that I have grievously sinned against all God's commandments, have never kept any of them,[2] and am still inclined to all evil,[3] yet God, without any merit of my own,[4] out of mere grace,[5] imputes to me the perfect satisfaction, righteousness, and holiness of Christ.[6] He grants these to me as if I had never had nor committed any sin, and as if I myself had accomplished all the obedi-

ence which Christ has rendered for me,[7] if only I accept this gift with a believing heart.[8]

[1]Rom. 3:21-28; Gal 2:16; Eph. 2:8, 9; Phil 3:8-11. [2]Rom. 3:9, 10. [3]Rom. 7:23. [4]Deut. 9:6; Ezek 36:22; Titus 3:4, 5. [5]Rom. 3:24; Eph. 2:8. [6]Rom. 4:3-5; 2 Cor. 5:17-19; 1 John 2:1, 2. [7]Rom. 4:24, 25; 2 Cor. 5:21. [8]John 3:18; Acts 16:30, 31; Rom. 3:22.

61. Q. Why do you say that you are righteous only by faith?
A. Not that I am acceptable to God on account of the worthiness of my faith, for only the satisfaction, righteousness, and holiness of Christ is my righteousness before God.[1] I can receive this righteousness and make it my own by faith only.[2]

[1]1 Cor. 1:30, 31; 2:2. [2]Rom. 10:10; 1 John 5:10-12.

LORD'S DAY 24

62. Q. But why can our good works not be our righteousness before God, or at least a part of it?
A. Because the righteousness which can stand before God's judgment must be absolutely perfect and in complete agreement with the law of God,[1] whereas even our best works in this life are all imperfect and defiled with sin.[2]

[1]Deut. 27:26; Gal 3:10. [2]Isa. 64:6.

63. Q. But do our good works earn nothing, even though God promises to reward them in this life and the next?[1]
A. This reward is not earned; it is a gift of grace.[2]

[1]Matt. 5:12; Heb. 11:6. [2]Luke 17:10; 2 Tim. 4:7, 8.

64. Q. Does this teaching not make people careless and wicked?
A. No. It is impossible that those grafted into Christ by true faith should not bring forth fruits of thankfulness.[1]

[1]Matt. 7:18; Luke 6:43-45; John 15:5.

LORD'S DAY 25

65. Q. Since then faith alone makes us share in Christ and all His benefits, where does this faith come from?
A. From the Holy Spirit,[1] who works it in our hearts by the preaching of the gospel,[2] and strengthens it by the use of the sacraments.[3]

[1]John 3:5; 1 Cor. 2:10-14; Eph. 2:8; Phil 1:29. [2]Rom. 10:17; 1 Peter 1:23-25. [3]Matt. 28:19, 20; 1 Cor. 10:16.

66. Q. What are the sacraments?
A. The sacraments are holy, visible signs and seals. They were instituted by God so that by their use He might the more fully declare and seal to us the promise of the gospel.[1] And this is the promise: that God graciously grants us forgiveness of sins and everlasting life because of the one sacrifice of Christ accomplished on the cross.[2]

[1]Gen. 17:11; Deut. 30:6; Rom. 4:11. [2]Matt. 26:27, 28; Acts 2:38; Heb. 10:10.

67. Q. Are both the Word and the sacraments then intended to focus our faith on the sacrifice of Jesus Christ on the cross as the only ground of our salvation?
A. Yes, indeed. The Holy Spirit teaches us in the gospel and assures us by the sacraments that our entire salvation rests on Christ's one sacrifice for us on the cross.[1]

[1]Rom. 6:3; 1 Cor. 11:26; Gal 3:27.

68. Q. How many sacraments has Christ instituted in the new covenant?
A. Two: holy baptism and the holy supper.[1]

[1]Matt. 28:19, 20; 1 Cor. 11:23-26.

LORD'S DAY 26

69. Q. How does holy baptism signify and seal to you that the one sacrifice of Christ on the cross benefits you?
A. In this way: Christ instituted this outward washing[1] and with it gave the promise that, as surely as water washes away the dirt from the body, so certainly His blood and Spirit wash away the impurity of my soul, that is, all my sins.[2]

[1]Matt. 28:19. [2]Matt. 3:11; Mark 16:16; John 1:33; Acts 2:38; Rom. 6:3, 4; 1 Peter 3:21.

70. Q. What does it mean to be washed with Christ's blood and Spirit?
A. To be washed with Christ's blood means to receive forgiveness of sins from God, through grace, because of Christ's blood, poured out for us in His sacrifice on the cross.[1] To be washed with His Spirit means

to be renewed by the Holy Spirit and sanctified to be members of Christ, so that more and more we become dead to sin and lead a holy and blameless life.[2]

[1]Ezek 36:25; Zech. 13:1; Eph. 1:7; Heb. 12:24; I Peter 1:2; Rev. 1:5; 7:14. [2]John 3:5-8; Rom. 6:4; I Cor. 6:11; Col. 2:11, 12.

71. Q. Where has Christ promised that He will wash us with His blood and Spirit as surely as we are washed with the water of baptism?
A. In the institution of baptism, where He says: Go therefore and make disciples of all nations, baptizing them in the name of the Father and of the Son and of the Holy Spirit[1]. He who believes and is baptized will be saved, but he who does not believe will be condemned.[2] This promise is repeated where Scripture calls baptism the washing of regeneration and the washing away of sins.[3]

[1]Matt. 28:19. [2]Mark 16:16. [3]Titus 3:5; Acts 22:16

LORD'S DAY 27

72. Q. Does this outward washing with water itself wash away sins?
A. No, only the blood of Jesus Christ and the Holy Spirit cleanse us from all sins.[1]

[1]Matt. 3:11; I Peter 3:21; I John 1:7.

73. Q. Why then does the Holy Spirit call baptism the washing of regeneration and the washing away of sins?
A. God speaks in this way for a good reason. He wants to teach us that the blood and Spirit of Christ remove our sins just as water takes away dirt from the body.[1] But, even more important, He wants to assure us by this divine pledge and sign that we are as truly cleansed from our sins spiritually as we are bodily washed with water.[2]

[1]I Cor. 6:11; Rev. 1:5; 7:14. [2]Mark 16:16; Acts 2:38; Rom. 6:3, 4; Gal 3:27.

74. Q. Should infants, too, be baptized?
A. Yes. Infants as well as adults belong to God's covenant and congregation.[1] Through Christ's blood the redemption from sin and the Holy Spirit, who works faith, are promised to them no less than to adults.[2] Therefore, by baptism, as sign of the covenant, they must be grafted into the Christian church and distinguished from the children of unbelievers.[3] This was done in the old covenant by circumcision,[4] in place of which baptism was instituted in the new covenant.[5]

[1]Gen. 17:7; Matt. 19:14. [2]Ps. 22:10; Isa. 44:1-3; Acts 2:38, 39; 16:31. [3]Acts 10:47; I Cor. 7:14. [4]Gen. 17:9-14. [5]Col. 2: 11-13.

LORD'S DAY 28

75. Q. How does the Lord's supper signify and seal to you that you share in Christ's one sacrifice on the cross and in all His gifts?
A. In this way: Christ has commanded me and all believers to eat of this broken bread and drink of this cup in remembrance of Him. With this command He gave these promises:[1] First, as surely as I see with my eyes the bread of the Lord broken for me and the cup given to me, so surely was His body offered for me and His blood poured out for me on the cross. Second, as surely as I receive from the hand of the minister and taste with my mouth the bread and the cup of the Lord as sure signs of Christ's body and blood, so surely does He Himself nourish and refresh my soul to everlasting life with His crucified body and shed blood.

[1]Matt. 26:26-28; Mark 14:22-24; Luke 22:19, 20; I Cor. 11:23-25.

76. Q. What does it mean to eat the crucified body of Christ and to drink His shed blood?
A. First, to accept with a believing heart all the suffering and the death of Christ, and so receive forgiveness of sins and life eternal.[1] Second, to be united more and more to His sacred body through the Holy Spirit, who lives both in Christ and in us.[2] Therefore, although Christ is in heaven[3] and we are on earth, yet we are flesh of His flesh and bone of His bones,[4] and we forever live and are governed by one Spirit, as the members of our body are by one soul.[5]

[1]John 6:35, 40, 50-54. [2]John 6:55, 56; I Cor. 12:13. [3]Acts 1:9-11; 3:21; I Cor. 11:26; Col. 3:1. [4]I Cor. 6:15, 17; Eph. 5:29, 30; I John 4:13. [5]John 6:56-58; 15:1-6; Eph. 4:15, 16; I John 3:24.

77. Q. Where has Christ promised that He will nourish and refresh believers with His body and blood as surely as they eat of this broken bread and drink of this cup?

A. In the institution of the Lord's supper: The Lord Jesus on the night when He was betrayed took bread, and when He had given thanks, He broke it and said, "This is my body which is for you. Do this in remembrance of Me." In the same way also the cup, after supper, saying, "This cup is the new covenant in My blood. Do this, as often as you drink it, in remembrance of Me." For as often as you eat this bread and drink the cup, you proclaim the Lord's death until He comes.[1] This promise is repeated by Paul where he says: The cup of blessing which we bless, is it not a participation in the blood of Christ? The bread which we break, is it not a participation in the body of Christ? Because there is one bread, we who are many are one body, for we all partake of the one bread.[2]

[1] I Cor. 11:23-26. [2] I Cor. 10:16, 17.

LORD'S DAY 29

78. Q. Are then the bread and wine changed into the real body and blood of Christ?
A. No. Just as the water of baptism is not changed into the blood of Christ and is not the washing away of sins itself but is simply God's sign and pledge,[1] so also the bread in the Lord's supper does not become the body of Christ itself,[2] although it is called Christ's body[3] in keeping with the nature and usage of sacraments.[4]

[1] Eph. 5:26; Titus 3:5. [2] Matt. 26:26-29.
[3] I Cor. 10:16, 17; 11:26-28. [4] Gen. 17:10, 11; Exod 12:11, 13; I Cor. 10:3, 4; I Peter 3:21.

79. Q. Why then does Christ call the bread His body and the cup His blood, or the new covenant in His blood, and why does Paul speak of a participation in the body and blood of Christ?
A. Christ speaks in this way for a good reason: He wants to teach us by His supper that as bread and wine sustain us in this temporal life, so His crucified body and shed blood are true food and drink for our souls to eternal life.[1] But, even more important, He wants to assure us by this visible sign and pledge, first, that through the working of the Holy Spirit we share in His true body and blood as surely as we receive with our mouth these holy signs in remembrance of Him,[2] and, second, that all His suffering and obedience are as certainly ours as if we personally had suffered and paid for our sins.[3]

[1] John 6:51, 55. [2] I Cor. 10:16, 17; 11:26.
[3] Rom. 6:5-11.

LORD'S DAY 30

80. Q. What difference is there between the Lord's supper and the papal mass?
A. The Lord's supper testifies to us, first, that we have complete forgiveness of all our sins through the one sacrifice of Jesus Christ, which He Himself accomplished on the cross once for all;[1] and, second, that through the Holy Spirit we are grafted into Christ,[2] who with His true body is now in heaven at the right hand of the Father,[3] and this is where He wants to be worshiped.[4] But the mass teaches, first, that the living and the dead do not have forgiveness of sins through the suffering of Christ unless He is still offered for them daily by the priests; and, second, that Christ is bodily present in the form of bread and wine, and there is to be worshiped. Therefore the mass is basically nothing but a denial of the one sacrifice and suffering of Jesus Christ, and an accursed idolatry.

[1] Matt. 26:28; John 19:30; Heb. 7:27; 9:12, 25, 26; 10:10-18. [2] I Cor. 6:17; 10:16, 17.
[3] John 20:17; Acts 7:55, 56; Heb. 1:3; 8:1.
[4] John 4:21-24; Phil 3:20; Col. 3:1; I Thess. 1:10.

81. Q. Who are to come to the table of the Lord?
A. Those who are truly displeased with themselves because of their sins and yet trust that these are forgiven them and that their remaining weakness is covered by the suffering and death of Christ, and who also desire more and more to strengthen their faith and amend their life. But hypocrites and those who do not repent eat and drink judgment upon themselves.[1]

[1] I Cor. 10:19-22; 11:26-32.

82. Q. Are those also to be admitted to the Lord's supper who by their confession and life show that they are unbelieving and ungodly?
A. No, for then the covenant of God would be profaned and His wrath kindled against the whole congregation.[1] Therefore, according to the command of Christ and

His apostles, the Christian church is duty-bound to exclude such persons by the keys of the kingdom of heaven, until they amend their lives.

[1]Ps. 50:16; Isa. 1:11-17; 1 Cor. 11:17-34.

LORD'S DAY 31

83. Q. What are the keys of the kingdom of heaven?
A. The preaching of the holy gospel and church discipline. By these two the kingdom of heaven is opened to believers and closed to unbelievers.[1]

[1]Matt. 16:19; John 20:21-23.

84. Q. How is the kingdom of heaven opened and closed by the preaching of the gospel?
A. According to the command of Christ, the kingdom of heaven is opened when it is proclaimed and publicly testified to each and every believer that God has really forgiven all their sins for the sake of Christ's merits, as often as they by true faith accept the promise of the gospel. The kingdom of heaven is closed when it is proclaimed and testified to all unbelievers and hypocrites that the wrath of God and eternal condemnation rest on them as long as they do not repent. According to this testimony of the gospel, God will judge both in this life and in the life to come.[1]

[1]Matt. 16:19; John 3:31-36; 20:21-23.

85. Q. How is the kingdom of heaven closed and opened by church discipline?
A. According to the command of Christ, people who call themselves Christians but show themselves to be un-christian in doctrine or life are first repeatedly admonished in a brotherly manner. If they do not give up their errors or wickedness, they are reported to the church, that is, to the elders. If they do not heed also their admonitions, they are forbidden the use of the sacraments, and they are excluded by the elders from the Christian congregation, and by God Himself from the kingdom of Christ.[1] They are again received as members of Christ and of the church when they promise and show real amendment.[2]

[1]Matt. 18:15-20; 1 Cor. 5:3-5; 11-13; 2 Thess. 3:14, 15. [2]Luke 15:20-24; 2 Cor. 2:6-11.

The Third Part
OUR THANKFULNESS

LORD'S DAY 32

86. Q. Since we have been delivered from our misery by grace alone through Christ, without any merit of our own, why must we yet do good works?
A. Because Christ, having redeemed us by His blood, also renews us by His Holy Spirit to be His image, so that with our whole life we may show ourselves thankful to God for His benefits,[1] and He may be praised by us.[2] Further, that we ourselves may be assured of our faith by its fruits,[3] and that by our godly walk of life we may win our neighbors for Christ.[4]

[1]Rom. 6:13; 12:1, 2; 1 Peter 2:5-10. [2]Matt. 5:16; 1 Cor. 6:19, 20. [3]Matt. 7:17, 18; Gal 5:22-24; 2 Peter 1:10, 11. [4]Matt. 5:14-16; Rom. 14:17-19; 1 Peter 2:12; 3:1, 2.

87. Q. Can those be saved who do not turn to God from their ungrateful and impenitent walk of life?
A. By no means. Scripture says that no unchaste person, idolater, adulterer, thief, greedy person, drunkard, slanderer, robber, or the like shall inherit the kingdom of God.[1]

[1]1 Cor. 6:9, 10; Gal 5:19-21; Eph. 5:5, 6; 1 John 3:14.

LORD'S DAY 33

88. Q. What is the true repentance or conversion of man?
A. It is the dying of the old nature and the coming to life of the new.[1]

[1]Rom. 6:1-11; 1 Cor. 5:7; 2 Cor. 5:17; Eph. 4:22-24; Col. 3:5-10.

89. Q. What is the dying of the old nature?
A. It is to grieve with heartfelt sorrow that we have offended God by our sin, and more and more to hate it and flee from it.[1]

[1]Ps. 51:3, 4, 17; Joel 2:12, 13; Rom. 8:12, 13; 2 Cor. 7:10.

90. Q. What is the coming to life of the new nature?
A. It is a heartfelt joy in God through Christ,[1] and a love and delight to live according to the will of God in all good works.[2]

[1]Ps. 51:8, 12; Isa. 57:15; Rom. 5:1; 14:17. [2]Rom. 6:10, 11; Gal 2:20.

91. Q. But what are good works?
A. Only those which are done out of true faith,[1] in accordance with the law of God,[2] and to His glory,[3] and not those based on our own opinion or on precepts of men.[4]

[1]John 15:5; Rom. 14:23; Heb. 11:6. [2]Lev 18:4; 1 Sam. 15:22; Eph. 2:10. [3]1 Cor. 10:31. [4]Deut. 12:32; Isa. 29:13; Ezek 20:18, 19; Matt. 15:7-9.

LORD'S DAY 34

92. Q. What is the law of the LORD?
A. God spoke all these words, saying: I am the LORD your God, who brought you out of the land of Egypt, out of the house of bondage.

1 You shall have no other gods before Me.
2. You shall not make for yourself a graven image, or any likeness of anything that is in heaven above, or that is in the earth beneath, or that is in the water under the earth; you shall not bow down to them or serve them; for I the LORD your God am a jealous God, visiting the iniquity of the fathers upon the children to the third and fourth generation of those who hate Me, but showing steadfast love to thousands of those who love Me and keep My commandments.
3. You shall not take the Name of the LORD your God in vain; for the LORD will not hold him guiltless who takes His Name in vain.
4. Remember the sabbath day, to keep it holy. Six days you shall labor, and do all your work; but the seventh day is a sabbath to the LORD your God; in it you shall not do any work, you, or your son, or your daughter, your manservant, or your maidservant, or your cattle, or the sojourner who is within your gates; for in six days the LORD made heaven and earth, the sea, and all that is in them, and rested the seventh day; therefore the LORD blessed the sabbath day and hallowed it.
5. Honour your father and your mother, that your days may be long in the land which the LORD your God gives you.
6. You shall not kill.
7. You shall not commit adultery.
8. You shall not steal.
9. You shall not bear false witness against your neighbor.
10. You shall not covet your neighbor's house; you shall not covet your neighbor's wife, or his manservant, or his maidservant, or his ox, or his ass, or anything that is your neighbor's.[1]

[1]Ex 20:1-17; Deut. 5:6-21.

93. Q. How are these commandments divided?
A. Into two parts. The first teaches us how to live in relation to God; the second, what duties we owe our neighbor. [1]

[1]Matt. 22:37-40.

94. Q. What does the LORD require in the first commandment?
A. That for the sake of my very salvation I avoid and flee all idolatry,[1] witchcraft, superstition,[2] and prayer to saints or to other creatures.[3] Further, that I rightly come to know the only true God,[4] trust in Him alone,[5] submit to Him with all humility[6] and patience,[7] expect all good from Him only,[8] and love,[9] fear,[10] and honor Him[11] with all my heart. In short, that I forsake all creatures rather than do the least thing against His will.[12]

[1]1 Cor. 6:9, 10; 10:5-14; 1 John 5:21. [2]Lev 19:31; Deut. 18:9-12. [3]Matt. 4:10; Rev. 19:10; 22:8, 9. [4]John 17:3. [5]Jer. 17:5, 7. [6]1 Peter 5:5, 6. [7]Rom. 5:3, 4; 1 Cor. 10:10; Phil 2:14; Col. 1:11; Heb. 10:36. [8]Ps. 104:27, 28; Isa. 45:7; James 1:17. [9]Deut. 6:5; (Matt. 22:37). [10]Deut. 6:2; Ps. 111:10; Prov 1:7; 9:10; Matt. 10:28; 1 Peter 1:17. [11]Deut. 6:13; (Matt. 4:10); Deut. 10:20. [12]Matt. 5:29, 30; 10:37-39; Acts 5:29.

95. Q. What is idolatry?
A. Idolatry is having or inventing something in which to put our trust instead of, or in addition to, the only true God who has revealed Himself in His Word.[1]

[1]1 Chron. 16:26; Gal. 4:8, 9; Eph. 5:5; Phil. 3:19.

LORD'S DAY 35

96. Q. What does God require in the second commandment?
A. We are not to make an image of God in any way,[1] nor to worship Him in any other manner than He has commanded in His Word.[2]

[1]Deut. 4:15-19; Isa. 40:18-25; Acts 17:29; Rom. 1:23. [2]Lev 10:1-7; Deut. 12:30; I Sam 15:22, 23; Matt. 15:9; John 4:23, 24.

97. Q. May we then not make any image at all?
A. God cannot and may not be visibly portrayed in any way. Creatures may be portrayed, but God forbids us to make or have any images of them in order to worship them or to serve God through them.[1]

[1]Ex 34:13, 14, 17; Num. 33:52; 2 Kings 18:4, 5; Isa. 40:25.

98. Q. But may images not be tolerated in the churches as "books for the laity"?
A. No, for we should not be wiser than God. He wants His people to be taught not by means of dumb images[1] but by the living preaching of His Word.[2]

[1]Jer. 10:8; Hab. 2:18-20. [2]Rom. 10:14, 15, 17; 2 Tim. 3:16, 17; 2 Peter 1:19.

LORD'S DAY 36

99. Q. What is required in the third commandment?
A. We are not to blaspheme or to abuse the Name of God by cursing,[1] perjury,[2] or unnecessary oaths,[3] nor to share in such horrible sins by being silent bystanders.[4] Rather, we must use the holy Name of God only with fear and reverence,[5] so that we may rightly confess Him,[6] call upon Him,[7] and praise Him in all our words and works.[8]

[1]Lev. 24:10-17. [2]Lev. 19:12. [3]Matt. 5:37; James 5:12. [4]Lev. 5:1; Prov 29:24. [5]Ps. 99:1-5; Isa. 45:23; Jer. 4:2. [6]Matt. 10:32, 33; Rom. 10:9, 10. [7]Ps. 50:14, 15; I Tim. 2:8. [8]Rom. 2:24; Col. 3:17; I Tim. 6:1.

100. Q. Is the blaspheming of God's Name by swearing and cursing such a grievous sin that God is angry also with those who do not prevent and forbid it as much as they can?
A. Certainly,[1] for no sin is greater or provokes God's wrath more than the blaspheming of His Name. That is why He commanded it to be punished with death.[2]

[1]Lev. 5:1. [2]Lev. 24:16.

LORD'S DAY 37

101. Q. But may we swear an oath by the Name of God in a godly manner?
A. Yes, when the government demands it of its subjects, or when necessity requires it, in order to maintain and promote fidelity and truth, to God's glory and for our neighbor's good. Such oath-taking is based on God's Word[1] and was therefore rightly used by saints in the Old and the New Testament.[2]

[1]Deut. 6:13; 10:20; Jer. 4:1, 2; Heb. 6:16. [2]Gen. 21:24; 31:53; Josh. 9:15; I Sam 24:22; I Kings 1:29, 30;.

102. Q. May we also swear by saints or other creatures?
A. No. A lawful oath is a calling upon God, who alone knows the heart, to bear witness to the truth, and to punish me if I swear falsely.[1] No creature is worthy of such honour.[2]

[1]Rom. 9:1; 2 Cor. 1:23. [2]Matt. 5:34-37; 23:16-22; James 5:12.

LORD'S DAY 38

103. Q. What does God require in the fourth commandment?
A. First, that the ministry of the gospel and the schools be maintained[1] and that, especially on the day of rest, I diligently attend the church of God[2] to hear God's Word,[3] to use the sacraments,[4] to call publicly upon the LORD,[5] and to give Christian offerings for the poor.[6] Second, that all the days of my life I rest from my evil works, let the LORD work in me through His Holy Spirit, and so begin in this life the eternal sabbath.[7]

[1]Deut. 6:4-9; 20-25; I Cor. 9:13, 14; 2 Tim. 2:2; 3:13-17; Titus 1:5. [2]Deut. 12:5-12; Ps. 40:9, 10; 68:26; Acts 2:42-47; Heb. 10:23-25. [3]Rom. 10:14-17; I Cor. 14:26-33; I Tim. 4:13. [4]I Cor. 11:23, 24. [5]Col. 3:16; I Tim. 2:1. [6]Ps. 50:14; I Cor. 16:2; 2 Cor. 8 and 9. [7]Isa. 66:23; Heb. 4:9-11.

LORD'S DAY 39

104. Q. What does God require in the fifth commandment?
A. That I show all honor, love, and faithfulness to my father and mother and to all those in authority over me, submit myself with due obedience to their good instruction and discipline,[1] and also have patience with their weaknesses and shortcomings,[2] since it is God's will to govern us by their hand.[3]

[1]Ex 21:17; Prov 1:8; 4:1; Rom. 13:1, 2; Eph. 5:21, 22; 6:1-9; Col. 3:18–4:1. [2]Prov. 20:20; 23:22; 1 Peter 2:18. [3]Matt. 22:21, Rom. 13:1-8; Eph. 6:1-9; Col. 3:18-21.

LORD'S DAY 40

105. Q. What does God require in the sixth commandment?
A. I am not to dishonour, hate, injure, or kill my neighbor by thoughts, words, or gestures, and much less by deeds, whether personally or through another;[1] rather, I am to put away all desire of revenge.[2] Moreover, I am not to harm or recklessly endanger myself.[3] Therefore, also, the government bears the sword to prevent murder.[4]

[1]Gen. 9:6; Lev. 19:17, 18; Matt. 5:21, 22; 26:52. [2]Prov. 25:21, 22; Matt. 18:35; Rom. 12:19; Eph. 4:26. [3]Matt. 4:7; 26:52; Rom. 13:11-14. [4]Gen. 9:6; Ex 21:14; Rom. 13:4.

106. Q. But does this commandment speak only of killing?
A. By forbidding murder God teaches us that He hates the root of murder, such as envy, hatred, anger, and desire of revenge,[1] and that He regards all these as murder.[2]

[1]Prov. 14:30; Rom. 1:29; 12:19; Gal 5:19-21; James 1:20; 1 John 2:9-11. [2]1 John 3:15.

107. Q. Is it enough, then, that we do not kill our neighbor in any such way?
A. No. When God condemns envy, hatred, and anger, He commands us to love our neighbor as ourselves,[1] to show patience, peace, gentleness, mercy, and friendliness toward him,[2] to protect him from harm as much as we can, and to do good even to our enemies.[3]

[1]Matt. 7:12; 22:39; Rom. 12:10. [2]Matt. 5:5; Luke 6:36; Rom. 12:10, 18; Gal 6:1, 2; Eph. 4:2; Col. 3:12; [3]Exod. 23:4, 5; Matt. 5:44, 45; Rom. 12:20.

LORD'S DAY 41

108. Q. What does the seventh commandment teach us?
A. That all unchastity is cursed by God.[1] We must therefore detest it from the heart[2] and live chaste and disciplined lives, both within and outside of holy marriage.[3]

[1]Lev 18:30; Eph. 5:3-5. [2]Jude 22, 23. [3]1 Cor. 7:1-9; 1 Thess. 4:3-8; Heb. 13:4.

109. Q. Does God in this commandment forbid nothing more than adultery and similar shameful sins?
A. Since we, body and soul, are temples of the Holy Spirit, it is God's will that we keep ourselves pure and holy. Therefore He forbids all unchaste acts, gestures, words, thoughts, desires,[1] and whatever may entice us to unchastity.[2]

[1]Matt. 5:27-29; 1 Cor. 6:18-20; Eph. 5:3, 4. [2]1 Cor. 15:33; Eph. 5:18.

LORD'S DAY 42

110. Q. What does God forbid in the eighth commandment?
A. God forbids not only outright theft and robbery[1] but also such wicked schemes and devices as false weights and measures, deceptive merchandising, counterfeit money, and usury;[2] we must not defraud our neigh-bor in any way, whether by force or by show of right.[3] In addition God forbids all greed[4] and all abuse or squandering of His gifts.[5]

[1]Ex 22:1; 1 Cor. 5:9, 10; 6:9, 10. [2]Deut. 25:13-16; Ps. 15:5; Prov 11:1; 12:22; Ezek 45:9-12; Luke 6:35. [3]Mic 6:9-11; Luke 3:14; James 5:1-6. [4]Luke 12:15; Eph. 5:5. [5]Prov. 21:20; 23:20, 21; Luke 16:10-13.

111. Q. What does God require of you in this commandment?
A. I must promote my neighbor's good wherever I can and may, deal with him as I would like others to deal with me, and work faithfully so that I may be able to give to those in need.[1]

[1]Isa. 58:5-10; Matt. 7:12; Gal 6:9, 10; Eph. 4:28.

LORD'S DAY 43

112. Q. What is required in the ninth commandment?
A. I must not give false testimony against anyone, twist no one's words, not gossip or slander, nor condemn or join in condemning anyone rashly and unheard.[1] Rather, I must avoid all lying and deceit as the devil's own works, under penalty of God's heavy wrath.[2] In court and everywhere else, I must love the truth,[3] speak and confess it honestly, and do what I can to defend and promote my neighbor's honor and reputation.[4]

[1]Ps. 15; Prov 19:5, 9; 21:28; Matt. 7:1; Luke 6:37; Rom. 1:28-32. [2]Lev 19:11, 12; Prov 12:22; 13:5; John 8:44; Rev. 21:8. [3]1 Cor. 13:6; Eph. 4:25. [4]1 Peter 3:8, 9; 4:8.

LORD'S DAY 44

113. Q. What does the tenth commandment require of us?
A. That not even the slightest thought or desire contrary to any of God's commandments should ever arise in our heart. Rather, with all our heart we should always hate all sin and delight in all righteousness.[1]

[1]Ps. 19:7-14; 139:23, 24; Rom. 7:7, 8.

114. Q. But can those converted to God keep these commandments perfectly?
A. No. In this life even the holiest have only a small beginning of this obedience.[1] Nevertheless, with earnest purpose they do begin to live not only according to some but to all the commandments of God.[2]

[1]Eccles. 7:20; Rom. 7:14, 15; 1 Cor. 13:9; 1 John 1:8. [2]Ps. 1:1, 2; Rom. 7:22-25; Phil 3:12-16.

115. Q. If in this life no one can keep the ten commandments perfectly, why does God have them preached so strictly?
A. First, so that throughout our life we may more and more become aware of our sinful nature, and therefore seek more eagerly the forgiveness of sins and righteousness in Christ.[1] Second, so that, while praying to God for the grace of the Holy Spirit, we may never stop striving to be renewed more and more after God's image, until after this life we reach the goal of perfection.[2]

[1]Ps. 32:5; Rom. 3:19-26; 7:7, 24, 25; 1 John 1:9. [2]1 Cor. 9:24; Phil 3:12-14; 1 John 3:1-3.

LORD'S DAY 45

116. Q. Why is prayer necessary for Christians?
A. Because prayer is the most important part of the thankfulness which God requires of us.[1] Moreover, God will give His grace and the Holy Spirit only to those who constantly and with heartfelt longing ask Him for these gifts and thank Him for them.[2]

[1]Ps. 50:14, 15; 116:12-19; 1 Thess. 5:16-18. [2]Matt. 7:7, 8; Luke 11:9-13.

117. Q. What belongs to a prayer which pleases God and is heard by Him?
A. First, we must from the heart call upon the one true God only, who has revealed Himself in His Word, for all that He has commanded us to pray.[1] Second, we must thoroughly know our need and misery, so that we may humble ourselves before God.[2] Third, we must rest on this firm foundation that, although we do not deserve it, God will certainly hear our prayer for the sake of Christ our Lord, as He has promised us in His Word.[3]

[1]Ps. 145:18-20; John 4:22-24; Rom. 8:26, 27; James 1:5; 1 John 5:14, 15; Rev. 19:10. [2]2 Chron. 7:14; 20:12; Ps. 2:11; 34:18; 62:8; Isa. 66:2; Rev. 4. [3]Dan. 9:17-19; Matt. 7:8; John 14:13, 14; 16:23; Rom. 10:13; James 1:6.

118. Q. What has God commanded us to ask of Him?
A. All the things we need for body and soul,[1] as included in the prayer which Christ our Lord Himself taught us.

[1]Matt. 6:33; James 1:17.

119. Q. What is the Lord's prayer?
A. Our Father who art in heaven, Hallowed be Thy Name. Thy kingdom come, Thy will be done, On earth as it is in heaven. Give us this day our daily bread; And forgive us our debts, As we also have forgiven our debtors; And lead us not into temptation, But deliver us from the evil one. For Thine is the kingdom, and the power, and the glory, for ever. Amen.[1]

[1]Matt. 6:9-13; Luke 11:2-4.

LORD'S DAY 46

120. Q. Why has Christ commanded us to address God as Our Father?
A. To awaken in us at the very beginning of our prayer that childlike reverence and trust toward God which should be basic to our prayer: God has become our Father through Christ and will much less deny us what we ask of Him in faith than our fathers would refuse us earthly things.[1]

[1]Matt. 7:9-11; Luke 11:11-13.

121. Q. Why is there added, Who art in heaven?

A. These words teach us not to think of God's heavenly majesty in an earthly manner,[1] and to expect from His almighty power all things we need for body and soul.[2]

[1]Jer. 23:23, 24; Acts 17:24, 25. [2]Matt. 6:25-34; Rom. 8:31, 32.

LORD'S DAY 47

122. Q. What is the first petition?
A. Hallowed be Thy Name. That is: Grant us first of all that we may rightly know Thee,[1] and sanctify, glorify, and praise Thee in all Thy works, in which shine forth Thy almighty power, wisdom, goodness, righteousness, mercy, and truth.[2] Grant us also that we may so direct our whole life – our thoughts, words, and actions – that Thy Name is not blasphemed because of us but always honored and praised.[3]

[1]Jer. 9:23, 24; 31: 33, 34; Matt. 16:17; John 17:3. [2]Ex 34:5-8; Ps. 145; Jer. 32:16-20; Luke 1:46-55, 68-75; Rom. 11: 33-36. [3]Ps. 115:1; Matt. 5:16.

LORD'S DAY 48

123. Q. What is the second petition?
A. Thy kingdom come. That is: So rule us by Thy Word and Spirit that more and more we submit to Thee.[1] Preserve and increase Thy church.[2] Destroy the works of the devil, every power that raises itself against Thee, and every conspiracy against Thy holy Word.[3] Do all this until the fulness of Thy kingdom comes, wherein Thou shalt be all in all.[4]

[1]Ps. 119:5, 105; 143:10; Matt. 6:33. [2]Ps. 51:18; 122:6-9; Matt. 16:18; Acts 2:42-47. [3]Rom. 16:20; I John 3:8. [4]Rom. 8:22, 23; I Cor. 15:28; Rev. 22: 17, 20.

LORD'S DAY 49

124. Q. What is the third petition?
A. Thy will be done, on earth as it is in heaven. That is: Grant that we and all men may deny our own will, and without any murmuring obey Thy will, for it alone is good.[1] Grant also that everyone may carry out the duties of his office and calling[2] as willingly and faithfully as the angels in heaven.[3]

[1]Matt. 7:21; 16:24-26; Luke 22:42; Rom. 12:1, 2; Titus 2:11, 12. [2]I Cor. 7:17-24; Eph. 6:5-9. [3]Ps. 103:20, 21.

LORD'S DAY 50

125. Q. What is the fourth petition?
A. Give us this day our daily bread. That is: Provide us with all our bodily needs[1] so that we may acknowledge that Thou art the only fountain of all good,[2] and that our care and labor, and also Thy gifts, cannot do us any good without Thy blessing.[3] Grant, therefore, that we may withdraw our trust from all creatures and place it only in Thee.[4]

[1]Ps. 104:27-30; 145:15, 16; Matt. 6:25-34. [2]Acts 14:17; 17:25; James 1:17. [3]Deut. 8:3; Ps. 37:16; 127:1, 2; I Cor. 15:58. [4]Ps. 55:22; 62; 146; Jer. 17:5-8; Heb. 13:5, 6.

LORD'S DAY 51

126. Q. What is the fifth petition?
A. And forgive us our debts, as we also have forgiven our debtors. That is: For the sake of Christ's blood, do not impute to us, wretched sinners, any of our transgressions, nor the evil which still clings to us,[1] as we also find this evidence of Thy grace in us that we are fully determined wholeheartedly to forgive our neighbor.[2]

[1]Ps. 51:1-7; 143:2; Rom. 8:1; I John 2:1, 2. [2]Matt. 6:14, 15; 18:21-35.

LORD'S DAY 52

127. Q. What is the sixth petition?
A. And lead us not into temptation, but deliver us from the evil one. That is: In ourselves we are so weak that we cannot stand even for a moment.[1] Moreover, our sworn enemies – the devil,[2] the world,[3] and our own flesh[4] – do not cease to attack us. Wilt Thou, therefore, uphold and strengthen us by the power of Thy Holy Spirit, so that in this spiritual war[5] we may not go down to defeat, but always firmly resist our enemies, until we finally obtain the complete victory.[6]

[1]Ps. 103:14-16; John 15:1-5. [2]2 Cor. 11:14; Eph. 6:10-13; I Peter 5:8. [3]John 15:18-21. [4]Rom. 7:23; Gal 5:17. [5]Matt. 10:19, 20; 26:41; Mark 13:33; Rom. 5:3-5. [6]I Cor. 10:13; I Thess. 3:13; 5:23.

128. Q. How do you conclude your prayer?
A. For Thine is the kingdom, and the power, and the glory, for ever. That is: All this we

ask of Thee because, as our King, having power over all things, Thou art both willing and able to give us all that is good,[1] and because not we but Thy holy Name should so receive all glory for ever.[2]

[1]Rom. 10:11-13; 2 Peter 2:9. [2]Ps. 115:1; Jer. 33:8, 9; John 14:13.

129. Q. What does the word Amen mean?
A. Amen means: It is true and certain. For God has much more certainly heard my prayer than I feel in my heart that I desire this of Him.[1]

[1]Isa. 65:24; 2 Cor. 1:20; 2 Tim. 2:13.

APPENDIX 6

THE CANONS OF DORDT

The Canons of Dordt

Formally Titled

The Decision of the Synod of Dordt on the Five Main Points of Doctrine in Dispute in the Netherlands

THE FIRST MAIN POINT OF DOCTRINE

Divine Election and Reprobation

The Judgment Concerning Divine Predestination

Which the Synod Declares to Be in Agreement with the Word of God

and Accepted Till Now in the Reformed Churches,

Set Forth in Several Articles

Article 1: God's Right to Condemn All People
Since all people have sinned in Adam and have come under the sentence of the curse and eternal death, God would have done no one an injustice if it had been His will to leave the entire human race in sin and under the curse, and to condemn them on account of their sin. As the apostle says: The whole world is liable to the condemnation of God (Rom. 3:19), All have sinned and are deprived of the glory of God (Rom. 3:23), and The wages of sin is death (Rom. 6:23).*

–*All quotations from Scripture are translations of the original Latin manuscript.–

Article 2: The Manifestation of God's Love
But this is how God showed His love: He sent His only begotten Son into the world, so that whoever believes in Him should not perish but have eternal life.

Article 3: The Preaching of the Gospel
In order that people may be brought to faith, God mercifully sends proclaimers of this very joyful message to the people He wishes and at the time he wishes. By this ministry people are called to repentance and faith in Christ crucified. For how shall they believe in Him of whom they have not heard? And how shall they hear without someone preaching? And how shall they preach unless they have been sent? (Rom. 10:14-15).

Article 4: A Twofold Response to the Gospel
God's anger remains on those who do not believe this gospel. But those who do accept it and embrace Jesus the Savior with a true and living faith are delivered through Him from God's anger and from destruction, and receive the gift of eternal life.

Article 5: The Sources of Unbelief and of Faith
The cause or blame for this unbelief, as well as for all other sins, is not at all in God, but in man. Faith in Jesus Christ, however, and salvation through Him is a free gift of God. As Scripture says, It is by grace you have been saved, through faith, and this not from yourselves; it is a gift of God (Eph. 2:8). Likewise: It has been freely given to you to believe in Christ (Phil. 1:29).

Article 6: God's Eternal Decision
The fact that some receive from God the gift of faith within time, and that others do

not, stems from his eternal decision. For all His works are known to God from eternity (Acts 15:18; Eph. 1:11). In accordance with this decision he graciously softens the hearts, however hard, of his chosen ones and inclines them to believe, but by his just judgment he leaves in their wickedness and hardness of heart those who have not been chosen. And in this especially is disclosed to us his act – unfathomable, and as merciful as it is just – of distinguishing between people equally lost. This is the well-known decision of election and reprobation revealed in God's Word. This decision the wicked, impure, and unstable distort to their own ruin, but it provides holy and godly souls with comfort beyond words.

Article 7: Election
Election or choosing is God's unchangeable purpose by which he did the following:

> Before the foundation of the world, by sheer grace, according to the free good pleasure of his will, he chose in Christ to salvation a definite number of particular people out of the entire human race, which had fallen by its own fault from its original innocence into sin and ruin. Those chosen were neither better nor more deserving than the others, but lay with them in the common misery. He did this in Christ, whom he also appointed from eternity to be the mediator, the head of all those chosen, and the foundation of their salvation. And so he decided to give the chosen ones to Christ to be saved, and to call and draw them effectively into Christ's fellowship through His Word and Spirit. In other words, he decided to grant them true faith in Christ, to justify them, to sanctify them, and finally, after powerfully preserving them in the fellowship of His Son, to glorify them.

God did all this in order to demonstrate His mercy, to the praise of the riches of His glorious grace.

As Scripture says, God chose us in Christ, before the foundation of the world, so that we should be holy and blameless before Him with love; he predestined us whom he adopted as His children through Jesus Christ, in Himself, according to the good pleasure of His will, to the praise of His glorious grace, by which he freely made us pleasing to Himself in His beloved (Eph. 1:4-6). And elsewhere, Those whom he predestined, he also called; and those whom he called, he also justified; and those whom he justified, he also glorified (Rom. 8:30).

Article 8: A Single Decision of Election
This election is not of many kinds; it is one and the same election for all who were to be saved in the Old and the New Testament. For Scripture declares that there is a single good pleasure, purpose, and plan of God's will, by which he chose us from eternity both to grace and to glory, both to salvation and to the way of salvation, which he prepared in advance for us to walk in.

Article 9: Election Not Based on Foreseen Faith
This same election took place, not on the basis of foreseen faith, of the obedience of faith, of holiness, or of any other good quality and disposition, as though it were based on a prerequisite cause or condition in the person to be chosen, but rather for the purpose of faith, of the obedience of faith, of holiness, and so on. Accordingly, election is the source of each of the benefits of salvation. Faith, holiness, and the other saving gifts, and at last eternal life itself, flow forth from election as its fruits and effects. As the apostle says, He chose us (not because we were, but) so that we should be holy and blameless before Him in love (Eph. 1:4).

Article 10: Election Based on God's Good Pleasure
But the cause of this undeserved election is exclusively the good pleasure of God. This does not involve his choosing certain human qualities or actions from among all those possible as a condition of salvation, but rather involves his adopting certain particular persons from among the common mass of sinners as his own possession. As Scripture says, When the children were not yet born, and had done nothing either good or bad..., she (Rebecca) was told, "The older will serve the younger." As it is written, "Jacob I loved, but Esau I hated" (Rom. 9:11-13). Also, All who were appointed for eternal life believed (Acts 13:48).

Article 11: Election Unchangeable
Just as God Himself is most wise, unchangeable, all-knowing, and almighty, so the election made by Him can neither be suspended nor altered, revoked, or annulled; neither can His chosen ones be cast off, nor their number reduced.

Article 12: The Assurance of Election
Assurance of this their eternal and unchangeable election to salvation is given to the chosen in due time, though by various stages and in differing measure. Such assurance comes not by inquisitive searching into the hidden and deep things of God, but by noticing within themselves, with spiritual joy and holy delight, the unmistakable fruits of election pointed out in God's Word – such as a true faith in Christ, a childlike fear of God, a godly sorrow for their sins, a hunger and thirst for righteousness, and so on.

Article 13: The Fruit of This Assurance
In their awareness and assurance of this election God's children daily find greater cause to humble themselves before God, to adore the fathomless depth of His mercies, to cleanse themselves, and to give fervent love in return to Him who first so greatly loved them. This is far from saying that this teaching concerning election, and reflection upon it, make God's children lax in observing His commandments or carnally self-assured. By God's just judgment this does usually happen to those who casually take for granted the grace of election or engage in idle and brazen talk about it but are unwilling to walk in the ways of the chosen.

Article 14: Teaching Election Properly
Just as, by God's wise plan, this teaching concerning divine election has been proclaimed through the prophets, Christ Himself, and the apostles, in Old and New Testament times, and has subsequently been committed to writing in the Holy Scriptures, so also today in God's church, for which it was specifically intended, this teaching must be set forth – with a spirit of discretion, in a godly and holy manner, at the appropriate time and place, without inquisitive searching into the ways of the Most High. This must be done for the glory of God's most holy name, and for the lively comfort of His people.

Article 15: Reprobation
Moreover, Holy Scripture most especially highlights this eternal and undeserved grace of our election and brings it out more clearly for us, in that it further bears witness that not all people have been chosen but that some have not been chosen or have been passed by in God's eternal election – those, that is, concerning whom God, on the basis of his entirely free, most just, irreproachable, and unchangeable good pleasure, made the following decision: to leave them in the common misery into which, by their own fault, they have plunged themselves; not to grant them saving faith and the grace of conversion; but finally to condemn and eternally punish them (having been left in their own ways and under his just judgment), not only for their unbelief but also for all their other sins, in order to display His justice. And this is the decision of reprobation, which does not at all make God the author of sin (a blasphemous thought!) but rather its fearful, irreproachable, just judge and avenger.

Article 16: Responses to the Teaching of Reprobation
Those who do not yet actively experience within themselves a living faith in Christ or an assured confidence of heart, peace of conscience, a zeal for childlike obedience, and a glorying in God through Christ, but who nevertheless use the means by which God has promised to work these things in us – such people ought not to be alarmed at the mention of reprobation, nor to count themselves among the reprobate; rather they ought to continue diligently in the use of the means, to desire fervently a time of more abundant grace, and to wait for it in reverence and humility. On the other hand, those who seriously desire to turn to God, to be pleasing to Him alone, and to be delivered from the body of death, but are not yet able to make such progress along the way of godliness and faith as they would like – such people ought much less to stand in fear of the teaching concerning reprobation, since our merciful God has promised that He will not snuff out a smoldering wick and that He will not break a bruised reed. However, those who have forgotten God and their Savior Jesus Christ

and have abandoned themselves wholly to the cares of the world and the pleasures of the flesh – such people have every reason to stand in fear of this teaching, as long as they do not seriously turn to God.

Article 17: The Salvation of the Infants of Believers
Since we must make judgments about God's will from His Word, which testifies that the children of believers are holy, not by nature but by virtue of the gracious covenant in which they together with their parents are included, godly parents ought not to doubt the election and salvation of their children whom God calls out of this life in infancy.

Article 18: The Proper Attitude Toward Election and Reprobation
To those who complain about this grace of an undeserved election and about the severity of a just reprobation, we reply with the words of the apostle, Who are you, O man, to talk back to God? (Rom. 9:20), and with the words of our Savior, Have I no right to do what I want with my own? (Matt. 20:15). We, however, with reverent adoration of these secret things, cry out with the apostle: Oh, the depths of the riches both of the wisdom and the knowledge of God! How unsearchable are His judgments, and His ways beyond tracing out! For who has known the mind of the Lord? Or who has been His counselor? Or who has first given to God, that God should repay him? For from Him and through Him and to Him are all things. To Him be the glory forever! Amen (Rom. 11:33-36).

Rejection of the Errors by Which the Dutch Churches Have for Some Time Been Disturbed

Having set forth the orthodox teaching concerning election and reprobation, the Synod rejects the errors of those

I. Who teach that the will of God to save those who would believe and persevere in faith and in the obedience of faith is the whole and entire decision of election to salvation, and that nothing else concerning this decision has been revealed in God's Word.

For they deceive the simple and plainly contradict Holy Scripture in its testimony that God does not only wish to save those who would believe, but that He has also from eternity chosen certain particular people to whom, rather than to others, He would within time grant faith in Christ and perseverance. As Scripture says, I have revealed your name to those whom you gave me (John 17:6). Likewise, All who were appointed for eternal life believed (Acts 13:48), and He chose us before the foundation of the world so that we should be holy... (Eph. 1:4).

II. Who teach that God's election to eternal life is of many kinds: one general and indefinite, the other particular and definite; and the latter in turn either incomplete, revocable, nonperemptory (or conditional), or else complete, irrevocable, and peremptory (or absolute). Likewise, who teach that there is one election to faith and another to salvation, so that there can be an election to justifying faith apart from a peremptory election to salvation.

For this is an invention of the human brain, devised apart from the Scriptures, which distorts the teaching concerning election and breaks up this golden chain of salvation: Those whom He predestined, He also called; and those whom He called, He also justified; and those whom He justified, He also glorified (Rom. 8:30).

III. Who teach that God's good pleasure and purpose, which Scripture mentions in its teaching of election, does not involve God's choosing certain particular people rather than others, but involves God's choosing, out of all possible conditions (including the works of the law) or out of the whole order of things, the intrinsically unworthy act of faith, as well as the imperfect obedience of faith, to be a condition of salvation; and it involves his graciously wishing to count this as perfect obedience and to look upon it as worthy of the reward of eternal life.

For by this pernicious error the good pleasure of God and the merit of Christ are robbed of their effectiveness and people are drawn away, by unprofitable inquiries, from the truth of undeserved justification and from the simplicity of the Scriptures. It also gives the lie to these words of the apostle: God called us with a holy calling, not in virtue of works, but in virtue of his own purpose and the grace which was given to us in Christ Jesus before the beginning of time (2 Tim. 1:9).

IV. Who teach that in election to faith a prerequisite condition is that man should rightly use the light of nature, be upright, unassuming, humble, and disposed to eternal life, as though election depended to some extent on these factors.

For this smacks of Pelagius, and it clearly calls into question the words of the apostle: We lived at one time in the passions of our flesh, following the will of our flesh and thoughts, and we were by nature children of wrath, like everyone else. But God, who is rich in mercy, out of the great love with which He loved us, even when we were dead in transgressions, made us alive with Christ, by whose grace you have been saved. And God raised us up with Him and seated us with Him in heaven in Christ Jesus, in order that in the coming ages we might show the surpassing riches of his grace, according to his kindness toward us in Christ Jesus. For it is by grace you have been saved, through faith (and this not from yourselves; it is the gift of God) not by works, so that no one can boast (Eph. 2:3-9).

V. Who teach that the incomplete and nonperemptory election of particular persons to salvation occurred on the basis of a foreseen faith, repentance, holiness, and godliness, which has just begun or continued for some time; but that complete and peremptory election occurred on the basis of a foreseen perseverance to the end in faith, repentance, holiness, and godliness. And that this is the gracious and evangelical worthiness, on account of which the one who is chosen is more worthy than the one who is not chosen. And therefore that faith, the obedience of faith, holiness, godliness, and perseverance are not fruits or effects of an unchangeable election to glory, but indispensable conditions and causes, which are prerequisite in those who are to be chosen in the complete election, and which are foreseen as achieved in them.

This runs counter to the entire Scripture, which throughout impresses upon our ears and hearts these sayings among others: Election is not by works, but by Him who calls (Rom. 9:11-12); All who were appointed for eternal life believed (Acts 13:48); He chose us in Himself so that we should be holy (Eph. 1:4); You did not choose me, but I chose you (John 15:16); If by grace, not by works (Rom. 11:6); In this is love, not that we loved God, but that He loved us and sent His Son (1 John 4:10).

VI. Who teach that not every election to salvation is unchangeable, but that some of the chosen can perish and do in fact perish eternally, with no decision of God to prevent it.

By this gross error they make God changeable, destroy the comfort of the godly concerning the steadfastness of their election, and contradict the Holy Scriptures, which teach that the elect cannot be led astray (Matt. 24:24), that Christ does not lose those given to Him by the Father (John 6:39), and that those whom God predestined, called, and justified, He also glorifies (Rom. 8:30).

VII. Who teach that in this life there is no fruit, no awareness, and no assurance of one's unchangeable election to glory, except as conditional upon something changeable and contingent.

For not only is it absurd to speak of an uncertain assurance, but these things also militate against the experience of the saints, who with the apostle rejoice from an awareness of their election and sing the praises of this gift of God; who, as Christ urged, rejoice with his disciples that their names have been written in heaven (Luke 10:20); and finally who hold up against the flaming arrows of the devil's temptations the awareness of their election, with the question Who will bring any charge against those whom God has chosen? (Rom. 8:33).

VIII. Who teach that it was not on the basis of His just will alone that God decided to leave anyone in the fall of Adam and in the common state of sin and condemnation or to pass anyone by in the imparting of grace necessary for faith and conversion.

For these words stand fast: He has mercy on whom He wishes, and He hardens whom He wishes (Rom. 9:18). And also: To you it has been given to know the secrets of the kingdom of heaven, but to them it has not been given (Matt. 13:11). Likewise: I give glory to you, Father, Lord of heaven and earth, that you have hidden these things from the wise and understanding, and have revealed them to little children; yes, Father, because that was your pleasure (Matt. 11:25-26).

IX. Who teach that the cause for God's sending the gospel to one people rather than to another is not merely and solely God's good pleasure, but rather that one people is better and worthier than the other to whom the gospel is not communicated.

For Moses contradicts this when he addresses the people of Israel as follows: Behold, to Jehovah your God belong the heavens and the highest heavens, the earth and whatever is in it. But Jehovah was inclined in his affection to love your ancestors alone, and chose out their descendants after them, you above all peoples, as at this day (Deut. 10:14-15). And also Christ: Woe to you, Korazin! Woe to you, Bethsaida! for if those mighty works done in you had been done in Tyre and Sidon, they would have repented long ago in sackcloth and ashes (Matt. 11:21).

THE SECOND MAIN POINT OF DOCTRINE

Christ's Death and Human Redemption Through It

Article 1: The Punishment Which God's Justice Requires
God is not only supremely merciful, but also supremely just. His justice requires (as he has revealed Himself in the Word) that the sins we have committed against His infinite majesty be punished with both temporal and eternal punishments, of soul as well as body. We cannot escape these punishments unless satisfaction is given to God's justice.

Article 2: The Satisfaction Made by Christ
Since, however, we ourselves cannot give this satisfaction or deliver ourselves from God's anger, God in His boundless mercy has given us as a guarantee His only begotten Son, who was made to be sin and a curse for us, in our place, on the cross, in order that he might give satisfaction for us.

Article 3: The Infinite Value of Christ's Death
This death of God's Son is the only and entirely complete sacrifice and satisfaction for sins; it is of infinite value and worth, more than sufficient to atone for the sins of the whole world.

Article 4: Reasons for This Infinite Value
This death is of such great value and worth for the reason that the person who suffered it is – as was necessary to be our Savior – not only a true and perfectly holy man, but also the only begotten Son of God, of the same eternal and infinite essence with the Father and the Holy Spirit. Another reason is that this death was accompanied by the experience of God's anger and curse, which we by our sins had fully deserved.

Article 5: The Mandate to Proclaim the Gospel to All
Moreover, it is the promise of the gospel that whoever believes in Christ crucified shall not perish but have eternal life. This promise, together with the command to repent and believe, ought to be announced and declared without differentiation or discrimination to all nations and people, to whom God in His good pleasure sends the gospel.

Article 6: Unbelief Man's Responsibility
However, that many who have been called through the gospel do not repent or believe in Christ but perish in unbelief is not because the sacrifice of Christ offered on the cross is deficient or insufficient, but because they themselves are at fault.

Article 7: Faith God's Gift
But all who genuinely believe and are delivered and saved by Christ's death from their sins and from destruction receive this favor solely from God's grace – which He owes to no one – given to them in Christ from eternity.

Article 8: The Saving Effectiveness of Christ's Death
For it was the entirely free plan and very gracious will and intention of God the Father that the enlivening and saving effectiveness of His Son's costly death should work itself out in all His chosen ones, in order that He might grant justifying faith to them only and thereby lead them without fail to salvation.

In other words, it was God's will that Christ through the blood of the cross (by which He confirmed the new covenant) should effectively redeem from every people, tribe, nation, and language all those and only those who were chosen from eternity to salvation and given to Him by the Father; that He should grant them faith (which, like the Holy Spirit's other saving gifts, He acquired for them by His death); that He should cleanse them by His blood from all their sins, both original and actual, whether committed before or after their coming to faith; that He should faithfully preserve them to the very end; and that He should finally present them to Himself, a glorious people, without spot or wrinkle.

Article 9: The Fulfillment of God's Plan
This plan, arising out of God's eternal love for His chosen ones, from the beginning of the world to the present time has been powerfully carried out and will also be carried out in the future, the gates of hell seeking vainly to prevail against it. As a result the chosen are gathered into one, all in their own time, and there is always a church of believers founded on Christ's blood, a church which steadfastly loves, persistently worships, and – here and in all eternity – praises Him as her Savior who laid down His life for her on the cross, as a bridegroom for his bride.

Rejection of the Errors

Having set forth the orthodox teaching, the Synod rejects the errors of those

I. Who teach that God the Father appointed His Son to death on the cross without a fixed and definite plan to save anyone by name, so that the necessity, usefulness, and worth of what Christ's death obtained could have stood intact and altogether perfect, complete and whole, even if the redemption that was obtained had never in actual fact been applied to any individual.

For this assertion is an insult to the wisdom of God the Father and to the merit of Jesus Christ, and it is contrary to Scripture. For the Savior speaks as follows: I lay down my life for the sheep, and I know them (John 10:15, 27). And Isaiah the prophet says concerning the Savior: When He shall make Himself an offering for sin, He shall see His offspring, He shall prolong His days, and the will of Jehovah shall prosper in His hand (Isa. 53:10). Finally, this undermines the article of the creed in which we confess what we believe concerning the Church.

II. Who teach that the purpose of Christ's death was not to establish in actual fact a new covenant of grace by His blood, but only to acquire for the Father the mere right to enter once more into a covenant with men, whether of grace or of works.

For this conflicts with Scripture, which teaches that Christ has become the guarantee and mediator of a better – that is, a new – covenant (Heb. 7:22; 9:15), and that a will is in force only when someone has died (Heb. 9:17).

III. Who teach that Christ, by the satisfaction which He gave, did not certainly merit for anyone salvation itself and the faith by which this satisfaction of Christ is effectively applied to salvation, but only acquired for the Father the authority or plenary will to relate in a new way with men and to impose such new conditions as He chose, and that the satisfying of these conditions depends on the free choice of man; consequently, that it was possible that either all or none would fulfill them.

For they have too low an opinion of the death of Christ, do not at all acknowledge the foremost fruit or benefit which it brings forth, and summon back from hell the Pelagian error.

IV. Who teach that what is involved in the new covenant of grace which God the Father made with men through the intervening of Christ's death is not that we are justified before God and saved through faith, insofar as it accepts Christ's merit, but rather that God, having withdrawn His demand for perfect obedience to the law, counts faith itself, and the imperfect obedience of faith, as perfect obedience to the law, and graciously looks upon this as worthy of the reward of eternal life.

For they contradict Scripture: They are justified freely by His grace through the redemption that came by Jesus Christ, whom God presented as a sacrifice of atonement, through faith in His blood (Rom. 3:24-25). And along with the ungodly Socinus, they introduce a new and foreign justification of man before God, against the consensus of the whole church.

V. Who teach that all people have been received into the state of reconciliation and into the grace of the covenant, so that no one on account of original sin is liable to condemnation, or is to be condemned, but that all are free from the guilt of this sin.

For this opinion conflicts with Scripture which asserts that we are by nature children of wrath.

VI. Who make use of the distinction between obtaining and applying in order to instill in the unwary and inexperienced the opinion that God, as far as He is concerned, wished to bestow equally upon all people the benefits which are gained by Christ's death; but that the distinction by which some rather than others come to share in the forgiveness of sins and eternal life depends on their own free choice (which applies itself to the grace offered indiscriminately) but does not depend on the unique gift of mercy which effectively works in them, so that they, rather than others, apply that grace to themselves.

For, while pretending to set forth this distinction in an acceptable sense, they attempt to give the people the deadly poison of Pelagianism.

VII. Who teach that Christ neither could die, nor had to die, nor did die for those whom God so dearly loved and chose to eternal life, since such people do not need the death of Christ.

For they contradict the apostle, who says: Christ loved me and gave Himself up for me (Gal. 2:20), and likewise: Who will bring any charge against those whom God has chosen? It is God who justifies. Who is he that condemns? It is Christ who died, that is, for them (Rom. 8:33-34). They also contradict the Savior, who asserts: I lay down my life for the sheep (John 10:15), and My command is this: Love one another as I have loved you. Greater love has no one than this, that one lay down his life for his friends (John 15:12-13).

THE THIRD AND FOURTH MAIN POINTS OF DOCTRINE

Human Corruption, Conversion to God, and the Way It Occurs

Article 1: The Effect of the Fall on Human Nature

Man was originally created in the image of God and was furnished in his mind with a true and salutary knowledge of his Creator and things spiritual, in his will and heart with righteousness, and in all his emotions with purity; indeed, the whole man was holy. However, rebelling against God at the devil's instigation and by his own free will, he deprived himself of these outstanding gifts. Rather, in their place he brought upon himself blindness, terrible darkness, futility, and distortion of judgment in his mind; perversity, defiance, and hardness in his heart and will; and finally impurity in all his emotions.

Article 2: The Spread of Corruption

Man brought forth children of the same nature as himself after the fall. That is to say, being corrupt he brought forth corrupt children. The corruption spread, by God's just judgment, from Adam to all his descendants – except for Christ alone – not by way of imitation (as in former times the Pelagians would have it) but by way of the propagation of his perverted nature.

Article 3: Total Inability

Therefore, all people are conceived in sin and are born children of wrath, unfit for any saving good, inclined to evil, dead in their sins, and slaves to sin; without the grace of the regenerating Holy Spirit they are neither willing nor able to return to God, to reform their distorted nature, or even to dispose themselves to such reform.

Article 4: The Inadequacy of the Light of Nature

There is, to be sure, a certain light of nature remaining in man after the fall, by virtue of which he retains some notions about God, natural things, and the difference between what is moral and immoral, and demonstrates a certain eagerness for virtue and for good outward behavior. But this light of nature is far from enabling man to come to a saving knowledge of God and conversion to Him – so far, in fact, that man does not use it rightly even in matters of nature and society. Instead, in various ways he completely distorts this light, whatever its precise character, and suppresses it in unrighteousness. In doing so he renders himself without excuse before God.

Article 5: The Inadequacy of the Law
In this respect, what is true of the light of nature is true also of the Ten Commandments given by God through Moses specifically to the Jews. For man cannot obtain saving grace through the Decalogue, because, although it does expose the magnitude of his sin and increasingly convict him of his guilt, yet it does not offer a remedy or enable him to escape from his misery, and, indeed, weakened as it is by the flesh, leaves the offender under the curse.

Article 6: The Saving Power of the Gospel
What, therefore, neither the light of nature nor the law can do, God accomplishes by the power of the Holy Spirit, through the Word or the ministry of reconciliation. This is the gospel about the Messiah, through which it has pleased God to save believers, in both the Old and the New Testament.

Article 7: God's Freedom in Revealing the Gospel
In the Old Testament, God revealed this secret of His will to a small number; in the New Testament (now without any distinction between peoples) he discloses it to a large number. The reason for this difference must not be ascribed to the greater worth of one nation over another, or to a better use of the light of nature, but to the free good pleasure and undeserved love of God. Therefore, those who receive so much grace, beyond and in spite of all they deserve, ought to acknowledge it with humble and thankful hearts; on the other hand, with the apostle they ought to adore (but certainly not inquisitively search into) the severity and justice of God's judgments on the others, who do not receive this grace.

Article 8: The Serious Call of the Gospel
Nevertheless, all who are called through the gospel are called seriously. For seriously and most genuinely God makes known in His Word what is pleasing to Him: that those who are called should come to Him. Seriously he also promises rest for their souls and eternal life to all who come to Him and believe.

Article 9: Human Responsibility for Rejecting the Gospel
The fact that many who are called through the ministry of the gospel do not come and are not brought to conversion must not be blamed on the gospel, nor on Christ, who is offered through the gospel, nor on God, who calls them through the gospel and even bestows various gifts on them, but on the people themselves who are called. Some in self-assurance do not even entertain the Word of life; others do entertain it but do not take it to heart, and for that reason, after the fleeting joy of a temporary faith, they relapse; others choke the seed of the Word with the thorns of life's cares and with the pleasures of the world and bring forth no fruits. This our Savior teaches in the parable of the sower (Matt. 13).

Article 10: Conversion as the Work of God
The fact that others who are called through the ministry of the gospel do come and are brought to conversion must not be credited to man, as though one distinguishes himself by free choice from others who are furnished with equal or sufficient grace for faith and conversion (as the proud heresy of Pelagius maintains). No, it must be credited to God: just as from eternity he chose his own in Christ, so within time he effectively calls them, grants them faith and repentance, and, having rescued them from the dominion of darkness, brings them into the kingdom of His Son, in order that they may declare the wonderful deeds of Him who called them out of darkness into this marvelous light, and may boast not in themselves, but in the Lord, as apostolic words frequently testify in Scripture.

Article 11: The Holy Spirit's Work in Conversion
Moreover, when God carries out this good pleasure in His chosen ones, or works true conversion in them, he not only sees to it that the gospel is proclaimed to them outwardly, and enlightens their minds powerfully by the Holy Spirit so that they may rightly understand and discern the things

of the Spirit of God, but, by the effective operation of the same regenerating Spirit, he also penetrates into the inmost being of man, opens the closed heart, softens the hard heart, and circumcises the heart that is uncircumcised. He infuses new qualities into the will, making the dead will alive, the evil one good, the unwilling one willing, and the stubborn one compliant; he activates and strengthens the will so that, like a good tree, it may be enabled to produce the fruits of good deeds.

Article 12: Regeneration a Supernatural Work
And this is the regeneration, the new creation, the raising from the dead, and the making alive so clearly proclaimed in the Scriptures, which God works in us without our help. But this certainly does not happen only by outward teaching, by moral persuasion, or by such a way of working that, after God has done His work, it remains in man's power whether or not to be reborn or converted. Rather, it is an entirely supernatural work, one that is at the same time most powerful and most pleasing, a marvelous, hidden, and inexpressible work, which is not lesser than or inferior in power to that of creation or of raising the dead, as Scripture (inspired by the author of this work) teaches. As a result, all those in whose hearts God works in this marvelous way are certainly, unfailingly, and effectively reborn and do actually believe. And then the will, now renewed, is not only activated and motivated by God but in being activated by God is also itself active. For this reason, man himself, by that grace which he has received, is also rightly said to believe and to repent.

Article 13: The Incomprehensible Way of Regeneration
In this life believers cannot fully understand the way this work occurs; meanwhile, they rest content with knowing and experiencing that by this grace of God they do believe with the heart and love their Savior.

Article 14: The Way God Gives Faith
In this way, therefore, faith is a gift of God, not in the sense that it is offered by God for man to choose, but that it is in actual fact bestowed on man, breathed and infused into him. Nor is it a gift in the sense that God bestows only the potential to believe, but then awaits assent – the act of believing – from man's choice; rather, it is a gift in the sense that he who works both willing and acting and, indeed, works all things in all people produces in man both the will to believe and the belief itself.

Article 15: Responses to God's Grace
God does not owe this grace to anyone. For what could God owe to one who has nothing to give that can be paid back? Indeed, what could God owe to one who has nothing of his own to give but sin and falsehood? Therefore the person who receives this grace owes and gives eternal thanks to God alone; the person who does not receive it either does not care at all about these spiritual things and is satisfied with himself in his condition, or else in self-assurance foolishly boasts about having something which he lacks. Furthermore, following the example of the apostles, we are to think and to speak in the most favorable way about those who outwardly profess their faith and better their lives, for the inner chambers of the heart are unknown to us. But for others who have not yet been called, we are to pray to the God who calls things that do not exist as though they did. In no way, however, are we to pride ourselves as better than they, as though we had distinguished ourselves from them.

Article 16: Regeneration's Effect
However, just as by the fall man did not cease to be man, endowed with intellect and will, and just as sin, which has spread through the whole human race, did not abolish the nature of the human race but distorted and spiritually killed it, so also this divine grace of regeneration does not act in people as if they were blocks and stones; nor does it abolish the will and its properties or coerce a reluctant will by force, but spiritually revives, heals, reforms, and – in a manner at once pleasing and powerful – bends it back. As a result, a ready and sincere obedience of the Spirit

now begins to prevail where before the rebellion and resistance of the flesh were completely dominant. It is in this that the true and spiritual restoration and freedom of our will consists. Thus, if the marvelous Maker of every good thing were not dealing with us, man would have no hope of getting up from his fall by his free choice, by which he plunged himself into ruin when still standing upright.

Article 17: God's Use of Means in Regeneration

Just as the almighty work of God by which he brings forth and sustains our natural life does not rule out but requires the use of means, by which God, according to his infinite wisdom and goodness, has wished to exercise his power, so also the aforementioned supernatural work of God by which he regenerates us in no way rules out or cancels the use of the gospel, which God in his great wisdom has appointed to be the seed of regeneration and the food of the soul. For this reason, the apostles and the teachers who followed them taught the people in a godly manner about this grace of God, to give Him the glory and to humble all pride, and yet did not neglect meanwhile to keep the people, by means of the holy admonitions of the gospel, under the administration of the Word, the sacraments, and discipline. So even today it is out of the question that the teachers or those taught in the church should presume to test God by separating what he in his good pleasure has wished to be closely joined together. For grace is bestowed through admonitions, and the more readily we perform our duty, the more lustrous the benefit of God working in us usually is and the better His work advances. To Him alone, both for the means and for their saving fruit and effectiveness, all glory is owed forever. Amen.

Rejection of the Errors

Having set forth the orthodox teaching, the Synod rejects the errors of those

I. Who teach that, properly speaking, it cannot be said that original sin in itself is enough to condemn the whole human race or to warrant temporal and eternal punishments.

For they contradict the apostle when he says: Sin entered the world through one man, and death through sin, and in this way death passed on to all men because all sinned (Rom. 5:12); also: The guilt followed one sin and brought condemnation (Rom. 5:16); likewise: The wages of sin is death (Rom. 6:23).

II. Who teach that the spiritual gifts or the good dispositions and virtues such as goodness, holiness, and righteousness could not have resided in man's will when he was first created, and therefore could not have been separated from the will at the fall.

For this conflicts with the apostle's description of the image of God in Eph. 4:24, where he portrays the image in terms of righteousness and holiness, which definitely reside in the will.

III. Who teach that in spiritual death the spiritual gifts have not been separated from man's will, since the will in itself has never been corrupted but only hindered by the darkness of the mind and the unruliness of the emotions, and since the will is able to exercise its innate free capacity once these hindrances are removed, which is to say, it is able of itself to will or choose whatever good is set before it – or else not to will or choose it.

This is a novel idea and an error and has the effect of elevating the power of free choice, contrary to the words of Jeremiah the prophet: The heart itself is deceitful above all things and wicked (Jer. 17:9); and of the words of the apostle: All of us also lived among them (the sons of disobedience) at one time in the passions of our flesh, following the will of our flesh and thoughts (Eph. 2:3).

IV. Who teach that unregenerate man is not strictly or totally dead in his sins or deprived of all capacity for spiritual good but is able to hunger and thirst for righteousness or life and to offer the sacrifice of a broken and contrite spirit which is pleasing to God.

For these views are opposed to the plain testimonies of Scripture: You were dead in your transgressions and sins (Eph. 2:1, 5); The imagination of the thoughts of man's heart is only evil all the time (Gen. 6:5; 8:21). Besides, to hunger and thirst for deliverance from misery and for life, and to offer God the sacrifice of a broken spirit is characteristic only of the regenerate and of those called blessed (Ps. 51:17; Matt. 5:6).

V. Who teach that corrupt and natural man can make such good use of common grace (by which they mean the light of nature) or of the gifts remaining after the fall that he is able thereby gradually to obtain a greater grace – evangelical or saving grace – as well as salvation itself; and that in this way God, for His part, shows Himself ready to reveal Christ to all people, since he provides to all, to a sufficient extent and in an effective manner, the means necessary for the revealing of Christ, for faith, and for repentance.

For Scripture, not to mention the experience of all ages, testifies that this is false: He makes known His words to Jacob, His statutes and His laws to Israel; he has done this for no other nation, and they do not know His laws (Ps. 147:19-20); In the past God let all nations go their own way (Acts 14:16); They (Paul and his companions) were kept by the Holy Spirit from speaking God's word in Asia; and When they had come to Mysia, they tried to go to Bithynia, but the Spirit would not allow them to (Acts 16:6-7).

VI. Who teach that in the true conversion of man new qualities, dispositions, or gifts cannot be infused or poured into his will by God, and indeed that the faith or believing by which we first come to conversion and from which we receive the name "believers" is not a quality or gift infused by God, but only an act of man, and that it cannot be called a gift except in respect to the power of attaining faith.

For these views contradict the Holy Scriptures, which testify that God does infuse or pour into our hearts the new qualities of faith, obedience, and the experiencing of His love: I will put my law in their minds, and write it on their hearts (Jer. 31:33); I will pour water on the thirsty land, and streams on the dry ground; I will pour out my Spirit on your offspring (Isa. 44:3); The love of God has been poured out in our hearts by the Holy Spirit, who has been given to us (Rom. 5:5). They also conflict with the continuous practice of the Church, which prays with the prophet: Convert me, Lord, and I shall be converted (Jer. 31:18).

VII. Who teach that the grace by which we are converted to God is nothing but a gentle persuasion, or (as others explain it) that the way of God's acting in man's conversion that is most noble and suited to human nature is that which happens by persuasion, and that nothing prevents this grace of moral suasion even by itself from making natural men spiritual; indeed, that God does not produce the assent of the will except in this manner of moral suasion, and that the effectiveness of God's work by which it surpasses the work of Satan consists in the fact that God promises eternal benefits while Satan promises temporal ones.

For this teaching is entirely Pelagian and contrary to the whole of Scripture, which recognizes besides this persuasion also another, far more effective and divine way in which the Holy Spirit acts in man's conversion. As Ezek. 36:26 puts it: I will give you a new heart and put a new spirit in you; and I will remove your heart of stone and give you a heart of flesh....

VIII. Who teach that God in regenerating man does not bring to bear that power of His omnipotence whereby he may powerfully and unfailingly bend man's will to faith and conversion, but that even when God has accomplished all the works of grace which he uses for man's conversion, man nevertheless can, and in actual fact often does, so resist God and the Spirit in their intent and will to regenerate him, that man completely thwarts his own rebirth; and, indeed, that it remains in his own power whether or not to be reborn.

For this does away with all effective functioning of God's grace in our conversion and subjects the activity of Almighty God to the will of man; it is contrary to the apostles, who teach that we believe by virtue of the effective working of God's mighty strength (Eph. 1:19), and that God fulfills the undeserved good will of His kindness and the work of faith in us with power (2 Thess. 1:11), and likewise that His divine power has given us everything we need for life and godliness (2 Peter 1:3).

IX. Who teach that grace and free choice are concurrent partial causes which cooperate to initiate conversion, and that grace does not precede – in the order of causality – the effective influence of the will; that is to say, that God does not effectively help man's will to come to conversion before man's will itself motivates and determines itself.

For the early church already condemned this doctrine long ago in the Pelagians, on the basis of the words of the apostle: It does not depend on man's willing or running but on God's mercy (Rom. 9:16); also: Who makes you different from anyone else? and What do you have that you did not receive? (1 Cor. 4:7); likewise: It is God who works in you to will and act according to His good pleasure (Phil. 2:13).

THE FIFTH MAIN POINT OF DOCTRINE

The Perseverance of the Saints

Article 1: The Regenerate Not Entirely Free from Sin

Those people whom God according to His purpose calls into fellowship with His Son Jesus Christ our Lord and regenerates by the Holy Spirit, he also sets free from the reign and slavery of sin, though in this life not entirely from the flesh and from the body of sin.

Article 2: The Believer's Reaction to Sins of Weakness

Hence daily sins of weakness arise, and blemishes cling to even the best works of God's people, giving them continual cause to humble themselves before God, to flee for refuge to Christ crucified, to put the flesh to death more and more by the Spirit of supplication and by holy exercises of godliness, and to strain toward the goal of perfection, until they are freed from this body of death and reign with the Lamb of God in heaven.

Article 3: God's Preservation of the Converted

Because of these remnants of sin dwelling in them and also because of the temptations of the world and Satan, those who have been converted could not remain standing in this grace if left to their own resources. But God is faithful, mercifully strengthening them in the grace once conferred on them and powerfully preserving them in it to the end.

Article 4: The Danger of True Believers' Falling into Serious Sins

Although that power of God strengthening and preserving true believers in grace is more than a match for the flesh, yet those converted are not always so activated and motivated by God that in certain specific actions they cannot by their own fault depart from the leading of grace, be led astray by the desires of the flesh, and give in to them. For this reason they must constantly watch and pray that they may not be led into temptations. When they fail to do this, not only can they be carried away by the flesh, the world, and Satan into sins, even serious and outrageous ones, but also by God's just permission they sometimes are so carried away – witness the sad cases, described in Scripture, of David, Peter, and other saints falling into sins.

Article 5: The Effects of Such Serious Sins

By such monstrous sins, however, they greatly offend God, deserve the sentence of death, grieve the Holy Spirit, suspend the exercise of faith, severely wound the conscience, and sometimes lose the awareness of grace for a time – until, after they have returned to the way by genuine repentance, God's fatherly face again shines upon them.

Article 6: God's Saving Intervention

For God, who is rich in mercy, according to his unchangeable purpose of election does not take his Holy Spirit from his own completely, even when they fall grievously. Neither does he let them fall down so far that they forfeit the grace of adoption and the state of justification, or commit the sin which leads to death (the sin against the Holy Spirit), and plunge themselves, entirely forsaken by Him, into eternal ruin.

Article 7: Renewal to Repentance

For, in the first place, God preserves in those saints when they fall his imperishable seed from which they have been born again, lest it perish or be dislodged. Secondly, by His Word and Spirit he certainly and effectively renews them to repentance so that they have a heartfelt and godly sorrow for the sins they have committed; seek and obtain, through faith and with a contrite heart, forgiveness in the blood of the Mediator; experience again the grace of a reconciled God; through faith adore His mercies; and from then on more eagerly work out their own salvation with fear and trembling.

Article 8: The Certainty of This Preservation

So it is not by their own merits or strength but by God's undeserved mercy that they neither forfeit faith and grace totally nor remain in their downfalls to the end and are lost. With respect to themselves this not only easily could happen, but also undoubtedly would happen; but with respect to God it cannot possibly happen, since His plan cannot be changed, His promise cannot fail, the calling according to His purpose cannot be revoked, the merit of Christ as well as His interceding and preserving cannot be nullified, and the sealing of the Holy Spirit can neither be invalidated nor wiped out.

Article 9: The Assurance of This Preservation

Concerning this preservation of those chosen to salvation and concerning the perseverance of true believers in faith, believers themselves can and do become assured in accordance with the measure of their faith, by which they firmly believe that they are and always will remain true and living members of the church, and that they have the forgiveness of sins and eternal life.

Article 10: The Ground of This Assurance

Accordingly, this assurance does not derive from some private revelation beyond or outside the Word, but from faith in the promises of God which he has very plentifully revealed in His Word for our comfort, from the testimony of the Holy Spirit testifying with our spirit that we are God's children and heirs (Rom. 8:16-17), and finally from a serious and holy pursuit of a clear conscience and of good works. And if God's chosen ones in this world did not have this well-founded comfort that the victory will be theirs and this reliable guarantee of eternal glory, they would be of all people most miserable.

Article 11: Doubts Concerning This Assurance

Meanwhile, Scripture testifies that believers have to contend in this life with various doubts of the flesh and that under severe temptation they do not always experience this full assurance of faith and certainty of perseverance. But God, the Father of all comfort, does not let them be tempted beyond what they can bear, but with the temptation he also provides a way out (1 Cor. 10:13), and by the Holy Spirit revives in them the assurance of their perseverance.

Article 12: This Assurance as an Incentive to Godliness

This assurance of perseverance, however, so far from making true believers proud and carnally self-assured, is rather the true root of humility, of childlike respect, of genuine godliness, of endurance in every conflict, of fervent prayers, of steadfastness in crossbearing and in confessing the truth, and of well-founded joy in God. Reflecting on this benefit provides an incentive to a serious and continual practice of thanksgiving and good works, as is evident from the testimonies of Scripture and the examples of the saints.

Article 13: Assurance No Inducement to Carelessness

Neither does the renewed confidence of perseverance produce immorality or lack of concern for godliness in those put back on their feet after a fall, but it produces a much greater concern to observe carefully the ways of the Lord which he prepared in advance. They observe these ways in order that by walking in them they may maintain the assurance of their perseverance, lest, by their abuse of his fatherly goodness, the face of the gracious God (for the godly, looking upon his face is sweeter than life, but its withdrawal is more bitter than death) turn away from them again, with the result that they fall into greater anguish of spirit.

Article 14: God's Use of Means in Perseverance

And, just as it has pleased God to begin this work of grace in us by the proclamation of the gospel, so he preserves, continues, and completes His work by the hearing and reading of the gospel, by meditation on it, by its exhortations, threats, and promises, and also by the use of the sacraments.

Article 15: Contrasting Reactions to the Teaching of Perseverance
This teaching about the perseverance of true believers and saints, and about their assurance of it – a teaching which God has very richly revealed in His Word for the glory of His name and for the comfort of the godly and which he impresses on the hearts of believers – is something which the flesh does not understand, Satan hates, the world ridicules, the ignorant and the hypocrites abuse, and the spirits of error attack. The bride of Christ, on the other hand, has always loved this teaching very tenderly and defended it steadfastly as a priceless treasure; and God, against whom no plan can avail and no strength can prevail, will ensure that she will continue to do this. To this God alone, Father, Son, and Holy Spirit, be honor and glory forever. Amen.

Rejection of the Errors

Concerning the Teaching of the Perseverance of the Saints

Having set forth the orthodox teaching, the Synod rejects the errors of those

I. Who teach that the perseverance of true believers is not an effect of election or a gift of God produced by Christ's death, but a condition of the new covenant which man, before what they call his "peremptory" election and justification, must fulfill by his free will.

For Holy Scripture testifies that perseverance follows from election and is granted to the chosen by virtue of Christ's death, resurrection, and intercession: The chosen obtained it; the others were hardened (Rom. 11:7); likewise, He who did not spare His own son, but gave Him up for us all – how will he not, along with Him, grant us all things? Who will bring any charge against those whom God has chosen? It is God who justifies. Who is he that condemns? It is Christ Jesus who died – more than that, who was raised – who also sits at the right hand of God, and is also interceding for us. Who shall separate us from the love of Christ? (Rom. 8:32-35).

II. Who teach that God does provide the believer with sufficient strength to persevere and is ready to preserve this strength in him if he performs his duty, but that even with all those things in place which are necessary to persevere in faith and which God is pleased to use to preserve faith, it still always depends on the choice of man's will whether or not he perseveres.

For this view is obviously Pelagian; and though it intends to make men free it makes them sacrilegious. It is against the enduring consensus of evangelical teaching which takes from man all cause for boasting and ascribes the praise for this benefit only to God's grace. It is also against the testimony of the apostle: It is God who keeps us strong to the end, so that we will be blameless on the day of our Lord Jesus Christ (1 Cor. 1:8).

III. Who teach that those who truly believe and have been born again not only can forfeit justifying faith as well as grace and salvation totally and to the end, but also in actual fact do often forfeit them and are lost forever.

For this opinion nullifies the very grace of justification and regeneration as well as the continual preservation by Christ, contrary to the plain words of the apostle Paul: If Christ died for us while we were still sinners, we will therefore much more be saved from God's wrath through Him, since we have now been justified by His blood (Rom. 5:8-9); and contrary to the apostle John: No one who is born of God is intent on sin, because God's seed remains in him, nor can he sin, because he has been born of God (1 John 3:9); also contrary to the words of Jesus Christ: I give eternal life to my sheep, and they shall never perish; no one can snatch them out of my hand. My Father, who has given them to me, is greater than all; no one can snatch them out of my Father's hand (John 10: 28-29).

IV. Who teach that those who truly believe and have been born again can commit the sin that leads to death (the sin against the Holy Spirit).

For the same apostle John, after making mention of those who commit the sin that leads to death and forbidding prayer for them (I John 5: 16-17), immediately adds: We know that anyone born of God does not commit sin (that is, that kind of sin), but the one who was born of God keeps himself safe, and the evil one does not touch him (v. 18).

V. Who teach that apart from a special revelation no one can have the assurance of future perseverance in this life.

For by this teaching the well-founded consolation of true believers in this life is taken away and the doubting of the Romanists is reintroduced into the church. Holy Scripture, however, in many places derives the assurance not from a special and extraordinary revelation but from the marks peculiar to God's children and from God's completely reliable promises. So especially the apostle Paul: Nothing in all creation can separate us from the love of God that is in Christ Jesus our Lord (Rom. 8:39); and John: They who obey His commands remain in Him and he in them. And this is how we know that he remains in us: by the Spirit he gave us (I John 3:24).

VI. Who teach that the teaching of the assurance of perseverance and of salvation is by its very nature and character an opiate of the flesh and is harmful to godliness, good morals, prayer, and other holy exercises, but that, on the contrary, to have doubt about this is praiseworthy.

For these people show that they do not know the effective operation of God's grace and the work of the indwelling Holy Spirit, and they contradict the apostle John, who asserts the opposite in plain words: Dear friends, now we are children of God, but what we will be has not yet been made known. But we know that when he is made known, we shall be like Him, for we shall see Him as he is. Everyone who has this hope in Him purifies himself, just as he is pure (I John 3:2-3). Moreover, they are refuted by the examples of the saints in both the Old and the New Testament, who though assured of their perseverance and salvation yet were constant in prayer and other exercises of godliness.

VII. Who teach that the faith of those who believe only temporarily does not differ from justifying and saving faith except in duration alone.

For Christ Himself in Matt. 13:20ff. and Luke 8:13ff. clearly defines these further differences between temporary and true believers: he says that the former receive the seed on rocky ground, and the latter receive it in good ground, or a good heart; the former have no root, and the latter are firmly rooted; the former have no fruit, and the latter produce fruit in varying measure, with steadfastness, or perseverance.

VIII. Who teach that it is not absurd that a person, after losing his former regeneration, should once again, indeed quite often, be reborn.

For by this teaching they deny the imperishable nature of God's seed by which we are born again, contrary to the testimony of the apostle Peter: Born again, not of perishable seed, but of imperishable (I Peter 1:23).

IX. Who teach that Christ nowhere prayed for an unfailing perseverance of believers in faith.

For they contradict Christ Himself when he says: I have prayed for you, Peter, that your faith may not fail (Luke 22:32); and John the gospel writer when he testifies in John 17 that it was not only for the apostles, but also for all those who were to believe by their message that Christ prayed: Holy Father, preserve them in your name (v. 11); and My prayer is not that you take them out of the world, but that you preserve them from the evil one (v. 15).

CONCLUSION

Rejection of False Accusations

And so this is the clear, simple, and straightforward explanation of the orthodox teaching on the five articles in dispute in the Netherlands, as well as the rejection of the errors by which the Dutch churches have for some time been disturbed. This explanation and rejection the Synod declares to be derived from God's Word and in agreement with the confessions of the Reformed churches. Hence it clearly appears that those of whom one could hardly expect it have shown no truth, equity, and charity at all in wishing to make the public believe:

– that the teaching of the Reformed churches on predestination and on the points associated with it by its very nature and tendency draws the minds of people away from all godliness and religion, is an opiate of the flesh and the devil, and is a stronghold of Satan where he lies in wait for all people, wounds most of them, and fatally pierces many of them with the arrows of both despair and self-assurance;

– that this teaching makes God the author of sin, unjust, a tyrant, and a hypocrite; and is nothing but a refurbished Stoicism, Manicheism, Libertinism, and Mohammedanism;

– that this teaching makes people carnally self-assured, since it persuades them that nothing endangers the salvation of the chosen, no matter how they live, so that they may commit the most outrageous crimes with self-assurance; and that on the other hand nothing is of use to the reprobate for salvation even if they have truly performed all the works of the saints;

– that this teaching means that God predestined and created, by the bare and unqualified choice of His will, without the least regard or consideration of any sin, the greatest part of the world to eternal condemnation; that in the same manner in which election is the source and cause of faith and good works, reprobation is the cause of unbelief and ungodliness; that many infant children of believers are snatched in their innocence from their mothers' breasts and cruelly cast into hell so that neither the blood of Christ nor their baptism nor the prayers of the church at their baptism can be of any use to them; and very many other slanderous accusations of this kind which the Reformed churches not only disavow but even denounce with their whole heart.

Therefore this Synod of Dordt in the name of the Lord pleads with all who devoutly call on the name of our Savior Jesus Christ to form their judgment about the faith of the Reformed churches, not on the basis of false accusations gathered from here or there, or even on the basis of the personal statements of a number of ancient and modern authorities – statements which are also often either quoted out of context or misquoted and twisted to convey a different meaning – but on the basis of the churches' own official confessions and of the present explanation of the orthodox teaching which has been endorsed by the unanimous consent of the members of the whole Synod, one and all.

Moreover, the Synod earnestly warns the false accusers themselves to consider how heavy a judgment of God awaits those who give false testimony against so many churches and their confessions, trouble the consciences of the weak, and seek to prejudice the minds of many against the fellowship of true believers.

Finally, this Synod urges all fellow ministers in the gospel of Christ to deal with this teaching in a godly and reverent manner, in the academic institutions as well as in the churches; to do so, both in their speaking and writing, with a view to the glory of God's name, holiness of life, and the comfort of anxious souls; to think and also speak with Scripture according to the analogy of faith; and, finally, to refrain from all those ways of speaking which go beyond the bounds set for us by the genuine sense of the Holy Scriptures and which could give impertinent sophists a just occasion to scoff at the teaching of the Reformed churches or even to bring false accusations against it.

May God's Son Jesus Christ, who sits at the right hand of God and gives gifts to men, sanctify us in the truth, lead to the truth those who err, silence the mouths of those who lay false accusations against sound teaching, and equip faithful ministers of his Word with a spirit of wisdom and discretion, that all they say may be to the glory of God and the building up of their hearers. Amen.

APPENDIX 7

PERSONAL INFORMATION SHEET*

Name:______________________________ Phone:____________________

Address: ____

____

Children's names and dates of birth:

Husband:____________________	Wife:________________________
Date of Birth __/__/ Home State:___	Date of Birth __/__/ Home State:___
Occupation:____________________	Occupation:____________________
Education Background:__________	Education Background:__________
Other Business Experience:	Other Business Experience:
Hobbies or Other Interests:	Hobbies or Other Interests:
Previous Church Affiliation:_______	Previous Church Affiliation:_______

The above information is requested so that we may each get to know one another better and draw on our individual talents. Please fill out those portions where you would like to share pertinent information.

SPECIAL INTERESTS AND TRAINING

Please indicate those areas of former service and/or present interest where you have been or may be useful to Christ and His Church:

CHURCH

___ Usher
___ Finance & Administration
___ Christian Education Committee
___ Evangelism & Missions Committee
___ Worship & Church Life Committee
___ Property Committee
___ Mercy & Service Committee
___ Other Activities (__________)

CHURCH SCHOOL

___ Attendance
___ Administrative Officer
___ Worship Leader
___ Children's Work
___ Teacher or Other Leader
  ___ Of Children
  ___ Of Youth
  ___ Of Adults
  ___ Of Special Children

OTHER ACTIVITIES

___ Women in Church
___ Men of the Church
___ Older Adult
___ Young Adult
___ Youth Work
___ Pianist
___ Weekday Bible School
___ Vacation Bible School
___ Scouting
___ Outpost Sunday School
___ Personal Evangelism

MUSIC

___ Choir
___ Solo
___ Instrument
___ Leading (__________________)

SERVICES

___ Typing
___ Mimeographing
___ Publicity
___ Telephoning
___ Corresponding
___ Waiting Tables
___ Cooking
___ Nursing
___ Visiting
___ Social Work
___ Using Car
___ Hospitality
___ Other (__________________)

HOBBIES

___ Recreation
___ Folk Games
___ Photography
___ Moving Pictures
___ Poster Making
___ Book Reviews
___ Art
___ Dramatics
___ Camping
___ Writing
___ Radio
___ Craft Work

SPECIAL TRAINING*

____

____

____

*Special training or experience valuable to the church, such as, business school, college, computer, church leadership courses, etc.

APPENDIX 8

BIBLE AND SERMON RECORD KEEPER*

Monday __/__/__

Scripture Read

Key Verses

List things for which to praise God or give thanks:

List of commands and any sins you need to confess:

List of doctrines taught and lessons learned:

Verses for meditation:

Tuesday __/__/__

Scripture Read

Key Verses

List things for which to praise God or give thanks:

List of commands and any sins you need to confess:

List of doctrines taught and lessons learned:

Verses for meditation:

Wednesday __/__/__

Scripture Read

Key Verses

List things for which to praise God or give thanks:

List of commands and any sins you need to confess:

List of doctrines taught and lessons learned:

Verses for meditation:

Thursday __/__/__

Scripture Read

Key Verses

List things for which to praise God or give thanks:

List of commands and any sins you need to confess:

List of doctrines taught and lessons learned:

Verses for meditation:

Friday __/__/__

Scripture Read

Key Verses

List things for which to praise God or give thanks:

List of commands and any sins you need to confess:

List of doctrines taught and lessons learned:

Verses for meditation:

Saturday __/__/__	Sunday __/__/__
Scripture Read Key Verses List things for which to praise God or give thanks: List of commands and any sins you need to confess: List of doctrines taught and lessons learned: Verses for meditation:	Scripture Read Key Verses List things for which to praise God or give thanks: List of commands and any sins you need to confess: List of doctrines taught and lessons learned: Verses for meditation:
A.M. Sermon Main Point: Main Heading: Paragraph summary of sermon: Verses for meditation:	P.M. Sermon Main Point: Main Heading: Paragraph summary of sermon: Verses for meditation:

* Appendix 7 and Appendix 8 can also be downloaded in PDF format from www.christianfocus.com.

Other Books of Interest
from
Christian Focus Publications

An Exposition on the Shorter Catechism

What is the Chief End of Man?

Alexander Whyte

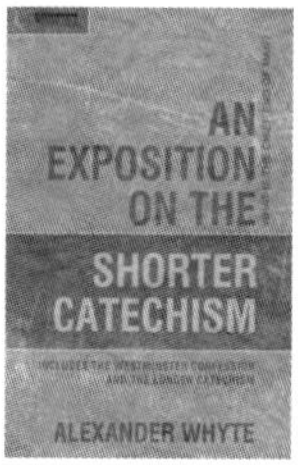

Alexander Whyte (1836-1921) is best known for his books on Bible Characters. A leading Scottish Churchman of the nineteenth and early twentieth centuries it is only to be expected that he turned his mind to the Shorter Catechism – that summary of Christian doctrine that was taught in schools and homes across Scotland and throughout the world. In a question and answer format the Shorter Catechism was written with uneducated layman in mind. Simple, direct and brief it was memorised by millions of people from all backgrounds. Its spiritual value has been proved again and again as it provides a base of solid Christian teaching that has stood the test of time.

This exposition is a treasure, as it adds some background and some explanation to the brevity that is obviously necessary in a catechism. Quoting from a wide range of Reformed and Puritan authors, Whyte provides useful application and illustrations that help illuminate the answers and will help us apply them to our lives.

ISBN 978-1-85792-250-9

The Reformed Faith

An Exposition of the
Westminster Confession of Faith

Robert Shaw

Foreword by Sinclair B. Ferguson

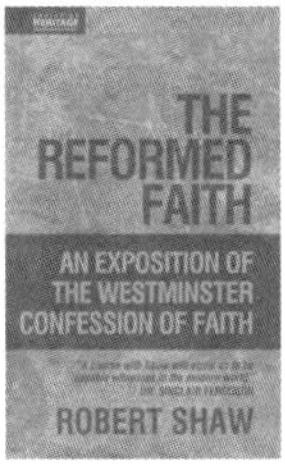

'His work provides a miniature course in theology. More than that, it explains, expounds and applies the whole gospel in a way that will explain the message of Scripture, illumine understanding, stimulate worship and strengthen Christian living. A course of private study with Shaw as teacher and companion will equip us to be intelligent and capable witnesses to Jesus Christ in the modern world – able to give a reason for the hope that the gospel gives us (1 Pet. 3:15)'.

Sinclair B. Ferguson,
First Presbyterian Church, Columbia, South Carolina

'...one of the best written and helpful expositions ever to appear. ...each category of doctrine is opened up with clarity and applied with warmth and spirituality. It is a handsome volume and is recommended highly.'

Evangelical Times

This book is a practical aid to help us understand and apply material in the Confession to our lives - making us live out our confession as individual Christians and as members of a worldwide church.

This book is the recognised companion volume to the Westminster Confession of Faith.

ISBN 978-1-84550-253-9

Christian Focus Publications

Our mission statement –

STAYING FAITHFUL
In dependence upon God we seek to impact the world through literature faithful to His infallible Word, the Bible. Our aim is to ensure that the Lord Jesus Christ is presented as the only hope to obtain forgiveness of sin, live a useful life and look forward to heaven with Him.

Our books are published in four imprints:

CHRISTIAN FOCUS

Popular works including biographies, commentaries, basic doc-trine and Christian living.

CHRISTIAN HERITAGE

Books representing some of the best material from the rich heritage of the church.

MENTOR

Books written at a level suitable for Bible College and seminary students, pastors, and other serious readers. The imprint includes commentaries, doctrinal studies, examination of current issues and church history.

CF4•K

Children's books for quality Bible teaching and for all age groups: Sunday school curriculum, puzzle and activity books; personal and family devotional titles, biographies and inspirational stories – because you are never too young to know Jesus!

Christian Focus Publications Ltd,
Geanies House, Fearn, Ross-shire,
IV20 1TW, Scotland, United Kingdom.
www.christianfocus.com